Diplomacy on Ice

DIPLOMACY ON ICE

Energy and the Environment in the Arctic and Antarctic

EDITED BY

Rebecca Pincus
Saleem H. Ali

Foreword by James Gustave Speth

Yale

UNIVERSITY PRESS

New Haven and London

Published with assistance from the Sustainable Minerals Institute, University of Queensland, Australia, and from the foundation established in memory of Amasa Stone Mather of the Class of 1907, Yale College.

Yale University Press books may be purchased in quantity for educational, business, or promotional use. For information, please e-mail sales.press@ yale.edu (U.S. office) or sales@yaleup.co.uk (U.K. office).

Figures prepared by Bill Nelson, except for figure 12.1.

Designed by James J. Johnson.
Set in Scala types by Newgen North America.
Printed in the United States of America.

Library of Congress Cataloging-in-Publication Data

Diplomacy on ice : energy and the environment in the Arctic and Antarctic / edited by Rebecca H. Pincus, Saleem H. Ali ; foreword by James Gustave Speth.
pages cm
Includes bibliographical references and index.
ISBN 978-0-300-20516-9 (hardback)
1. Geopolitics—Polar regions.   2. Polar regions—International status.
3. Energy development—Environmental aspects—Polar regions.   I. Pincus, Rebecca H., editor of compilation.   II. Ali, Saleem H. (Saleem Hassan), 1973– editor of compilation.
G593.D57 2015
919.8—dc23
2014014291

A catalogue record for this book is available from the British Library.

This paper meets the requirements of
ANSI/NISO z39.48-1992 (Permanence of Paper).

10 9 8 7 6 5 4 3 2 1

This volume is dedicated to all those scholars who commit to work in extreme environments and have a planetary vision of diplomacy.

Why then do we feel this strange attraction for these polar regions, a feeling so powerful and lasting, that when we return home we forget the mental and physical hardships, and want nothing more than to return to them? Why are we so susceptible to the charm of these landscapes when they are so empty and terrifying?

—JEAN-BAPTISTE CHARCOT

Contents

Foreword by James Gustave Speth xi
Preface xiii

Introduction: A Cold Prelude to a Warming World
SALEEM H. ALI AND REBECCA PINCUS I

Part I The Law: Legal Structures in Polar Regions II

1. *Polar Environmental Governance and Nonstate Actors*
SÉBASTIEN DUYCK 13

2. *Interlinkages in International Law: The Convention on Biological Diversity as a Model for Linking Territory, Environment, and Indigenous Rights in the Marine Arctic*
BETSY BAKER 41

3. *An Erosion of Confidence?*
The Antarctic Treaty System in the Twenty-first Century
DANIELA LIGGETT 61

4. *Invasive Species in the Arctic: Concerns, Regulations, and Governance*
KAMRUL HOSSAIN 72

5. *Managing Polar Policy through Public and Private Regulatory Standards: The Case of Tourism in the Antarctic*
MICHELE ZEBICH-KNOS 94

Part 2 **Critical Actors: Power Dynamics and
             Driving Forces in Polar Regions   111**

6. *From Energy to Knowledge? Building Domestic Knowledge-
   Based Sectors around Hydro Energy in Iceland and Greenland*
   RASMUS GJEDSSØ BERTELSEN AND KLAUS GEORG HANSEN   113

7. *Arctic Melting Tests the United Nations Convention on the Law of the Sea*
   ASIM ZIA, ILAN KELMAN, AND MICHAEL H. GLANTZ   128

8. *Growth Imperative: Intermediaries, Discourse Frameworks, and the Arctic*
   ARTHUR MASON   141

9. *Connecting China through "Creative Diplomacy": Greenland,
   Australia, and Climate Cooperation in Polar Regions*
   DAMIEN DEGEORGES AND SALEEM H. ALI   151

10. *Security in the Arctic: A Receding Wall*
    REBECCA PINCUS   161

Part 3 **Community: Human Rights, Indigenous Politics, and
             Collective Learning   169**

11. *Using Human Rights to Improve Arctic Governance*
    REBECCA BRATSPIES   171

12. *Cooperative Food Sharing in Sheshatshiu: Uncovering Scenarios to
    Support the Emergent Capacity of Northern Communities*
    DAMIÁN CASTRO, GLEN LESINS, RACHEL HIRSCH, AND KAZ HIGUCHI   186

13. *Crossing the Land of Indigenous People in the Arctic: Comparison of
    Russian and North American Experiences of Economic Growth and
    Human Rights in Energy and Infrastructure Projects*
    NATALIA YAKOVLEVA AND RICHARD GROVER   198

14. *Emergent Cooperation, or, Checkmate by Overwhelming Collaboration:
    Linear Feet of Reports, Endless Meetings*
    GLENN W. SHEEHAN AND ANNE M. JENSEN   213

15. From Northern Studies to Circumpolar Studies: In the Field and in the Ether
KATHLEEN OSGOOD AND STEVEN B. YOUNG   224

Epilogue
REBECCA PINCUS   235

Selected Resources   239
List of Contributors   269
Index   275

Foreword

The polar regions of the planet remain underappreciated in discussions of global development. Often they draw attention when major ecological crises emerge such as ozone depletion in the Antarctic or the melting of the Greenland ice sheet in the Arctic. It is high time that the international community consider these regions more deliberately as part of diplomatic engagement. Rebecca Pincus and Saleem Ali's work in developing this admirable volume is a pioneering effort to provide rigorous scholarly research that is still accessible to policymakers in this arena.

During my time as the administrator of the United Nations Development Program in the 1990s, the issue of human development in the Arctic first caught my attention. Later in 2004, UNDP published the first Arctic Regional Human Development Report, raising issues further developed here. By then I had moved on to be dean of the Yale School of Forestry and Environmental Studies, where I followed the work of coeditor Saleem H. Ali, who is also an alumnus of the school. His research attempts to find paths by which environmental conflicts can be transformed into opportunities for cooperation.

Pincus and Ali have assembled an impressive team of researchers with vast field experience in the polar regions. As international efforts move forward to negotiate binding agreements on challenges like climate change, such work can provide indispensable guidance.

It is also fitting that the state of Vermont, a community that I now call home and that has led the way in championing innovative approaches to social and environmental problems, was an incubator for this volume, in the form of the Institute for Environmental Diplomacy and Security at the University of Vermont.

I look forward to following the work of these researchers and hope that policy-makers and students alike will read this volume with an eye toward constructive engagement on polar diplomacy in years to come.

James Gustave Speth
Vermont Law School
South Royalton, Vermont, USA

Preface

Discussion and thinking about this volume began in 2010, over the course of several conversations between the editors and some contributors about the overheated media portrayal of impending conflict in the Arctic. We felt that this characterization was both flawed and dangerous, and wished there were a more nuanced perspective, as well as a focus on diplomacy and the potential for cooperation. As our thinking coalesced into a book project, the Antarctic element became inescapable as a needed counterpoint. The lessons from the Antarctic Treaty System, the similarities and differences between the poles, and the uncertain future of contested issues in Antarctica all seemed clearly requisite to any fresh conversation about the Arctic.

Fundamentally, that is the point of this volume: to bring a new perspective on the potential for cooperative conduct by international players on polar issues. So much has been written about the potential for conflict, environmental destruction, and upheaval from climate change, but it often feels like the same terrain is retread over and over again. We felt that voices and perspectives that were more solution-oriented were missing, and that we could bring together researchers through a rigorous peer-review process to further these conversations in academia and in the policymaking arena.

Our contributors bring a diversity of expertise to the volume. Many hail from the Arctic or have done extensive work there, and their research spans a variety of disciplines, from law to geography to botany. We asked each to provide a chapter that raised a new question about polar governance, or identified an issue that had been overlooked to date in discussions about the poles. The resulting volume is therefore highly eclectic and aims to illustrate the complexity of the Arctic and Antarctic regions. The collision of different perspectives sheds new light on the

issues, and often permits insights to be realized. We also note that the contributors endeavored to be very applied and policy-relevant in the final analysis.

We are grateful to all our contributors, who have shared their research and
patiently endured the review process, and to Yale University Press for the vote
of confidence to publish the book. Funding support for part of this research and
publication were also provided by the University of Queensland, Australia, and
the Brian Bronfman Family Foundation in Canada.

Ultimately, the success of this volume will be judged by how students of international relations and policymakers embrace these ideas and use them for improving environmental and social relations in the polar regions.

Introduction
A Cold Prelude to a Warming World
SALEEM H. ALI AND REBECCA PINCUS

It is now indisputable that the polar regions of the earth are thawing rapidly. Arctic temperatures have risen more than twice as fast as the global average over the past half-century. If the speed of change continues, a largely ice-free Arctic in the summer months is likely by 2040—up to forty years earlier than was anticipated in the most recent assessment report by the Intergovernmental Panel on Climate Change (IPCC). The last time the Arctic was unquestionably free of summertime ice was 125,000 years ago, at the height of the last major interglacial period, known as the Eemian.[1] On the southern pole the changes are comparably dramatic albeit with less international contention. The Antarctic warming is partly related to ambient temperature changes but is also due to warming ocean currents that are making their way more easily to this region, leading to break-off of ice shelves that were stable for thousands of years. This is a planetary change of monumental proportions.

Whether or not these changes are anthropogenic is irrelevant to the theme at hand since the speed of changes necessitates adaptive governance mechanisms. The changing environment will have as-yet unknown effects, but already poses new challenges and opportunities. The retreat of polar ice is opening new possibilities for ship transit and traffic in and across the Arctic; in addition, current estimates describe enormous quantities of petroleum and natural gas in the region that will be increasingly available for exploitation as thawing progresses. While bracing for adverse ecosystem impacts, states are simultaneously seeking to engage the resource and transit opportunities flowing from the Arctic melt. On the southern pole, the decades-old Antarctic Treaty, which entered into force in 1961, expanded dramatically in 2010, although it continues to reserve Antarctica as a peaceful region devoted to scientific research and ecological preservation. However, increased fishing and tourism pressure are impacting the region at the same time that the changing climate clouds the future.

Much of the popular discussion of the warming poles has focused on the potential for greater conflict; the "race" or "war" for the Arctic is a common theme
in recent works on this topic. The aim of this volume is to consider the reverse—
how cooperation through skillful framing of issues and creative diplomacy may be
equally plausible. Despite such a positive prospective approach, we are not sanguine
about the gravity of incipient conflicts that exist and the fragility of any cooperation
that might arise. Our goal is to recognize these conflicts but to not be deterministic
about them. Rather, this book aims to use conflict analysis as a means of fostering
better diplomacy. Given the demographic prominence of the Arctic compared to the
Antarctic, the book and its arguments have greater emphasis on the Arctic. However, we are very cognizant of some ecological similarities between both poles and
the importance of comparisons where appropriate. An important starting point for
comparisons in the context of political geography is the Cold War, when the world
was also figuratively polarized between the Soviet Union and the United States.
Competition between these two powers for ascendency in scientific achievement
was just as strong as their caustic race for weapons. Nevertheless, in the context of
Antarctica both sides cooperated on a treaty. In the Arctic there was less cooperation despite unusual historic contracts such as Russia's sale of Alaska to the United
States in 1867. In this introduction, our substantive aim is to present this context as
a way to frame the rest of the analysis as a post–Cold War phenomenon.

Situating Security: Shadows of the Cold War and Cultural Theorizing

Arctic states are increasing their polar capabilities in order to take advantage
of increasing accessibility, as well as demonstrate sovereign rights or claims over
Arctic holdings, on- or offshore, that they previously left undeveloped. Russia has
embarked upon an extensive development of Arctic capabilities, including ordering several new, very powerful icebreakers, as well as deploying army brigades to
the Arctic. The US government has been keeping an eye on these developments;
the US Army War College devoted an entire monograph to "Russia in the Arctic"
in 2011, noting "aggressive" Russian claims in the polar region.[2] Canada has also
recently ordered new icebreakers and offshore patrol vessels, and has stepped up
Arctic training for Canadian troops. NATO has increased Arctic activity with Cold
Response 2012, a large-scale military exercise involving NATO countries and Swedish personnel war-gaming in challenging Arctic conditions. The United States has
also begun to devote attention to the Arctic region. In 2009, the US Navy published
an "Arctic Roadmap" that laid out action items, strategic objectives, and desired
outcomes in the Arctic region.[3] This document notes the possibilities of increased
activity in the Arctic as warming continues, and states, "While the United States has
stable relationships with other Arctic nations, the changing environment and competition for resources may contribute to increasing tension, or, conversely, provide
opportunities for cooperative solutions" (US Navy Arctic Roadmap, 2009, p. 8).

Not only are there crucial differences between indigenous and outsider perceptions of the region, but there are also differences across national boundaries and cultures. It is critical to examine the impact of national culture on treatments of the Arctic. Of particular importance may be the impact of culture on militarization and security in the Arctic as popular rhetoric stirs fears of forthcoming conflict. The recognition that national culture influences security practices has deep historical roots.

Cultural theorizing informed US strategy during World War II, when cultural anthropologists were employed by the military to analyze the "national character" of the Axis powers and describe the "nature of the enemy."[4] Another wave of strategic culture studies emerged in the later Cold War period as some scholars pointed to cultural differences between the United States and the Soviet Union to explain and predict different strategic "predispositions" and choices.[5] Alastair Johnston states that, "most of those who use the term 'culture' tend to argue, explicitly or implicitly, that different states have different predominant strategic preferences that are rooted in the early or formative experiences of the state, and are influenced to some degree by the philosophical, political, cultural, and cognitive characteristics of the state and its elites."[6] This approach stands in marked contrast to the realist approach to explaining and predicting state behavior, which presumes state rationality. Katzenstein provides this justification for looking beyond traditional rational models: "Perspectives that neglect social factors foreclose important avenues for empirical research and theoretical insight that are relevant for explaining specific aspects of national security."[7] The co-occurrence of significant energy-related security threats in the early twenty-first century, in particular climate change, may have created enough pressure to change a long-entrenched strategy and culture of energy in the military.

Redefining National Security in the American Context

Since the rise of the nation-state system, threats to national security have primarily come from outside, specifically from other nation-states. A divide existed between the military, which protected the state from external attack and waged war against other states, and the police force, which enforced domestic laws and fought crime internally. The longstanding divide between domestic and external notions of security, between policing and war fighting, no longer makes sense given the fragmented threat landscape. Until recently, war was conceptualized differently, as described movingly by General Wesley Clark: "In World War II, Korea, Vietnam, and afterward, the US armed forces sought an enemy, focused on him, trained to beat him. It was a heroic image—the bayonet assault, the airborne jump, clearing the caves of Iwo Jima, the cliffs at Pointe du Hoc at Normandy. These were the forces of twentieth-century warfare, of mass armies and the battles of state against state."[8] Military might and territory were the primary tangible loci of power and security. In the introduction to their classic *International Politics*, Art and Jervis sum up the "security dilemma" facing all states in purely state-state terms: "The security dilemma means that an action-reaction spiral can occur between two states or among several of them, forcing each to spend ever larger sums on arms to be no more secure than before. All will run faster merely to stay where they are."[9] This summary is accurate, and may have been comprehensive until recently. Spending alone no longer determines defense against the threat posed by an enemy. Strategists and planners must not only guard against threats posed by states, but now need to also consider nonstate threats.

Military planners during the World War II era envisioned virtually a second frontier, the "strategic frontier," marked by US bases ringing the Atlantic and Pacific. US forces were expected to exercise hegemonic force over these oceans, and within the strategic frontier as well, as well as "counter any threats" beyond this frontier.[10] The concept underlying the frontier of bases was "defense in depth," with a goal of keeping enemies as geographically distant from the United States as possible. The planners behind this "strategic frontier" defense strategy had much narrower assumptions about the threats facing the United States: "Since attacks against the United States could only emanate from Europe and Asia."[11] The same approach was undertaken in the Arctic during the Cold War.

The militarization of the Arctic followed a path similar to the nuclear arms race. Despite the low probability of "attack," a deterrent capability was argued to assure mutual security. Nobel laureate Thomas C. Schelling was among the major strategic thinkers during this period.[12] New theory was needed beyond pure military strategy to accommodate this new, surpassingly destructive generation of weaponry. Strategic alternatives to nuclear warfare, and theories constraining strategy (such as deterrence) were needed. American security strategy was challenged by the development of nuclear weapons, since the new goal was to avoid war entirely through effective deterrence. Huntington summarized this new paradigm: "The success of foreign policy now depended more upon what military forces were maintained rather than how those military forces were used. Indeed, if the proper decisions were made . . . it would seldom be necessary to use the forces and weapons."[13] Rather than planning for battlespace operations, strategists now planned for deterrence; rather than strategizing how to best defeat the enemy, the focus was now on how to apply pressure without antagonizing.

Furthermore, the concept of security and of the enemy was almost entirely bundled into the USSR and the Soviet sphere of influence. As Rothkopf summarizes it, "The Soviet Union and the Cold War were the defining factors in virtually all US foreign policy at that time. They were the elephants, or, more appropriately, the bears in the room in every discussion."[14] National security planners focused their efforts on a variety of tactics to "put the squeeze on the Russians," deny Soviet expansion, and encourage the spread of liberal democracy in Western Europe and Asia.[15] Policymakers under Truman, however, recognized the efficacy of economic aid in achieving security goals, and military planners supported the rebuilding of Europe under the Marshall Plan, "strengthening the economic and social dikes against Soviet communism" in a broader-angle approach to containing and challenging the Soviet threat.[16]

Vietnam, and a series of smaller engagements through the 1970s, '80s, and '90s, added a new challenge for presidential administrations: media and public scrutiny. Again, new technology changed the previous relationship between the administration, the military, and the public. Proliferating media tools have enabled unprecedented public access to the operations of US forces overseas. How operations will play in the media has become an element that administrations must consider when weighing decisions on the use of force. In this case, the development of satellites set journalists free from military censors (previously, media reports were transmitted through military communications lines), enabling the public to see unfiltered news reports for the first time. That this revolution in media technology occurred during the era of Vietnam meant that the difference between what had been previously filtered out by military censors and what began to be sent over satellites was quite significant, and caused a deep and lasting rift between the military and the news media.[17] A similar liberation of media with the advent of the Internet is particularly palpable among remote indigenous communities that previously had little or no voice.

Recently, the rise of global terrorism again shifted US understanding of "security" and forced a radical shift in thinking about war and conflict. No longer is conflict seen largely as either a state-state or interstate problem. As such, it is also neither seen to have a strictly military solution. Donald Snow defines terrorism and other new threats as "semimilitary": they contain elements of traditional military threats and responses, but also aspects that involve politics and law enforcement, among others.[18] Furthermore, given that attacks today can come from a variety of conventional and unconventional weapons and delivery systems, much more than military might needs to be applied to the problem of national security. Former national security advisor Condoleezza Rice noted this problem: "[The] transnational threats [that] became the dominant factor in American foreign policy, if you think about it, [are] not only transnational, they're transfunctional, and that means they cross all kinds of jurisdictional boundaries in the government."[19]

Such concerns are remnants of the Cold War and have particular salience in the Arctic. However, the trust deficit is augmented by a race for scarce resources as well. "Threat" in this context is no longer a physical fear of attack but a fear of access to a zero-sum game of finite essential commodities. In particular, as fossil fuel supplies dwindle, the poles are likely to be the final frontier in the quest for carbon energy.

Energy Security

We depend on energy supplies to sustain, and not only to grow, our economy. Energy powers our army, navy, and air force, as well as our satellites and high-tech information technology. Energy underlies our foreign relations with other nations, whether they supply us with energy, purchase it from us, compete for it, or offer bargaining chips for third-party interests. Jon Barnett described "energy security" quite simply as *"the theory and practice of securing energy for the nation-state."*[20]

Although Barnett's quote, above, seems to leave out the demand side of energy consumption in favor of a focus on supply management, it sums up briefly the importance of energy availability to national security. It is readily apparent that the modern way of life is energy-intensive: for electricity, transportation, heating, and other diverse and important uses. In addition, the national security apparatus is also heavily energy-dependent in our age of modern warfare. It is therefore incumbent upon the government to secure energy supplies, or access to energy, as part of any comprehensive security program.

Furthermore, it is widely acknowledged that the United States, like or perhaps to a greater extent than many developed states, relies heavily upon plentiful and relatively inexpensive supplies of carbon-based energy, primarily oil, coal, and natural gas. The pursuit and maintenance of this goal is the realm of "energy security." As a vital national interest, there is always the possibility of "direct" military intervention in the pursuit of energy security.[21] The United States, however, seeks a more stable international environment where energy is continually available to the market.[22]

When assessing the security of an energy source, important factors include reliability, affordability (which is really price volatility), and availability. Many now argue for the inclusion of environmental sustainability as well.[23] Raphael and Stokes call a state energy-secure when the following conditions are met:

> Energy sources must be large enough to meet the needs of the political community (the energy demands), which include all military, economic and societal activity. These sources must be able to deliver such quantities of energy in a reliable and stable manner, and for the foreseeable future. As soon as these conditions are not met, there exists a problem of energy (in)security.[24]

The effort to increase energy security in the United States has been on-again, off-again for several decades, arguably with inadequate results.[25] As described by Jonathan Elkind, US pursuit of energy security has been "narrow," ignoring environmental sustainability, and has been "episodic," reacting to cyclical energy price spikes rather than driving market conditions proactively.[26] When prices return to acceptable levels, the perception of crisis fades and attention is diverted, "even as the energy intensity of its economy remains substantially undiminished."[27] For example, following the oil crisis of the early 1970s, several laws were passed aimed at increasing the United States' energy security: the Department of Energy Organization Act,[28] the National Energy Act,[29] the Crude Oil Windfall Profit Tax Act, and the Energy Security Act. However, we are not appreciably less dependent on oil today.

Over the same time frame, a number of potentially disruptive factors have also emerged on the global energy market: these include climate change most obviously, but also the rise of international terrorism, and increased energy demand by US competitors.[30] In response, "core powers are increasingly militarizing their approach to energy security,"[31] tightly linking narrow security concepts with energy policy decisions. The concept of energy security can be framed as well in terms of the threat of terrorism or direct attack, either upon vulnerable energy installations like nuclear power plants or fuel refineries, or energy transfer mechanisms like pipelines.[32] All of these considerations around the national energy supply translate into governmental efforts to manage the inherent risk and uncertainty of the global market for energy, which rests upon variable factors at several levels: planetary supply, political brokering, natural disasters, and market forces. All of these forces affect the equation; all must be weighed and managed by energy security practitioners and policymakers.[33]

The polar regions are at the heart of this scramble for energy security. They have not yet been fully explored; their smaller populations have a greater challenge to contend with impacts of extraction. The ecological sensitivity of these regions remains a cause for international concern. Negotiating the ecological and the economic salience of these regions collectively provides us with diplomatic opportunities. Tradeoffs and compromises in the broader spirit of global environmental governance may well be possible and move us beyond the old Cold War paradigm that has plagued the Arctic. Lessons instead from the southern pole, where science played a role in diplomacy and the negotiation of the Antarctic Treaty, could be invoked here. Within the Antarctic Treaty itself, there are provisions for mineral resource extraction, but these have been placed in abeyance until they might be economically feasible. The time may soon be approaching within the twenty-first century when this prospect is also possible. *Diplomacy on Ice* aims to provide coherent guidance on how to address this transformation of our physical and political environment to foster constructive engagement.

Structure of the Book

Given the unique physical geographies of the polar regions, novel forms of governance have been suggested to grapple with the remoteness of sparse polar populations. Communities in these regions are highly dependent on seasonal changes as well as on external sources for amenities provided by the market economy. The first section of the book, "The Law: Legal Structures in Polar Regions," addresses the legal and governance structures that currently shape polar activities and decision making. By starting with the law as it currently exists, we hope to take a clear-eyed view of opportunities and challenges relating to governance at the poles.

Part 1 opens with a chapter that introduces the concept of governance and its extension into polar issues, in particular relating to the environment. Although very different, both the Arctic and Antarctic regions provide interesting laboratories for questioning traditional assumptions of sovereignty and developing new governance norms. The second chapter uses the Convention on Biological Diversity as a model to link territorial issues with environmental and human rights interests in the marine Arctic, with an argument that the proliferation of narrowly focused legal structures impedes strong governance, and that states would be well served by identifying areas of linkage among treaties and using these links to improve the flow of information and policymaking. In chapter 3, we take a hard look at the Antarctic Treaty System and learn about its challenges, strengths, and the promise it holds for adapting to the twenty-first century. Chapter 4 examines the legal structures that may help address the serious issue of invasive species and their threat to biodiversity in the Arctic region, and questions whether these legal tools will be adequate to address a new and growing threat. The final chapter in this section returns to the Antarctic with a look at the issue of tourism and the legal structures that affect tourists at the South Pole, in a careful analysis of the unique difficulty of achieving environmental goals on a continent without geographically defined sovereign states, where tourism presents a potentially grave threat to ecological stability.

Part 2 of the book, "Critical Actors: Power Dynamics and Driving Forces in Polar Regions," examines several of the important forces pushing change at the poles. The rich natural resources of the Arctic, in particular energy and minerals, are a clear magnet for international attention, from governments and corporations alike. We begin with a chapter addressing the fascinating history of Iceland's development of its geothermal energy resources, and the lessons this may offer to another emerging Arctic microstate, Greenland. The authors provide a compelling narrative for the Iceland case study, and note that Iceland's use of energy profits to develop a knowledge-based economy allowed it to move beyond resource exploitation while building domestic capacity. Next, in chapter 7, the issue of climate change and the Convention on the Law of the Sea are tackled head-on. The authors explore whether UNCLOS is capable of handling sovereignty and property rights in the Arctic, and how the energy resources in question play into global climate projections. Next, chapter 8 examines the nuts and bolts of how development is being operationalized in the polar regions by considering the "growth imperative," which still remains dominant in development discourse. This fascinating chapter upends conventional assumptions about development, growth, and Arctic energy resources, and urges readers to take a closer look at how Arctic discourses shape policy. In chapter 9, the authors take a close look at Greenland and Australia to argue that the particular geographic attributes of these two enormous islands offer opportunities for "creative diplomacy" on issues including climate change and energy security. Finally in this section, in chapter 10 the issue of Arctic security is examined as a prime driver of policy and strategy in the region.

The final section of the book, "Community: Human Rights, Indigenous Politics, and Collective Learning," turns to the communities of the Arctic and the critical issue of human rights. Due to low population and a legacy of poor treatment, community relations have historically been neglected in the polar regions, but this has changed dramatically in the last few decades as the rights of indigenous people rise as an international norm. Part 3 of the book suggests that rather than viewing community concerns as a potential source of conflict, we consider how lessons from communities on resource sharing can provide diplomatic opportunities. Chapter 11 presents a legal analysis of the prospects for using human rights issues to strengthen Arctic governance, with a persuasive argument that protecting the fragile Arctic region, while respecting the interests of Arctic communities, is a challenge that requires more effective governance tools than currently available. In chapter 12, the authors use a case study approach to examine the traditional reliance on solidarity and co-operation within Arctic communities, and how these values may help adaptation succeed in a warming climate. Chapter 13 addresses the community impacts of energy and infrastructure projects in the Arctic. Since development often negatively impacts the natural resources upon which indigenous communities depend, particularly game, Arctic communities may be forced to bear the costs of development when the benefits of these projects flow far away. In chapter 14, the authors take us to northern Alaska, with a scathing and unique look at the dark side of inclusive participation, concluding that culturally appropriate ways of engagement are essential to prevent community resilience from being undermined. Finally, chapter 15 analyzes the remarkable evolution of knowledge in the circumpolar world as the Internet revolutionizes information sharing and education. The authors illuminate the evolution of circumpolar studies as a discipline and a means of empowering Arctic communities and students.

We conclude the book with a synthesis of key points that policymakers should consider to reconcile science and economic necessity in the polar regions. Looking back, and looking forward, we hope to shine some light on the path to achieving polar peace—protecting the fragile environments of the poles, respecting and empowering Arctic communities, ensuring responsible development, and above all enshrining dialogue and diplomacy as the preferred means of resolving disputes.

Notes

1. Michael H. Field, Brian Huntley, and Helmut Muller, "Eemian Climate Fluctuations Observed in a European Pollen Record," in *Nature* 371 (6500) (27 October 1994): 779–783.

2. Document accessible at: http://www.strategicstudiesinstitute.army.mil/europe-russia/.

3. Details at: http://www.navy.mil/navydata/infoIndex.asp.

4. Ruth Benedict's *The Chrysanthemum and the Sword*, on Japanese culture, is a classic example (Boston: Houghton Mifflin, 1946). See also Michael C. Desch, "Culture Clash: Assessing the Importance of Ideas in Security Studies," *International Security* 23(1) (1998): 144–145.

5. Alastair Iain Johnston, "Thinking About Strategic Culture," *International Security* 19(4) (1995): 32.

6. Ibid., 34.

7. Peter J. Katzenstein, ed., *The Culture of National Security* (New York: Columbia University Press, 1996), introduction, p. 21.

8. General Wesley A. Clark, *Winning Modern Wars* (New York: Public Affairs, 2003), 165.

9. Robert J. Art and Robert Jervis, eds., *International Politics: Enduring Concepts and Contemporary Issues*, 8th ed. (New York: Pearson, 2007), 2.

10. Melvyn P. Leffler, "The American Conception of National Security and the Beginnings of the Cold War, 1945–48," *American Historical Review* 89(2) (1984): 349.

11. Ibid., 350.

12. Thomas C. Schelling, "The Diplomacy of Violence," in *International Politics*, Robert J. Art and Robert Jervis, eds., 8th ed. (New York: Pearson, 2007), 158.

13. Samuel P. Huntington, *The Common Defense: Strategic Programs in National Politics* (New York: Columbia University Press, 1961), 23.

14. David J. Rothkopf, *Running the World: The Inside Story of the National Security Council and the Architects of American Power* (New York: Public Affairs, 2005), 128.

15. Melvyn P. Leffler, "The American Conception of National Security," 368–370.

16. Assistant Secretary of War Peterson, quoted in Melvyn P. Leffler, "The American Conception of National Security," 371.

17. Donald M. Snow, *National Security for a New Era*, 3rd ed. (New York: Pearson Education, 2008), 92–93.

18. Ibid., 168.

19. Quoted in David J. Rothkopf, *Running the World*, 405.

20. Jon Barnett, *The Meaning of Environmental Security: Ecological Politics and Policy in the New Security Era* (New York: Zed Books, 2001), 34.

21. Jan H. Kalicki and David L. Goldwyn, eds., *Energy and Security: Toward a New Foreign Policy Strategy* (Washington, D.C.: Woodrow Wilson Center Press, 2005), 411.

22. Isabel Studer and Carol Wise, eds., *Requiem or Revival? The Promise of North American Integration* (Washington, D.C.: Brookings Institution Press, 2007), 233.

23. Jonathan Elkind, "Energy Security: Call for a Broader Agenda," in *Energy Security*, Carlos Pascual and Jonathan Elkind, eds. (Washington, D.C.: Brookings Institution Press, 2010), 121.

24. Sam Raphael and Doug Stokes, "Energy Security," in *Contemporary Security Studies*, Alan Collins, ed., 2nd ed. (Oxford: Oxford University Press, 2010), 379.

25. Elkind, "Energy Security," 120.

26. Ibid.

27. Ibid.

28. Michael W. Grainey, "Recent Federal Energy Legislation: Towards a National Energy Policy At Last?," in *Lewis and Clark Law School Journal of Environmental Law*, 12 Envtl. L. (1981): 29, citing 42 U.S.C. §§7101–7352 (Supp. III 1979).

29. Ibid.

30. Raphael and Stokes, "Energy Security," 379–381.

31. Ibid.

32. Kalicki and Goldwyn, *Energy and Security*, 412.

33. Studer and Wise, *Requiem or Revival?*, 214.

PART ONE

The Law
Legal Structures in Polar Regions

We may brave human laws, but we cannot resist natural ones.
—JULES VERNE

A LTHOUGH much about the future of the polar regions is called into question by the pace and projected scale of change, no discussion is complete without a consideration of the governance structures already in place. Many international legal structures apply at the poles, and these will shape the future course of human activity in the region. The following chapters tackle some of the important governance structures that apply at the poles, and offer both critiques and recommendations for future adaptations.

Given the shared nature of both poles—the Antarctic as a region of peaceful international cooperation and scientific discovery, and the Arctic as an international ocean, albeit one ringed by national territory—the ability of the global community to create structures that will protect these fragile ecosystems, while satisfying the demand for human access and activity, is clearly critical. In addition, current and future changes can only be fully understood when placed in the context of what has come before. The history of polar governance has been written about thoroughly by others and is beyond the scope of this volume, but authors in the first section provide snapshots of critical issues of polar governance that place later discussions in context.

In particular, Sébastien Duyck in chapter 1 starts off with an analysis of the role of nonstate actors in environmental governance in polar regions, offering insight into the ways in which decision making about the Arctic and Antarctic could be expanded to more participatory models. In chapter 2, Betsy Baker continues the focus on environmental governance with an examination of the overlapping issues of territorial conflict, environmental protection, and human rights in the Arctic.

In the third chapter, Daniela Liggett provides an overview of the history of the Antarctic Treaty System (ATS) and the challenges it faces in the twenty-first century. The ATS stands out as a remarkable act of cooperation by its signatories, and its preservation of the Antarctic as a region of peaceful scientific exploration provides inspiration for the future of polar governance. However, the ATS is a relic from another era of international relations, and the future of the ATS and Antarctica depends on successful adaptation to the new realities of the international political and economic system.

Moving into specific challenges to polar governance, in chapter 4 Kamrul Hossain examines the threat posed by invasive species in the Arctic, and what governance structures exist to help combat this challenge. In chapter 5, Michele Zebich-Knos offers a clear and concise picture of the multiple issues associated with tourism in the Antarctic region, and the difficulties of managing economic activity in an international region that is both irresistibly compelling to outsiders but at terrible risk from their presence.

All of these chapters serve to illustrate the broader conclusion that old models of governance will not be adequate to address the multifaceted challenges of the twenty-first century, when climate change will cause widespread geostrategic change and a much wider group of states will seek to pursue strategic interests at both poles. It remains to be seen whether the international community can make positive change, both by modifying existing governance structures and by creating new ones, and successfully ease the transition into a new polar order.

1. *Polar Environmental Governance and Nonstate Actors*

SÉBASTIEN DUYCK

From International to Global Governance

The role and nature of sovereign states have been profoundly affected over the past two decades by many external and internal pressures related, among other factors, to the end of the Cold War, the emergence of transnational corporations with global economic impact, the development of new technologies, and the multiplication of unconventional security threats. These developments have supported the emergence of a discourse addressing this shift from government to governance, the latter notion being more encompassing. This trend is exemplified by the comparison of the outcomes of the major United Nations conferences dedicated to sustainable development. While the 1992 Rio Conference resulted in the adoption of major international legally binding agreements, the outcomes of the World Summit on Sustainable Development ten years later emphasized the opportunity for the conclusion of "type II partnerships," defined as voluntary and multi-stakeholders initiatives.[1] This approach was reiterated at the 2012 United Nations Conference on Sustainable Development (Rio Plus 20) with the creation of a registry of "voluntary commitments" by states, intergovernmental organizations, and stakeholders.[2]

The increasing recognition of the role of nonstate actors, however, did not lead to a demise of the central role of sovereign states or to "governance without governments," but rather contributes to the emergence of a new form of governance.[3] The UN Commission on Sustainable Development emphasized, for instance, that "partnerships," while contributing to the implementation of intergovernmental decisions, should neither divert resources from nor substitute for these commitments. Increasingly faced with challenges lying beyond the competences and capacities of the nation-states, governments are increasingly engaging new sets of actors in cooperative experiments in order to address these problems "through multi-party collaborative governance arrangements that pool, recombine, and coordinate the deployment of the varied resources and competencies of multiple actors."[4]

While this evolution provides the general background of this study, this chapter considers more specifically whether—and how—these new forms of governance have developed in polar environmental governance. Beyond the occurrence of relatively similar climate, the two polar regions present essential different characteristics. The South Pole is located at the core of a vast landmass free from long-term human activities beyond scientific research. In contrast, the Arctic is centered on an ocean, which is variably ice-covered. Local and indigenous communities have occupied most of the Arctic coastal areas for hundreds or thousands of years. While conservation of the scientific and aesthetic values of the continent are the main objective of current human endeavors in the Antarctic, the High North is perceived as a region rich in natural resources where economic activities are expected to proliferate, taking advantage of new physical conditions resulting from climate change. The historical contexts in which governance regimes have developed in both regions constitute another major difference between these polar experiences. The Antarctic Treaty System was established during the Cold War in order to guarantee that the continent would not become the source or theater of open conflicts between states, whereas Arctic governance emerged in an era during which the international community progressively acknowledged the role of nonstate actors in environmental governance.[5]

Despite these differences, both regions share several common patterns, for instance in relation to challenges to the traditional understanding of the concept of national sovereignty. In the Arctic, the presence of indigenous people contributes to the questioning of sovereignty as a prerogative of sovereign states only. In 2009, the leaders of Inuit communities pointed out, "'sovereignty' is a term that has often been used to refer to the absolute and independent authority of a community or nation both internally and externally. Sovereignty is a contested concept, however, and does not have a fixed meaning. Old ideas of sovereignty are breaking down as different governance models, such as the European Union, evolve."[6]

The relevance of the traditional concept of national sovereignty remains questioned in the context of the Antarctic, as states have maintained conflicting positions with regard to territorial claims on the continent. Many states and intergovernmental organizations have even proposed to regulate the continent according to the principle of the common heritage of mankind. The UN General Assembly adopted for instance in 1989 a resolution calling for the "establishment . . . of Antarctica as a nature reserve or a world park . . . for the benefit of all mankind," giving leverage to those calling for the recognition of Antarctica as a region beyond national jurisdiction.[7] Disputes over the application of the concept of the nation-state strengthen the question of the central role of sovereign states and provide an opportunity for the recognition of other actors: "Popular myths about the operation of the state system in Antarctica . . . could be used to construct an argument for a large NGO role in Antarctic affairs. . . . Thus, if state-based mechanisms are inadequate, then nonstate mechanisms such as NGOs should come into their own."[8]

In this context, the polar regions provide a unique opportunity to investigate how national states have responded in practice to the questioning of the concept of sovereignty. The lessons learned from these experiences provide valuable examples of inclusive forms of environmental governance regimes. In some instances, they also highlight the resilience of the traditional models of international relations and the resistance of states to alternative models of regional cooperation.

The first section of this chapter will provide a brief introduction to the emerging forms of governance and the role herein of a diverse set of new players. Undermining the hegemony of sovereign states as the sole relevant actors of international relations, nonstate actors—both nongovernmental and governmental—claim a growing role in decision making and have occasionally succeeded in securing the recognition of a greater role in regional governance. Building on the recognition of the existence of very atypical circumstances for the exercise of national sovereignty, the second section explores in more depth how environmental institutions established in both polar regions address the participation of various nonstate actors. While in some cases the approaches adopted are simply illustrative of general trends in international law, both Antarctic and Arctic models of cooperation have also experienced more inclusiveness toward specific sections of civil society. The chapter concludes with a survey of the trends currently affecting Arctic governance and the threats or opportunities for local stakeholders and right-holders.

Stakeholder Participation

For more than three centuries, international relations have been framed by the paradigm of Westphalian sovereignty, defined by the 1648 Treaty of Münster, which established a new system of world order on the basis of the emergence of sovereign nation-states. While this model still persists to a certain extent, over the past sixty years several actors have challenged the hegemony of nation-states as the sole actors of world politics, thus contributing to the transition from international to global governance.

Public Participation

The importance of the participation of nonstate actors in decision making has been recognized repeatedly as a key element of sustainable development. The 1987 report of the World Commission on Environment and Development referred to the importance of providing nongovernmental organizations (NGOs) access to information, opportunities to participate in decision-making processes on environmental matters, and access to legal remedies.[9] The Rio Declaration on Environment and Development elevated public participation as a principle of sustainable development: "Environmental issues are best handled with participation of all concerned citizens, at the relevant level. At the national level, each individual shall have appropriate access to information concerning the environment that is held by public authorities" (1992 Rio Declaration, Principle 10).[10]

Agenda 21—the implementation plan of the Rio Declaration—comprises a full section dedicated to the critical role of the "commitment and genuine involvement of all social groups."[11] Agenda 21's main contribution to the framing of the role of stakeholders consisted in the identification of nine major groups representing the interests of these social groups. The UN Economic Commission for Europe (UNECE) adopted a legally binding agreement in 1998 to implement Principle 10 of the Rio Declaration.[12] More recently, during the 2012 Rio Plus 20 Conference several Latin American states initiated a process to consider opportunities for the adoption of a similar instrument in the region.[13]

Effective participation of stakeholders in international forums provides added value, including the provision of a unique set of expertise and information—both technical and practical, the capacity to act as bridge builders between diverging national positions, and an increased legitimacy.[14] Nevertheless, nonstates remain invited in international decision making mainly under the terms of *observer* status, rather than as participants. The Brundtland Report noted in 1987 that improvements to the participatory rights of civil society should not only take place at the domestic level, calling for the "establish[ment] or strengthen[ing] of procedures for official consultation and more meaningful participation by NGOs in all relevant intergovernmental organizations."[15] All major UN declarations on sustainable development have since then referred to the importance of increasing the role of civil society at all levels of decision making.[16] The UNECE addressed this gap in the pan-European context with the adoption in 2005 of the Almaty Guidelines on the promotion of the principles of the Aarhus Convention in international forums. These guidelines constitute the first international instrument providing a detailed set of principles regarding the procedural rights of civil society in intergovernmental processes.[17]

The Role of Private Actors in International Governance

The role of the private sector in environmental governance was highlighted at the 1992 Rio Earth Summit, businesses and industries constituting one of the nine major groups identified in Agenda 21.[18] Private governance requires more than a partial withdrawal of the state and ad hoc cooperation among private actors; it builds on a conscious development of institutionalized interactions among business sector entities, based on the recognition of the legitimacy of a new governance model guaranteeing the permanence of the norms.[19] In their essay on the emergence of global administrative law, Kingsbury, Krisch, and Stewart identify two trends in the development of the role of private entities in international governance.[20] Global regulation is increasingly framed by structures involving both governmental actors and private entities in what the authors described as "hybrid intergovernmental-private administration." Additionally, Kingsbury et al. noted that private actors have also seized many opportunities to fill the gaps in intergovernmental governance by carrying out regulatory functions themselves. In relation to environmental issues, this second approach includes more specifically nongovernmental certification schemes and the adoption of self-regulatory regimes by private actors. The establishment of private certification schemes as a tool of environmental governance gained momentum, for example, in the field of sustainable forest management, when at the 1992 Rio Conference states failed to reach consensus on the regulation of forest exploitation and trade in timber; the resulting absence of a normative framework created the condition favorable to the emergence of a new form of regulation with the development of the Forest Stewardship Council (FSC) certification. The FSC is a voluntary, market-based mechanism that relies for its effective implementation on the participation of both businesses and nongovernmental organizations. This experience demonstrated the potential for the private sector to deliver regulatory schemes in fields that intergovernmental processes failed to address through legally binding instruments.[21] Such self-regulatory regimes raise questions concerning classic notions of legitimacy, accountability, and effectiveness in international politics. Such private regulatory actors do not rely on accountability mechanisms comparable to those of national governments, and the norms they adopt lack the legitimacy of state consent, which traditionally served as the main source of the legitimacy for international norms.[22]

Environmental Institutions and Multilayered Governance

An International Role for Local and Regional Authorities

While foreign policy is not a prerogative of local authorities, the importance of their role in the effective implementation of environmental policy provides an argument in favor of their involvement in decision-making processes on sustainable development. The 1972 Stockholm Declaration highlighted that "[l]ocal and national governments will bear the greatest burden for large-scale environmental policy and action within their jurisdictions."[23] Beyond this assessment, the role of local and regional authorities is, however, largely disregarded in international governance. Both the Stockholm and Rio declarations lacked references to the role of local authorities in environmental governance. Agenda 21 emphasized the participation of local authorities as a "determining factor" in fulfilling the objectives of Agenda 21.[24] The document also required UN bodies to provide similar opportunities for their participation in the work of the United Nations as those granted to NGOs.[25] More than a decade later, the High-Level Panel of Eminent Persons on United Nations–Civil Society Relations noted the lack of engagement of the UN with local authorities and highlighted the need for the UN to work more closely with all elected representatives: "In an era when decentralization is shaping the political landscape as powerfully as globalization, it is also important for the United Nations to find deeper and more systematic ways to engage with elected representatives and authorities at the local level."[26]

Cities have been particularly successful over the past years, for instance, in establishing partnerships with intergovernmental organizations, in particular as recipients of development funding.[27] The recognition of local governments as one

of the nine major groups of stakeholders has, however, provided different results related to the recognition of the democratic legitimacy of local governments. This recognition has contributed to granting local governments opportunities to participate
in decision making in a manner similar to other nonstate actors. At the same time,
some of the UN processes have adopted a one-size-fits-all approach to nonstate actors' engagement, resulting in the imposition of a ceiling to the participation of local
governments.[28] In this context, the argument has been made that global governance
would take democracy seriously only if "localities [would] become equal partners in
the formation and adjudication of international norms."[29] Furthermore, increasing
constraints imposed by international norms on the political choices of local authorities provide additional support to calls for the greater participation of subnational
decision makers to international governance.[30]

Cooperation among Intergovernmental Institutions

The progressive shift from international governance to global governance has not
only resulted in a growing engagement of actors involved at the national and local
levels. The role of intergovernmental organizations in new forms of governance is
also developing. While these organizations are originally established by a delegation
of authority from national governments, they have gained an increasing amount of
autonomy from their principals.[31]

The importance of these new forms of international cooperation involving the
participation of several international institutions is highlighted, for instance, by the
2007 pilot initiative of the UN Development Group "delivering as one," through
which UN agencies involved in projects related to development aim at increasing
the effectiveness of their work through the streamlining of their intervention in
target countries.[32]

The importance of such cooperation among intergovernmental organizations is
particularly significant in the field of global environmental governance, with more
than five hundred multilateral agreements adopted and two hundred organizations
or secretariats established during the past decades. Furthermore, the overlap between the competences of these numerous environmental IGOs and the activities of
IGOs focused primarily on other issues continues to grow as the limits of these various political fields become increasingly blurred. While the growing delegation of
authority to intergovernmental organizations raises legitimacy issues,[33] the mutual
recognition of intergovernmental organizations through the granting of observer
status also reinforces the legitimacy of each organization.[34]

Cooperation between intergovernmental organizations is an element of the governance of both polar regions, perhaps most particularly in relation to the Antarctic
regime.[35] This aspect of polar governance will, however, not be covered in detail in
this chapter, which will mainly focus on the participation in governance of various
nongovernmental and subnational actors. Intergovernmental organizations active
in the polar regions and not referred to in this chapter have not achieved such a de-

gree of autonomy from their primaries as other supranational organizations might have achieved.

The Experience of Decades of Polar Governance

Governance of the Antarctic

Originally, the main purpose of the Antarctic Treaty was to address disputes related to claims of national sovereignty over the Antarctic. As emphasized in its first articles, the main objectives of the treaty are to ensure the peaceful use of the continent by all contracting parties and to guarantee the freedom to conduct scientific research. With other concerns emerging over uses of the continent, a more complex regime—the Antarctic Treaty System (ATS)—was progressively established to complement the provisions of the Antarctic Treaty. The participation of nonstate actors in this regime will be studied in the following subsections along the three stages identified by Herr in the evolution of the role of NGOs in Antarctic governance.[36]

The Science-Policy Interface

The promotion of scientific research has been a cornerstone of the ATS since the early years of the regime, Article 2 of the Antarctic Treaty providing that "freedom of scientific investigation in Antarctica and cooperation toward that end . . . shall continue, subject to the provisions of the present Treaty."[37] In the years following the adoption of the Antarctic Treaty, the Special Committee on Antarctic Research (SCAR)[38] was the only nongovernmental actor playing a role in the implementation and development of the regime as a scientific organization. The SCAR raison d'être is the promotion and coordination of scientific research in the Antarctic. While independent from the structure established under the Antarctic Treaty, SCAR closely cooperates with the ATS in a "mutually beneficial relationship."[39] The Agreed Measures for the Conservation of Antarctic Fauna and Flora adopted in 1964 already included a direct reference to the conservation principles adopted by SCAR.[40]

The 1972 Convention for the Conservation of Antarctic Seals (hereinafter Seal Convention) marked a turning point in the integration of nonstate actors in polar governance. The important delegation of functions from its intergovernmental bodies to a scientific nongovernmental organization was described as "the peak of NGO status under any international legal instrument."[41] The Seal Convention requests that the contracting parties report both to other parties and to SCAR on the issuance of special permits, as well as on information required from the annexes.[42] It further defines the tasks of SCAR, inviting the committee to assess the information provided to it and to propose recommendations on scientific programs and amendments to the convention. It further invites SCAR to report on the impact of the harvest of any particular species and to notify the depository of the convention when it foresees catch limits to be exceeded. Finally, the convention highlights the opportunity for cooperation between SCAR and the UN Food and Agriculture Organization (FAO) and allows the former to seek FAO's assistance.[43] The parties to the convention established a mechanism, however, to repeal all or part of this delegation in case of a significant increase of the industry being regulated. The convention provides that, in case of a significant increase in commercial sealing, the parties might decide by a two-thirds majority to establish a scientific advisory committee to which some or all of the functions delegated to SCAR would be reallocated.[44]

More recent agreements such as the 1980 Convention for the Conservation of Antarctic Marine Living Resources (CCAMLR) and the Environmental Protocol have, however, discontinued this approach of delegating tasks to a specific nongovernmental scientific organization. Following the current practice of many international regimes, both of these agreements instead rely on the establishment of their own intergovernmental scientific committees. Thus the parties no longer have the need to position SCAR at the center of the regime as the main provider of scientific input to the decision-making process. The role of the scientific community is thus mainly limited to the status of observers to the same extent as other NGOs (see hereinafter). Both of the agreements contain specific references mandating that their institutions take into consideration the work done by relevant technical and scientific organizations.[45]

Status and Role of Environmental NGOs in the Development of the Antarctic Treaty System

Originally, scientific organizations were the only nonstate actors participating to some extent in the ATS.[46] A second phase began in the 1970s in the context of the growth of environmental concerns and of the organization of the UN Conference on Human Environment, when grassroots and advocacy organizations became involved with issues related to Antarctic governance.[47] In 1978, several NGOs created the Antarctic and Southern Ocean Coalition (ASOC) as an umbrella organization advocating stronger environmental protection on the continent and greater participation of civil society in the process.[48] While most of the intergovernmental meetings remained closed to observers until the end of the 1980s, NGOs dealt with this constraint by relying mainly on indirect mechanisms of participation, such as through the organization of their own events to which governmental representatives were invited. Supportive governments also adopted the practice of including representatives from civil society in their national delegations.[49]

A third stage toward greater inclusiveness of the Antarctic regime debuted in 1987 with the progressive recognition of a more formal role for civil society. Greenpeace and ASOC attempted to exploit new opportunities to participate in decision making as the CCAMLR provided a formal status for NGOs. According to the provisions of the CCAMLR, both commission and scientific committee might enter in agreement with relevant organizations and invite observers to their meetings.[50]

After a rather complicated and equivocal application process,[51] ASOC was formally invited to attend a meeting of the commission established by the CCAMLR in 1987, while the application of Greenpeace was rejected.[52] Under the umbrella of ASOC several of its member organizations have since then attended the meetings of the commission.[53] The rules of procedure for both commission and scientific committee define in similar terms the participation of observers.[54] The chairpersons of each institution can decide to invite new observer organizations to attend meetings, in which case a decision is made by the relevant body on the acceptance of observers to its meeting. Unless otherwise decided, observers might attend all sessions without taking part to vote. They might also submit documents, and, at the discretion of the chairperson, deliver statements during meetings. In practice several additional representatives from civil society attend the meetings of the commission as advisers to national delegations.

In 1987, the consultative parties also amended the rules of procedure of the Antarctic Treaty Consultative Meeting (ATCM) in order to allow for the participation of observers.[55] The 1988 Convention on the Regulation of Antarctic Mineral Resource Activities (CRAMRA) also provided for cooperation with international organizations, including nongovernmental organizations, having a scientific, technical, or environmental interest in Antarctica.[56] The convention never entered into force, however, due to the withdrawal of the support of Australia and France. NGOs played an informal yet determining role in shaping the emerging regime as they successfully prevented the adoption of the convention and created momentum for the consecutive negotiations of the more ambitious Environmental Protocol.[57]

Building on the experience of the CCAMLR, ASOC was granted the status of "invited experts" for the meeting of the consultative parties to the Antarctic Treaty in 1991.[58] Greenpeace adopted for a few years the unusual approach of following the practice of states interested in receiving an enhanced role in the ATS. Since the status of consultative parties was conditional on the operation of a scientific base on the continent, the organization decided to establish and operate its own base. It also conducted monitoring visits in other national scientific bases, asserting that this action demonstrated that it was at least as serious as the consultative states in its interest on the continent.[59]

The provisions of the Antarctic Treaty limit, however, to what extent the status of NGOs can be enhanced without an amendment to the treaty. The adoption of the Environmental Protocol provided an opportunity to implement comprehensively the more inclusive approach to NGOs already adopted by the previous convention. The protocol thus contains provisions allowing "relevant scientific, environmental and technical organizations which can contribute [to the work of the Committee for Environmental Protection (CEP)] to participate as observers at the [CEP] sessions."[60] The rules of procedure of the CEP are similar to those of the previous agreements adopted under the ATS, observers having the right to take part in discussions and table documents but not to vote.[61] This opportunity remains subject to the decision of the CEP, with approval by the ATCM. Based on these developments, NGOs have

been able to contribute further to Antarctic governance, both in supporting the consultative parties on substantive discussions, as well as in affirming the legitimacy of
the whole regime.[62]

Antarctic Governance and the Private Sector: Toward the End of a Regime of Exception?

Until the 1980s, the business sector was absent from the governance of the Antarctic. The agreements and measures adopted under the frame of the ATS had little
direct economic impact on their operations. This context changed in 1980 with the
adoption of the Convention for the Conservation of Antarctic Marine Living Resources to regulate fisheries in the Southern Ocean. According to the provisions of
the CCAMLR, both commission and scientific committees might enter in agreement with relevant organizations and invite observers to their meetings.[63] Private
entities involved in toothfish fisheries established the Coalition of Legal Toothfish
Operators (COLTO) in 1987 as a nongovernmental organization in order to represent their interests, in particular against illegal unregulated and unreported (IUU)
fishing.[64] COLTO obtained observer status to the CCAMLR commission in 2003,
enabling representatives to attend meetings. Prior to its first participation in a meeting of the commission, COLTO contributed to the proceedings by submitting for
consideration a report on IUU fishing in the area covered by the CCAMLR, providing a list of vessels involved in illegal activities and registered in ten states that
were parties to the convention. The contracting parties, in particular China, Chile,
Russia, and Uruguay, met this initiative with strong resistance.[65] Since this meeting,
relations between COLTO and the commission have improved. COLTO's membership has for instance contributed financially to the work of the CCAMLR.[66]

The lack of adequate regulation of the growing tourism industry is a notable gap
in the regime established by the Environmental Protocol. In order to address this
lacuna, several contracting states promoted the idea of adoption of a specific annex
to regulate the activities of tourist operators and nongovernmental organizations.
However, while governments had been able to adopt sectoral regulatory frameworks
prior to the development of industrial fisheries and mineral exploitation, tour operators were already active in the region by the time the parties to the ATS began to
consider the need for specific related arrangements. Once the consultative parties
began to discuss whether to regulate tourism, the industry created the International
Association of Antarctic Tour Operators (IAATO) in 1991 to represent and advocate
its interests. This organization was first acknowledged in the context of the ATS
with its invited expert status at the Venice informal meeting convened to discuss
tourism regulation prior to the XVII Consultative Meeting. By then, IAATO had
adopted its own guidelines to limit the environmental impacts of tourism.[67] These
self-regulations made a case against the development of further intergovernmental
rules.[68] Facing the opposition of several other parties, the proposal for adoption of a
specific annex was abandoned, resulting in the adoption of two weaker measures.[69]
Furthermore, these measures have not yet entered into force due to a particularly

low number of ratifications.[70] Thus the regulation of tourism in the Antarctic currently relies on self-regulation adopted by the industry. Another argument promoting self-regulation of tourism in the region can be debated from the perspective of effectiveness. The complicated nature of jurisdiction over tourism operators—most notably the issue of flags of convenience—represents a substantial obstacle to the effective implementation of any measures adopted in the frame of the protocol.[71] Bastmeijer noted in 2004, however, a regression of confidence among consultative parties that self-regulation was adequate. Issues related to the cumulative impacts of tourism were discussed at the XXVII ATCM with more focus than at any previous meeting, suggesting the possibility of a new stage of tourism regulation in the Antarctic.[72]

The self-regulatory approach to Antarctic tourism favored by the consultative parties has recently been challenged by the adoption of regulations through the International Maritime Organization (IMO). In 2010, the Marine Environment Protection Committee amended Annex I of the International Convention for the Prevention of Pollution from Ships (MARPOL) in order to bar the use and carriage of heavy-grade oil below 60 degrees latitude south from August 1, 2011.[73] Implementation of this rule has led to the first drastic reduction in pollution through regulation affecting tourism in the region. In addition, the IMO is currently developing its International Code of Safety for Ships Operating in Polar Waters (Polar Code). While originally scheduled to enter into force in 2013, adoption of the Polar Code has been postponed with negotiations continuing in spring 2014. The entry into force of the code will further impact Antarctic tourist operators, limiting the capacity of the industry to self-regulate in order to avoid mandatory standards. In this context, the ability of IAATO to avoid international regulation of Antarctic tourism activities seems to fade as the stakes are raised by the growing scale of the activity.

Twenty Years of Arctic Governance

Up to the 1990s, global geopolitical interests particularly dominated international relations in the Arctic, the region being located directly between the two main opponents of the Cold War. The historic speech delivered by Mikhail Gorbachev in Murmansk in 1987 opened a new era for Arctic cooperation as the Soviet leader declared that it was "appropriate to examine the idea of cooperation between all people also from the standpoint of the situation in the northern part of this planet."[74] The Nordic states took initiatives to ensure the follow-up of this declaration and launched processes for regional cooperation. In 1989, Finland organized the Rovaniemi Conference, which included all Arctic nations and initiated the process that resulted in the adoption of the Arctic Environmental Protection Strategy (AEPS) two years later. While implementing the AEPS, the Arctic states also built on the strategy and established the Arctic Council in 1996 as a more formal forum for regional cooperation.[75] While the Arctic Council is the most prominent forum for Arctic governance, additional regional processes have also been established to foster transboundary collaboration.[76] The Barents Euro-Arctic Region (BEAR), for instance, relies on an alternative model of governance involving several levels of transboundary cooperation.

The following subsections will analyze three aspects of Arctic governance from the perspective of nonstate actors. The first case study will highlight how the procedures of the Arctic Council provide only limited opportunities for NGOs to participate in the work of the Council, as the status of observer limits the influence of civil society; the following subsections will consider more innovative mechanisms for the participation of indigenous peoples' organizations (IPOs) in the proceedings of the Arctic Council and of local governments in the case of the BEAR cooperation.

Stakeholders and Observers

When the AEPS was adopted, the Arctic states granted to the IPOs a status of observers similar to the role attributed to other civil society actors.[77] In the subsequent process leading to the establishment of the Arctic Council, the Task Force on Sustainable Development and Utilization (TFSDU) highlighted in similar terms the importance of enabling the participation of both local communities and indigenous peoples.[78] The TFSDU recognized for instance that "the inclusion of the indigenous people and local communities in the decision-making process will enhance the legitimacy of the decisions made and will facilitate compliance."[79] The Ottawa Declaration establishing the Arctic Council further refers in its preamble to the desire to "ensure full consultation with and the full involvement of indigenous people and their communities and other inhabitants of the Arctic in such activities."[80] The operative paragraphs of the declaration and the rules of procedure of the Arctic Council, however, create distinct rules for the participation of indigenous peoples and other communities.

Nongovernmental organizations can participate in the work of the Arctic Council under the status of observer. The status can be granted by the members of the Council provided that applicants can prove that their participation can "contribute to the work" of the Council.[81] In practice this criterion has been used in a political manner in order to prevent the participation of organizations and states that do not share some of the vision of the Arctic states.[82] To respond to the increasing interest of non-Arctic states in gaining the status, the Senior Arctic Officials (SAOs) at the Arctic Council adopted a clearer set of criteria that applicants should respect in order to become observers.[83] The *Arctic Council Observer Manual for Subsidiary Bodies* was developed and adopted by the SAOs ahead of the Kiruna ministerial meeting.[84] The manual describes logistical arrangements to accommodate the presence of observers and defines their role in relation to the subsidiary bodies of the Arctic Council.

The rules of procedure provide a rather limited role for observers, mainly restricted to attendance at meetings, submission of relevant documents, and minor participation during the sessions other than ministerial meetings, at the discretion of the chair.[85] The chair of any of the subsidiary bodies and working groups can also decide to invite on an ad hoc basis other organizations and individuals who have a specific expertise relevant to a specific meeting.[86] Observers might contribute to a greater extent to the projects of the working groups.[87] The new guidelines on the role of observers provide that, "while the primary role of observers is to observe the work of the Arctic Council, observers should continue . . . their engagement in the Arctic Council primarily at the level of working groups."[88] Currently, most NGOs with observer status are environmental NGOs, other observers representing research institutions, regional authorities, or local interests such as reindeer herders.[89] Despite the rather passive role foreseen for NGOs with observer status, it is interesting to note that these organizations have the same formal status as non-Arctic states and intergovernmental organizations with observer status.[90]

The Special Status of Permanent Participants

During the first years of Arctic cooperation under the AEPS, the importance of the participation of indigenous peoples was progressively emphasized, particularly in the context of the adoption of the Rio Declaration in 1992 and its Principle 22 recognizing the importance of the participation of indigenous people in environmental management. The process leading to the creation of the Arctic Council offered an opportunity to review their status and to formalize the stronger role played by indigenous peoples' organizations in Arctic cooperation.[91] An Indigenous Peoples' Secretariat was created in 1994 in order to support the participation of IPOs in Arctic governance. Negotiations leading to the establishment of the Arctic Council considered the opportunity for equal participation of both IPOs and states, including, for instance, the former as cosignatories to the Ottawa Declaration.

Due to the lack of support of the United States, however, the status of IPOs in Arctic cooperation was only elevated to an intermediary level with the adoption of the Ottawa Declaration on the Establishment of the Arctic Council.[92] The declaration created the category of "Permanent Participants" for the three IPOs already recognized as observers under the Arctic Environmental Protection Strategy.[93] A procedure was also created for the recognition of additional IPOs as Permanent Participants.[94] The objective of the creation of this specific status is to "provide for active participation and full consultation with the Arctic indigenous representatives within the Arctic Council," the rules of procedure further providing that this principle should apply "to all meetings and activities of the Arctic Council."[95] The Ottawa Declaration also provided for the continuation of the Indigenous Peoples' Secretariat.[96] The newly established Permanent Secretariat of the Arctic Council is also mandated to "provide services" to the Permanent Participants.[97] The establishment of the Permanent Secretariat is expected to benefit the Permanent Participants.[98]

According to the rules of procedure, Permanent Participants have participatory rights almost equal to those of the member states to the Council, except for the right to vote; Koivurova and Heinämäki described this status as "close to a de facto power of veto should they all reject a particular proposal."[99] The rights of Permanent Participants listed in the rules of procedure allow them to play a role both prior to the meetings in agenda setting as well as during all meetings themselves. Permanent Participants have also been heavily involved in the activities of each of the six working groups established under the Arctic Council, and contributed to other ad hoc initiatives. The Arctic Marine Shipping Assessment and the report on Best Practices in Ecosystem-Based Oceans Management in the Arctic both contain, besides national sections, a specific section dedicated to indigenous knowledge and experience.[100] In this context, the recognition of the status of Permanent Participants at the Arctic Council constitutes an example of best practices in relation to the participation of indigenous peoples in environmental governance.[101]

Another Forum for Arctic Cooperation: The Barents Euro-Arctic Region

Among the other forums for environmental governance in the Arctic, the model of cooperation adopted by the Barents Euro-Arctic Council (BEAC) is particularly enriching from the viewpoint of transnational governance. The Barents Euro-Arctic Region was established after the end of the Cold War in order to transform a heavily militarized region into an area for political collaboration focused on regional sustainable development.[102] The Kirkenes Declaration in 1993 established a unique bicameral institutional structure with representation of both national interests and local governments.[103] Similar to the development of the Arctic Council, the BEAR cooperation has relied on soft-law documents rather than building on a legally binding agreement.[104]

With regard to international cooperation, governments take part in the BEAC gathering at a ministerial level on a biannual basis, thus constituting a traditional platform for international dialogue. The representation of the interests of indigenous peoples is currently channeled through the Working Group on Indigenous Peoples (WGIP). Membership to the WGIP includes one Saami representative from each of the countries as well as one Vespian and one Nenets representative, with three organizations represented as observers.[105] The WGIP is established as a permanent working group, contributes directly to the work of both the BEAC and the Barents Regional Council (BRC), and is supported by a secretariat currently located in Lovozero, Russia.[106] In the Declaration on the Twentieth Anniversary of the Barents Euro-Arctic Cooperation, the prime ministers taking part in the BEAR reiterated indigenous peoples' "right to participate in decision making in matters that would affect their rights."[107] The declaration also called for a strengthening of indigenous peoples' representation in the Barents cooperation.[108] Participation of other segments of civil society is comparatively limited, despite the fact that the 1993 terms of reference for the BEAC also created a status of observers for NGOs. In related working groups, special advisory bodies have been created to enable the representation of businesses and youth.

The Barents Regional Council is established to foster cooperation among representatives of regional governments; each of the thirteen regions taking part in the Barents cooperation participate, together with representatives of three indigenous peoples' organizations, in the annual meetings of the BRC. The BRC further relies on the work of its five regional working groups for the sectoral implementation of decisions, each working group gathering representatives from each regional administration working on a similar field.

The BEAR thus represents a model of regional governance with regard to the participation of different layers of public authority. In this cooperation a large role is foreseen for the representatives of regional administrations. This transboundary cooperation does not require the systematic approval of national governments to engage in joint projects across borders. Cooperation at the regional level has been particularly productive in supporting the emergence of "professional networks" among administration officials across borders and trust building among different administrative cultures.[109] Zimmerbauer noted through his empirical research, however, the important framing role played by top-down processes in the development of the Barents cooperation and its impact on the shaping of the BEAR institutions.[110]

Pressures on Arctic Governance: Toward More Inclusive or More Classic Governance?

Climate change has undeniably become the single most important natural factor impacting the development of both polar regions. Its impact in the Arctic, however, has led to more radical social and economic consequences than its consequences in Antarctica. In the latter region, the impact of climate change still remains mainly limited to environmental and scientific implications. In this context, climate change has not yet arisen as a major issue challenging the current Antarctic regime, while it certainly contributes greatly to fostering discussions related to Arctic governance.[111]

The previous section highlighted the fact that, despite allowing only limited participation from other stakeholders, the current structure of the Arctic Council provides a usually high level of participation of IPOs. While this status might serve as an example of best practices in other forums, recent developments related to Arctic governance constitute both a threat to and an opportunity for the continuation of these inclusive procedures.

The Arctic Five: Establishment of a Closed Forum for Ocean Issues

The rapidly evolving economic context in the Arctic is currently a source of great pressure on the way in which Arctic states have cooperated up to now. The Arctic Ocean is now perceived as a strategic asset due to both the opening of new sea routes and the amount of mineral resources stored under the seabed.[112] This shift toward seeing the Arctic through an economic perspective has affected the vision of the eight Arctic states for the governance of the region, and has brought substantial political pressure from external actors. Both of these developments are likely to present challenges and opportunities for the inclusion of nonstate actors in environmental governance. The increasing focus on the ocean itself in Arctic politics has revealed the potential tensions between the five Arctic coastal states on the one hand and Finland, Iceland, and Sweden on the other hand, the latter three lacking an Arctic Ocean coastline. The Arctic coastal states engaged in 2008 in a new model of regional governance with the convening of a meeting focused on maritime issues, to which neither the noncoastal states nor the Permanent Participants were invited.

The declaration resulting from the meeting emphasized the coastal states' vision for Arctic Ocean management: "[b]y virtue of their sovereignty, sovereign rights and jurisdiction in large areas of the Arctic Ocean the five coastal states are in a unique position to address these possibilities and challenges."[113]

Iceland reacted to the initiative in expressing its concerns about such discussions sidelining the Arctic Council.[114] These developments might lead the three noncoastal states to provide strong support for the current structure of the Arctic Council in order to maintain their role at the core of decisions impacting Arctic governance, consequently supporting the continuation of the status of the Permanent Participants. Indigenous Peoples' Organizations expressed their opposition to any political discussions taking place at the regional level without the presence of the Permanent Participants. The Inuit Circumpolar Council (ICC), representing communities in half of the Arctic states, issued a strong statement to highlight its particular vision of sovereignty: "The conduct of international relations in the Arctic and the resolution of international disputes in the Arctic are not the sole preserve of Arctic states or other states; they are also within the purview of the Arctic's indigenous peoples. The development of international institutions in the Arctic, such as multilevel governance systems and indigenous peoples' organizations, must transcend Arctic states' agendas on sovereignty and sovereign rights and the traditional monopoly claimed by states in the area of foreign affairs."[115]

Since the 2008 Ilulissat Arctic Conference, cooperation between the five Arctic coastal states has continued, both at the political and at a technical level, furthering consideration among the five coastal states of opportunities to address the issue of high Arctic fisheries. The meeting of the coastal states has, however, attracted less outrage from other regional stakeholders, possibly due to the lower level of visibility associated with the process and to the more focused agenda of the discussion.

Diverging Views over the Role and Responsibility of Observers

External actors are also pressing the Arctic Council to adopt a new approach for Arctic governance that would leave greater space for the participation of non-Arctic states.[116] The number of non-Arctic states expressing interest in playing a role in regional politics has recently increased. The Kiruna ministerial meeting granted permanent observer status to six additional non-Arctic states, including prominent geopolitical players such as China and Japan. The number of observer states now exceeds the number of parties. Some of the current permanent observers have expressed their frustration with the current status of non-Arctic states.[117] In reaction to these developments, some of the Arctic states, most notably Russia and Canada, reiterated that non-Arctic states had only a very limited role to play in the governance of the region.

This context could possibly support the claims of local nonstate actors for a continuation and a strengthening of their status in the proceedings of the Arctic Council. Indeed, the inclusion of the Permanent Participants in regional decision making contributes to increasing the legitimacy of the Arctic Council.[118] Under current circumstances, the Arctic states can make the case that the model of the Arctic Council is sufficiently inclusive as it involves local communities and IPOs, possibly to a larger extent than any other international regime. The Senior Arctic Officials also adopted criteria for the admission of permanent observers. In the context of the tensions raised by the EU ban on imports of seal hunt products and of strong concerns raised about the impact of the ban on Inuit communities,[119] the criteria include the necessity for applicant states to "respect the values, interests, culture and traditions of Arctic indigenous peoples and other Arctic inhabitants" and to "have demonstrated a political willingness as well as financial ability to contribute to the work of the Permanent Participants and other Arctic indigenous peoples."[120] These additional expectations contribute to strengthen the position of Arctic nonstate actors vis-à-vis non-Arctic states, a situation thus implicitly accepted by all new applicants to permanent observer status; this also implies mandatory financial support from non-Arctic states to the activities of the Permanent Participants.[121]

Recent Institutional Developments at the Arctic Council

The ongoing process toward institutionalization of the Arctic Council and the trend toward the adoption of more formal agreements might pose another potential challenge to the status of the Permanent Participants and other observers. At its 2011 and 2013 ministerial meetings, the Arctic Council adopted the first two legally binding instruments negotiated under its auspices aimed at establishing a legal framework facilitating cooperation among the eight parties.

Despite the stakes that local governments or representatives of the shipping and aeronautical industries might have, the 2011 Agreement on Aeronautical and Maritime Search and Rescue contains no reference to any role for nonstate actors.[122] Participation of these stakeholders is provided for neither in relation to implementation of the agreement nor as observers at future meetings taking place under the agreement.

The 2013 Agreement on Cooperation on Marine Oil Pollution Preparedness and Response in the Arctic does refer to the role of stakeholders.[123] The agreement notes the important role of indigenous peoples, local communities, local and regional governments, and individual Arctic residents and recognizes the expertise of "various stakeholders."[124] The agreement provides that information exchanged among parties shall be made publicly available.[125] Stakeholders shall be invited to participate "when appropriate" in the planning and execution of joint exercises and training mandated under the agreement.[126] The agreement includes, however, no provision defining a role for stakeholders in decision making, such as through participation in the Conference of the Parties established by the agreement.

Among the decisions reached during the Nuuk ministerial meeting to strengthen the Arctic Council, the Arctic states agreed to establish a Permanent Secretariat in Tromsø.[127] The Permanent Secretariat is mandated to facilitate exchange of information between observers, Permanent Participants, and Arctic states.[128] In relation to access to information, the Permanent Secretariat should take actions "facilitating and improving the quality and availability of information on the Arctic Council" as well as "recording, maintaining and posting, as appropriate, the records of the Arctic Council."[129] While such functions could benefit nonstate actors in facilitating access to relevant documents in relation to the activities and proceedings of the Arctic Council, these provisions fall short of providing clear access to information policy such as in relation to the Antarctic Treaty System.[130] Whereas there are still opportunities to strengthen this role, the establishment of the Permanent Secretariat of the Arctic Council provides benefits for nonstate actors involved in regional governance.

The practice of the Arctic Council of establishing ad hoc task forces more regularly, including for the negotiations of the Search and Rescue Agreement, might further jeopardize the inclusiveness of the Arctic Council. Task forces, as ad hoc bodies, are not constrained by the formal rules of procedure of the Arctic Council but might operate under their own terms of reference. The task force negotiating the agreement did not allow for the participation of observers in its proceedings, despite the positive experiences of former task forces with regard to the inclusion of observers.[131] The 2011 Senior Arctic Officials report refers to the growing use of task forces in the substantive work of the Arctic Council and confirms that the mode of operation of the task force will be determined in a case-by-case basis.[132] The reliance on task forces weakens the position of Permanent Participants and observers, their participation requiring a case-by-case confirmation for each task force—an additional requirement compared to the modalities of the working groups. The Kiruna ministerial meeting established four additional task forces, thus increasing reliance on these informal settings.[133]

Such developments have raised concern over the ability of the Arctic states to accept the continuation of the current status of Permanent Participants in a more formal context. No principles of international law preclude the inclusion of nonstate actors in global governance. Koivurova noted nevertheless that the increase of formalism in Arctic governance might involve a new set of actors and interests within the administration of the participating states, thus potentially threatening the current relative inclusiveness of the Arctic Council.[134]

On the basis of their empirical study of the Council, Kankaanpää and Young recommended in 2012 the reform of the Sustainable Development Working Group in order to interact with stakeholders and further implement Agenda 21 across all sectors of activities of the Council.[135]

A New Role for the Private Sector in Arctic Governance

Since prior to the beginning of its presidency, Sweden indicated its interest to consider the contribution of businesses to fostering sustainable development in the Arctic. Prior to the 2011 Nuuk ministerial meeting, the Senior Arctic Officials already recommended that ministers take note of the intention of the Swedish chairmanship to address the issue.[136] As it took over the chairmanship, Sweden defined Corporate Social Responsibility (CSR) as a priority of its work in the Sustainable

Development Working Group (SDWG), leading to the organization of two thematic workshops and an informal dialogue with businesses. This work resulted in the development of a publicly available information tool. For the period 2013–2015, the SDWG will continue to address CSR and sustainable business in the Arctic as a crosscutting project drawing from existing international CSR frameworks.[137]

In the context of the positive experience of the SDWG in its interactions with the private sector in the CSR project, the Arctic Council decided at the Kiruna ministerial meeting to establish a task force dedicated to the creation of a circumpolar business forum.[138] The task force builds the participation of the Arctic states and Permanent Participants, as well as invited experts representing industry. It is mandated to provide rapid results in order to launch the circumpolar business forum—renamed Arctic Economic Council—in spring 2014.

In Kankaanpää and Young's empirical study, industry was rated as having very little impact on the work of the Arctic Council.[139] Among the grounds invoked as justifying the establishment of the task force, the SAO referred to the interest of industry to "engage directly with key governance forums" and referred to the potential benefits of more direct linkage for several areas of work undertaken by the Council.[140] The mandate emphasizes explicitly the role of the Arctic Economic Forum as "a mechanism to allow business and industry to engage with the Arctic States and Permanent Participants," thus allowing for the private sector to provide direct policy input to the work of the Arctic Council.

Conclusions

In both polar regions, governments have developed innovative approaches to regional governance, allowing the participation of nonstate actors to a larger extent than is commonly the case at the global level. In some cases inclusive decision-making procedures of these regimes allow for an unprecedented level of participation by specific groups of stakeholders. In the ATS, the parties to the Seal Convention have granted a central role in its regime to the Scientific Committee on Antarctic Research (SCAR), a nongovernmental scientific organization. The convention not only identifies various tasks for the organization, but also imposes obligations toward SCAR on its state parties. In the context of Arctic governance, the status of Permanent Participants has enabled the effective participation of indigenous peoples in the work of the Arctic Council. Through this status, IPOs have been able to take part in the proceedings of the Council to an even greater extent than other states with observer status. The Barents Euro-Arctic Region provides a third interesting example of a new form of participatory governance with its reliance on transboundary cooperation between national and regional administrations. In addition, nonstate actors have also come to play an important external role in relation to polar governance, capitalizing on the emotional symbolism of the regions. These developments led Spectar to predict in 1999 the end of the hegemony of state actors in Antarctic governance. The author analyzed "the coming of age of NGOs" in the process leading to the abandonment of the Convention on the Regulation of Antarctic

Mineral Resource Activities and the impact of this successful campaign in the promotion of "a non state-centered and progressive jus gentium publicum in the new
millennium."[141]

While the decision-making procedures of several regional institutions indeed allow for an unprecedented level of participation by specific groups of stakeholders,
there is, however, no uniform approach to the participation of nonstate actors in
the various regimes of polar governance. Each regime has established its own set of
rules for participation at the proceedings of other stakeholders. Despite the unique
conditions prevailing in both polar regions, many developments related to the inclusiveness of the Antarctic Treaty System and of the Arctic Council seem to follow
the general trends of global environmental governance rather than to constitute a
unique pattern. Within the ATS, as in other international environmental processes,
the role of NGOs evolved mainly in the eighties, in the context of the emergence of
the concept of sustainable development and the accompanying recognition of the
importance of stakeholder participation. The recognition of a role for the private
sector in the regime also echoes a more general pattern toward partnerships with
business entities and greater reliance on corporate social responsibility to promote
the implementation of development policies. Beyond the example provided by the
Antarctic regime, corporations have worked over the past decades to promote adoption of self-regulatory schemes rather than international norms, both through participation in the intergovernmental process and in preemptively adopting codes of
conduct in order to avoid further governmental regulation. As suggested earlier in
this chapter, however, self-regulatory options raise questions concerning accountability, legitimacy, and effectiveness, as the norms adopted in such a context lack the
legitimacy of state consent.

The question of the role of different groups of stakeholders in international environmental governance has recently been at the core of discussions related to the
reform of the institutional framework for sustainable development, in particular
during the process leading to the 2012 United Nations Conference on Sustainable
Development (Rio Plus 20 Conference).[142] The outcome of the conference reiterated the principle of public participation, as well as provided a concrete mandate
to strengthen the participation of stakeholders, both specifically in the proceedings
of the institutions created or reformed in Rio but also more generally throughout
global environmental governance.[143] The study of best practices related to nonstate
actors' engagement in the various regimes established in the polar regions could
thus provide valuable examples of approaches and procedures that could be implemented more broadly.

A perceptive analysis of the role and status of nonstate actors in polar environmental governance also highlights a more nuanced conclusion. With additional
distance, the experience in Antarctic governance has demonstrated that while the
interface between policy and science remains particularly important for governance
of the pole, state actors have retained their central role in governance of the region. The establishment of intergovernmental scientific bodies in the agreements
adopted under the ATS since the adoption of the Seal Convention indeed proves

that there is no irresistible trend toward more participatory governance. This lesson might also prove relevant in the Arctic context. In the 1990s, the definition of the status of Permanent Participants constituted a major step toward more participatory governance. While this approach constitutes nowadays a model to be applied under other international agreements, the role of indigenous peoples in Arctic governance could potentially be undermined under a set of both internal and external pressures.

Climate change contributes to modifying the balance between the interests of several actors in the Arctic, leading to a questioning of the current model for regional cooperation. Despite the growing discourse on the diminishing role of nation-states and the emergence of new forms of governance and new status for nonstate actors, the overall conclusion of the study of stakeholder participation in polar governance demonstrates that this development is not a linear process. While both Arctic and Antarctic players have innovated in the development of new forms of cooperation between states and other actors, the central role of the nation-states has remained the key figure of all regimes described previously. Herr reached the following conclusion fifteen years ago in relation to the inclusiveness of the Antarctic regime, an analysis that appears to be relevant not only to the Antarctic nowadays but also to some extent to the Arctic context: "The state system has demonstrated a considerable degree of resilience in Antarctica even though it has been forced to operate without the substantial prop of national sovereignty."[144]

One can expect, perhaps more than anywhere else, that the consequences of climate change in the polar regions will continue to challenge existing institutions and modes of cooperation, in particular as new economic opportunities emerge. During recent years, the interest and engagement of environmental organizations and the business sector have considerably increased in the Arctic in relation to potential fossil fuel extraction and the development of new fisheries. These developments confront the states involved in regional governance with the need to arbitrate between priorities and values that are difficult to reconcile.

Notes

1. See World Summit on Sustainable Development Declaration, para. 16 and 18.
2. See Rio Plus 20 Voluntary Commitments, http://www.uncsd2012.org/voluntary commitments.html. Accessed 27 September 2013.
3. See James N. Rosenau and Ernst Otto Czempiel, *Governance without Government: Order and Change in World Politics* (Cambridge: Cambridge University Press, 1992).
4. Bradley C. Karkkainen, "Post-Sovereign Environmental Governance," *Global Environmental Politics* 4(1) (2004): 76.
5. Koivurova highlights the positive influence that the UN Conference on Environment and Development had on the increasing role of indigenous peoples in Arctic governance. Timo Koivurova, "The Status and Role of Indigenous Peoples in Arctic International Governance," *Yearbook of Polar Law* 3 (2011): 177.
6. Inuit Circumpolar Council, Circumpolar Inuit Declaration on Sovereignty in the Arctic, April 2009, para. 2.1, http://inuitcircumpolar.com/files/uploads/icc-files/declaration12x18vice chairssigned.pdf. Accessed 27 September 2013.

7. United Nations General Assembly, 44th session, Resolution 44/124 B, December 1989, para. 6.

8. Richard A. Herr, "The Changing Roles of Non-Governmental Organizations in the Antarctic Treaty System," in *Governing the Antarctic: The Effectiveness and Legitimacy of the Antarctic Treaty System*, ed. Olav Schram Stokke and Vidas Davor (Cambridge: Cambridge University Press, 1996), 91.

9. World Commission on Environment and Development, *Our Common Future* (Oxford: Oxford University Press, 1987).

10. United Nations, 1992 Rio Declaration on Environment and Development, Principle 10.

11. UN Conference on Environment and Development, Agenda 21, sec. 3.

12. UN Convention on Access to Information, Public Participation in Decision-Making and Access to Justice in Environmental Matters (Aarhus Convention) 1998, *International Legal Materials (ILM)* 38 (1999), in force 30 October 2001.

13. UN Declaration on the Application of Principle 10 of the Rio Declaration on Environment and Development, 27 June 2012, UN Doc. A/CONF.216/13.

14. See, generally, Kal Raustiala, "States, NGOs, and International Environmental Institutions," *International Studies Quarterly* 41 (1997).

15. World Commission on Environment and Development (1987), Chap. 12, para. 73, supra note 9.

16. UN, 1992 Rio Declaration, Principle 10, Johannesburg Declaration on Sustainable Development 2002, para. 26; and Outcome of the 2012 Rio Conference on Sustainable Development, sec. II.C.

17. UNECE Guidelines on Promoting the Application of the Principles of the Aarhus Convention in International Forums (Almaty Guidelines), sec. I.1, Document ECE/MP.PP/2005/2/Add.5.

18. UN, Agenda 21, chap. 30.

19. Robert Falkner, "Private Environmental Governance and International Relations: Exploring the Links," *Global Environmental Politics* 3(2) (2003): 73.

20. Benedict Kingsbury, Nico Krisch, and Richard Stewart, "The Emergence of Global Administrative Law," *Law and Contemporary Problems* 68 (2005): 22–23.

21. For a broader introduction to the development of the FSC as an example of private governance, see Steven Bernstein and Benjamin Cashore, "Nonstate Global Governance: Is Forest Certification a Legitimate Alternative to a Global Forest Convention?" in *Hard Choices, Soft Law: Voluntary Standards in Global Trade, Environment, and Social Governance*, ed. John J. Kirton and M. J. Trebilcoc (Hants: Ashgate, 2004).

22. Daniel M. Bodansky, "The Legitimacy of International Governance: A Coming Challenge for International Environmental Law?" in *American Journal of International Law* 7(1) (1999): 605.

23. 1972 Stockholm Declaration on the Human Environment, preamble, Recital 7.

24. UN, Agenda 21, chap. 28.1.

25. UN, Agenda 21, chap. 28 on Local Authorities' initiatives in support of Agenda 21 and chap. 23, para. 3.

26. Report of the Panel of Eminent Persons on United Nations–Civil Society Relations (also known as the Cardoso Report), UN Doc. A/58/817:10, and more generally para. 117–119.

27. Ileana M. Porras, "The City and International Law: In Pursuit of Sustainable Development," *Fordham Urban Law Journal* 3 (2009): 552ff.

28. In the international climate regime, for instance, representatives of locally elected officials have been considered up to 2010 as one of the segments of civil society. In 2010, the specific nature of local governments compared to other groups of stakeholders was for the first time acknowledged in this regime with a reference to the recognition of *"the important role and value of the participation of all stakeholders*, both governmental and non-governmental" (empha-

sis mine). Report of the UNFCCC Subsidiary Body for Implementation on its thirty-third session, FCCC/SBI/2010/27, para. 143.

29. Yishai Blank, "Localism in the New Global Legal Order," *Harvard International Law Journal* 47(1) (2006).

30. Gerald Frug and David Barron, "International Local Government Law," *The Urban Lawyer* 38(1) (2006): 1–62.

31. Frank Biermann and Philipp Pattberg, "Global Environmental Governance: Taking Stock, Moving Forward," *Annual Review of Environment and Resources* 33 (2008): 281.

32. See the Report of the High-level Panel on United Nations System-wide Coherence in the Areas of Development, Humanitarian Assistance and the Environment, UN Doc. A/61/583 (2006).

33. See Daniel C. Esty, "Good Governance at the Supranational Scale: Globalizing Administrative Law," *Yale Law Journal* (2006): 1502.

34. Peter Willetts, "Transnational Actors and International Organizations in Global Politics," in *The Globalization of World Politics*, ed. J. B. Baylis and S. Smith, 2nd ed. (Oxford: Oxford University Press, 2001), text box 15.12.

35. The Antarctic Treaty System (ATS) has for instance a long history of cooperation with the International Whaling Commission.

36. See Richard Herr for a description of the evolving role of the NGOs in the ATS. Herr, "Changing Roles," supra note 8, 96–106.

37. Antarctic Treaty, 402 UN Treaty Series (UNTS) 71 (1959), Art. 2.

38. SCAR will later become the Scientific Committee on Antarctic Research. SCAR was established by the International Council of Scientific Unions as an organization entirely dedicated to the issue of Antarctic science. See http://www.scar.org/. Accessed 27 September 2013.

39. Richard Fifield, *International Research in the Antarctic* (Oxford: Oxford University Press, 1987), 1–2.

40. Agreed Measures for the Conservation of Antarctic Fauna and Flora, Recommendation ATCM III–VIII (1964), Preamble.

41. Lee Kimball, "The Role of Non-governmental Organizations in Antarctic Affairs," in Christopher Joyner and Sudhir Chopra, *The Antarctic Legal Regime* (Dordrecht: Martinus Nijhoff, 1988), 44.

42. Convention for the Conservation of Antarctic Seals, UNTS 175 (1972), Art. 4 and 5.

43. Ibid., Art. 4.4–4.6.

44. Ibid., Art. 6.1.c.ii.

45. Convention on the Conservation of Antarctic Marine Living Resources (CCAMLR), (1980) 19 *ILM* 841; Art. 15.3 in relation to the CCAMLR Scientific Committee and Environmental Protocol; Art. 10.1 in relation to the Antarctic Treaty Consultative Meeting.

46. Lee Kimball noted such a lack of recognition for NGOs was not in conformity with the practices of the UN at that time. See Kimball, "The Role of Non-governmental Organizations," supra note 41, at 56.

47. Ibid., at 36, establishing the parallel between the growth of the involvement of environmental NGOs in Antarctic matters and the general context.

48. See ASOC web page: http://asoc.nonprofitsoapbox.com/about/history. Accessed 27 September 2013.

49. J. N. Barnes, "Environmental Protection and the Future of the Antarctic: New Approaches and Perspectives Are Necessary," in *The Antarctic Treaty Regime: Law, Environment and Resources*, ed. Gillian D. Triggs (Cambridge: Cambridge University Press, 1989), 153–154.

50. CCAMLR, Art. 23.3 and 23.4.

51. For a rather critical study of the approach of the commission to the recognition of observers, see Matthew Howard, "The Convention on the Conservation of Antarctic Marine Living Resources: A Five-Year Review," *International and Comparative Law Quarterly* 38(104) (1989).

52. The commission decided to accept only the application of ASOC on the basis of the fact that it is an umbrella organization; see report of the third meeting of the Commission, para. 54ff. This acceptance was, however, preceded by a rather long application process, including the requirement that the applicant NGOs state that they support the objectives of the convention prior to consideration of their application. Francisco Vicuna, *Antarctic Mineral Exploitation—The Emerging Legal Framework* (Cambridge: Cambridge University Press, 1988), 468.

53. See participant lists for the meetings of the commission, available from the web page of the CCAMLR: http://www.ccamlr.org/. Accessed 27 September 2013.

54. Rules of procedure of the Commission, part VI, and Rules of procedure of the Scientific Committee, part X.

55. XIV ATCM, Report para. 8ff.

56. Convention on the Regulation of Antarctic Mineral Resource Activities, 27 *ILM* 868 (1988), Art. 34.3 and 34.4.

57. J. M. Spectar, "Saving the Ice Princess: NGOs, Antarctica and International Law in the New Millenium," *Suffolk Transnational Law Review* 23 (1999): 81ff.; Margaret Clark, "The Antarctic Environmental Protocol: NGOs in the Protection of Antarctica," in *Environmental NGOs in World Politics*, ed. Thomas Princen and Matthias Finger (London: Routledge, 1994), 167ff. See also Vidas noting that concerns raised by environmental NGOs over the CRAMRA contributed in several countries to the adoption of national positions supportive to a new and more ambitious protocol. Davor Vidas. "The Protocol on Environmental Protection to the Antarctic Treaty: A Ten-Year Review," *Yearbook of International Co-operation on Environment and Development* 3 (2002): 52.

58. ASOC was invited for the first time to a meeting of the consultative parties during the XVI ATCM held in Bonn, October 1991.

59. See Clark, "Antarctic Environmental Protocol," supra note 57, at 164–165. See also Greenpeace's own reporting on the activities for their base, in John May, *The Greenpeace Book of Antarctica: A New View of the Seventh Continent*, 2nd ed. (New York: Doubleday, 1989), 172.

60. Protocol on Environmental Protection to the Antarctic Treaty, 30 *ILM* 1455, Art. 11.4. The protocol also provides that the report of each session shall be circulated to the observers attending this particular session. Protocol, Art. 11.5.

61. Revised Rules of Procedure for the Committee for Environmental Protection (2011), Rules 4(c), 6 and 12.

62. Herr, "The Changing Roles of Non-governmental Organizations," supra note 8, at 108.

63. CCAMLR, Art. 23.3 and 23.4.

64. See the articles of association of COLTO, available at http://www.colto.org/images/COLTO-revised-FINAL-Constitution-May-2011.pdf. Accessed 27 September 2013.

65. See report of the XXII meeting of the commission, para. 14.25–14.42.

66. See report of the XXIX meeting of the commission, para. 4.78.

67. In 1993, two years after its establishment, IAATO adopted two sets of guidelines, addressed respectively to Antarctica tour operators and to Antarctica visitors. See C. Michael Hall and Stephen J. Page, *The Geography of Tourism and Recreation: Environment, Place and Space* (London: Routledge, 2003), 317.

68. See Kees Bastmeijer and Ricardo Roura, "Regulating Antarctic Tourism and the Precautionary Principle," *American Journal of International Law* 98(4) (2004): 774–775.

69. Mike G. Richardson, "Regulating Tourism in the Antarctic: Issues of Environment and Jurisdiction," in *Implementing the Environmental Protection Regime for the Antarctic*, ed. Davor Vidas (Dordrecht: Kluwer, 2000), 79. Interestingly, environmental NGOs usually supportive of tighter environmental regulations, such as ASOC, did not provide the expected support to the proposal, partly due to their own interest in not having their own landings on the continent further regulated.

70. The two measures are Measure 4 (2004) on Insurance and Contingency Planning for Tourism and Non-governmental Activities in the Antarctic Treaty Area, and Measure 15 (2009) on the Landing of Persons from Passenger Vessels in the Antarctic Treaty Area.

71. Richardson, "Regulating Tourism in the Antarctic," supra note 69, at 81–83.

72. Bastmeijer and Roura, "Regulating Antarctic Tourism and the Precautionary Principle," supra note 68, at 775–777. For a discussion of ethical differences in relation to nature among consultative parties as the deeper roots of the inability of the ATCM to regulate the issue of tourism, see also Kees Bastmeijer and Machiel Lamers, "Reaching Consensus on Antarctic Tourism Regulation: Calibrating the Human-Nature Relationship?" in *New Issues in Polar Tourism*, ed. D. Mueller, L. Lundmark, and H. Lemelin (Heidelberg: Springer Verlag, 2012).

73. Resolution MEPC.189(60), adopted on 26 March 2010 (addition of a new chapter 9 to MARPOL Annex I).

74. Speech available at: www.barentsinfo.fi/docs/Gorbachev_speech.pdf. Accessed 27 September 2013.

75. Ottawa Declaration on the establishment of the Arctic Council (1996) [hereinafter Ottawa Declaration].

76. See Sébastien Duyck, "Participation of Non-state Actors in Arctic Environmental Governance," *Nordia Geographical Publications* 40(4) (2012).

77. Arctic Environmental Protection Strategy—The Declaration on the Protection of the Arctic Environment (Rovaniemi Declaration), Rovaniemi, Finland, 14 January 1991, at 42.

78. Eva Carina Keskitalo, *Negotiating the Arctic: The Construction of an International Region* (London: Routledge, 2004), 83–98.

79. Task Force on Sustainable Development and Utilization, Draft no. 3, 1995.

80. Ottawa Declaration, Preamble.

81. Arctic Council Rules of Procedure, contained in SAO report (1998 Iqaluit), Annex 1.

82. See, for an early example of the refusal to grant the status of observer to an NGO (the International Fund for Animal Welfare) on the basis of its stand with regard to sealing: Keskitalo, *Negotiating the Arctic*, supra note 78, at 93.

83. Nuuk Declaration on the occasion of the Seventh Arctic Council Ministerial Meeting, 12 May 2011, p. 2, deciding to apply the criteria proposed by the SAOs to new applicants. The list of the criteria is available in the 2011 SAO report, Annex 1: "The criteria for admitting observers and role for their participation in the Arctic Council," 50.

84. *Arctic Council Observer Manual for Subsidiary Bodies, Senior Arctic Officials Report to Ministers* (Kiruna, Sweden, 12 May 2011), 90–96.

85. Arctic Council Rules of Procedure, Rules 37 and 38, completed by the 2011 SAO report, Annex 1, 50–51.

86. Arctic Council Rules of Procedure, Rule 39.

87. The Arctic Environmental Protection Strategy for instance led to the establishment of the Conservation of Arctic Fauna and Flora Working Group on the basis of the reference to the need for the Arctic states to "seek to create a distinct forum for scientists, indigenous peoples and conservation managers engaged in Arctic flora, fauna and habitat," AEPS, 38.

88. *Arctic Council Observer Manual for Subsidiary Bodies.*

89. In 2014, the eleven NGOs with observer status were as follows: Advisory Committee on Protection of the Seas (ACOPS), Arctic Circumpolar Gateway, Association of World Reindeer Herders (AWRH), Circumpolar Conservation Union (CCU), International Arctic Science Committee (IASC), International Arctic Social Sciences Association (IASSA), International Union for Circumpolar Health (IUCH), International Work Group for Indigenous Affairs (IWGIA), Northern Forum (NF), University of the Arctic (UArctic), World Wide Fund for Nature–Global Arctic Program (WWF).

90. For further discussion of the role and status of non-Arctic states, see Piotr Graczyk and Timo Koivurova, "A New Era in the Arctic Council's External Relations? Broader Consequences of the Nuuk Observer Rules for Arctic Governance," *Polar Record*, 2013.

91. See Koivurova, "The Status and Role of Indigenous Peoples in Arctic International Governance," supra note 5.

92. David Scrivener, "Arctic Environmental Cooperation in Transition," *Polar Record* 35(192) (1999): 54.

93. Ottawa Declaration, para. 2.

94. The Ottawa Declaration stipulates organizations representing the interests of several indigenous peoples in the same country or representing a single indigenous people residing in several countries. Besides the Inuit Circumpolar Council (ICC), the Russian Association of the Indigenous Peoples of the North (RAIPON), and the Saami Council recognized as Permanent Participants in 1996, the Aleut International Association (AIA), the Arctic Athabaskan Council, and the Gwich'in Council International have also obtained this status.

95. Arctic Council Rules of Procedure, Rule 5.

96. Ottawa Declaration, para. 8.

97. Terms of Reference of the Permanent Secretariat of the Arctic Council, DMM02, 15 May 2012, Stockholm, Sweden, para. 2.2.

98. Nikolas Sellheim, "The Establishment of a Permanent Arctic Council Secretariat: Challenges and Opportunities," in *The Arctic Council: Its Place in the Future of Arctic Governance*, ed. Thomas Axworthy, Timo Koivurova, and Waliul Hasanat (Walter and Duncan Gordon Foundation, 2012), 76.

99. Timo Koivurova and Leena Heinämäki, "The Participation of Indigenous Peoples in International Norm-Making in the Arctic," *Polar Record* 42:221 (2006): 104.

100. Arctic Marine Shipping Assessment, particularly section 5, "Scenarios, Futures and Regional Futures" to 2020; section 6 on "Human Dimensions"; and "Best Practices in Ecosystem-Based Oceans Management," 11–18.

101. Leena Heinämäki, "Towards an Equal Partnership between Indigenous Peoples and States: Learning from Arctic Experiences?" *The Yearbook of Polar Law* 3 (2009): 209.

102. Sigve R. Leland and Alf Håkon Hoel, "Learning by Doing: The Barents Cooperation and Development of Regional Collaboration in the North," in *The New Northern Dimension of the European Neighborhood*, ed. Pami Aalto, Helge Blakkisrud, and Hanna Smith (Brussels: Centre for European Policy Studies, 2008), 37–38.

103. Kirkenes Declaration, Conference of Foreign Ministers on Co-operation in the Barents Euro-Arctic Region, 11 January 1993. For more elaboration on the structure of the BEAR, see S. G. Sreejith, "Subjective Environmentalism: The Barents Euro-Arctic Council and Its Climate Change Policy," in *Climate Governance in the Arctic*, ed. Timo Koivurova, Carina Keskitalo, and Nigel Bankes (Berlin: Springer, 2009), 389.

104. For a discussion of the legal nature of the BEAR cooperation, see, generally, Waliul Hasanat, "Cooperation in the Barents Euro-Arctic Region in the Light of International Law," *Yearbook of Polar Law* 2 (2010): 299.

105. Observers to the WGIP are currently the Saami Council, the Russian Association of the Indigenous Peoples of the North (RAIPON), and the Association of World Reindeer Herders. The former two are Permanent Participants at the Arctic Council while the third is a permanent observer.

106. For further description of the Working Group on Indigenous Peoples, see Waliul Hasanat, "A unique arrangement of soft-law cooperation in the Barents Region," in *Politics of Development in the Barents Region*, ed. Monica Tennberg (Rovaniemi: Lapland University Press, 2012), 73.

107. Declaration on the Twentieth Anniversary of the Barents Euro-Arctic Cooperation (Kirkenes, Norway, 3–4 June 2013), at 3, available at http://www.barentsinfo.fi/beac/docs/Barents_Summit_Declaration_2013.pdf. Accessed 27 September 2013.

108. Ibid., at 6.

109. Leland and Hoel, "Learning by Doing: The Barents Cooperation," supra note 102, at 50–52.

110. Kaj Zimmerbauer, "Unusual Regionalism in Northern Europe: The Barents Region in the Making," *Regional Studies* 47(1) (2013).

111. See, for instance, Rayfuse on upcoming challenges for Arctic governance when assessing climate impacts in the polar region: Rosemary Rayfuse, "Melting Moments: The Future of

Polar Oceans Governance in a Warming World," *Review of European Community and International Environmental Law* 16(2) (2007).

112. United States Geological Survey, Circum-Arctic Resource Appraisal: Estimates of Undiscovered Oil and Gas North of the Arctic Circle (2008).

113. Ilulissat Declaration, Arctic Ocean Conference, Greenland, May 2008.

114. See Icelandic statement, Meeting of Senior Arctic Officials, Final Report, Narvik, Norway, 28–29 November 2007.

115. Inuit Circumpolar Declaration on Arctic Sovereignty, para. 4.2.

116. See for instance the Warsaw Meeting of Arctic Council Observer States organized at the initiative of the Polish Ministry of Foreign Affairs, 26 March 2010.

117. Following the refusal of the participation of France in the intergovernmental negotiations within the Search and Rescue Task Force, French Ambassador for the Polar Regions Michel Rocard listed his concerns in a letter dated 8 May 2011 to the Danish Foreign Minister, Lene Espersen, chairperson of the Arctic Council at the time.

118. Koivurova, "The Status and Role of Indigenous Peoples in Arctic International Governance," supra note 5, at 181.

119. See for instance Kamrul Hossain, "The EU Ban on the Import of Seal Products and the WTO Regulations: Neglected Human Rights of the Arctic Indigenous Peoples?" *Polar Record*, 2013.

120. Accreditation and Review of Observers, Annex 2 to Arctic Council Rules of Procedure, SAO Report to Ministers, Kiruna, Sweden, para. 6.

121. Graczyk and Koivurova, "A New Era in the Arctic Council's External Relations?" supra note 90, at 9.

122. Agreement on Aeronautical and Maritime Search and Rescue in the Arctic, signed in Nuuk, Greenland, 12 May 2011.

123. Agreement on Cooperation on Marine Oil Pollution Preparedness and Response in the Arctic, signed in Kiruna, Sweden, 15 May 2013.

124. Ibid., preamble, recital 12 and 13.

125. Ibid., Art. 12.2.

126. Ibid., Art. 13.3.

127. Nuuk Declaration, supra note 83, at 2.

128. Arctic Council Secretariat, Terms of Reference, supra note 97, para. 2.2.

129. Ibid.

130. Sellheim, "The Establishment of a Permanent Arctic Council Secretariat," supra note 98, at 72ff.

131. The Task Force on Short-Lived Climate Forcers and the Task Force for Institutional Issues are based on more participatory terms of reference.

132. Annex to the May 2011 SAO report, at 50.

133. The task force established focus on the creation of a circumpolar business forum, arrangements on actions to achieve enhanced black carbon and methane emission reductions, the development of an action plan or other arrangement on oil pollution prevention, and improved scientific research cooperation among the eight Arctic states.

134. Timo Koivurova, "Alternatives for an Arctic Treaty—Evaluation and a New Proposal," *Review of European Community and International Environmental Law* 17:1 (2008): 25.

135. Paula Kankaanpää and Oran R. Young, "The Effectiveness of the Arctic Council," *Polar Research* 31 (2012): 31.

136. SAO Report to Ministers, Nuuk, Greenland, 2011, at 28.

137. SAO Report to Ministers, Kiruna, Sweden, at 56.

138. Kiruna Declaration on the occasion of the Eighth Arctic Council Ministerial Meeting, 15 May 2013, at 4.

139. Kankaanpää and Young, "The Effectiveness of the Arctic Council," supra note 135.

140. SAO Report to Ministers, Kiruna, Sweden, at 73–74.

141. Spectar, "Saving the Ice Princess," supra note 57, at 58.

142. See UN Resolution on Implementation of Agenda 21, the Programme for the Further Implementation of Agenda 21 and the Outcomes of the World Summit on Sustainable Development, UN Doc. A/Res/64/236 (2010).

143. Outcome of the 2012 Rio Conference on Sustainable Development. For a general re-affirmation of the principle of public participation, see paras. 42–55; concerning the role of stakeholders in the High Level Forum, para. 85; and a strengthened United Nations Environment Program (UNEP), para. 88. More recently, this emphasis has led to the adoption by the UN General Assembly of procedures allowing for a greater involvement of nonstate actors. UN Doc. A/67/L.72.

144. Herr, "The Changing Roles of Non-governmental Organizations," supra note 8, at 96.

2. Interlinkages in International Law
The Convention on Biological Diversity as a Model for Linking Territory, Environment, and Indigenous Rights in the Marine Arctic

BETSY BAKER

Treaties relevant to the Arctic abound. Some resolve territorial boundaries; they are largely bilateral. Some address environmental problems; these are overwhelmingly multilateral and not specific to the Arctic. Some address the rights of indigenous peoples; these are almost exclusively internal to the individual Arctic states and their indigenous populations, but global human rights norms are increasingly relevant to these concerns.[1] The problem is that the proliferation of multilateral agreements has generally made it more, not less, difficult for states to coordinate and effectively enforce the numerous obligations to assess, report, and exchange information in ways that solve the individual problems the agreements were designed to address. This chapter suggests how states in the Arctic can identify treaty interlinkages between three sectors—territorial concerns, the environment, and indigenous rights—and use these connections to improve not only the flow of information between various agreements by which these sectors are bound but also how they implement their international obligations in Arctic-specific settings.

The twenty-first-century Arctic is changing physically, biologically, and geopolitically, with effects arising in the region as well as in areas well beyond. Permafrost thaw, sea ice melt, and warming trends in the terrestrial and marine Arctic are leading to new ranges for flora, fauna, and vector-borne disease; to increased shipping; to greater industrial and tourist activity; and to other opportunities and threats that do not stop at national boundaries.[2] In the face of this change, states are slowly increasing transboundary and circumpolar cooperation by building on existing bilateral and multilateral agreements and gradually expanding the work of multiactor forums such as the Arctic Council. Through this state practice, international law is itself adapting to change in the Arctic.

This chapter uses the Convention on Biological Diversity (CBD) and its application to marine biodiversity to examine how states can work within and beyond the limitations of territorially based international law to better keep pace with changes in the Arctic.[3] State actors have proven only partly capable of shifting from a boundary-based practice of sovereignty and territorial integrity to acknowledging and acting upon indigenous rights and environmental concerns in the marine Arctic. In part, this is because the majority of instruments with which states must work are state-based treaties and declarations. It is also in part because international human rights law and international environmental law have their own limitations when it comes to dovetailing with each other and with traditional territorially "bounded" international law.[4]

This work builds on the proposal that states can provide better practical solutions for the changing Arctic by weaving more tightly together those norms and principles that are common to three strands of international law: (i) the international law of territory and boundaries; (ii) international environmental law; and (iii) international indigenous rights law.[5] To test this proposal, this chapter uses the CBD to examine how states have made and can continue to draw connections between principles and instruments from each of the three strands in ways that are relevant to the Arctic, and in ways that are in keeping with basic precepts of international law for reconciling conflicts between treaties. The CBD involves all three strands, both in the original convention text and in subsequent implementation measures. It thus has the potential to serve as a model for an Arctic-focused, intertreaty information exchange mechanism to help Arctic states harmonize and improve their implementation of obligations in all three areas. Making such connections will allow Arctic states to better fulfill their responsibilities under international law to their people and the environment, and to provide an integrated model of international law to address concerns that international law itself has grown too fragmented.[6]

Part I of this chapter recalls how the eight Arctic states—Canada, Denmark/Greenland, Finland, Iceland, Norway, Sweden, the Russian Federation, and the United States—have organized Arctic decision making through the Arctic Council. The Council's work necessarily involves all three strands of international law. Cooperation on issues of sustainable development and protecting the Arctic, its residents, and its environment is a central purpose of the Council. States remain its sole decision makers, but the Permanent Participants who represent the North's indigenous peoples also participate in Arctic Council deliberations, as nonstate actors. This flexibility and integration render the Arctic Council more permeable than classic structures of international law and potentially more able to connect all three strands simultaneously rather than keeping them unduly segregated.

Part II discusses the 1992 Convention on Biological Diversity, which is primarily an instrument of international environmental law yet incorporates elements of traditional territorially based international law and expressly interacts with indigenous practices, knowledge, and innovation. Because this chapter focuses on marine biodiversity, the section also introduces the UN Convention on the Law of the Sea as a more territorially based multilateral agreement yet one that necessarily engages with the CBD on issues of marine biodiversity.

Part III examines how coordination between the CBD and other biodiversity-related treaties has helped turn information-based requirements into more effective tools for achieving those treaties' purposes. It considers how the Arctic states can apply similar information exchange mechanisms for better coordination between Arctic-relevant instruments from all three areas of international law considered here—territory, environment, and indigenous rights.

The chapter concludes in Part IV by showing that the Arctic states, whether acting alone or in the Arctic Council, can learn from the CBD's innovations in coordinating information exchange and implementation mechanisms with other treaty bodies and entities. If the Arctic states apply a similar approach in the Arctic, they can improve information exchange and build upon it. This will help them gradually adjust the fundamental understanding of what it will take to sustain life and prosperity in a changing Arctic: not simply more information gathering and exchange for the sake of compliance, but information for the sake of smart, sustainable solutions to real-time problems. The fact that the key Arctic players—its peoples and its states—are relatively few allows them to build on what they have in common: a once ice-bound yet changing geography, stable governments, developed economies, subsistence and cold-based cultures, and centuries of resilience and adaptation to change. In short, the chapter proposes improving on the existing information-based adaptation model to translate international legal obligations of Arctic states into solutions for their shared concerns.

I. The Arctic Council: Supplementing State-Based Decision Making with Indigenous Participation

In the broader context of subsiding Cold War tensions and increasing environmental awareness, in 1991 the eight Arctic states (A8) agreed to an Arctic Environmental Protection Strategy (AEPS).[7] Groups representing indigenous peoples of the North assisted as observers in preparing the AEPS, as did three non-Arctic states and three inter- and nongovernmental organizations.[8] The A8 committed to a joint action plan that included research cooperation and data sharing on sources and effects of pollutants in the Arctic, assessment of potential environmental impacts of development, and implementation of measures to "control pollutants and reduce their adverse effects to the Arctic environment."[9] Five years later the A8 signed the Ottawa Declaration establishing the Arctic Council as a "high level forum to: provide a means for promoting cooperation, coordination and interaction among the Arctic states, with the involvement of the Arctic indigenous communities and other Arctic inhabitants on common Arctic issues."[10]

The Ottawa Declaration elevated the indigenous representative groups, now numbering six,[11] from observers to Permanent Participants, a category "created to provide for active participation and full consultation with the Arctic indigenous representatives within the Arctic Council."[12] Non-Arctic states and other entities are still categorized as observers.[13]

At the 2013 Ministerial meeting in Kiruna, Sweden, the Arctic Council ministers admitted six additional non-Arctic states as observers.[14] This step related to larger institutional reforms, which also included establishing a permanent secretariat in

Tromsø, Norway.[15] The so-called Nuuk Observer Rules were adopted at the 2011 Ministerial in Greenland.[16] Those rules require states and other entities applying for observer status to be evaluated as to whether they "Respect the values, interests, culture and traditions of Arctic indigenous peoples and other Arctic inhabitants" and "Have demonstrated a political willingness as well as financial ability to contribute to the work of the Permanent Participants and other Arctic indigenous peoples."[17] To date, the relatively small number of primary players in the Arctic—the eight Arctic states and the six Permanent Participants—generally enter into a close working relationship with Arctic Council observers. That dynamic may change now that the total of non-Arctic state observers has doubled to twelve. This change makes all the more important the requirement that non-Arctic observers respect and contribute to the work of the Arctic indigenous peoples.

While the Arctic Council is state-based, it is not an intergovernmental organization (IGO), does not possess legal personality, and is neither a creature of international law nor completely state-centric.[18] It is, however, Arctic-centric. The key to the Arctic Council's potential to address challenges effectively in the changing Arctic lies in the Council's Arctic-centrism, its non-IGO status, and its sui generis membership comprising Arctic states and Permanent Participants. Combined, these factors give the Council enough flexibility, and arguably a mandate, to weave the three strands of territorial, indigenous, and environmental international law more closely together for "common arctic issues."[19]

As state members of the Arctic Council, the A8 nations still act individually to implement obligations under non-Arctic treaties by which they are bound.[20] Acting collectively, through nonbinding recommendations and guidelines, the A8 can—and do—highlight what common or compatible principles these treaties contain.[21] This is a first step in coordinating how the states fulfill their obligations under sector-specific treaties that are relevant to one or more of the three strands. They should do so more intentionally as an Arctic bloc in appropriate forums (for example, treaty bodies and negotiating conferences), to draw Arctic-specific connections between the information-based and other obligations they have in all three areas of international law. The A8 must, of course, exercise this flexibility in keeping with the "conflict provisions" of the treaties to which they belong individually; these determine which agreement prevails when they contain contradictory terms.[22] Not all of the A8 belong to all Arctic-relevant treaties. For example, Canada, the Russian Federation, and the United States are not party to the OSPAR Convention (Convention for the Protection of the Marine Environment of the North-East Atlantic of 22 September 1992 (amended and updated text available at www.ospar.org). Further, the United States is not party to the Convention on Biological Diversity and has yet to accede to the Law of the Sea Convention.

The Arctic Council ministers adopted an Arctic Marine Strategic Plan (AMSP) in 2004, the same year as the release of the Arctic Climate Impact Assessment (ACIA), a groundbreaking report by the International Arctic Science Committee (IASC) and the Arctic Council that drew the world's attention to the Arctic as a bellwether for changes in the world's climate.[23] Among its many recommendations, the ACIA called for "improved capacity to monitor and understand changes in the Arctic" and urged action "to improve and enhance long-term biodiversity monitoring." For its part, the AMSP is based on principles and approaches that "include sustainable development, precaution, polluter pays, integrated management and an ecosystem-based approach" drawn from instruments such as the Rio Declaration and Agenda 21, the Convention on Biological Diversity, the Johannesburg Plan of Implementation from the World Summit on Sustainable Development, "and the Arctic Council's founding documents."[24] Those founding documents include the AEPS and the Ottawa Declaration discussed above, the latter of which affirms the A8's commitment to the Arctic's indigenous people and communities, to sustainable development and use of Arctic resources, and to protecting the Arctic environment and ecosystems and maintaining Arctic biodiversity.

The eight state members of the Arctic Council still prefer to channel any binding legal instruments through their individual diplomatic and ministerial offices. In this way, they maintain their state prerogative as the only official voice for their respective national-territorial interests, even as their actions as Arctic Council member states may address issues that fall under the other two strands—indigenous rights and environmental protection—of international law. The 2011 Arctic Search and Rescue Agreement and the 2013 Oil Spill Response and Preparedness Agreements were negotiated under Arctic Council auspices, but both are instruments the states themselves created and not an output of the Arctic Council.[25] Taken together, these two agreements raise the question of whether the Arctic Council states might eventually generate binding instruments qua Arctic Council or, at a minimum, coordinate reporting requirements and linkages between treaties to which all eight states are party.[26] At the least, with these two agreements the Arctic Council has proved itself a powerful convening forum for the negotiation of international agreements.

II. The Convention on Biological Diversity: Anchored In but Moving Beyond the International Law of Territory

The 1992 Convention on Biological Diversity is a global convention to which all Arctic states except the United States are party. It combines aspects of all three strands of international law under discussion in this chapter: territorial, environmental, and indigenous interests, if not rights per se. Article 3 of the CBD combines the first two strands: "States have, in accordance with the Charter of the United Nations and the principles of international law, the sovereign right to exploit their own resources pursuant to their own environmental policies, and the responsibility to ensure that activities within their jurisdiction or control do not cause damage to the environment of other States or of areas beyond the limits of national jurisdiction."

How the CBD approaches territory explains in part why terrestrial biodiversity generally enjoys more protected areas in the Arctic than does marine biodiversity.[27] The CBD "recognizes that states have sovereign rights over their own biological resources and legal requirements are to be implemented in national legal frameworks."[28] Thus, CBD member states implement their obligations in national law, on national territory and in areas where they exercise full sovereignty, constrained only by the terms of the treaties to which they are party. By contrast, coastal states have sovereign rights, but not always full sovereignty, over their marine areas, depending on which marine area is involved.

Under the global 1982 UN Convention on the Law of the Sea (UNCLOS or the LOS Convention), coastal states' sovereignty over their marine areas diminishes as one moves seaward: from internal waters to territorial sea to the Exclusive Economic Zone (EEZ) to the continental shelf to the high seas and "the Area" (the seabed and subfloor beyond national jurisdiction). Like the CBD, UNCLOS is firmly grounded in the principle of state sovereignty over natural resources. Like the CBD, UNCLOS also incorporates components of international environmental law, although it covers a much wider range of legal matters, including transit rights and freedoms, marine scientific research, and dispute settlement. UNCLOS Part XII established a new regime for protection and preservation of the marine environment, obliging coastal and noncoastal states alike in Article 192 and acknowledging in Article 193 the rights of states to exploit their own resources subject to this obligation.[29]

UNCLOS was groundbreaking in introducing the EEZ and tying coastal state jurisdiction over different maritime zones to graduated degrees of sovereign rights and obligations, including environmental protection. Regarding a coastal state's continental shelf, for example, under UNCLOS Article 77 a coastal state exercises "sovereign rights for the purpose of exploring it and exploiting" its living and nonliving natural resources. However, these rights are not the same as the full sovereignty enjoyed on land or in a coastal state's internal waters. On the high seas, which are also areas beyond national jurisdiction (ABNJ), all states enjoy certain passage and resource freedoms. Because no state has jurisdiction over ABNJs, some states that are party to both the UNCLOS and the CBD are interested in establishing a cooperative regime for protecting marine biodiversity.[30]

Global in scope, UNCLOS also calls for regional cooperation for, inter alia, "the protection and preservation of the marine environment, taking into account characteristic regional features" (Art. 197). One example is the OSPAR Convention for the Protection of the Marine Environment of the North-East Atlantic that includes part of the Arctic.[31] The five Arctic states in Europe—Denmark/Greenland, Finland, Iceland, Norway, and Sweden—are party; the three remaining Arctic states of Canada, Russia, and the United States are not. OSPAR contrasts states' gradated rights in various ocean zones with the freedom of the high seas. It turns this tension into an opportunity for its contracting parties to collaborate for marine environmental protection in the region: "The OSPAR Convention recognizes the jurisdictional rights of states over the seas and the freedom of the high seas, and, within this framework, the application of main principles of international environmental policy to prevent and eliminate marine pollution and to achieve sustainable management of the maritime area."[32] The "main principles of international environmental policy" for OSPAR include those articulated at the 1972 Stockholm UN Conference on the Human Environment and at the 1992 Rio UN Conference on Environment and Development, which also produced the CBD.[33]

The CBD, too, expressly invokes the Stockholm and Rio Declarations together with UNCLOS Part XII and its Article 197 on regional cooperation.[34] The CBD includes marine biodiversity in its definition of biodiversity: "'Biodiversity' means the variability among living organisms from all sources including, inter alia, terrestrial, marine, and other aquatic ecosystems and ecological complexes of which they are a part: this includes diversity within species, between species, and of ecosystems (Art. 2)."

The CBD provides in Article 22(2) that "Contracting Parties shall implement this Convention with respect to the marine environment consistently with the rights and obligations of States under the law of the sea." The phrase "law of the sea" encompasses customary international law and other marine treaties, so is broader than UNCLOS. Still, Article 22 was included in part to acknowledge the potential conflicts between the CBD and UNCLOS.[35]

The CBD and UNCLOS, neither of which are specific to the Arctic, are seen as taking different approaches to marine living and genetic resources. The CBD is considered more protective and conservation oriented; UNCLOS more management oriented and possibly more open to use and development of the resources.[36] However, this difference is largely "in approach, not in obligation" to protecting and conserving these resources.[37] The difference may be traceable in part to the more environmental and conservational focus of the CBD compared to the more territorial and zonal foundations of UNCLOS. The differences between the CBD and UNCLOS can be seen not only as tensions but as offering potential for coordination.[38] While "[t]here is no hierarchy of treaties in international law," most modern treaties contain conflict clauses.[39] These apply only as between parties to the conventions.

III. CBD Mechanisms for Interlinkages with Other Entities

One impetus for creating treaty interlinkages is to improve overall implementation of the agreements in question. With respect to multilateral environmental agreements (MEAs), a 2001 United Nations Environment Program (UNEP) report identified several crosscutting priorities for all MEAs that would help improve how effectively they are implemented. These priorities included a "strengthened scientific basis for decision-making; strengthened international partnerships" and "compliance and monitoring of implementation of the convention" in question.[40] The CBD has developed various mechanisms to create linkages with other international instruments and entities, including those that do not focus primarily on biodiversity.[41]

CBD Interlinkages with Other Biodiversity Instruments

Biodiversity treaties enjoy a long history of exchange and management of information among one another.[42] The CBD has been at the forefront of improved information management internally and in cooperation with other agreements, through intertreaty linkages.[43] Long sees the CBD "actively pursu[ing] institutional linkages, perhaps more so than any other international environmental regime, by identifying and promoting connections with other regimes and institutions that can promote biodiversity preservation."[44] Internally, the CBD has developed the Biodiversity Clearing House Mechanism (CHM) for its own purposes, which include improving global information regarding implementation of the CBD. Externally, the Liaison Group of Biodiversity Related Conventions (LGB) is a prime example of how the CBD engages in intertreaty linkages.[45] The LGB involves the secretariats of six international instruments that focus significantly on biodiversity[46] in coordinating efforts to improve cooperation, communication, harmonization, and implementation of their respective instruments.[47]

CBD Interlinkages with Marine Biodiversity Initiatives

The CBD has also developed parallel programs with instruments that are not biodiversity-specific but do relate to the marine environment.[48] Early on, at the second meeting of the CBD Conference of Parties (CoP) held in Jakarta in 1995, the CoP instructed the CBD Executive Secretary to consult with the UN Office for Ocean Affairs and Law of the Sea to study the relationship between the CBD and the LOS Convention "with regard to the conservation and sustainable use of genetic resources on the deep seabed."[49] Some ten years later, in 2004, the UN General Assembly established an Ad Hoc Open-ended Informal Working Group to study issues relating to the conservation and sustainable use of marine biological diversity beyond areas of national jurisdiction (the ABNJ Working Group).[50] This ABNJ Working Group includes issues of Arctic marine biodiversity in its program.[51]

In light of the General Assembly's ABNJ Working Group activity, the CBD CoP invited its own members and other states to consider related issues, including those that might fall under the purview of the International Maritime Organization (IMO) and the Food and Agriculture Organization (FAO).[52] In 2012, the ABNJ Working Group recommended convening intersessional workshops on whether to elaborate a possible implementing agreement under the LOS Convention.[53] The CBD will necessarily be involved in plans for any international instrument for the conservation and sustainable use of marine biodiversity in ABNJ that might emerge in other forums.[54]

CBD Interlinkages on Arctic Issues

The CBD Secretariat has entered into memoranda of understanding (MOUs) or developed joint work plans to address Arctic issues with secretariats of other instruments and with nontreaty entities. One is its MOU with GRID-Arendal, UNEP's information office, the purpose of which is to enhance cooperation on issues of common interest.[55] These include "communication and outreach, tourism and biodiversity and joint activities regarding Arctic biodiversity," as well as implementing the strategic plan of the CBD clearing-house mechanism (CHM) discussed above.[56]

The CBD also has an MOU with the Conservation of Arctic Flora and Fauna (CAFF) Working Group of the Arctic Council.[57] The MOU contains very general objectives such as: "sharing knowledge, creating awareness and enhancing capacity for implementation of the [CBD] in the Arctic Region, as appropriate. Governments and other Stakeholders may see the activities of CAFF and the CBD as mutually supportive."[58]

The CBD-CAFF MOU "Objectives may also include other areas of cooperation as may be mutually determined by both parties." This last phrase provides a window to expand cooperation to more concrete activities, such as CAFF's contributions to the CBD's ongoing programs of global biodiversity assessment, the Arctic Biodiversity Assessment (ABA),[59] and the Circumpolar Biodiversity Monitoring Program.[60]

The ABA is a major scientific study whose recommendations the Arctic Council ministers adopted at their 2013 Kiruna Ministerial.[61] One ABA recommendation is to "mainstream biodiversity," incorporating it into all of its actions and deliberations.[62]

Mainstreaming biodiversity

4. Require the incorporation of biodiversity objectives and provisions into all Arctic Council work and encourage the same for on-going and future international standards, agreements, plans, operations and/or other tools specific to development in the Arctic. This should include, but not be restricted to, oil and gas development, shipping, fishing, tourism and mining.

Such a recommendation lays the groundwork for all Arctic Council member states to speak in an "Arctic voice" in shaping the discussion of biodiversity.

Even the structure of ABA recommendations reflects the need for interlinkage with other entities. The introduction to the ABA recommendations specifies that they are "aimed primarily at the Arctic Council, its member states and Permanent Participants," and that "Success in conserving Arctic biodiversity, however, also depends upon actions by non-Arctic states, regional and local authorities, industry and all who live, work and travel in the Arctic. These recommendations may, therefore, also provide a guide for action for states, authorities, and organizations beyond the Arctic Council. Some of the ABA recommendations directly encourage cooperation with those outside the Arctic Council process."[63]

These recommendations thus provide additional foundation for Arctic states to engage individually or collectively in other forums even if they are not party to the CBD or other relevant biodiversity conventions. The fact that the Arctic Council Ministers adopted the recommendation adds a layer of nonbinding but persuasive authority for its member states to cooperate "with those outside the Arctic Council process" as well.

CBD and CAFF also cooperate on the Circumpolar Biodiversity Monitoring Program (CBMP), which is considered as a "valuable contribution to the CBD 2010 target and to the implementation of the target as a whole."[64] This example of an Arctic Council working group helping a multilateral convention meet its implementation goals has potential model character for treaty interlinkage. As Marauhn notes, the CBMP "is strategically linked to other international conservation programmes," in addition to the CBD.[65] These include the AMAP Working Group of the Arctic Council, the International Polar Year, and the International Arctic Science Committee, the last of which is an Arctic Council observer.[66]

While the Arctic Council may not yet be at a point where it can convene Arctic focus groups of the various biodiversity conventions, the CHM and LGB may eventually serve as models for intertreaty information sharing, coordinated for Arctic-specific purposes through the Arctic Council. CAFF's development of the Arctic Biodiversity Data Service (ABDS) moves in this direction. ABDS is "a coordinated web-based data management system that accesses, integrates, displays and analyzes biodiversity data according to various user needs."[67] CAFF anticipates that its collaboration with other biodiversity actors "will provide answers to questions not previously attained on a circumpolar scale, and will lead to a broader understanding of the Arctic environment and the effects of various stressors on biodiversity and ecosystem integrity." Possible interlinkages between the ABDS exist with the Intergovernmental Platform on Biodiversity and Ecosystem Services (IPBES) launched in April 2012.[68]

CBD Interlinkages on Climate

The CBD, through its CoP, has created other intertreaty linkages, for example in tasking the CBD Subsidiary Body on Scientific, Technical and Technological Advice (SBSTTA) to work with the UN Framework Convention on Climate Change (UNFCCC) and the Intergovernmental Panel on Climate Change (IPCC). The three groups are to "prepare scientific advice in collaboration with the appropriate bodies of the UNFCCC in order to integrate biodiversity considerations in the implementation of the UNFCCC and the Kyoto Protocol."[69] Marauhn provides a detailed analysis of how the resulting CBD Ad Hoc Technical Expert Group on Biodiversity and Climate Change (AHTEG) can address climate change issues in the Arctic.[70] He identifies as weaknesses the fact that not all of the same states belong to each of the treaties involved, which leaves open the possibility of conflicting obligations.[71] This may in turn prevent a "move toward increased coherence in the interpretation and application of multilateral environmental agreements"; one country, either by objecting or not participating, can prevent the establishment of formal links between two regimes.[72]

The fact that coordination between treaties is still done largely as bilateral cooperation between states makes for inconsistent application of treaties throughout a region.[73] The Arctic Council, as a multilateral forum for eight states that sometimes are but often are not all parties to any given international instrument, has the potential to overcome this patchwork approach. It can do so not by addressing how the Arctic states are implementing individual treaty responsibilities (which is beyond its competence) but by providing neutral information-based tools that each state, party or not to a specific instrument, can use to tackle on its own terms the problems that gave rise to that instrument.

The CBD and Indigenous Rights

The UNCLOS Working Group on marine biodiversity in areas beyond national jurisdiction (ABNJ Working Group), introduced above, addresses concerns arising from the territorial and environmental strands of international law.[74] Turning to the third strand of international law that is the subject of this chapter, the inclusion of indigenous interests arises under Article 8(j) of the CBD. Article 8(j) lays the groundwork for the CBD member states and the CBD Secretariat to incorporate indigenous interests into the CBD's activities, including interactions with working groups of other conventions. The Ad Hoc Open-ended Working Group on Article 8(j) and Related Provisions meets intersessionally on such matters.[75]

The CBD itself mentions indigenous interests only twice, in the preamble and in Article 8, regarding "In-Situ Conservation" of biodiversity.[76] Under Article 8, each contracting party "shall, as far as possible and as appropriate,"

(a) Establish a system of protected areas or areas where special measures need to be taken to conserve biological diversity; and . . .

(j) Subject to its national legislation, *respect, preserve and maintain knowledge, innovations and practices of indigenous and local communities embodying traditional lifestyles relevant for the conservation and sustainable use of biological diversity* and promote their wider application with the approval and involvement of the holders of such knowledge, innovations and practices and encourage the equitable sharing of the benefits arising from the utilization of such knowledge, innovations and practices (emphasis added).

The CBD contracting parties, working groups, and other bodies have involved indigenous participants in Arctic-relevant projects.[77] An example is the convening of the International Expert Meeting on Responses to Climate Change for Indigenous and Local Communities and Their Impact on Traditional Knowledge Related to Biological Diversity in the Arctic Region, and its information document presented to the ninth meeting of the CBD CoP in May 2008.[78]

The preeminent statement of the rights of indigenous peoples, the nonbinding UN Declaration on the Rights of Indigenous Peoples (UNDRIP) is global in reach.[79] With respect to resources, UNDRIP Article 32(2) provides that "States shall consult and cooperate in good faith with the indigenous peoples concerned through their own representative institutions in order to obtain their free and informed consent prior to the approval of any project affecting their lands or territories and other resources, particularly in connection with the development, utilization or exploitation of mineral, water or other resources."

Reliance on the provisions of the CBD alone would scarcely bring indigenous rights robustly into Arctic marine resource decisions. However, when CBD working groups elaborate on such texts and create linkages to entities like the United Nations Permanent Forum on Indigenous Issues, they contribute to helping these rights take shape.[80]

Arctic indigenous groups have invoked UNDRIP in regionally specific declarations.[81] The Inuit Circumpolar Council (ICC) issued a Circumpolar Inuit Declaration on Sovereignty in the Arctic in 2009 and a Circumpolar Inuit Declaration on Resource Development Principles in Inuit Nunaat in 2011.[82] The ICC declarations have no force as international law but they do reference international declarations and bodies by name and draw on certain principles of international law. For example, the sovereignty declaration provides at section 1.3: "Inuit are a People. . . . As a people, we enjoy the rights of all peoples. These include the rights recognized in and by various international instruments and institutions, such as the Charter of the United Nations; the International Covenant on Economic, Social and Cultural Rights; the International Covenant on Civil and Political Rights; the Vienna Declaration and Program of Action; the Human Rights Council; the Arctic Council; and the Organization of American States." Section 1.4 identifies the rights and responsibilities of all indigenous peoples as including those recognized by the UN Permanent Forum on Indigenous Issues, the UN Expert Mechanism on the Rights of Indigenous Peoples, the 2007 UN Declaration on the Rights of Indigenous Peoples (UNDRIP), and others.

The June 2013 Alta Outcome Document of a preparatory conference for the World Conference on Indigenous Peoples combines numerous references to international agreements, sovereignty, and resource rights but, significantly, makes no mention of either biodiversity or environment.[83] Importantly for the Arctic, the Alta Outcome Document also adds specific reference to ice throughout, which was not called out in the UNDRIP but rather subsumed under general references to water.[84] The Outcome Document Theme 1 refers specifically to the need to implement indigenous rights "consistent with State's obligations under international law, the UN Charter, the Declaration and Treaties and agreements concluded with Indigenous Peoples and Nations."[85] In discussing UN system action for the implementation of the rights of indigenous peoples, the Outcome Document does not mention the CBD or any convention by name but it does "recommend that more Indigenous candidates with expertise on Indigenous Peoples' rights be appointed to Treaty monitoring bodies."[86] The Arctic Council is ideally suited to recommend such indigenous experts by drawing on the work of the Permanent Participants in its working groups.

IV. CBD Interlinkages and Lessons for Information Exchange in the Arctic

As seen in the emerging practice of MOUs between the CBD and the Arctic Council working groups, the two entities have effectively linked their respective mechanisms to help each reach their stated goals. They have done so largely by coordinating work programs of their respective subsidiary bodies. Both entities also have formal mechanisms to incorporate indigenous perspectives into their internal activities. Permanent Participant status in the Arctic Council provides a much more robust formal structure than the CBD has for ensuring that indigenous representatives are integrally involved in decision making. Accordingly, the Arctic Council can leverage this key component of its identity to affect how CBD-related initiatives are carried out through the Arctic Council and its working groups.

The Arctic Council can also leverage its proven information-producing capacity to build on the fact that the CBD "is an instrument which, by its fundamental approach and design, can realize its objectives through the implementation of other international agreements."[87] Even though the Arctic Council is not an "international agreement" per se, it is based on a declaration of its eight members "recognizing the Arctic Council's significance and intending to promote its results."[88] Arctic Council working group outputs—including sophisticated Arctic-specific studies on biodiversity, climate, black carbon, human health, oil and gas development, shipping, and a range of other topics—have the potential to be of great use to convention secretariats and other convention bodies and working groups seeking scientific and indigenous studies to inform decision making.

Precisely because the Arctic Council is neither based on a treaty nor an intergovernmental organization it is in a position to broker cooperation "between organs established by multilateral environmental agreements" or other instruments to which its eight member states are parties.[89] It may even be able to do so for instruments to which not all eight states belong. It would do so not for purposes of compliance or reporting, a role that exceeds its competence, but for purposes of sharing information necessary to good policymaking. The Arctic Council's newly established Secretariat might assist in this regard, although the Arctic Council's continued lack of legal personality raises the question of whether the Secretariat has the legal competence to enter into such agreements.[90]

The Arctic Council's long track record in producing valuable studies and other information for decision makers renders it especially well placed to provide Arctic-specific information linkages between agreements to which at least some of the Arctic states are party. This is all the more important given that "[m]any Memoranda in the environmental context do not regulate the issue" of information flow between two agreements.[91] MOUs, as nonbinding agreements, are not seen as suitable instruments for promoting activities relating to binding obligations arising under other instruments.[92] By contrast, the Arctic Council is a forum where its members approach issues of common Arctic concern whether or not they are party to a specific instrument.

Factors affecting the potential for successful partnerships and joint activities of treaty bodies include "the number of participating treaties and the issue addressed by partnerships."[93] These factors can also be applied to potential joint activities between treaty bodies such as convention secretariats with a nontreaty body—for example, the Arctic Council. The fact that a large number of treaties have potential relevance to the Arctic might at first be seen as precluding a successful partnership between the Arctic Council and the treaty bodies of the relevant instruments.[94] However, the interlinkages could start small, involving only those agreements to which all or most of the eight Arctic states are party.[95]

Alternatively, interlinkage could start by focusing on a narrow set of issues, such as those associated with offshore oil and gas development. For example, the Arctic Ocean Review recommended that the Arctic Council "should promote interactions with the appropriate international treaty bodies on offshore oil and gas issues that address for example discharges, oil spill preparedness and response, and environmental monitoring. This could include coordinating information exchange on reporting, monitoring, assessment and/or other requirements under relevant entities, encouraging inclusion of science and traditional knowledge, and keeping abreast of Arctic-specific developments relevant to the appropriate instruments."[96]

To what does better information exchange lead? At a project level it could lead to better decision making on siting offshore industrial activity or vessel routing schemes. At the process level, when similar information is being gathered for different instruments, it can lead to "avoiding duplication of effort in reporting processes; increasing efficiency and reducing the burden of reporting [under multiple agreements]; and improving access to reported information."[97] Practical lessons learned from a pilot project involving four countries and eight biodiversity-related treaties[98] include "Interlinkages . . . the fact that information requested for one convention might address an information requirement in another convention, and appropriate steps taken to share information and approaches."[99]

Arctic states have begun to act collectively to address some of their physical infrastructure needs through instruments such as the 2011 Arctic Search and Rescue Agreement.[100] They now have the opportunity to address their shared information needs by creating and strengthening interlinkages with international instruments that address issues of common Arctic concern.

Notes

1. See, e.g., The Western Arctic (Inuvialuit) Claims Settlement Act, S.C. 1984, c. 24 (Can.), authorizing the land claims settlement agreed to in the 5 June 1984 Inuvialuit Final Agreement (IFA) between the Committee for Original Peoples' Entitlement (COPE) and Canada. Such bilateral agreements are not discussed further in this chapter.

2. See, e.g., National Oceanic and Atmospheric Administration (NOAA), "Arctic Report Card: Update for 2012," available at http://www.arctic.noaa.gov/reportcard; and Birgitta Evengard and Rainer Sauerborn, "Climate change influences infectious diseases both in the Arctic and the tropics: Joining the dots," Global Health Action, vol. 2 (2009), eISSN 1654–9880.

3. Convention on Biological Diversity of 22 May 1992 (1760 United Nations Treaty Series 143).

4. Lenna Heinämäki, "Rethinking the Status of Indigenous Peoples in International Environmental Decision-Making: Pondering the Role of Arctic Indigenous Peoples and the Challenge of Climate Change," in T. Koivurova et al. (eds.), Climate Governance in the Arctic (Berlin: Springer, 2009), 207–262.

5. Betsy Baker, "International Law and the Arctic: How territoriality, human rights and the environment can shape shared sovereignty," in R. Murray and A. D. Nuttal (eds.), Interna-

tional Security and the Arctic: Examining the Theories and Policies of Circumpolar Politics (Cambria, 2014), in press; manuscript on file with author.

6. See, e.g., Matthew Craven, "Unity, Diversity and the Fragmentation of International Law," *Finnish Yearbook of International Law* 1 (2003): 5; Harro van Asselt et al., "Global Climate Change and the Fragmentation of International Law," *Law and Policy* 30 (2008): 423, 426.

7. Arctic Environmental Protection Strategy (AEPS) of 14 June 1991, *International Legal Materials (ILM)* 30 (1991): 1624. See also Declaration on the Establishment of the Arctic Council 1996–Ottawa Declaration (available at http://library.arcticportal.org/1270/). On pre–Arctic Council collaboration amongst Arctic states see E. C. H. Keskitalo, *Negotiating the Arctic: The Construction of an International Region* (New York: Routledge, 2004), 47ff.; Olav Schram Stokke and Geir Hønneland, *International Cooperation and Arctic Governance: Regime Effectiveness and Northern Region Building* (New York: Routledge, 2007); and Oran Young and Gail Osherenko (eds.), *Polar Politics: Creating International Environmental Regimes* (Ithaca: Cornell University Press, 1993), 96–151.

8. These nine entities are listed in the AEPS as "observers" assisting with its preparation: Inuit Circumpolar Conference, Nordic Saami Council, USSR Association of Small Peoples of the North; Germany, Poland, and the United Kingdom; UN Environment Programme (UNEP), UN Economic Commission for Europe (UNECE), and the International Arctic Science Committee (IASC). The Ottawa Declaration creating the Arctic Council established two different categories, "Permanent Participant" for indigenous representation and "Observer" for inter- and nongovernmental organizations and non-Arctic states. See Declaration on the Establishment of the Arctic Council of 19 September 1996 (Ottawa Declaration). This and all other Ministerial Declarations and Arctic Council documents are available at www.arctic-council.org.

9. AEPS, supra note 7, p. 2.

10. Ottawa Declaration, supra note 7, para. 1(a): Referring to "common Arctic issues," the Ottawa Declaration specifies in a footnote that "The Arctic Council should not deal with matters related to military security."

11. Aleut International Association (AIS), Arctic Athabaskan Council, Gwich'in Council International, Inuit Circumpolar Council (ICC—previously the Inuit Circumpolar Conference), the Russian Association of the Indigenous Peoples of the North (RAIPON), and the Saami Council.

12. Ottawa Declaration, para. 2.

13. Before 2013, the non-Arctic state observers were France, Germany, Netherlands, Poland, Spain, and the United Kingdom. At the May 2013 Ministerial meeting of the Arctic Council, six more states were added to the existing state observers: the People's Republic of China, Indonesia, Italy, Japan, Republic of Korea, and Singapore. A partial list of IGO observers include the OSPAR Treaty, the Nordic Council of Ministers, UNDP, and UNEP GRID-Arendal; NGO observers include the International Arctic Science Committee, the Northern Forum, and the World Wide Fund for Nature–Global Arctic Program (WWF).

14. Primary documents from the 2013 Ministerial are available at http://www.arctic-council.org/index.php/en/events/meetings-overview/kiruna-ministerial-2013.

15. E. J. Molenaar, "Current and Prospective Roles of the Arctic Council System within the Context of the Law of the Sea," *International Journal of Marine and Coastal Law* 27 (2012): 553–595.

16. The Nuuk Observer Rules are contained in Annex 1 to the Report of the May 2011 Senior Arctic Officials Meeting (available at www.arctic-council.org), 50–51.

17. Nuuk Observer Rules, ibid.

18. See, e.g., Evan Bloom, "Establishment of the Arctic Council," *American Journal of International Law* 93 (July 1999): 712–722 (re: no legal personality); Timo Koivurova and David VanderZwaag, "The Arctic Council at 10 Years: Retrospect and Prospects," *University of British Columbia Law Review* 40 (2007): 121–194 (re: state-based; relationship to international law).

19. Ottawa Declaration, supra note 7, para. 1(a).

20. For a discussion of Arctic state membership in various agreements relevant to the Arctic Ocean, see PAME, The Arctic Ocean Review Project, Final Report (Phase II 2011–2013), Kiruna, May 2013. Protection of the Arctic Marine Environment (PAME) Secretariat, Akureyri (2013) (AOR Report).

21. See, e.g., the PAME *Arctic Offshore Oil and Gas Guidelines*, 2009, 6–7: "Arctic offshore oil and gas activities should be based on the principles of the precautionary approach, polluter pays, sustainable development, and continuous improvement." These guidelines do not identify the principles with specific treaties, but cite Articles 15 and 16 of the Stockholm Declaration.

22. See, e.g., CBD, supra note 3, Art. 22.2. On conflicts between the CBD and other agreements generally, see Rüdiger Wolfrum and Nele Matz, *Conflicts in International Environmental Law* (Berlin: Springer, 2003), 172ff.

23. PAME Secretariat, Arctic Council Arctic Marine Strategic Plan, Akureryri (2004) (AMSP); the AMSP is being revised for 2014. ACIA Secretariat, Arctic Council, Arctic Climate Impact Assessment (2005), available at http://www.acia.uaf.edu/pages/scientific.html.

24. PAME Secretariat, Arctic Council Arctic Marine Strategic Plan (AMSP), Akureryri (2004), part 8, sec. 6.0.

25. Agreement on Cooperation in Aeronautical and Maritime Search and Rescue in the Arctic of 12 May 2011 (available at www.arctic-council.org) (Arctic SAR Agreement). Agreement on Cooperation on Marine Oil Pollution Preparedness and Response in the Arctic, 15 May 2013, available at http://www.state.gov/r/pa/prs/ps/2013/05/209406.htm). The much older 1974 International Agreement on the Conservation of Polar Bears is the only other legal agreement binding all eight states in an Arctic context. Agreement on the Conservation of Polar Bears, January 1974, *ILM* 13:13–18.

26. See, generally, Erik Jaap Molenaar, "Current and Prospective Roles of the Arctic Council System within the Context of the Law of the Sea," *International Journal of Marine and Coastal Law* 27 (2012): 553–595.

27. Kathryn I. Johnsen, Bjorn Alfthan, Lawrence Hislop, and Janet F. Skaalvik (eds.), *Protecting Arctic Biodiversity*, United Nations Environment Programme, GRID-Arendal (2010), available at www.grida.no, 34: "While increased action outside the Arctic is urgently required, Arctic nations need to substantially increase the extent of protected areas, especially in the coastal zone as well as the marine environment. Currently, only a fraction of the marine environment is protected, and an even lesser part adjacent to terrestrial protected areas, so crucial in the Arctic ecosystems. Protection of areas still remains one of the most effective tools available in management of Arctic resources, and so is the development of co-management programmes."

28. Johnsen et al., ibid., 24.

29. UNCLOS Art. 192: "States have the obligation to protect and preserve the marine environment." Art. 193: "States have the sovereign right to exploit their natural resources pursuant to their environmental policies and in accordance with their duty to protect and preserve the marine environment."

30. For a discussion of marine biodiversity in areas beyond national jurisdiction (ABNJ) see Rosemary Rayfuse, "Protecting Marine Biodiversity in Polar Areas Beyond National Jurisdiction," *Review of European Community and International Environmental Law* 17(1) (2008): 3–13.

31. The OSPAR Convention, supra note 20, establishes "The Arctic" as its Region 1, which constitutes some 40 percent of the OSPAR maritime region; see http://www.ospar.org/content/content.asp?menu=00420211000000_000000_000000.

32. OSPAR "Principles" as presented at http://www.ospar.org/content/content.asp?menu=00320109000000_000000_000000.

33. Ibid.

34. CBD, supra note 3, preamble.

35. Wolfrum and Matz, *Conflicts in International Environmental Law*, supra note 22, p. 16.

36. Ibid., 16ff.

37. Ibid.

38. Ibid., 27, identifying other potential conflicts between the two agreements, including the CBD's detailed provisions on access and benefit sharing.

39. Ibid., 120: "The starting point for a discussion of the reliance upon the law of treaties as a solution to treaty conflicts is the principle that there is no hierarchy in international law."

40. UNEP, International Environmental Governance: Multilateral Environmental Agreements, Meeting of the Open-Ended Intergovernmental Group of Ministers or Their Representatives on International Environmental Governance, New York, 18 April 2001, 12–13, quoted in Johnsen et al., supra note 27, *Protecting Arctic Biodiversity*, 28.

41. Johnsen et al., supra note 27, *Protecting Arctic Biodiversity*, 25, list the Ramsar Convention on Wetlands; the UNESCO Convention concerning the Protection of World Cultural and Natural Heritage; the Convention on Migratory Species and associated agreements, such as the Agreement on the Conservation of African-Eurasian Migratory Waterbirds (AEWA); and the Convention on International Trade in Endangered Species of Wild Fauna and Flora; and state that "Regional and/or species-specific agreements, such as the Bern Convention on the Conservation of European Wildlife and Natural Habitats, the International Convention for the Regulation of Whaling (ICRW), and the Agreement on the Conservation of Polar Bears, are also highly relevant to the conservation of Arctic biodiversity."

42. Wolfrum and Matz, *Conflicts in International Environmental Law*, supra note 22, p. 172, citing, e.g., T. H. Johnson, I. K. Krain, and M. V. Sneary, *Feasibility Study for a Harmonised Informations Management Infrastructure for Biodiversity-related Treaties* (World Conservation Monitoring Center [WCMC], 1998).

43. On treaty interlinkages generally, see W. Bradnee Chambers, *Interlinkages and the Effectiveness of Multilateral Environmental Agreements* (Tokyo: United Nations University Press, 2008); on the Liaison Group of Biodiversity Conventions (LGB), see Chambers p. 70, n. 80. See also the CBD discussion of cross-convention engagement at its eighth CoP, UNEP, "Cooperation with Other Conventions, Organizations and Initiatives and Engagement of Stakeholders, Including Options for a Global Partnership" (note by the Executive Secretary, UNEP/CBD/COP/8/25, 21 January 2006).

44. Andrew Long, "Developing Linkages to Preserve Biodiversity" (paper presented at the 2011 Vermont Law School Colloquium on Environmental Scholarship, on file with author), published as "Developing Linkages to Preserve Biodiversity," *Yearbook of International Environmental Law* 21(1) (2010): 41–80; published online 14 March 2012, p. 21.

45. The LGB is distinct from a joint liaison group established in 2001 between the CBD, the UN Convention on Climate Change, and the UN Convention to Combat Desertification.

46. Listed chronologically: Convention on Wetlands of International Importance, Especially as Waterfowl Habitat, 2 February 1971, TIAS No. 11,084, 996 UNTS 245 [Ramsar Convention]; Convention Concerning the Protection of the World Cultural and Natural Heritage, 16 November 1972, 1037 UNTS 151, 27 UST 37 [World Heritage Convention]; Convention on International Trade in Endangered Species of Wild Fauna and Flora, 3 March 1973, 27 UST 1087, 993 UNTS 243 [CITES]; Convention on the Conservation of Migratory Species of Wild Animals, 23 June 1979, 1990 UKTS No. 87 [Bonn Convention]; Convention on Biological Diversity, 5 June 1992, 31 *ILM* 818 (1992) [CBD]; The International Treaty on Plant Genetic Resources for Food and Agriculture, FAO/RES/3 (3 November 2001).

47. CBD CoP 7 Decision VII/26, Cooperation with other conventions and international organizations and initiatives, 2004. For a history of the Liaison Group of Biodiversity Related Conventions see Long, "Developing Linkages to Preserve Biodiversity," supra note 44.

48. For an excellent study of international efforts regarding Arctic (and Antarctic) marine biodiversity, see Rayfuse, "Protecting Marine Biodiversity in Polar Areas Beyond National Jurisdiction," supra note 30, 3–13.

49. UNEP, Report of the Second Meeting of the Conference of the Parties to the Convention on Biological Diversity, UNEP/CBD/COP/2/19, para. 12, 16 (30 November 1995), http://www .cbd.int/doc/meetings/cop/cop-02/official/cop-02-19-en.pdf.

50. Oceans and the Law of the Sea, G.A. Res. 59/24, Doc. A/Res/59/24, para. 73 (2004).

51. The working group produced a new Strategic Plan for Biodiversity 2011–2020 that specifically addressed Arctic issues. Letter dated 30 June 2011 from the cochairs of the Ad Hoc Open-ended Informal Working Group to the President of the General Assembly, A/66/119 para. 11.

52. See, e.g., UNEP, Report of the Expert Workshop on Scientific and Technical Aspects Relevant to Environmental Impact Assessment in Marine Areas Beyond National Jurisdiction, UNEP/CBD/SBSTTA/14 INF/5 (8 March 2010) at http://www.cbd.int/doc/meetings/sbstta/ sbstta-14/information/sbstta-14-inf-05-en.pdf.

53. United Nations General Assembly, Letter dated 8 June 2012 from the cochairs of the Ad Hoc Open-ended Informal Working Group to the President of the General Assembly, A/67/95.

54. United Nations General Assembly, Letter dated 30 June 2011 from the cochairs of the Ad Hoc Open-ended Informal Working Group to the President of the General Assembly, A/66/119.

55. Information on GRID-Arendal is available at www.grida.no/.

56. See UNEP/CBD/COP/Bur/2008/1/4, 12 December 2007, Report on Activities of the Secretariat on the Implementation of the Work Programme of the Convention and Its Protocol, p. 52, item 16. A related press release is available at www.cbd.int/doc/press/2007/pr-2007-10 -30-grid-arendal-en.pdf. The CHM strategic plan is contained in annex I to CBD CoP decision VIII/11.

57. See, e.g., UNEP/CBD/SBSTTA/15/WG.2/CRP.2, 9 November 2011, recalling the Resolution on Cooperation between the Secretariats of the Convention on Biological Diversity and the Conservation of Arctic Flora and Fauna Working Group. Other Arctic Council working groups also have MOUs with treaty bodies; see, e.g., the Arctic Marine Assessment Program (AMAP) working group MOU with the OSPAR Commission (information available at http://www.ospar .org/content/content.asp?menu=0016), and plans for an MOU with the Stockholm Convention on Persistent Organic Pollutants (AMAP, AMAP Report 2010:2, Minutes of the 23rd AMAP WG Meeting San Francisco, 11–12 February 2010, p. 8, available at www.amap.no).

58. Conservation of Arctic Flora and Fauna (CAFF), 2013, CBD-CAFF Resolution on Cooperation, 2.

59. See Conservation of Arctic Flora and Fauna (CAFF), 2013, Arctic Biodiversity Assessment (ABA): Report for Policy Makers. CAFF, Akureyri, Iceland, available at www.arctic biodiversity.is.

60. See, e.g., CBD SBSTTA 14, 10–21 May 2010, Nairobi, Kenya. Recommendation XIV/16. New and emerging issues: "3. Invites the Arctic Council to provide relevant information and assessments of Arctic biodiversity, in particular information generated through the Circumpolar Biodiversity Monitoring Program (CBMP) of the Arctic Council's Conservation of Arctic Flora and Fauna Working Group, for consideration by the Subsidiary Body on Scientific, Technical and Technological Advice."

61. Arctic Council Secretariat, Kiruna Declaration on the Occasion of the Eighth Ministerial Meeting of the Arctic Council, MM08, 15 May 2013, available at www.ArcticCouncil.is, 4.

62. ABA, supra note 59, at Recommendation 4.

63. ABA Report for Policy Makers, supra note 59, p. 17.

64. Thilo Marauhn, "The Potential of the Convention on Biological Diversity to Address the Effects of Climate Change in the Arctic," in T. Koivurova et al. (eds.), Climate Governance in the Arctic (Berlin: Springer, 2009), 263–286, 277–278, citing a 2002 CAFF decision.

65. Marauhn, ibid., 278.

66. Marauhn, ibid.

67. CAFF Progress Report, Senior Arctic Officials Meeting, Luleå, Sweden, 8–9 November 2011, p. g.

68. On the connection between IPBES and marine biodiversity, see B. Baker, "Marine Biodiversity, Ecosystem Services and Better Use of Science Information," in H. Scheiber and M. Kwon (eds.), *Securing the Ocean for the Next Generation*, Papers from the Law of the Sea Institute–Korea Institute of Ocean Science and Technology Conference held in Seoul, Korea, May 2012, published at http://www.law.berkeley.edu/15589.htm (2013).

69. Marauhn, "The Potential of the Convention on Biological Diversity," supra note 64, p. 270. See also CBD CoP Decision VII/15 of 2004, which "invites parties and bodies to make use of the report on climate change and biodiversity prepared by the AHTEG in order to promote synergies." Beyond this, SBSTTA welcomes the report of the Ad Hoc Technical Expert Group on Biodiversity and Climate Change (AHTEG)—"as scientific advice."

70. Marauhn, "The Potential of the Convention on Biological Diversity," supra note 64, 269ff.

71. Marauhn, ibid., 273–274.

72. Marauhn, ibid., 274.

73. Marauhn, ibid.

74. Rayfuse, "Protecting Marine Biodiversity in Polar Areas," supra notes 30 and 48.

75. 2013 marked the eighth meeting of the working group. The Provisional Agenda for the eighth meeting, in Montreal, Canada, 7–11 October 2013, included "5. Recommendations from the United Nations Permanent Forum on Indigenous Issues and 6. Connecting traditional knowledge systems and science, such as under IPBES, including gender dimensions." UNEP/CBD/WG8J/8/1, 6 March 2013.

76. CBD, supra note 3, preamble: "Recognizing the close and traditional dependence of many indigenous and local communities embodying traditional lifestyles on biological resources, and the desirability of sharing equitably benefits arising from the use of traditional knowledge, innovations and practices relevant to the conservation of biological diversity and the sustainable use of its components . . ."

77. See, e.g., CoP decision VIII/5, Art. 8(j) and related provisions (2006), http://www.cbd.int/doc/decisions/COP-08-dec-en.pdf.

78. See, e.g., Decisions Adopted by the Conference of the Parties to the Convention on Biological Diversity at Its Ninth Meeting, Bonn, 19–30 May 2008, Unep/Cbd/Cop/9/29, Decision Ix/13, Article 8(j) and Related Provisions, p. 117, referencing work that produced the study "Indigenous Peoples and Traditional Knowledge Related to Biological Diversity and Responses to Climate Change in the Arctic Region," published by the Ministry of the Environment of Finland (2008), introduction.

79. Declaration on the Rights of Indigenous Peoples, G.A. Res. 61/295, U.N. Doc. A/Res/61/295 (13 September 2007). On the declaration in general, see E. G. Claire Charters and Rodolfo Stavenhagen, International Work Group for Indigenous Affairs (IWGIA), *Making Declarations Work: The United Nations Declaration on the Rights of Indigenous Peoples*, Doc. 127 (Copenhagen: IWGIA, 2009).

80. See, e.g., Provisional Agenda, supra note 75, item 5, "Recommendations from the United Nations Permanent Forum on Indigenous Issues."

81. No reference to UNDRIP appears in the Kuellnegk Neark Declaration of the Twentieth Saami Conference, 2 to 4 May 2013, Murmansk, Russia, even though the Saami were involved in the creation of UNDRIP. See www.galdu.org/govat/doc/1305_kuellnegk_neark_declaration_final.pdf.

82. Available at http://inuitcircumpolar.com/files/uploads/icc-files/declaration12x18vicechairssigned.pdf.

83. Alta Outcome Document, Global Indigenous Preparatory Conference for the United Nations High Level Plenary Meeting of the General Assembly to be known as the World Conference on Indigenous Peoples, 10–12 June 2013, Alta, available at http://wcip2014.org/1530.

84. Alta Outcome Document, ibid., preamble, "We Indigenous Peoples, have the right of self determination and permanent sovereignty over our lands, territories, resources, air, ice, oceans and waters, mountains and forests." See also pp. 2, 3, 5, and 7.

85. Alta Outcome Document, Theme 1.1, p. 3.

86. Alta Outcome Document, Theme 2.7, p. 5.

87. Wolfrum and Matz, *Conflicts in International Environmental Law*, supra note 22, p. 77.

88. Ottawa Declaration, supra note 7, penultimate clause.

89. Wolfrum and Matz, *Conflicts in International Environmental Law*, supra note 22, 340ff. and 194–209, and Marauhn, "The Potential of the Convention on Biological Diversity," supra note 64, n. 33.

90. Marauhn, "The Potential of the Convention on Biological Diversity," supra note 64, p. 274.

91. Wolfrum and Matz, *Conflicts in International Environmental Law*, supra note 22, pp. 173–174, noting that the secretariats of the CBD and Ramsar Convention on the Conservation of Wetlands, and the CBD and Bonn Agreement do not regulate the question of information exchange.

92. On the imprecision and nonbinding character of MOUs generally, see David Llewellyn and Maureen Tehan, "'Treaties,' 'Agreements,' 'Contracts' and Commitments'—What's in a Name? The Legal Force and Meaning of Different Forms of Agreement Making," Melbourne Law School, Legal Studies Research Paper No. 134, October 2004, 9ff., available at http://ssrn.com/abstract=815324.

93. Wolfrum and Matz, *Conflicts in International Environmental Law*, supra note 22, p. 174.

94. The Arctic Ocean Review Final Report examines almost twenty instruments that are relevant to the marine Arctic alone, excluding discussion of the terrestrial Arctic. See AOR Report, supra note 20.

95. E.g., the Convention on International Trade in Endangered Species of Wild Fauna and Flora (CITES), the 1973 International Convention for the Prevention of Pollution from Ships, its 1978 Protocol, known as MARPOL 73/78, and three of its six Annexes—I (oil), II (noxious liquid substances in bulk), and III (harmful substances, packaged).

96. AOR Report, supra note 20, Executive Summary, Recommendation 16.

97. UNEP—World Conservation Monitoring Center, Workshop Report, "Towards the harmonization of national reporting to biodiversity-related treaties, A workshop convened by UNEP-WCMC in cooperation with the governments of Belgium and the UK," Haasrode, Belgium, 22–23 September 2004, Doc: AEWA/StC Inf. 2.5, 11 November 2004, 1.

98. UNEP-WCMC Workshop Report, ibid., 3.i, p. 2.

99. UNEP-WCMC Workshop Report, ibid., 3.iii, p. 3.

100. Arctic SAR Agreement, supra note 25.

3. An Erosion of Confidence?
The Antarctic Treaty System in
the Twenty-first Century

DANIELA LIGGETT

Over the last sixty years, Antarctica moved from the periphery of global political awareness and from being a frontier for exploration, adventure, and notions of political sovereignty at "the bottom of the world" to one of the focal points of international discussion, especially in the context of climate change, as a place where sovereignty matters were set aside and where peace and science were moved to the fore. At the same time, the notion of suspended sovereignty, which has been described as an ingenious agreement to disagree, has been contested as rooted in an intrinsically colonial system of the past that might not stand up in the contemporary world (Hemmings, 2008).

Conventionally praised as a successful governance system and a dedicated environmental regime, the Antarctic Treaty System (ATS) has recently come under criticism for its lack of confidence in Antarctic exceptionalism and a lack of administrative capacity to deal with the growing complexity of human activities and environmental concerns in the Antarctic (Hemmings, 2009). The spirit of peaceful cooperation during the 1957–1958 International Geophysical Year (IGY) and the limited number of parties involved in the negotiation of the 1959 Antarctic Treaty contributed to the adoption of consensus-based decision making as one of the principles upon which the Antarctic Treaty was to rest. More than half a century later, consensus is still required for political decision making within the framework of the Antarctic Treaty System, yet the number of states involved in Antarctic governance has grown from twelve to fifty. Challenges confronting Antarctic Treaty Consultative Parties (ATCPs) have increased in scale and complexity and test the robustness and success of the Antarctic Treaty System. Diverging national interests, the frozen yet unresolved sovereignty issues, and the cautious avoidance of contentious geopolitical matters during Antarctic Treaty Consultative Meetings (ATCMs) have further contributed to what appears to be a lack of enthusiasm and urgency with regard to how ATCPs approach challenging matters such as the increase of commercial activity in Antarctica; scientific whaling; internal pressures arising from sovereignty claims and the continental shelf delimitation; and external factors such as climate change.

This chapter will provide a brief overview of the development of the Antarctic Treaty System and will discuss the challenges faced by the ATS in the twenty-first century. Threats to the stability and continued success of the ATS will be examined and compared to its flexibility and capacity to react to a changing environment.

The Roots and Development of the Antarctic Treaty System

> The Antarctic has been a political laboratory where the respec-
> tive merits of jurisdiction based on territory and on nationality have
> been fought out in debate marked by forbearance—a tribute to those
> who engaged in the debates but, more than anything, to the unique
> and all-pervading nature and force of the Antarctic itself.
> —HEAP (2007, P. 86)

The history of human activity in the Antarctic is very brief compared to other landmasses on earth. Active geographic and scientific exploration in Antarctica only occurred in the last two centuries. In the nineteenth century, commercial exploitation through sealing and whaling in the Antarctic and sub-Antarctic dominated, but in the early twentieth century, the Antarctic seemed to gain strategic political importance. Between 1908 and 1957, seven states (Argentina, Australia, Chile, France, New Zealand, Norway, and the United Kingdom) made claims to territorial sovereignty over parts of Antarctica (Triggs, 2011). During this period of increasing politicization of Antarctica, interest in the future of Antarctica was expressed by public figures, such as the son of Ernest Shackleton or the president of the American Polar Society, as well as by political and nongovernmental groups (e.g., the Women's International League for Peace and Freedom), international organizations (e.g., UNESCO), and governments (Jacobsson, 2011).

The 1940s and early 1950s saw an increasing militarization of human activities in the Antarctic (Summerhayes and Beeching, 2007). Military operations in the Antarctic, assertions of sovereignty, tensions surrounding overlapping claims in the Antarctic Peninsula region, and the unstable global political situation that culminated in the Cold War represented signs of potential conflict that states feared could be exploited by rival states (Beck, 2010; Rothwell and Nasu, 2008). A variety of solutions were proposed, ranging from a temporary suspension of territorial rights (Chile-Escudero Proposal), United Nations trusteeship (United States), to a pure condominium (United Kingdom) (Jacobsson, 2011). None of these proposals found wide acceptance, however, and concerns by nonclaimant states grew. India, for instance, approached the United Nations with the request for the UN to assume responsibility for the governance of Antarctica (Rothwell, 1996).

As diplomats struggled to find a resolution for the tensions in Antarctica, science came to their aid with the 1957–1958 International Geophysical Year. The peaceful and productive scientific collaboration during the IGY is said to have contributed to the formulation of the 1959 Antarctic Treaty (Jacobsson, 2011; Summerhayes, 2008).[1] In fact, aside from considerations of political security emphasized above, the security to continue undertaking scientific research was an important factor that led to the negotiation of the Antarctic Treaty (Rothwell and Nasu, 2008).

The Antarctic Treaty, which has been regarded as being "amongst the most successful multilateral agreements negotiated in the twentieth century" (Joyner, 2008, p. 61) and which has been described as "elegant in its simplicity" (Berkman, 2010, p. 7), gives free access to the Antarctic Treaty area south of 60° S latitude for peaceful purposes and scientific activity. Despite this honorable focus of the treaty, the creation of a continent dedicated to peace and science resulted not so much from altruism but from the recognition by states of what they stood to lose if they did not provide for the continued denuclearized and demilitarized status of the Antarctic continent (Beck, 2010). Article IV of the Antarctic Treaty is a true masterpiece of diplomacy as it protects the position of claimant and nonclaimant states as well as the position of the two states (the United States and Russia) that reserved their basis to a claim.[2] The treaty succeeded in preventing military conflict in the Antarctic, and it has been applauded as saying "only what . . . had to be said to provide a framework within which peace could be maintained and no more, but how it was to be maintained was left to the parties" (Heap, 2007, p. 86).

The treaty itself did not set out to protect the Antarctic environment per se (Polk, 1998). Reflecting the political environment of the time it was drafted, the treaty focused more on political security than environmental protection. The treaty provided, however, the foundations of environmental governance in the Antarctic (Hemmings, 2010), in that its drafters were mindful of future developments when they safeguarded the right of the parties to develop new regulatory mechanisms that targeted "matters of common interest" such as the "preservation and conservation of living resources in Antarctica" (Article IX of the Antarctic Treaty).[3] As such, Article IX facilitated the growth from one international agreement into the Antarctic Treaty System (Jacobsson, 2011), which is the "whole complex of arrangements made for the purpose of regulating relations among states in the Antarctic" (Heap, 2007, p. 82). Aside from the Antarctic Treaty itself, the ATS encompasses a range of recommendations, measures, decisions, and resolutions concluded at annual Antarctic Treaty Consultative Meetings, as well as three conventions addressing the Conservation of Antarctic Seals (1972), the Conservation of Antarctic Marine Living Resources (CCAMLR, 1980), and the Regulation of Antarctic Mineral Resource Activities (CRAMRA, 1988). After its creation, CRAMRA was blocked by leading Antarctic states such as Australia and France, and never entered into force (Rothwell, 2010). Instead, the gap it left was replaced by the Protocol on Environmental Protection to the Antarctic Treaty (Madrid Protocol), which contained many of the environmental impact assessment tools elaborated in CRAMRA. The Madrid Protocol went further than CRAMRA by prohibiting any mineral resource activities in the Antarctic. It was also the first to regulate all human activities in the Antarctic (Heap, 2007). Since the adoption of the Madrid Protocol, the ATS has put a great

deal of emphasis on environmental security (Rothwell and Nasu, 2008), with some
contentious environmental issues receiving more attention.[4]

Initially criticized as a "closed club" (Rothwell and Nasu, 2008, p. 15), the ATS
has been exposed to greater public scrutiny over the mining debate and has opened
up considerably to NGOs and other parties outside the ATS since the 1980s (Dodds,
2010a). Its membership expanded, and the institution itself has been adapted
and strengthened over time, reacting to a changing political environment (Dodds,
2010a), and has increased and diversified its activities (Hemmings, 2008). After
prolonged discussion at ATCMs, the decision was made to establish a secretariat in
Buenos Aires, Argentina. This institutional strengthening tied the existing membership together in terms of collective responsibility; it helped build trust and cement
interstate and interpersonal relationships; it also gave the ATS greater institutional
legitimacy in a transformed, decolonizing world (Dodds, 2010a).

So far, the ATS has been relatively successful and able to deal with challenges
as they arose, including the critical move from negotiating a mining convention to
abandoning this convention and developing an environmental agreement instead
(Rothwell and Nasu, 2008). At the same time, an increasing number of internal
and external challenges are confronting the ATS. Some scholars question the capacity of the ATS to deal with these challenges. The following section will give an
overview of some of the issues challenging the ATS and will discuss the regime's
stability.

Contemporary Challenges to the Stability of the ATS

In essence the managerial challenges pertaining to the Antarctic can be summarized as being largely a function of the region's diminishing isolation in a
variety of political, scientific, commercial, cultural and environmental contexts.
—DODDS (2010A, P. 115)

So far, the Antarctic Treaty System has shown significant resilience and has successfully weathered storms challenging its stability. The ATS was seriously tested in
the 1980s, when it was on the brink of negotiating a convention to regulate mineral
resource extraction. At the UN General Assembly, the system was then criticized as
being "an elitist, secretive, anachronistic old boy's club" by a Malaysian-led initiative
(Jabour and Weber, 2008, p. 36). The consequent focus of the UN on the future of
Antarctica under ethical considerations of fairness, along with the re-evaluation of
its status as a global commons and the call for an opening of the ATS to developing
states, put considerable pressure on the ATS (Buck, 1998; Herber, 2007). At that
time, the ATS succeeded in making changes to the regime and its membership,
which quieted the voices of criticism (Dodds, 2010a). The membership of the ATS
drastically expanded and opened up to include less powerful states to a greater extent. The ATS began to show greater transparency and engagement with the media,
and the mineral resources convention was abandoned and replaced by a comprehensive agreement protecting the Antarctic environment and prohibiting mineral

resource exploration and extraction. As a result, the controversial question of how Antarctic resources were to be shared between claimant and nonclaimant states, including states that were not Antarctic Treaty signatory states, became irrelevant, and UN debates over the future of Antarctica lost momentum (Dodds, 2010a; Herber, 2007; Tracey, 2001).

Despite the resilience the ATS has shown with regard to past challenges, and the cooperative spirit with which ATS states responded to these challenges, a range of new issues that emerged over the last ten years poses a significant threat to the stability and integrity of the ATS (Joyner, 2008). These new challenges appear to be "fuelled mostly by accelerating globalization . . . [and] could eat away at that cooperative underpinning of the Antarctic Treaty regime, especially if ATCP governments opt to press for narrow-minded interests at the expense of what is good for the whole Treaty membership" (Joyner, 2008, p. 30). Table 3.1 provides a categorized overview of the challenges faced by the ATS as discussed in the scholarly literature.

There appears to be considerable debate concerning the seriousness of individual challenges. Joyner (2008), for instance, argues that issues that the ATS has been confronted with since the 1980s, such as climate change, tourism, and IUU fishing (illegal, unreported, and unregulated fishing), while constituting challenges that will still need to be addressed, are not as pressing as bioprospecting, the delimitation of the outer continental shelf, or whaling. Other scholars argue that the inability of treaty parties (along with CCAMLR members) to effectively address the problem of IUU fishing, which threatens the sustainability of marine living resources, or the differences of opinion on how to regulate Antarctic tourism impose greater pressures on the ATS. However, scholars agree on two main points. The first is that most of the contemporary challenges faced by the ATS reflect increasing global concerns surrounding resource security, indicative of an era characterized by accelerating globalization, growing world population, and diminishing natural resources. Consequently, the delicate matter of who can access resources—now and in the future—becomes increasingly significant, in and beyond the Antarctic region. Article 7 of the Madrid Protocol currently prohibits any mineral resource activities in the Antarctic that are not related to scientific research.[5] Nonetheless, states seem to wish to secure their rights for a potential future exploitation of resources, e.g., of potential offshore hydrocarbon resources on the continental shelf.

A second point is that the contested notion of ownership to parts of the Antarctic fundamentally weakens the ATS (Beck, 1990; Molenaar, 2005); in the context of managing Antarctica, sovereignty always creeps in as a central issue and, as Rothwell (2010, p. 17) highlights, "sovereignty was and still remains one of the principle reasons for human endeavor in Antarctica." Sovereignty matters have largely been dormant, but might be reignited by Antarctica's prospective resources; if awakened, they have the potential to pose a significant threat to the Antarctic regime (Rothwell, 2010). Maintaining the current situation of (suspended) sovereignty claims might endanger not only the political sustainability of the ATS but also the environmental sustainability of the Antarctic, as claimant states might push for retrieving benefits from resource exploitation in "their" territories (Hemmings, 2008).

Table 3.1: Contemporary challenges faced by Antarctic Treaty consultative parties

Challenge	Nature of the challenge	Legal basis/conflict	References
Biological prospecting	There is a lack of consensus regarding the status of bio-prospecting, i.e., as a research activity or as a commercial pursuit, which has significant implications for how it should be treated, who should have access to natural resources in Antarctica, and how any benefits should be shared.	Art. III (Antarctic Treaty), requiring scientific cooperation and the free sharing of scientific information, vs. patenting endeavors necessitating privacy surrounding research findings or methodologies.	Jacobsson (2011); Joyner (2008; 2011); Leary (2008; 2009); Rothwell and Nasu (2008)
Whaling	Political tensions exist between Australia and Japan due to Japanese whaling activities in parts of the Australian-claimed sector of the Southern Ocean. Because of the unresolved sovereignty situation, jurisdiction over the management of marine resources is ambiguous and contested. Jurisdiction by coastal states is not internationally recognized, and the development of alternative regulatory mechanisms has been impeded by the suspension of existing sovereignty claims.	Art. 2 and 3 (Madrid Protocol), committing Parties to comprehensive environmental protection and the planning of activities in a way that avoids detrimental effects on flora or fauna, and Art. VI (CCAMLR) ensuring that all Parties retain the rights and obligations imposed on them by the International Convention for the Regulation of Whaling (ICRW).	Dodds (2010a); Hemmings (2008); Joyner (2008; 2011); Rothwell and Nasu (2008); Scott (2010); Triggs (2011)
IUU Fishing	The sustainable management of Southern Ocean fisheries through CCAMLR (Convention on the Conservation of Antarctic Marine Living Resources) is under significant pressure from illegal, unreported, and unregulated fishing, which raises concerns about environmental and resource security.	CCAMLR regulations requiring Parties to ensure compliance with CCAMLR fisheries management and to cooperate with ATCPs.	Dodds (2010a); Hemmings (2008); Rothwell and Nasu (2008)
Submissions to the UN Commission on the Limits of the Continental Shelf (CLCS)	According to the 1982 UN Convention on the Law of the Sea (UNCLOS), states could make submissions to the CLCS to extend their territorial seas to the outer edge of the continental margin. All seven Antarctic claimant states have made preliminary, partial, or full submissions to the CLCS covering their Antarctic claims, in some cases in conjunction with more general submissions. Should these submissions be considered as new claims, extensions of existing claims, or merely part of extant claims?	Art. IV (Antarctic Treaty), resembling an "agreement to disagree" on existing claims and suspending the latter, vs. Art. 76 (UNCLOS), allowing for an extension of the territorial sea to the edge of the continental margin, up to 350 nautical miles.	Dodds (2010a; 2010b); Hemmings (2008; 2010); Jacobsson (2011); Joyner (2008; 2011); Triggs (2011); Weber (2011)

Tourism	Tourism activities in the Antarctic have drastically increased and diversified since the 1990s. One cruise ship sank in the Antarctic in 2007. There is general disagreement about the regulation of Antarctic tourism among Treaty Parties, and any benefits Parties derive from tourism are currently not shared.	The Madrid Protocol applies to all human activity, including tourism, but focuses only on potential environmental impacts of tourism and not on political, jurisdictional, sociocultural, or economic challenges.	Dodds (2010a); Hemmings (2008); Orheim et al. (2011); Triggs (2011)
Climate change	Climate change is often considered an external factor that can be dealt with from a scientific perspective. The focus on climate change science has drawn attention away from the development of normative responses to assessing and managing human activities in the Antarctic in a responsible way such that the human footprint and greenhouse gas emissions are minimized.	Art. 3 (Madrid Protocol) requiring a minimization of adverse environmental impacts vs. global environmental regimes (e.g., Kyoto Protocol) aiming at achieving a reduction of greenhouse gas emissions, which have to be administered by regional regimes (such as the ATS) to a greater extent.	French and Scott (2009); Joyner (2011); Orheim et al. (2011); Rothwell and Nasu (2008)
Jurisdiction all limitations	Nationality-based jurisdiction in conjunction with the unresolved status of jurisdiction over individuals who are not official observers or science personnel on exchange has led to a jurisdictional void whenever state Parties choose not to cooperate in the investigation of legal matters.	Art. VIII (Antarctic Treaty), stipulating nationality-based jurisdiction, and Art. IV (Antarctic Treaty) suggesting that existing claims are merely suspended but not void.	Scott (2010)
Conflict	The conflict between Argentina and the United Kingdom with regard to sovereignty over the Falkland Islands / Las Malvinas has significant bearing on the relationship between these two countries and their level of cooperation within the ATS. Furthermore, extreme environmental interventions (e.g., activities of antiwhaling groups with regard to Japanese whaling) might fall into this category.	Various (very much depending on the specific case)	Triggs (2011)

As matters of resource security coupled with the problematic situation of un-resolved sovereignty, which the Antarctic Treaty has not been designed to solve (Dodds, 2010a), the aforementioned challenges pose a significant threat to the sta-bility of the ATS. Developed as "a surrogate governing body to resolve tensions be-tween various institutions that have interests in the continent" (Polk, 1998, p. 1395), cooperation and comradeship form the very basis of the ATS. The founders of the Antarctic Treaty went so far as to require all decisions to be by consensus in an effort to retain the cooperative spirit under which the treaty was conceived. This may have worked well with the group of twelve original signatory states, but it poses a much greater challenge in a system that now comprises fifty signatory states, twenty-nine of which are ATCPs with the right to partake in decision making. The growth of the ATS decision-making body in numbers has overtaken its institutional development, which seems to have come to a standstill (Hemmings, 2008).

Furthermore, the ATS is faced with a changing external environment to which it may no longer be well suited. In some respects, the ATCM, which effectively facilitates the administration of an entire continent, may be "the victim of its own success," as the former executive secretary of the ATS muses (Huber, 2011, p. 92). He contends that "the ATCM is . . . an intensely conservative and complacent group where agreements are negotiated in a confidential, clubby atmosphere, far away from the public and media, and where change is usually resisted" (Huber, 2011, p. 93). Having an integral actor from within the ATS express such concern, if not ex-asperation, about the processes and procedures driving the regime can be regarded as evidence of an erosion of confidence in the ability of the ATS to adequately and effectively respond to contemporary and future challenges. Similarly, the reported reluctance of parties to discuss questions related to the regulatory effectiveness of how the ATS is administered or how mechanisms agreed upon are implemented, and the parties' sensitivity when it comes to matters of sovereignty or institutional development (Huber, 2011) reflect a lack of confidence in their own right. This ero-sion of confidence has also been commented on by scholars like Hemmings, who observes that "Antarctica today appears to be significantly more unstable than at any previous time since the adoption of the Antarctic Treaty" (2009, p. 56). A sense of instability of the ATS and lack of confidence in it might hint that the robustness of the regime is withering away. The regime's robustness is reflected by the capacity of the ATS to react to disturbances while maintaining its integrity, i.e., pursuing its objectives and maintaining certain desirable characteristics despite changes in other systems or components (Carlson and Doyle, 2002; Dodds, 2010a; Rothwell and Nasu, 2008; Young, 1998). From this, it follows that regime flexibility is of utmost importance (Young, 1994; Young, 1998). Considerable flexibility has been built into the ATS right from the start, and wisely so. Regulatory mechanisms can be added and amended, as we have seen over the years with the growth of the ATS, but the core of the regime and the decision-making procedures remain stable. Rules and procedures of the regime have not kept pace with external and internal develop-ments, however, and an increase in the number of ATCPs means that despite an inbuilt flexibility, decision making can be glacially slow due to the dependence on consensus (Huber, 2006).

The flexibility of a regime to react to disturbances needs to be matched by its capacity to enforce mechanisms that reflect changing parameters. In the ATS, enforcement is still largely based on goodwill. Similarly, transparency, which has a direct bearing on enforceability of any measures as it raises awareness, understanding, and compliance (Ostrom, 2005), is also principally a matter of political will. Whereas information sharing is heralded by the Antarctic Treaty, it is not necessarily followed through to the same extent by all parties (Huber, 2011). Clearly, incentives for reporting are needed, routines should be developed for self-assessment and reporting, technical obstacles to reporting need to be removed, and decisions not to report need to be discouraged.

The ATS in the Twenty-first Century

> While the ATS is not likely to disappear, its capacity to manage and regulate will continue to be challenged by actors, events and processes which one day might include mineral exploitation—the contested sovereignty of the region remains a haunting presence.
> —DODDS (2010A, P. 115)

While matters of institutional design and regime flexibility and transparency can be easily considered from a purely regional perspective and with internal processes in mind, what is also crucial is how an environmental regime or treaty system can adapt to changing external factors. Many of the challenges discussed in this chapter arise from globalization, a changing world order, and the pressing need for resource and environmental security. These challenges may be considered as resulting from external forces, but they are inherently a test for the robustness and stability of the ATS and its internal mechanisms. How the ATCPs respond to these challenges will prove whether the ATS has outlived its time or whether it can successfully adapt to the political realities of the twenty-first century.

Due to its reliance on consensus decision making and political will regarding the implementation of any measures and reporting, the ATS can only be as strong as its individual parties. It also requires all parties to be pulling in the same direction on a path strewn with challenges in the form of external forces acting upon the ATS as well as an internal struggle for cohesion and the accommodation of a growing membership. As highlighted in this chapter, at the juncture of external challenges and internal struggle lies the complicated matter of unresolved sovereignty. The latter was clearly the product of the time when the Antarctic Treaty was drafted and was, at this time, an ingenious solution to seemingly insurmountable differences between states. More than fifty years later, the suspension of sovereignty claims in the Antarctic appears to be considered more critically (Scott, 2010), and scholars are asking whether the considerations behind Article IV are intrinsically colonial and outdated and whether Article IV will, in fact, suffice over the next fifty years (Hemmings, 2008). Hemmings eloquently posits that "the past need not be an appropriate guide to the future" (2008, p. 82) and that the sovereignty claims neither have sufficient international support nor are they ethically defendable at current times.

So, where is the ATS heading from here? Are the ATCPs ready to follow recommendations by scholars who call for a greater internationalization of Antarctica and adoption of a common heritage of mankind regime, one that sees sovereignty claims disestablished and the ATS continuing to manage the region, but on behalf of all of humankind with a set of agreed principles at its core (Scott, 2010)?[6] At the moment, there do not seem to be any signals that any of the claimant states are willing to give up their claims for a greater common good. In fact, the submissions made to the Commission on the Limits of the Continental Shelf (CLCS) indicate efforts to strengthen Antarctic territorial claims and prepare for a time when mineral resource exploitation might be feasible. However, as Hemmings (2008) already points out, the realization and protection of territorial sovereignty by the claimants is, at least in regard to New Zealand and Australia, unrealistic from an economic, logistical, political, and managerial perspective. Pertinent questions—about what will happen if the ATS continues on the path that the regime is currently following and about what feasible alternative pathways there are—have been, to some extent, explored in this chapter but need to be moved out of the academic into the political realm. For the ATS to remain strong in the twenty-first century, political will to cooperate is not enough but needs to be matched by openness for reflection, reassessment, and confidence in the regime in such a way that political processes and regime effectiveness can be critically examined and monitored and potentially drastic steps to bring the regime in line with the contemporary global environment are taken into serious consideration.

Notes

1. It is worth noting that Bulkeley (2010, p. 10) disputes this assertion and contends that "[t]he IGY did not inspire or initiate the diplomatic process that eventually resulted in the Treaty." Instead, he suggests that calls for an internationalization of Antarctica and scientific collaboration preceded the IGY and that the IGY might have been a proof of concept (of peaceful collaboration, involving different nations which included the Soviet Union) rather than its origin.

2. Article IV of the Antarctic Treaty suspended the seven existing territorial claims by Argentina, Australia, Chile, France, New Zealand, Norway, and the United Kingdom; protected the basis to claim by the United States and Russia; and gave signatories to the AT the nonprejudicial option to accept or reject any or all existing claims or basis to claim. As such, Article IV resembles an agreement to disagree and acted as the sine qua non for the Antarctic Treaty itself.

3. This paved the way for the transformation of the Antarctic Treaty into an environmental regime with the Madrid Protocol as the focal point of environmental protection.

4. Examples include the Japanese scientific whaling program and climate change as external forces with serious implications for Antarctic politics as well as the Antarctic environment. Climate change, however, so far has been neglected when it comes to developing normative responses (French and Scott, 2009; Rothwell and Nasu, 2008).

5. A review of the Protocol may be requested by any contracting party in 2048, and modifications to the Protocol can then be proposed, but to be adopted they require the approval of 75 percent of the ATCPs who initially adopted the Protocol (see Article 25 of the Madrid Protocol). In addition, the modification of Article 7 requires the existence or adoption of a legally binding regime addressing Antarctic mineral resource activities at the time the modification to the Protocol is proposed (Article 25(5) of the Madrid Protocol).

6. Scott (2010) argues that the ATS is the most appropriate and pragmatic regime to extend trusteeship over Antarctica to all of humankind and contends that the UN is not equipped to take on the institutional oversight of a huge uninhabited continent.

4. Invasive Species in the Arctic: Concerns, Regulations, and Governance

KAMRUL HOSSAIN

In most literature, numerous terminologies are utilized in referring to invasive species. Such terminologies are used interchangeably and include nonindigenous species, alien species, immigrated species, or nonnative species, among others. Invasive species are species that include plants, animals, and microorganisms that did not originally develop in a particular region, but are introduced either accidently or deliberately. Their introduction may take place via the importing, for limited purposes, of species which then escape.[1] In most cases, the so-called four T's—trade, transport, travel, and tourism—are responsible for the introduction of invasive alien species.[2] Increased Internet sales of horticultural plants, insects, and exotic animals may also contribute to the introduction of invasive species since such sales and the postal screening processes associated with them are mostly unregulated or poorly regulated.[3] In addition, human or anthropogenic impact on the environment facilitates the development of invasive species outside of their past or present natural distribution range.[4] By whatever means they are introduced, in most cases, invasive species pose a significant threat to the environment and to their new habitat. They threaten biodiversity by behaving as predators, competitors, parasites, or pathogens when establishing themselves in a new place.[5] They ultimately disrupt the development and growth of native species. Invasive species also carry the potential risk of introducing foreign diseases.[6] The adverse effects of their introduction include: concerns regarding public health, disruption of the balance of the ecosystem, the extinction of native species, as well as the risk of losing culture and livelihood of the local human (and indigenous) communities that rely on a particular ecosystem.[7]

Regional concerns regarding the potentially detrimental effects of introduction of invasive species in the Arctic are relatively new and are primarily associated with the rapid rise in temperature resulting from climate change. The Arctic temperature is rising at twice the pace of other regions, leading to the rapid melting of sea ice (Arctic Council, Arctic Climate Impact Assessment [ACIA], 2005). Consequently, the

Arctic marine area is increasingly opening for navigation; in particular, the regional seas adjacent to coastal areas are now largely ice-free during summer months. A large part of the Arctic Ocean is also ice-free for a short duration during the summer months. Open access to these marine waters with increased navigation establishes situations where nonnative species may be carried into the region. At present, four ways of tracing the presence of invasive species in the Arctic ecosystem via marine navigation are by examining ship ballast water, hull fouling, cargos, and causalities. The introduction of invasive species into the Arctic may also take place via land-based sources. The release of living modified organisms resulting from biotechnology, the impact of globalization, including increased international trade, tourism, and other large-scale economic activities such as mining and mineral activities, as well as overall infrastructure development, generate scenarios where invasive species may be introduced.

The Arctic Climate Impact Assessment, reported by the Arctic Council and the International Arctic Science Committee, with reference to the findings indicated by the International Conservation Union (IUCN), states that, of three indicators that threaten Arctic ecosystems, invasive species are the second most threatening (the other indicators are energy development and climate change).[8] The introduction of invasive species contributes to loss of biodiversity, habitat change, and fragmentation in the region.[9] The Arctic's sensitive ecosystems, dependent on the preservation of a unique ecological balance, may suffer significant adverse consequence resulting from the introduction of invasive species. Moreover, the human community in the region, including indigenous communities relying on traditional lands and nature for their survival and livelihood, will be threatened in diverse ways, such as by the foods that they consume, which may carry viruses, and by the loss of biospecies that serve to maintain their tradition-based culture and the subsistence economy linked to biodiversity management on the lands where they live.[10]

This chapter first addresses the specific adverse consequences that invasive species may have on an ecosystem in general at various latitudes, and, in particular, on the Arctic ecosystem. Subsequently, it focuses on the available international legal mechanisms applicable in addressing concerns resulting from the introduction of invasive species. It also analyzes possible measures available to reduce the multifaceted risks caused by invasive species. Finally, the analysis brings particular concerns into the framework of the Arctic governance regime with the motive of examining whether there are adequate legal means to address this particular issue in the Arctic context.

Drivers of Invasive Species and Potential Adverse Consequences

Several factors contribute to the invasion of nonnative species into foreign environments. The most important invasion question depends on the degree of interdependence among global change drivers, such as climate change, global trade, and habitat modification. Climate change is one of the main factors that create a favorable environment where nonnative species adapt well in order to survive and develop. For example, many wildlife pathogens benefit from climate change as warmer temperatures typically increase their virulence by supporting growth, reproduction, and higher transmission rates.[11] Climate change has been identified as the most contemporary danger to biodiversity in a number of ways, including its effects on the population dynamics of invasive species.[12] The Intergovernmental Panel on Climate Change (IPCC) estimated that global average air temperatures are expected to rise an additional 1.8°C to 4.0°C by the end of this century.[13] Linked to this warming temperature, the increased emission of CO_2 is expected to disproportionately promote plant growth for some invasive species, disrupting the balance of the native ecosystem.[14] Climate change and biological invasion interact with one another; they are, thus, interconnected and interdependent.[15] They affect human health and well-being through their impact on resources, goods, and services provided by ecosystems.[16] Invasive species, pressured by climate change, reshuffle the landscape of agricultural services and resources including food, fuel, fiber, and forests. The modification of land use due to climate change provides yet another risk to the existence of native biodiversity.[17] Climate change also affects marine and aquatic ecosystems by, for example, contributing to fisheries collapse and opening new potential niches for tolerant invasive species in the marine environment. It has also been evidenced that climate change may alter the efficacy of management strategies for invasive species. Due to climate change, extreme events—cyclones, floods, droughts, and fires—will increase.[18] They kill or weaken native species over large areas and serve as major triggers for invasions.[19] These are likely to result in the spreading of pests and weeds; moreover, human activity, especially recovering after such extreme events, also facilitates invasion.[20] Such invasions, along with other climate change impacts, can further influence weather and climate conditions. In some regions, the combined effect of climate change and invasive species is likely to increase the frequency of wildfires, which will further facilitate the establishment of fire-adapted invasive species, providing fuels for more frequent and intensive fires.[21]

The transportation of goods and materials in international trade, as well as human movement (e.g., tourism) from one part of the globe to the other, causes an increase in the spread of invasive plants, animals, and microbes worldwide.[22] As free trade impacts exporting and importing nations and expedites globalization, it also plays a significant role in contributing to the introduction of invasive species.[23] Globalization and free trade stimulate the spread of economically important species, such as those used in temperate or tropical regions in establishing pine, rubber, oil palm, pineapple, and coffee plantations, as well as soybean, cassava, maize, sugar cane, and wheat, among others, far from their place of origin; in these processes, the accidental spread of species through a variety of pathways may occur.[24] In recent years, the transportation of nonnative species including weeds and pest animals has dramatically increased due to international trade and travel.[25] Both the intentional (such as species traded for forestry and agriculture) and accidental (such as species transported through ballast water) spread of invasive species will occur as a result of international trade.[26] Transportation includes the direct trade of live animals and plants as food, marine and freshwater species for aquaculture, pests, horticultural species, species for research, fur farming and hunting, and others.[27] International trade presents a challenge to environmental planners: on the one hand, it is important to control the negative impacts of invasive species, while on the other hand, imposing and enforcing regulations on international trade is a difficult task in today's globalized world. Invasive species, however, are a counterexample to unrestricted free trade. Free trade that includes exotic hitchhikers (e.g., zebra mussels in the Great Lakes) is not good for the environment or for the people who depend on the environment's ecosystem services.[28] It is costly to search for and remove invasive species that have entered into a new environment via negligent trade practices.

Habitat modification is another driver of the introduction of invasive species. It is broadly defined as encompassing a range of effects—from the creation of entirely novel habitats to slight changes in abiotic conditions due to the presence or biological activity of a species.[29] It is not clear how habitat modification effectively contributes to the introduction of nonnative marine species. However, the alteration of a habitat leads a particular ecosystem to suffer from physical stress.[30] This, in turn, facilitates the growth of nonnative species. The Global International Waters Assessment (GIWA) conducted by the United Nations Environment Program (UNEP) suggests that habitat modification has led to the proliferation of invasive species in coastal and fresh water systems.[31] The assessment highlights the environmental impacts of invasive species in almost half of the GIWA regions.[32] Due to the alteration of habitats, increased numbers of invasive species are often seen in areas disturbed by human activity. Some of these species have special characteristics that allow them to survive better in altered habitat in comparison to their native ecosystem. In marine areas, invasions also depend on water quality conditions.[33] Zebra mussels are, for example, tolerant of a wide range of environmental conditions.[34]

It is estimated that 480,000 alien species have been introduced into varied ecosystems across the globe.[35] Although not all invasive species are detrimental to their host environment, many are harmful to native ecosystems, leading to major environmental and economic problems worldwide.[36] They also have large-scale social impacts.[37] Invasive species are ranked as one of the top two threats to the survival of endangered species, the other being habitat destruction.[38] Invasive species can originate from any part of the world due to deliberate human action, by accident, or through negligence. Once introduced, they ultimately increase in numbers and density as well as in geographic range.[39] Human-induced actions multiply the number of invasive species causing native species problems within their common range.[40] Invasive species eventually become a form of biological pollution.[41] By dominating a region, they disrupt wilderness or particular habitats, leading to loss of biodiversity and disruption of natural control of biodiversity. They may also damage crops, harm human health, and alter ecosystem functions and the structure of the landscape.[42] Invasive species have been identified as a significant threat to aquatic habitats.[43] Their introduction also contributes to the spread of infectious diseases. While their introduction increases concerns over human health, extinction of native species, as well as impacts on regional economies, there are, however, some positive effects, especially in the cases of invasions associated with climate change, including the impacts of some invasive pests.[44] Many nonnative species have been introduced for economic and ecological purposes.[45] For example, nonnative fish may provide excellent sport fishing; plants can provide food, fodder, timber, and energy, while insects can provide biological controls.[46] Despite the benefit they add to some native species, their success sometimes comes at a cost to other native species.[47] Introduced species can carry a heavy price tag in terms of reduced crop and livestock production, loss of native biodiversity, increased production costs, and so forth.[48]

Arctic Concerns

The introduction of invasive species into the Arctic environment necessitates research and monitoring to understand and cope with impacts.[49] The study by Lassuy and Lewis, "Invasive Species (Human Induced)" in the 2011 *Arctic Biodiversity Assessment*, suggests that the introduction of over a dozen invasive plant species in the Canadian Arctic, as well as in the sub-Arctic, presents a risk for the entirety of the Arctic region.[50] Global warming, leading to environmental change in the Arctic, allows for invasion opportunities. As temperature rise in the Arctic is occurring at twice the rate observed in the rest of the world, the rapid melting of sea ice creates increasingly open access to the region, facilitating more frequent navigation and maritime commercial activities, as noted above. The two major sea routes—the Northwest Passage and the Northern Sea Route—are now open for longer periods of time than before. Shipping and commercial activities are projected to gradually rise in the near future. In line with this development, it is expected that the region is likely to see an increased introduction of nonnative species to its ecosystem. A report from the *Guardian* Environment Network suggests that an increasing number of brown bears and a succession of other animals such as red foxes, white-tailed deer, Pacific salmon, and killer whales have begun to show up in areas traditionally occupied by polar bears, Arctic foxes, caribou, Arctic char, and beluga whales.[51]

A number of studies reveal that the risks of invasion in the Arctic rise due to increased shipping, energy development, mineral exploration, and associated shorebased developments, such as ports, roads, and other human responses.[52] Trans-Arctic shipping, particularly between the North Atlantic and North Pacific, potentially represents a vector for the transfer of species to new areas.[53] Shipping sources as well as dual pressure of both climate change and globalization create pathways for the introduction of nonnative species in the Arctic region.[54] Additionally, other human-induced actions in the Arctic, such as increasing oil and gas activities, will risk the introduction of invasive species and will intensify the need for stringent cleaning and monitoring requirements.[55]

Whereas the consequences of the introduction of invasive species into the Arctic require more extensive studies, adverse consequences have been referred to in various literatures.[56] The Arctic Climate Impact Assessment report, for example, provided that the warming of the Arctic will cause a shift in vegetation zones, leading to a wide range of impacts in terms of animal species diversity, range, and distribution.[57] Potential pressure on biodiversity resulting from the introduction of invasive species contributes to biodiversity loss, which eventually affects humans' ability to use that biodiversity.[58] It is evident that warming climatic conditions prevailing in the Arctic would cause critical consequences for Arctic species and ecosystems.[59] The risk in the Arctic is associated with the fact that the introduction of invasive species will decrease stability while at the same time it will increase uncertainty in ecosystem functioning.[60] For example, in the past, the introduction of rodent species—predatory rats—has proven to have devastating ecological effects on islands harboring nesting seabirds in Arctic Alaska.[61] Additionally, there have been reported cases where killer whales, moving into the Arctic from southern waters, have eaten beluga whales and narwhal, thus suggesting that Arctic animals may be unable to compete with their southern cousins.[62] Moreover, the movement of southern species into the Arctic may lead to interbreeding, which may result in hybrid creatures. The most notorious example of this is, of course, the "grolar bear" hybrid produced by the interbreeding of polar and grizzly bears.[63] As a result, there may be a reduction in the unique gene pool that has helped Arctic animals adapt to the region's harsh environment. The combination of habitat loss or alteration with increased pressure from competitive invasive species may lead to extinction of native Arctic species.[64] In addition, as southern species move north to the Arctic, they may carry new diseases with them, adding another challenge to Arctic ecosystems.[65]

Regulations Related to Invasive Species

As environmental problems related to invasive species have recently received considerable attention at the international level, regulation pertaining to the prevention of negative consequences of invasive species has been of particular significance. A set of established principles of international environmental law, a number of multilateral environmental agreements, and numerous other nonbinding guidelines are applicable in addressing concerns related to invasive species.[66] The legally nonbinding principles of international environmental law, as they exist, are particularly important in this regard, both in adopting legal rules and in interpreting existing rules. Principle 15 of the Rio Declaration, for example, examines precautionary measures that go well beyond ordinary prevention mechanisms in the face of scientific uncertainty. Scientific certainty in regard to the introduction of invasive species is imperfect. It may not be readily known, for example, whether certain ballast water contains invasive species and whether they are able to arrive, survive, and thrive in their new environment. Preemptive measures are an important factor, however, to prevent continued introduction of invasive species, as it is certain that inappropriate plant and animal introductions have contributed to biodiversity loss.[67] These concerns are reflected in the UN Convention on Biological Diversity adopted in 1992.

On a general level, international regulations that directly or indirectly address invasive species may be classified in several categories. These include customary international law, multilateral environmental agreements, and trade-related regulations under the auspices of the World Trade Organization (WTO). In addition, there are nonbinding guidelines, adopted by various institutions, which also play a significant role in controlling and preventing the introduction of harmful invasive species. In order to coherently analyze these regulations, they are discussed within the categories of universal regulations, multilateral environmental agreements, regulation relating to international trade, and soft law measures.

Universal regulations provide a general duty for states. They can be found both in customary laws as well as in treaty laws that are universal in nature. Customary international law provides a duty to take appropriate measures to prevent transboundary environmental harm. Such responsibility has been affirmed in several international tribunals and has now been established as one of the core principles of international environmental law. It also plays a significant role in analyzing existing rules. Therefore, it is the duty of states to take effective measures in their territory so that no harm, intentional or unintentional, from the spread of invasive species may occur in a transboundary context. The UN Convention on the Law of the Sea (LOS Convention) and the UN Convention on Biological Diversity (CBD) are universally oriented legal mechanisms that directly apply in relation to the prevention of harmful consequences of invasive species by requiring state parties to adopt effective measures.

Chapter XII of the LOS Convention deals with the control, prevention, and reduction of marine environmental pollution from multidimensional sources. Articles 192 and 196(1) are particularly applicable here. The former provides the general obligation to protect and preserve the marine environment; the latter obliges states to take necessary measures to tackle environmental harm, for example, from the intentional and accidental introduction of alien or new species harmful to the environment. A general obligation is entailed upon the flag, coastal, and port states to engage in the protection of the marine environment. However, to specifically deal with concerns arising out of each particular source, contracting states are required to become parties to the relevant international and regional legal instruments. Specifically, in the case of invasive species it is argued that states are encouraged to be parties to the International Convention for the Control and Management of Ships' Ballast Water and Sediments (not yet in force), which would provide precise regulation for the management of ballast water so that the chance of introducing invasive species may be minimized.[68]

As for the Convention on Biological Diversity, Article 8(h) requires states to "prevent introduction of, control or eradicate those alien species which threaten ecosystem, habitats or species." In regard to biotechnology, Article 8(g) requires the parties to establish or maintain means to regulate, manage, or control the risks associated with the use and release of living modified organisms resulting from biotechnology which are likely to have adverse environmental impacts that could affect the conservation and sustainable use of biological diversity, taking also into account risks to human health. The CBD is, however, a framework convention, which, like the LOS Convention mentioned above, requires precise rules to be found elsewhere. The most detailed rules regarding invasive species come from the International

Plant Protection Convention (IPPC)[69] and the nonbinding guidelines adopted under the auspices of the CBD.[70] In this connection, the Cartagena Protocol on Biosafety, negotiated under the CBD, is also worth mentioning. The protocol addresses the international movement of living modified organisms with the aim of minimizing the chance of introduction of such organisms that might present an invasive threat to the environment.

Apart from the LOS Convention and the CBD, the UN Framework Convention on Climate Change (UNFCCC) is relevant in the context of invasive species as changes in temperature and rainfall patterns can induce new invasions and exacerbate existing invasions, necessitating specific regulations to address mitigation and adaptation to climate change. The Kyoto Protocol is an example in the mitigation of climate change via which states commit to the reduction of greenhouse gas emissions. It is also important to note that measures relating to animal health and disease control are coordinated under the auspices of an international agreement administered by the Office International des Épizooties (OIE).[71] Its functions include informing members of outbreaks of contagious diseases of animals; enabling members to take preventive action; and providing them with information on the most effective methods of controlling animal disease. The OIE formulates guidelines for the control of animal diseases; it has, for example, recently adopted the Aquatic Animal Health Code 2007 and the Terrestrial Animal Health Code 2007. These codes standardize health and quarantine regulations for animals and animal products for member states and provide general obligation for exporting and importing states.

A number of multilateral environmental agreements are applicable in the regulation of invasive species. The International Convention for the Control and Management of Ships' Ballast Water and Sediments (BWM) adopted by the International Maritime Organization (IMO), referred to above, provides specific rules to prevent the potentially devastating effects of the spread of harmful aquatic organisms carried by ships' ballast water from one region to another.[72] The general obligation incurred by states is found in Article 2, which stipulates state parties' commitment to prevent, minimize, and ultimately eliminate the transfer of harmful aquatic organisms and pathogens through the control and management of ships' ballast water and sediments. The convention provides several measures to be undertaken by state parties that include reception facilities (Article 5), research and monitoring (Article 6), survey, certification, and inspection (Articles 7 and 9), technical assistance, and regional cooperation (Article 13). In addition, the annexes attached to the convention provide standards and requirements to which states commit in order to ensure that ships comply.

The International Plant Protection Convention,[73] also referred to above, applies primarily to quarantine of pests in international trade. The convention creates an international regime to prevent the spread and introduction of plant and plant product pests, premised on the exchange of phytosanitary certificates between importing and exporting countries' national plant protection offices. Parties establish national plant protection organizations according to the convention with the related authority for quarantine control, risk analysis, and other measures required to prevent the establishment and spread of all invasive alien species that, directly or indirectly, are pests of plants (Article IV). By virtue of Article VIII, parties agree to exchange information and develop international standards for phytosanitary measures, which include agreements on definitions (terminology) and working procedures.

The Cartagena Protocol on Biosafety aims at minimizing the chance of introduction of genetically modified organisms harmful to the environment. In accordance with Article 4, the protocol applies to the transboundary movement, transit, handling, and use of all living modified organisms that may have adverse effects on the conservation and sustainable use of biological diversity, and on human health. The state party is under an obligation to immediately notify affected or potentially affected states, as well as the Biosafety Clearing House and, where relevant, international organizations, of the unintentional release of living modified organisms with the potential for transboundary movement.[74] The parties to the protocol also undertake the adoption of necessary measures with adequate safety standards in handling, packaging, and transporting living modified organisms so that no adverse consequences occur.[75] However, most of the big Arctic players, including Canada, Russia, and the United States, are not parties to the Cartagena Protocol. The requirement for the prevention of transboundary movement or introduction of invasive species may be found in the Convention on the Law of Non-navigational Uses of International Watercourses.[76] Article 22 of the convention suggests that states shall take all necessary measures to prevent the introduction of species, alien or new, into an international watercourse, which may have effects detrimental to the ecosystem of the watercourse resulting in significant harm to other watercourse states.

The Convention on Wetlands of International Importance, commonly known as the Ramsar Convention, is a treaty for conservation and sustainable utilization of wetlands, which recognizes the fundamental ecological function of wetlands and their economic, cultural, scientific, and recreational value.[77] Through the resolutions adopted in the Conference of Parties (CoP), the convention calls upon the parties "to address the problems posed by invasive species in wetland ecosystems in a decisive and holistic manner making use of the tools and guidance developed by various institutions and processes, including any relevant guidelines or guiding principles adopted under other conventions."[78] The CoP resolution VIII.18 in Valencia in 2002, highlighting the risks associated with the introduction of invasive species, suggested a number of recommendations requiring state parties to develop tools, assess risks, cooperate with other relevant international organizations, and take effective national measures.[79]

The Convention on International Trade in Endangered Species of Wild Fauna and Flora (CITES) is one of the largest conservation agreements aiming to ensure sustainable international trade in specimens of wild animals and plants. The CoP 14 within the convention dealt with trade in alien invasive species.[80] Acknowledging the fact that alien species may pose a significant threat to biodiversity and that species of fauna and flora in commercial trade are likely to be introduced to new habitat as a result of international trade, the resolution recommended that states consider specific regulations in dealing with trade in live animals or plants. The resolution also recommends that the states consult the management authority of a proposed country of import when considering exports of potentially invasive species; consider the opportunity of synergy between CITES and the CBD; and explore cooperation and collaboration on the introduction of potentially alien invasive species.[81]

The Convention on Migratory Species of Wild Animals requires range states to control the introduction of invasive alien species or to eliminate them if they present a threat to endangered migratory species.[82] Article III (4)(c) clearly stipulates that regarding migratory species that are endangered and listed in Appendix I of the convention, a range state endeavors to use appropriate measures to prevent, reduce, or control factors that further endanger species. These include strictly controlling the introduction of or eliminating previously introduced exotic species. Article IV (4) suggests that parties take further action by concluding agreements to protect any population or any geographically separate part of the population of any native species or lower taxon of wild animals that may periodically cross one or more national jurisdiction boundaries.

Addressing concerns specific to the Antarctic, the Convention on the Conservation of Antarctic Marine Living Resources (CCAMLR) in Article II (3)(c) requires parties to prevent changes or minimize the risk of changes in the marine ecosystem, taking into account available knowledge of the effect of the introduction of alien species. The Protocol to the Antarctic Treaty on Environmental Protection also suggests that animal or plant species not native to the Antarctic Treaty Area shall not be introduced onto land or ice shelves, or into water in the Antarctic Treaty Area except in accordance with a permit.[83]

In addition, the Agreement Concerning Cooperation in the Quarantine of Plants and Their Protection Against Pests and Diseases[84] requires state parties to apply measures to prevent the introduction from one country into another, in exported consignments of goods or by any other means, of quarantinable plant pests, diseases, or weeds specified in lists drawn up by agreement between the parties concerned.[85] Article I of the Convention on the Prohibition of the Development, Production and Stockpiling of Bacteriological [biological] and Toxin Weapons and on Their Destruction—or, the Biological Weapons Convention or BWC—prohibits parties from developing, producing, stockpiling, acquiring, or retaining microbial or other biological agents that are not justified by an exclusively peaceful purpose. Article II of the convention requires parties to destroy or divert all such agents within nine months of the convention entering into force.

Today, international trade is mainly regulated under the auspices of the World Trade Organization. The objectives of the WTO are threefold: trade liberalization, economic development, and the optimal use of the world's resources. The WTO seeks to achieve such objectives by adopting measures to remove what members deem to be unnecessary barriers to trade; these objectives, however, must be compatible with protection and preservation of the environment. One of the main principles of the WTO is nondiscrimination, which is to be applied in the three main areas of trade—products, services, and intellectual property. The idea is that WTO member countries cannot discriminate their trading partners. Any special favor is mutually accorded among members of the WTO, such as the maintenance of lower customs duty rates for members' respective products. As a result, member countries do not generally discriminate between their own and foreign products. There are exception clauses, however, mainly based on the grounds of environmental protection, including plant and human health; such exceptions are nevertheless only permissible under strict conditions.

Over the past two decades, the connection between trade and the environment has frequently been articulated. As a response to the growing demand for such issue-linkage, the Uruguay Round of trade negotiations of the WTO settled the reconstitution of a Committee on Trade and the Environment (CTE)[86] in order to examine the interaction between trade and environmental measures, trade measures used for environmental purposes, and the effects of trade liberalization on the environment.[87] The CTE has not yet recommended any modification to WTO regulations, but has held that current WTO laws provide sufficient scope for the protection of the environment, explicitly referring to the Agreement on Sanitary and Phytosanitary Measures (SPS) and the Technical Barriers to Trade (TBT) Agreement.[88] The General Agreement on Tariffs and Trade (GATT) contains three important provisions to protect the environment and human health, which may be expanded to deal with exotic species. These provisions include the SPS Agreement, the TBT Agreement, and Article 20: General Exceptions, which protect the right of members to take any necessary measures to protect human, animal, or plant life or health.[89] According to subarticle (b) of GATT Article 20, a restriction may only be imposed when it is necessary to protect human, animal, or plant life or health. Subarticle (g) provides that restrictive measures are compatible if they relate to the conservation of exhaustible natural resources and if such measures are effectively taken in conjunction with restrictions on domestic production or consumption. As mentioned, environmental standards may also be set under GATT's TBT Agreement, which is meant for internationally agreed upon and harmonized standards so that regulations, standards, testing, and certification procedures do not create "unnecessary obstacles." However, countries are allowed to impose stricter standards than other countries if they wish to protect "human, animal or plant life or health . . . [and] the environment."[90] The SPS Agreement appears to be the most applicable WTO regulation in connection with invasive alien species.[91]

The Agreement on Sanitary and Phytosanitary Measures has scope in terms of exemptions from the fundamental nondiscrimination principle of the WTO based on environmental grounds. The SPS Agreement deals with health risks coming from pests, contaminants, and other disease-causing agents, as well as contaminants and toxins in foods, which have environmental components. It promotes international standards for risk prevention upon which trade restriction may be based, but allows countries to set higher standards of safety if there are reasons based on scientific evidence.[92] Under the SPS Agreement, countries are required to use a common set of procedures for evaluating risks of contamination in internationally traded commodities; the procedures promote the fundamental right of countries to protect the health and life of people, animals, and plants against pests, diseases, and other threats to health.[93] The SPS Agreement establishes the basic framework and requirements for member countries' national regulations regarding the import of products that may contain alien species harmful to public health, animals, or plant life. Several decisions of the WTO Appellate Body have ruled that the implementation of particular measures addressing invasive alien species have been inconsistent with the SPS Agreement.[94] It must be noted that the WTO body of law has not been consistent in its case rulings on matters relating to trade measures and environmental protection.[95]

Nevertheless, to the extent that the central purpose of the SPS Agreement is to protect plant and animal health from the risk of pests and diseases, it is argued that uncertainties regarding risks posed by invasive alien species should be removed and strong prevention measures should be adopted.[96] The SPS Agreement, which encourages countries to harmonize their SPS measures on a wide basis by supporting their quarantine measures on relevant science-based international standards, mentions specific cooperative international standard-setting bodies. These include the Codex Alimentarius Commission, the International Plant Protection Convention (IPPC), and the Office International des Épizooties (OIE) for food safety, plant, and animal health standards, respectively. The SPS Agreement, relevant to invasive species that are pests or diseases, helps members protect human, animal, and plant life or health from risks arising due to the entry, establishment, or spread of pests, diseases, or disease-carrying organisms, and it prevents or limits other damage that may potentially be caused by such entry.[97]

Apart from the regulations mentioned above, there are a number of nonbinding guiding principles adopted within the functions of relevant institutions for the protection of the environment from the adverse consequences of invasive species. The Secretariat of the UN Convention on Biological Diversity has, for example, taken further steps in developing guiding principles for the prevention, introduction, and mitigation of the impacts of alien species. In the fifth meeting of the subsidiary body on scientific, technical, and technological advice of the CBD, held in January–February 2000, a list of guiding principles was developed for the prevention and control of the introduction of alien invasive species.[98] These principles include, among others, the precautionary approach, the ecosystem approach, cooperation, and capacity building, as well as mitigation. They were first presented to the CBD CoP 5 in May 2000. The International Conservation Union has also developed guidelines for the prevention of biodiversity loss caused by alien invasive species. IUCN provides guidance on preventing the introduction or reintroduction of alien invasive species, and on eradication and control.[99] With a view to Article 8(h) of the CBD, the aim of these guidelines is to help address and prevent the loss of native biological diversity caused by the biological invasion of alien invasive species. The Global Invasive Species Program (GISP), established in 1997 to address global threats caused by invasive species and to support the implementation of Article 8(h) of the CBD, in collaboration with the Scientific Committee on Problems of the

Environment (SCOPE), CAB International (CABI), and the IUCN–World Conservation Union in partnership with the United Nations Environment Program (UNEP), also developed the Global Strategy on Invasive Alien Species in 2000.[100]

Prior to the convention concluded in 2004, the International Maritime Organization adopted Guidelines for the Control and Management of Ships' Ballast Water to Minimize the Transfer of Harmful Aquatic Organisms and Pathogens, which provide flag administrations and state port authorities with guidance on procedures, minimizing the risk of transfer of harmful aquatic organisms via ships' ballast water and sediments.[101] The guidelines also provide a ballast water management plan that includes a procedure for the safe exchange of ballast at sea, for the precautionary practice to minimize the uptake of organisms, the removal of sediment and avoidance of unnecessary discharge. In relation to the introduction of nonnative species, the UN Food and Agricultural Organization (FAO) is responsible for codes of conduct on responsible fisheries, on the import and release of biological control agents, and on the import and release of exotic biological control agents.[102] The aim is to facilitate the safe import and release of exotic biological control agents by introducing procedures of an internationally acceptable level for all public and private entities involved. This is particularly the case where national legislation to regulate their use does not exist or is inadequate.

Arctic Governance Addressing Invasive Species

Although the problems of invasive species in the Arctic are relatively new, it is evident that the consequences of increased warming in the Arctic resulting from climate change will lead to a rise in invasive species. Such an increase is likely to contribute to a loss of Arctic biodiversity and a threat to ecosystem functions. It is essential to see how this is addressed by Arctic governance mechanisms; while there is no comprehensive instrument, there is a fragmented legal regime conceived of both multilateral environmental agreements (MEAs) and soft law instruments. In recent years, there has been enthusiasm among a number of scholars regarding the importance of adopting a comprehensive nonsectoral Arctic-specific treaty. It is argued that such a treaty would provide a better governance mechanism in tackling Arctic challenges.[103] Such arguments have, nonetheless, found no substantial support from the five Arctic Ocean coastal states, as the 2008 Ilulissat Declaration clearly denounced the need for such a new international Arctic instrument.[104] Instead, it has been argued that the law of the sea including the LOS Convention provides the necessary legal framework regarding the rights and obligations of Arctic littoral states.[105] The Ilulissat Declaration clearly stated that the law of the sea provides a "solid foundation" for the responsible management of the Arctic Ocean through national implementation and application of relevant provisions.[106] The declaration also acknowledged the "stewardship" responsibilities of coastal states via existing soft law instruments, such as regional cooperative mechanisms under the Arctic Council.[107] Although the nonlittoral Arctic states, as well as indigenous groups, were not included in discussions, it has become apparent that there is no political will, at least in the foreseeable future, for a unified binding governance regime.[108]

It should be noted that, despite the existence of a number of MEAs applicable to the Arctic in regard to invasive species, there is still a lack of sufficient data for a comprehensive understanding of the region in terms of knowledge of its biodiversity. An increased and targeted prevention effort to limit the influx of invasive species in the Arctic is particularly required.[109] Although the recognition of traditional and local knowledge provides important information in prevention efforts, unless targeted management plans are accomplished, the high risk of the introduction of invasive species will cause significant adverse impacts. To date, efforts to protect Arctic biodiversity are based, for the most part, on the precautionary principle, which in itself does not provide any binding commitments for states.[110] It is, however, important to introduce such precautionary measures within the governance mechanism. In the Arctic, the governance regime on invasive species has to be seen in existing MEAs, as well as in other soft law arrangements undertaken by the Arctic Council.

Multilateral Environmental Agreements

A number of MEAs are relevant in addressing concerns about invasive species in the Arctic. They, however, do not sufficiently address the potential challenges in the Arctic context. Some of these MEAs are universal in scope with applicability in the Arctic. Others have a limited range of applicability in a regional context and are either applicable to the Arctic as a whole, or to a part of it. The most relevant universal legislations include: the LOS Convention,[111] UN Framework Convention on Climate Change and its Kyoto Protocol, the CBD, the UNESCO Convention on the Protection of the World Cultural and Natural Heritage,[112] the Convention on International Trade in Endangered Species of Wild Fauna and Flora,[113] the Ramsar Convention, the Stockholm Convention on Persistent Organic Pollutants,[114] and the Convention on Migratory Species.[115] Not all eight Arctic states are parties to all of these MEAs. For example, the United States is not a party to the LOS Convention, the CBD, or the Kyoto Protocol. The trade regulations within the WTO may also be applicable with reference to the introduction of invasive species. With Russia's joining in the WTO in December 2011, all eight Arctic states are members of the WTO.[116] The IMO-adopted conventions are particularly relevant in the Arctic context—for example, the MARPOL Convention concerning marine pollution from ships. The IMO International Convention for the Control and Management of Ships' Ballast Water and Sediments, as referred to elsewhere in this chapter, is directly relevant regarding invasive species, but the convention has not yet entered into force.[117]

Apart from these universally applicable conventions, there are other MEAs, limited in scope, that many of the Arctic states are party to. These MEAs may be relevant in the Arctic context in their ability to address concerns regarding invasive species. The International Convention for the Regulation of Whaling,[118] the Agreement on the Conservation of Polar Bears,[119] and the Convention for the Protection of the Marine Environment of the North-East Atlantic (OSPAR) are worth mentioning.[120] Although reference to the introduction of invasive species in these MEAs is ambiguous, it is important to note that the OSPAR Commission, the administering body within the convention in 2008 (along with the Helsinki Commission, which is the administering body within the Convention on the Protection of the Marine Environment in the Baltic Sea Area), jointly undertook the initiatives—which partly cover the Arctic Ocean—to safeguard the marine environment from invasive species both in the northeast Atlantic and in the Baltic Sea.[121] These conventions (OSPAR and Baltic Sea) place voluntary guidelines on the shipping industry and request that vessels entering the concerned waters exchange all of their ballast tanks at least two hundred nautical miles from the nearest land in water that is at least two hundred meters deep.[122]

The Arctic Council

The Arctic Council is an intergovernmental cooperative body established by all eight Arctic nations. In addition to states, indigenous groups are also represented in the Arctic Council.[123] The Council encourages continuous dialogue among scientists, policy planners, political-level decision makers, and Arctic residents, including indigenous peoples. The decision making is heavily based on scientific information influenced by the traditional knowledge of the indigenous peoples. The tasks of several Arctic Council working groups, including the Conservation of Arctic Flora and Fauna (CAFF), the Protection of Arctic Marine Environment (PAME), and the Arctic Monitoring and Assessment Program (AMAP), are relevant in the context of invasive species. The CAFF provides information on conservation strategies, undertakes assessments of climate change in the circumpolar region, maintains a circumpolar network of protected areas, documents traditional ecological knowledge, undertakes the assessment of the conservation value of sacred sites of indigenous peoples, assesses the conservation status of Arctic migratory birds, and develops integrated ecosystem management strategies. In 2010, CAFF adopted the Arctic Biodiversity Assessment in which it addressed concerns about invasive species, among others.[124] However, the stronger emphasis on possible threats from the introduction of invasive species and on their control within the Arctic Council was addressed by the PAME working group, which conducted the Arctic Marine Shipping Assessment (AMSA). The report of the assessment was published in 2009 and addressed concerns related to invasive species. The assessment conducted a baseline survey of aquatic species in major recipient ports in the Arctic region in order to carry out a risk assessment of the introduction of invasive species under current international standards in order to determine the need for Arctic-specific protection.[125] The working group recommended that the Arctic states consider ratification of the IMO International Convention for the Control and Management of Ships' Ballast Water and Sediments as soon as possible. The recommendation also urged Arctic states to assess the risk of introducing invasive species, through ballast water and other means, so that adequate prevention measures can be implemented in waters under their jurisdiction.[126]

The Way Forward

Greater research effort must be devoted to the issue of invasive species, and the effects of their introduction, in the Arctic. Rapid changes, however, require attention in regard to assessing the scope of introduction and the associated challenges. This chapter has attempted to investigate this novel challenge. While addressing the possible challenges, this chapter has also discussed the available regulatory mechanisms that may be applicable in mitigating the problems associated with invasive species. The findings suggest that introduction of invasive species into the Arctic may take place through both land- and marine-based sources; the marine-based sources are of a wider and therefore more concerning scale. While, as noted, more research on this issue is needed, particularly in the context of the Arctic, according to the literature available the consequences in the Arctic may be devastating unless an effective governance regime addressing this particular challenge is established.

The Arctic requires a holistic approach in terms of its biodiversity conservation and management. Such an approach needs to accommodate the global impacts of climate change and biodiversity loss in the Arctic, and balance both environmental and economic interests. It is optimistic to believe that such a holistic governance approach will be realized; in the interim, an ad hoc governance regime through the networks of multilateral environmental agreements, along with strengthened Arctic Council initiatives, could serve as an arena for dialogue, and could initiate "targeted activities" to help prevent and control the introduction of invasive species in the Arctic.[127]

Notes

1. Jeff McNeely, "Invasive Species: A Costly Catastrophe for Native Biodiversity," *Land Use and Water Resources Research* 1 (2001) 2 at 2.

2. Stas Burgiel, Greg Foote, et al., "Invasive Alien Species and Trade: Integrating Prevention Measures and International Trade Rules," *Center for International Environmental Law* (CIEL) (2006) at 6.

3. Stas Burgiel, Greg Foote, et al., ibid., at 22.

4. P. Genovesi and C. Shine, "European Strategy on Invasive Alien Species. Nature and Environment," n. 137 (Strasbourg: Council of Europe 2004), at 67.

5. Tim Low, "Climate Change and Invasive Species: A Review of Interaction" (Biological Diversity Advisory Committee, 2005–2007), Commonwealth of Australia, 2008, at http://www.environment.gov.au/biodiversity/publications/pubs/interactions-cc-invasive.pdf (accessed 20 January 2012).

6. See David Pimentel et al., "Economic and environmental threats of alien plant, animal, and microbe invasions, Agriculture," *Ecosystems and Environment* 84 (2001) 1–20 at 12–13.

7. Introduction of invasive species contributes to habitat fragmentation, resulting in direct extinction of existing species and aiding the process of further extinctions. This ultimately disrupts the balance of the ecosystem. See Craig R. Allen, Alan R. Johnson, and Leslie Parris, "A

framework for spatial risk assessments: Potential impacts of nonindigenous invasive species on native species," *Ecology and Society* 11(1) (2006): 39.

8. ACIA Secretariat, Arctic Council, Arctic Climate Impact Assessment (2005), available at http://www.acia.uaf.edu/pages/scientific.html; ACIA: *Arctic Climate Impact Assessment* (Cambridge: Cambridge University Press, 2005), 575.

9. Craig R. Alan (2006), supra note 7.

10. Kathrine I. Johnsen, Björn Alfthan, et al. (eds.), *Protecting Arctic Biodiversity: Limitations and Strengths of Environmental Agreements*, United Nations Environment Program, GRID-Arendal, Norway (2010) at 29–44, at: http://www.grida.no/_res/site/file/publications/arctic-biodiv/arcticMEAreport_screen.pdf (accessed 24 February 2012).

11. See Tim Low, supra note 5.

12. See, for example, Stanley W. Burgiel and Adrianna A. Muir, "Invasive Species, Climate Change and Ecosystem-Based Adaptation: Addressing Multiple Drivers of Global Change," *Global Invasive Species Program*, September 2010 at 9, http://data.iucn.org/dbtw-wpd/edocs/2010–054.pdf (accessed 20 November 2012).

13. See S. Solomon, D. Qin, M. Manning, Z. Chen, et al. (eds.), *Contribution of Working Group I to the Fourth Assessment Report of the Intergovernmental Panel on Climate Change* (Cambridge: Cambridge University Press, 2007).

14. P. D. Moore, "Favoured aliens for the future," *Nature* 427(6975) (2004): 594.

15. Raphael K. Didham, Jason M. Tylianakis, Neil J. Gemmell, Tatyana A. Rand, and Robert M. Ewers, "Interactive effects of habitat modification and species invasion on native species decline," *Trends in Ecology and Evolution* 22(9) (2007): 490.

16. "Invasive Species and Climate Change," December 9, 2010, US Department of the Interior, http://www.invasivespecies.gov/ISAC/White%20Papers/Climate_Change_White_Paper_FINAL_VERSION.pdf (accessed 20 November 2012).

17. See "Invasive Species and Climate Change," ibid. See also Tim Low, supra note 5, regarding mobile animals, such as birds, butterflies, dragonflies, and marine species quickly relocating in response to climate change. Most native plants and the less mobile animals may be unable to migrate at the pace required by climate change. As a result, in both cases incursions occur rapidly; many weeds and other pests, for example, spread faster than native species because, among other reasons, they are regularly transported by people.

18. Stanley W. Burgiel and Adrianna A. Muir, supra note 12.

19. Tim Low, supra note 5.

20. Tim Low, ibid. See also Stanley W. Burgiel and Adrianna A. Muir, supra note 12. Both intentional and unintentional human responses to climate change influence the impact of invasive species.

21. "Invasive Species and Climate Change," supra note 16.

22. David Pimentel et al. (2001), supra note 6 at 3.

23. Michael Margolis and Jason F. Shogren, "How Trade Politics Affect Invasive Species Control," *Discussion Paper* 04–07, January 2004, http://www.rff.org/documents/RFF-DP-04-07.pdf (accessed 20 November 2012).

24. Jeff McNeely, supra note 1.

25. Tim Low, supra note 5.

26. Piero Genovesi and Riccardo Scalera, "Toward a Blacklist of Invasive Alien Species Entering Europe through Trade, and Proposed Responses," https://wcd.coe.int/wcd/com.instranet.InstraServlet?command=com.instranet.CmdBlobGet&InstranetImage=1298206&SecMode=1&DocId=1438902&Usage=2 (accessed 12 February 2012).

27. Ibid.

28. Michael Margolis and Jason F. Shogren, supra note 23.

29. Laura F. Rodriguez, "Can invasive species facilitate native species? Evidence of how, when, and why these impacts occur," *Biological Invasions* (2006) 8 at 929.

30. Laura F. Rodriguez, ibid., at 927.

31. The GIWA Final Report, "Global International Waters Assessment, Challenges to International Waters—Regional Assessments in a Global Perspective," United Nations Environment Program (2006), at 72.

32. Ibid., at 79.

33. Adrienne Pappal, "Marine Invasive Species: State of the Gulf of Maine Report," Marine Life/Gulf of Maine Area Program (2010).

34. Zebra Mussel (*Dreissena polymorpha*), http://www.invadingspecies.com/Invaders.cfm ?A=page&PID=1 (accessed 13 June 2012).

35. David Pimentel et al., (2001) supra note 6 at 3.

36. David Pimentel et al., ibid., p. 3.

37. Stas Burgiel, Greg Foote, et al., supra note 2 at 5.

38. Stas Burgiel, Greg Foote, et al., ibid., at 5.

39. Stas Burgiel, Greg Foote, et al., ibid., at 6.

40. Tim Low, supra note 5.

41. Stas Burgiel, Greg Foote, et al., supra note 2 at 6.

42. Tim Low, supra note 5.

43. Alice Reaveley, Karen Bettink, and Leonie Valentine, "Impacts of Introduced Species on Biodiversity," in Barbara A. Wilson and Leonie E. Valentine (eds.), *Biodiversity values and threatening processes of the Gnangara groundwater system*, Department of Environment and Conservation (2009) at 7, http://www.water.wa.gov.au/sites/gss/Content/reports/Chapter%208%20 Impacts%20of%20Introduced%20Species%20on%20Biodiversity.pdf (accessed 14 February 2012).

44. Tim Low, supra note 5.

45. Many such introduced species, such as corn, wheat, rice, domestic chicken, cattle, and others, are economically beneficial and now provide more than 98 percent of the world food supply. See David Pimentel et al., supra note 6 at 1.

46. Jeff McNeely, supra note 1 at 5.

47. Tim Low, supra note 5.

48. Jeff McNeely, supra note 1 at 5. See also Stanley W. Burgiel and Adrianna A. Muir, supra note 12.

49. See Dennis R. Lassuy and Patrick N. Lewis, "Invasive Species (Human Induced)," *Arctic Biodiversity Assessment* (Arctic Council, April 2011) at: http://www.arcus.org/files/page/ documents/1622/invasivespecies.pdf (accessed 20 January 2012). See also AMSA: "Environmental Considerations and Impacts," *Arctic Marine Shipping Assessment* (AMSA) (Arctic Council, 2009), 150, at: http://www.arctic.gov/publications/AMSA/environmental.pdf (accessed 20 January 2012).

50. Dennis R. Lassuy and Patrick N. Lewis, "Invasive Species (Human Induced)," *Arctic Biodiversity Assessment*, supra note 49.

51. "Warming Arctic brings invasion of southern species," at: http://www.guardian.co.uk/ environment/2011/feb/14/warming-arctic-southern-species (accessed 23 August 2011).

52. See, for example, Dennis R. Lassuy and Patrick N. Lewis, supra note 49.

53. AMSA, supra note 49 at 151.

54. See Stas Burgiel and Greg Foote (2006), supra note 2 at 22.

55. Dennis Lassuy and Patrick N. Lewis, supra note 49 at 48.

56. See, for example, *Arctic Biodiversity Assessment* (2011), *Arctic Marine Shipping Assessment* (2009), *Arctic Climate Impact Assessment* (2005): supra note 8.

57. *Arctic Climate Impact Assessment* (2005), supra note 8.

58. Dennis Lassuy and Patrick N. Lewis, supra note 49 at 46.

59. Kathrine I. Johnsen, Björn Alfthan, et al. (eds.) (2010), supra note 10 at 29–44.

60. Dennis R. Lassuy and Patrick N. Lewis, supra note 49.

61. In the Aleutian Islands, located in the North Pacific Arctic in Alaska, the invasive rodent species Norway rats (*Rattus norvegicus*) were established over two hundred years ago because

of a Japanese shipwreck, and have caused huge impacts on the seabirds of the islands. The US government has adopted an eradication project to restore the native biological diversity. See S. E. Ebbert and G. V. Byrd, "Eradication of invasive species to restore natural biological diversity on the Alaska Maritime National Refuge," in C. R. Veitch and M. N. Clout (eds.), *Turning the Tide: The Eradication of Invasive Species* (Gland, Switzerland and Cambridge: International Conservation Union [IUCN], 2004): 102. See also AMSA, supra note 49 at 151.

62. "Warming Arctic brings invasion of southern species," supra note 51.

63. Bruce Barcott, "Grolar Bears and Narlugas: Rise of the Arctic Hybrid," *On Earth* (December 2010), at: http://www.onearth.org/article/grolar-bears-and-narlugas-rise-of-the-arctic -hybrids (accessed 12 June 2012).

64. "Warming Arctic brings invasion of southern species," supra note 51.

65. See "The Future of Marine Mammals in a Changing Arctic," Oceans North Canada, http://oceansnorth.org/future-marine-mammals-changing-arctic (accessed 12 June 2012).

66. Principles of international environmental law have been developed by means of both customary jurisprudence and norms adopted in the remarkable conferences in connection to the environment, such as the 1972 Stockholm Conference on Human Environment and the 1992 Rio Conference on Environment and Development.

67. Agenda 21—an action plan, was adopted at the Rio Conference in 1992: http://sustain abledevelopment.un.org/content/documents/Agenda21.pdf. United Nations Convention on Biological Diversity, *International Legal Materials* 31 (1992): 818.

68. The International Convention for the Control and Management of Ships' Ballast Water and Sediments, concluded 13 February 2004, not in force, IMO Doc. BWM/CONF/36, 16 February 2004.

69. The International Plant Protection Convention of 1997 is the second revised text of the International Plant Protection Convention of 1951 (revised 28 November 1979), adopted 17 November 1997, [2005] ATS No. 23 (entered into force 2 October 2005). As of November 2007, the International Plant Protection Convention 1997 (IPPC) had 166 parties.

70. The Guiding Principles for the Prevention, Introduction and Mitigation of Impacts of Alien Species that Threaten Ecosystems, Habitats or Species; see also IUCN Guidelines for the Prevention of Biodiversity Loss Caused by Alien Invasive Species.

71. International Agreement for the Creation at Paris of an International Office for Dealing with Contagious Diseases of Animals, and Annex 1924, adopted 25 January 1924 [1925] ATS No. 15 (entered into force 12 January 1925); Office International des Épizooties (OIE). As of November 2007 the OIE had 173 members.

72. See the International Convention for the Control and Management of Ships' Ballast Water and Sediments. Adoption: 13 February 2004; Entry into force: twelve months after ratification by thirty States, representing 35 percent of world merchant shipping tonnage.

73. As of September 2011, the IPPC has 177 contracting parties. See https://www.ippc.int/index.php?id=1110618&L=0 (accessed 24 January 2012).

74. Article 17.1.

75. Article 18.1.

76. Full text of the convention is available at: http://untreaty.un.org/ilc/texts/instruments/english/conventions/8_3_1997.pdf (24 January 2012).

77. Full text of the convention is available at: http://www.ramsar.org/cda/en/ramsar-home/main/ramsar/1_4000_0__ (24 January 2012).

78. See Resolution VIII.18, Resolutions of the 8th meeting of the Conference of the Parties, Invasive species and wetlands, Valencia, Spain, 18–26 November 2002, http://www.ramsar .org/pdf/res/key_res_viii_18_e.pdf (24 January 2012).

79. See Resolution VIII.18, Resolutions of the 8th meeting of the Conference of the Parties, Invasive species and wetlands, Valencia, Spain, 18–26 November 2002, http://www.ramsar .org/pdf/res/key_res_viii_18_e.pdf (24 January 2012).

80. Resolution Conf. 13.10 (Rev. CoP14)—1 "Trade in alien invasive species," http://www .cites.org/eng/res/all/13/E13–10R14.pdf (24 January 2012).

81. Ibid.

82. See Article III.

83. Article 4(1) of Annex II.

84. Agreement Concerning Cooperation in the Quarantine of Plants and Their Protection Against Pests and Diseases, Sofia, 14 December 1959, http://sedac.ciesin.org/entri/texts/ quarantine.of.plants.1959.html (24 January 2012).

85. Article VI.

86. See Setareh Khalilian, "The WTO and Environmental Provisions: Three Categories of Trade and Environmental Linkage," *Keil Working Papers* 1485 (2009): 2. The CTE was originally set up in the 1970s but had stopped meeting. At the Uruguay setting the CTE was set up to meet at least twice a year.

87. See WTO Trade and Environmental Ministerial Decision, 14 April 1994, GATT Doc. MTN.TNC/MIN (94)/Rev. 1, (1994) 33 I.L.M. 1267.

88. See Setareh Khalilian, supra note 86 at 2.

89. Jeff McNeely, supra note 1 at 7.

90. See Article 2.2 TBT, which states:

Members shall ensure that technical regulations are not prepared, adopted or applied with a view to or with the effect of creating unnecessary obstacles to international trade. For this purpose, technical regulations shall not be more trade-restrictive than necessary to fulfil a legitimate objective, taking account of the risks non-fulfilment would create. Such legitimate objectives are, inter alia: national security requirements; the prevention of deceptive practices; protection of human health or safety, animal or plant life or health, or the environment. In assessing such risks, relevant elements of consideration are, inter alia: available scientific and technical information, related processing technology or intended end-uses of products.

91. Stas Burgiel, Greg Foote, et al., supra note 2 at 21.

92. See Article 2(1) of the SPS Agreement: The members have the right to take measures but only when they are necessary under the Agreement, whereas Article 2(2) states that "necessary" measures to be taken shall be based on scientific principles.

93. Stas Burgiel, Greg Foote, et al., supra note 2 at 21.

94. Stas Burgiel, Greg Foote, et al., ibid., at 10.

95. Setareh Khalilian, supra note 86 at 3.

96. Stas Burgiel, Greg Foote, et al., supra note 2 at 10.

97. Perry Polar and Ulrike Krauss, "Status of International Legislative Framework for the Management of Invasive Alien Species in the Wider Caribbean Region," www.cabi.org (24 January 2012).

98. "Alien Species: Guiding Principles for the Prevention, Introduction and Mitigation of Impacts, Subsidiary Body of Scientific, Technical and Technological Advice," Fifth Meeting, Montreal, 31 January–4 February 2000.

99. "IUCN Guidelines for the Prevention of Biodiversity Loss Caused by Alien Invasive Species." The guidelines were approved at the 51st Meeting of the International Conservation Union Council, Gland, Switzerland, February 2000, at: http://www.issg.org/pdf/guidelines_iucn.pdf (24 January 2012).

100. The draft of the strategy can be found at: http://www.cites.org/common/com/AC/16/ E16-Inf-12.pdf (24 January 2012).

101. Resolution A. 868(20), Assembly of the International Maritime Organization, IMO, as publication number IMO-661E, ISBN 92–801–1454–9. Adopted 27 November 1997.

102. Code of conduct for the import and release of exotic biological control agents, http://www.fao.org/docrep/x5585e/x5585eoi.htm (24 January 2012).

103. See one such proposal with a suggestion for a comprehensive treaty in T. Koivurova and E. Molenaar, "International Governance and Regulation of the Marine Arctic (Part III: A Proposal for a Legally Binding Instrument)," World Wide Fund for Nature (WWF)–International Arctic Program, Oslo, 8 February 2010.

104. The Ilulissat Declaration was adopted by the five Arctic coastal states on 28 May 2008; it reaffirmed that the UN Convention on the Law of the Sea (UNCLOS or the LOS Convention) provides the legal framework for the Arctic marine area. The declaration emphasized the delimitation of the outer continental shelf and the protection of the marine environment, including the ice-covered areas, which are covered by the law of the sea, and the commitment of the coastal states to the orderly settlement of any overlapping claims. See: Danish Ministry of Foreign Affairs, The Ilulissat Declaration 2008, http://www.oceanlaw.org/downloads/arctic/Ilulissat_Declaration.pdf (24 January 2012).

105. The basic objective of the LOS Convention is to establish "[. . .] legal order for the seas and oceans which will facilitate international communication, and will promote the peaceful uses of the seas and oceans, the equitable and efficient utilisation of their resources, the conservation of their living resources, and the study, protection and preservation of the marine environment." See: Preamble, United Nations Convention on the Law of the Sea (LOS Convention), http://www.un.org/Depts/los/convention_agreements/convention_overview_convention.htm (24 January 2012).

106. See Ilulisaat Declaration, supra note 104.

107. Ilulissat Declaration, ibid.

108. See, for example, Clive Schofield, Tavis Potts, and Ian Townsend-Gault, "Boundaries, Biodiversity, Resources, and Increasing Maritime Activities: Emerging Oceans Governance Challenges for Canada in the Arctic Ocean," 34 *Vermont Law Review* (2009) at 55.

109. Dennis Lassuy and Patrick N. Lewis, supra note 49 at 48.

110. Kathrine I. Johnsen, Björn Alfthan, et al. (eds.) (2010), supra note 10 at 34.

111. Although the United States has not yet been a party to the LOS Convention, it is legally bound by most of the provisions of the convention as customary norm since the convention is mainly the codification of the customary law of the sea.

112. All Arctic states are parties to the convention.

113. All Arctic states, but Greenland, are parties to the convention.

114. All Arctic states, but Greenland, are parties to the convention.

115. Among the Arctic states, Denmark, Finland, Norway, and Sweden are parties to the convention. Both the United States and Russia are only signatories to the MOU.

116. After eight years of negotiation starting from 1993, Russia's accession to the WTO was adopted on 10 November 2011. See http://www.wto.org/english/thewto_e/acc_e/a1_russie_e.htm (24 January 2012).

117. The convention is available at: http://www.imo.org/About/Conventions/ListOfConventions/Pages/Default.aspx (24 January 2012).

118. Except Canada and Iceland, all other Arctic states are parties to the convention.

119. This is the only treaty that concluded only among the eight Arctic states.

120. The parties to the convention are only the European Arctic states, except Russia. The treaty does not cover all of the Arctic Ocean, though it covers part of the Arctic waters.

121. The convention does not cover Arctic waters, but Denmark, Finland, Russia, and Sweden are parties to the convention; http://www.helcom.fi/Convention/en_GB/convention/ (24 January 2012).

122. "Winning the war on invasive species" (2008), http://www.ospar.org/content/news_detail.asp?menu=00600725000000_000004_000000 (24 January 2012).

123. The Arctic Council was formally established in 1996 as a regional intergovernmental forum for sustainable development. The Council is the replacement of the Arctic Environmen-

tal Protection Strategy (AEPS) established in 1991. The members of the Arctic Council include Canada, Denmark, Finland, Iceland, Norway, Russia, Sweden, and the United States. It has a mandate to address Arctic-wide environmental, social, and economic challenges. Environmental monitoring and assessment are a key element of the Arctic Council agenda. The Council works through six working groups: Arctic Monitoring and Assessment Program (AMAP), Protection of Arctic Marine Environment (PAME), Conservation of Arctic Flora and Fauna (CAFF), Sustainable Development Working Group, Emergency Prevention, Preparedness and Response (EPPR), and Arctic Contaminants Action Program (ACAP). Several of these working groups deal with the issues that have relevance in addressing concerns about invasive species. See Arctic Council and Its Working Groups at: http://www.arctic-council.org/ (24 January 2012).

124. "Arctic Biodiversity Trends" (2010), at: http://abt.arcticportal.org/images/stories/report/pdf/Key_Findings.pdf.

125. See AMSA, supra note 49 at 150.

126. See The Arctic Marine Shipping Assessment Recommendations at: http://www.pame.is/amsa/on-focus/81-the-arctic-marine-shipping-assessment-recommendations (24 January 2012).

127. See Kathrine I. Johnsen, Björn Alfthan, et al., eds. (2010), supra note 10 at 37.

5. Managing Polar Policy through Public and Private Regulatory Standards
The Case of Tourism in the Antarctic

MICHELE ZEBICH-KNOS

Tourism in a Scientific Environment

Antarctica is situated in a resource-rich yet remote area that increasingly attracts visitors, from scientists to tourists. This chapter frames Antarctica within a case study approach that examines the role of polar diplomacy in the management of tourist travel to the continent. It also seeks to broaden the scholarly and applied understanding of how visits to Antarctica are managed by a global community of actors who share an interest in that continent's physical environment. Such policy management requires the integration of governmental outputs in the form of subnational management activities, multilateral cooperation under the Antarctic Treaty System (ATS) umbrella, and contributions from nongovernmental organizations (NGOs) and the private sector. The private business sector contributes to the increased importance of voluntary private regulatory standards especially as they relate to tourism around the Antarctic Peninsula. The chapter will examine both public regulations and private voluntary standards to better understand how a continent devoid of geographically defined sovereign states in the normal global system can operate to achieve environmental and other operational goals.

While the Antarctic Treaty regards this continent as the domain of scientific exploration and understanding, the reality is that tourists—especially to the Antarctic Peninsula—outnumbered scientists by the early 1990s, and became firmly entrenched by the twenty-first century.[1] Tourism increased from 27,537 visitors in the 2003–2004 travel season to 33,824 in 2010–2011. Visits were as high as 46,069 in the 2007–2008 season prior to the global economic downturn, but remain steady at the 30,000-plus mark since 2008–2009.[2] By the 1990s we began to see what we might call an *environmental risk cluster* developing around the Antarctic Peninsula. It is evident that scientists can cause environmental harm and put themselves in dangerous situations, but their familiarity with Antarctica, cold-weather training, and desire to conduct government-funded research are factors that facilitate regulatory control of this population. Should a scientist or research group based at McMurdo research station not follow proper protocol, and if the National Science Foundation's Office of Polar Programs learns of the offending activity, action may be taken and ultimately end project funding. Stays at research stations are approved by the host government with a process akin to the issuing of a visa by sovereign states.

Japanese tourists must first acquire approval from their Ministry of the Environment Biodiversity Policy Division before traveling to Antarctica; no other state has such stringent regulatory control over its own citizen-tourists.[3] No such leverage exists to manage the tourist who has a one-time association with the continent and its surrounding waters. The high number of tourist ships in and around the Antarctic Peninsula poses a threat to the area's rich flora and fauna; it also presents a safety hazard to tourists, many of whom have little understanding of Antarctica's very real dangers. Tour operators and travel agents are in the business of transforming dreams into trips and are less apt to send their clients to the International Association of Antarctica Tour Operators (IAATO) website where they can read about ship accidents, groundings, and even the 2007 sinking of a tourist vessel. This less knowledgeable but numerous population challenges the existing ATS regulatory structure that is more geared to overseeing scientific research and facilities than to dealing with tourists. Since the mid-1990s, however, the Antarctic Treaty parties began to recognize the need for significant tourism regulatory standards. In light of this emerging process, this chapter focuses on tourists—and their impact on the environment—rather than scientists as they fit into the Antarctic regulatory structure, but does so with the recognition that most regulations impact both the scientific and tourist populations.

Antarctica is the world's largest ice mass, with 98 percent of its surface covered by ice. It also accounts for 90 percent of the world's ice and contains 70 percent of the world's fresh water.[4] The Southern Ocean around the continent is home to marine fauna such as seals, penguins, and whales, and the continent holds touristic appeal for its pristine yet harsh environment. This same environment attracts scientists who seek to better understand the continent's natural resources, geologic structures, and atmospheric issues, especially those related to climate change. Exploration of such an inhospitable and remote part of the earth presents an attraction to tourists and scientists alike, if for no other reason than to say, "I've been to the ice."

A General Regulatory Framework

Antarctica's attraction partially explains the increase in tourism to the continent and its surrounding waters over the last thirty years. The increase in human activity—with its incipient environmental consequences—poses potential threats to the continent and its surrounding waters, and thus necessitates a regulated structure within which to operate. Some, like Oran Young, refer to the Antarctic Treaty System as a regime with its treaty structure ranging from the Antarctic Treaty (1959) to the Convention for the Conservation of Antarctic Seals (1972).[5] Young also places this regime in the context of an international space which lies outside the domestic jurisdiction of individual states.[6]

Yet, an additional dimension must be added to the regime framework, and that is the role of regulation. Regulations, and subsequent rules, normally appear after a state's domestic governance system enacts a law, or after a bilateral or multilateral treaty is ratified in order to facilitate policy implementation. In turn, the regulatory process begets rules and standards that serve as guidelines for achieving goals set forth in laws or treaties. Mattli and Woods (2009) remind us of the difference between national and global regulation. While the former deals with hard rules backed by government enforcement mechanisms, global regulation frequently relies upon soft law and voluntary standards whose enforcement authority takes hold only if states and the private sector choose to respond. National regulation often relies upon command-and-control methods while global regulation is heavily reliant upon diplomatic persuasion and cooperation.

General standards created by the Antarctic Treaty Conference of Parties, called General Guidelines for Visitors to the Antarctic—or Antarctic Tourism Guidelines, for short— were, for example, subsequently adopted by IAATO, a private sector organization that develops, adopts, and implements its own operational standards.[7] This private-public sector relationship forms the basis for maintaining a safe environment for Antarctica's flora and fauna as well as tourists; public sector output from the Conference of Parties is thus translated into IAATO standards as this private organization seeks to maintain a harmonious relationship with states involved in formulating Antarctic Treaty policies. The scientific visitor, however, comes under another rigorous set of government standards from his or her country of origin as well as those specified by the research station's host country. Adherence to the rules set forth by the US National Science Foundation's Office of Polar Programs, for instance, is highly recommended if an Antarctic scientist wishes to continue his or her research.

This chapter examines the global aspects of Antarctic regulatory policy as manifested by the Antarctic Treaty (1959) and other related treaties, and how policymaking for the polar south remains closely aligned to cooperative diplomacy among states, as well as the role played by private sector nongovernmental organizations—business sector NGOs, as well as environmental NGOs. Normally, we think of policymaking and implementation by governmental regulatory entities as the purview of domestic actors within a state. Antarctica represents a unique polar environment, however, in which diplomats, participants in the Conference of Parties meetings, and international functionaries from the Antarctic Treaty Secretariat often become not only policymakers, but also purveyors of rules and regulations for daily operation and environmental conservation. These rules and regulations are then implemented by the public and private sectors and, while slow moving, the process works fairly well. Private organizations such as the Antarctic and Southern Ocean Coalition (ASOC) and the International Association of Antarctica Tour Operators also contribute feedback to an international body of rules and regulations that deal specifically with Antarctic tourism. However, there is no Antarctic police force to enforce compliance; rather, compliance is generally self-imposed.

Before proceeding to an examination of specific Antarctic regulatory standards, let us first define some key terms, theories, and general conceptual underpinnings of the regulatory process. Regulatory standard-setting (RSS) as defined by Mattli and Woods is the "organization and control of economic . . . and social activities by means of making, implementing, monitoring, and enforcing of rules—even though RSS rules are voluntary."[8] Mattli and Woods emphasize that RSS is a *voluntary* process, which distinguishes it from mandatory regulatory compliance within states; in principle and practice within states, we see that domestic governmental rules and regulations are normally not voluntary. This changes once we move to the global arena where regulations created to implement treaty provisions can suffer from an enforcement dilemma. Due to lack of enforcement, such global regulations may become more like private voluntary standards than domestic regulations promulgated by the US Environmental Protection Agency, for example.

To further complicate the situation, successful Antarctic management relies on a large degree of voluntary compliance to regulations simply because isolation precludes frequent verification. Who will monitor the scientific team once it is out in the field? The team self-monitors each member much as tourists and their tour operator implement the Antarctic Tourism Guidelines. Infractions to the guidelines are generally corrected on-site by another tourist or tour guide, but not by the sudden appearance of enforcement police with authority to punish the tourist.

Global RSS bodies include the International Organization for Standardization (ISO) and the Codex Alimentarius Commission. The ISO is a private organization that defines itself as "a nongovernmental organization that forms a bridge between the public and private sectors."[9] The Codex Alimentarius Commission is an international governmental organization (IGO) created by the UN Food and Agriculture Organization and the UN World Health Organization that blends private and public aspects of standard-setting by working with NGOs and IGOs alike.[10] For our purposes, global RSS bodies also include the Antarctic Treaty Secretariat and the International Association of Antarctica Tour Operators. The former is an international governmental organization formed to administer the Antarctic Treaty; it works with NGOs, but its official membership consists of states. IAATO views itself as an international organization in the geographic sense; nevertheless, it is a private organization whose hundred-plus members include private tour operators, not governments.[11] Article 3 of the IAATO bylaws on membership states that members "are experienced organizers that operate travel programs to the Antarctic and/or sub-Antarctic islands."[12]

According to Drezner, global regulatory standards benefit private firms by simplifying "production processes."[13] In the case of Antarctic tourism, standards enable IAATO to label noncompliant members and nonmembers as *outliers* who, in turn, risk a poor reputation in the global marketplace. One might say that IAATO functions partially as the Better Business Bureau of Antarctic tourism. The incentive to conform to IAATO guidelines is a way to keep mandatory state enforcement at bay. If IAATO does not self-police its members, and if tour operators disregard Antarctic Treaty policies and standards, cooperation among private and public stakeholders would decline. This could lead Antarctic Treaty parties to adopt and enforce more stringent regulatory measures. One could say that this is what happened with the enactment in August 2011 of strict International Convention for the Prevention of Pollution from Ships (MARPOL) fuel standards for vessels traveling in and around Antarctica. The new fuel oil standards affecting large cruise ships coming to the region were enacted after many years of concern over their increased traffic in Antarctic and sub-Antarctic waters.

Drezner clarifies the relationship between international governmental organizations and nongovernmental ones, by noting that IGOs are formed by states while NGOs are the "creation of like-minded private individuals who share a founding idea."[14] A caveat should be added to Drezner's explanation—while IGOs represent a vast array of states with diverse domestic viewpoints and levels of economic and political sophistication, business sector NGOs such as IAATO represent a single body of constituents, i.e., that of Antarctic tour operators. State actors and their relevant domestic subactors, such as the National Science Foundation's Office of Polar Programs (OPP) or the Australian Antarctic Division (AAD), have multiple constituencies ranging from political and economic interests to the general public—to name but three. Unlike the domestic arena, there are not many business sector NGOs competing over tourism-related issues in the Antarctic, which gives IAATO an advantage when offering input into the policymaking and regulatory process. It has the opportunity to exert such influence every two years at the Antarctic Treaty Conference of Parties meetings in which NGOs like IAATO and ASOC hold participant, nonvoting status.

Let us conclude this general explanation of how the regulatory process and subsequent standard-setting applies to the Antarctic by recognizing Abbott and Snidal's conceptual framework, which they call the *Governance Triangle*.[15] The Governance Triangle is a means to conceptually map RSS within a transnational regulatory space populated by states, IGOs, NGOs, and even private sector firms. For our purposes we modify this heuristic tool to demonstrate the relationship between hard and soft Antarctic-related outcomes such as laws, treaties, and, most importantly, guidelines, that derive from both private and public sector actors. Abbott and Snidal remind us that to be effective, an institution within this regulatory framework must exhibit competence in four areas: independence, representativeness, expertise, and operational capacity.[16] It behooves us to examine how the relevant actors exhibit these four competencies; whether the existing regulatory process for safeguarding the Antarctic environment runs as effectively as possible; and whether anything else can be added to the process in order to enhance positive environmental outcomes.

Environmental Theories Applied to the Antarctic

Complementing this overall framework are various environmental regulatory theories that apply to the Antarctic case. Foremost among them is the precautionary principle, which urges those making policy or regulations to take action before damage occurs. The precautionary principle is often applied in Antarctica to prevent oil spills, biological contamination by nonnative species of flora and fauna, and to ensure the safety of not only the continent itself, but also of visitors to the icy south—i.e., scientists and tourists. Resolution 7 of the 2009 Antarctic Treaty Consultative Meeting clearly illustrates this approach in its general principles, noting, "decisions on tourism should be based on a pragmatic and precautionary approach, that incorporates an evaluation of risks."[17]

Should an accident occur, the "polluter-pays" approach should come into play and the offending state be held responsible for the cleanup. However, liability for Antarctic accidents is a sore subject that has yet to be resolved by Antarctic Treaty System parties. Sunstein (2002) adheres to the idea of imposing fees on polluting firms and industries that will lead to higher prices and thereby decrease consumption, reducing impacts. For Antarctic tourism operators, polluter-pays might mean that an offending firm would be expected to pay for an oil spill or other environmental damage. Enforcement of such a scheme would take place in the tourism operator's home country of business, or the ship's flag state. An operator may see payment as a goodwill gesture needed to ensure harmonious relations with its trading partners and IAATO. If an operator shirks responsibility, this might mean marginalization by IAATO—and loss of the valuable advertising credential of IAATO membership. Membership in IAATO holds strong sway for tourists who book trips to Antarctica, as it implies that the tour operator is knowledgeable and in compliance—albeit voluntary—with IAATO standards. In short, IAATO membership translates into a useful marketing tool by ensuring peace of mind for the tourist that he or she will pay for a worthwhile and safe Antarctic trip.

Another theory that holds relevance to our case is "race-to-the-top." This theory regards a well-constructed regulatory system with demanding regulations and standards as a means to improve health, safety, and the environment. It also fits our Antarctic example. In race-to-the-top, states with the lowest amount of stringent environmental, health, labor, and safety regulations and enforcement—usually less-developed countries—are then obliged to reach for higher standards or risk being closed out of the trade arena for certain products. This is especially true, for instance, for foodstuffs, about which health concerns of importing states are considerable. Higher standards imposed in the global trade arena may serve to uplift a state's own citizens through enactment of such labor and environmental regulations that may spill into the domestic arena. For example, shrimp processing for export is often in the same facility as shrimp processed for domestic consumption; thus we see a spillover benefit to locals. In a subsequent section we will examine the 2011 ban on ships traveling to Antarctic waters that use heavy oil, which is a way to impose a higher environmental protection standard that also indirectly contributes to passenger safety.

The theoretical opposite, race-to-the-bottom, assumes an economically competitive global system in which states lower their regulatory demands in order to compete with other states with less stringent regulations and rules. Hence, globalization fosters a race to the bottom where states with the lowest, rather than the highest, standards benchmark the level of human rights, environmental security, and individual well-being. Production moves to states with the least regulations. Since Antarctic Treaty parties are generally not involved in extensive trade in Antarctica, and its management relies so heavily on cooperative diplomacy within the Antarctic Treaty System, a race-to-the-bottom trend seems less applicable to our examination in this chapter.

Antarctic Treaty System: Public Sector Policies and Regulations

Before we examine the private sector role in standards implementation, it behooves us to start with public sector outputs since Antarctic policy first emanates from there. The Antarctic Treaty System is the common term for the series of treaties that focus on Antarctica as well as the framework under which Antarctic administration occurs. The primary treaties include the Antarctic Treaty (1959); the Protocol on Environmental Protection to the Antarctic Treaty, or Madrid Protocol (1991); the Convention for the Conservation of Antarctic Seals (1972); and the Convention on the Conservation of Antarctic Marine Living Resources (CCAMLR, 1980). The Antarctic Treaty Secretariat is headquartered in Buenos Aires, Argentina, and is the administrative body whose main task is to coordinate ATS requirements, the main one being the annual Antarctic Treaty Consultative Meeting (ATCM). The ATCM is specified in Article IX of the Antarctic Treaty; attending parties were originally twelve in number. Today, thirty-seven states have joined the Antarctic Treaty as contracting parties and can participate in the consultative meetings as long as they are actively engaged in "conducting substantial research" in Antarctica.[18] Among the thirty-seven states that have ratified the treaty, there are currently sixteen consultative parties with full decision-making power and twenty-one nonconsultative parties who can attend the ATCMs, but do so without decision-making capability.[19]

The Secretariat also coordinates Special Antarctic Treaty Consultative Meetings, diplomatic conferences, and meetings of experts. This corpus of meetings is the setting in which to formulate policy and create regulations in accordance with Antarctic treaties. Polar diplomacy takes place at these meetings, which function under a tiered operational system. First, there are consultative parties with full decision-making status, next come the twenty-one states with nonconsultative party status, and observers who include representatives from the Commission for the Conservation of Antarctic Marine Living Resources, the Scientific Committee on Antarctic Research, and the Council of Managers of National Antarctic Programs (COMNAP). Finally, there are NGOs that, while not technically holding observer status, are able to attend meetings and submit documents, as are representatives from other international organizations.[20] NGOs typically fall under the "expert" or guest category.

It is in this environment that meeting participants discuss Antarctic issues and share information that can lead to policy revisions and regulations. To facilitate the management process, issues are generally broken down into categories of subjects including peaceful use and inspections; science and operations; environmental protection; climate change; bioprospecting; minerals; and tourism.

For the Thirty-fourth Antarctic Treaty Consultative Meeting, held in Buenos Aires from 20 June to 1 July 2011, three expert groups submitted reports. They included IAATO, the Antarctic and Southern Ocean Coalition, and the International Hydrographic Organization (IHO).[21] For the 2011 ATCM meeting as with previous ones, IAATO's report reflected its desire to work in accordance with Article III(2) of the Antarctic Treaty and to support the management of its members' activities in and around Antarctica. IAATO reiterated its desire to promote best practices in the Antarctic tourism industry and portrayed itself as a team player, much as it has done in previous ATCM meetings. To that end, IAATO demonstrated its active participation in many Antarctic conferences and IGO meetings, thus reinforcing the idea that polar diplomacy is a dynamic process with governmental and nongovernmental stakeholders actively pursuing dialogue and information sharing. During the 2010–2011 reporting period IAATO's select interface with governmental actors included participation in the following activities:

- Attendance at a 12 May 2011 meeting with the Australian Antarctic Division (AAD) and other stakeholders in a roundtable at AAD offices in Tasmania;
- Participation in a Nonnative Species Workshop and other meetings at COMNAP XXII in Buenos Aires;
- Presentation at COMNAP XXII on a risk-assessment approach at the International Maritime Organization (IMO) Polar Code talks;
- Served as advisor for Cruise Lines International at the IMO's Design and Equipment Subcommittee in London and provided input into development of a Polar Code;
- Attended the May 2011 Conservation of Antarctica Workshop in South Africa hosted by the Scientific Committee on Antarctic Research (SCAR).[22]

The distinction between private and public actors at policymaking meetings is one in which the final decisions remain in the hands of state actors and not NGOs (see table 5.1). Since IGOs often include NGOs in their meetings, one might be misled to assume that there is greater equality than first meets the eye, but NGOs represent specific interests and are more akin to domestic US lobbies than equal partners. While policymaking power clearly resides with the consultative parties to the Antarctic Treaty, NGOs like IAATO certainly play a valuable role as disseminators of information and *translators* of policy and subsequent regulations to their members who interface with tourists.

It is not, after all, members of the Antarctic Treaty Secretariat staff who interface directly with tourists on the Antarctic Peninsula, but the tour guide who represents the tour operator. That tour operator may well be an IAATO member. Because of this important connection to those in the field, state actors and IGOs realize that a working relationship is beneficial to regulatory implementation.

How the process works is best demonstrated by the various ATS tourism documents that specify regulations and guidelines for tourists and expedition leaders. The main documents include the Environmental Protocol, *Guidance for Visitors to*

Table 5.1: International organizations instrumental in the creation and maintenance of Antarctic policies and regulations

Organization	Role	Type
Antarctic and Southern Ocean Coalition (ASOC)	Creates and submits reports to Antarctic Treaty System meetings, especially those of the Antarctic Treaty Consultative Parties and the Committee on Environmental Protection (CEP).	NGO
Antarctic Treaty Secretariat	Oversees operation of the Antarctic Treaty System. Facilitates exchanges, maintains databases, disseminates information, and coordinates Antarctic Treaty Consultative Meetings.	IGO
Commission for the Conservation of Antarctic Marine Living Resources	Supports implementation and compliance of the Convention for the Conservation of Antarctic Marine Living Resources. Reviews information on illegal, unreported, and unregulated fishing. Maintains a data center.	IGO
Council of Managers of National Antarctic Programs (COMNAP)	Supports national Antarctic programs. Created *Antarctic Flight Information Manual* for communication frequencies and landing sites in Antarctica. Maintains *Ship Position Reporting System*.	IGO
International Association of Antarctica Tour Operators (IAATO)	Represents Antarctic tour operators. Promotes safe travel to Antarctica and maintains databases promoting this goal. Works with IGOs to support Antarctic conservation through responsible tourism.	NGO
International Hydrographic Organization (IHO)	Supports navigational safety and protection of the marine environment. Facilitates accurateness in nautical charts and documents.	IGO
Scientific Committee on Antarctic Research (SCAR)	Coordinates and promotes scientific research in Antarctica. A committee of the International Council for Science, SCAR represents government and private sector scientists.	NGO

IGO = International governmental organization; NGO = Nongovernmental organization

the Antarctic Attached to Recommendation XVIII-1 (1994), *General Guidelines for Visitors to the Antarctic Attached to Resolution 3* (2011), and *ATCM Measures on Tourism and Site Guidelines for Visitors.* These documents are numerous and not especially relevant to the tourist. What is relevant is that the IAATO-member tour guide provides a PowerPoint lecture to tourists while on board ship so that everyone is versed on the *General Guidelines for Visitors to the Antarctic.* The lecture includes mention that all visits to Antarctica "should be conducted in accordance with the Antarctic Treaty" and that respect for wildlife, vegetation, and historic areas calls for specific dos and don'ts. Tourists are provided with a list that is tailored to their specific type of tourism. If traveling by a touring ship, they may not be told, for example, "do not use guns or explosives," which is part of the guidelines. Instead, they will hear guidelines including "maintain an appropriate distance from wildlife . . . in general don't approach closer than five meters," "carefully wash boots and clean all equipment . . . before bringing them to Antarctica," "do not deposit any litter," and "do not take souvenirs." The antimicrobial boot wash quickly becomes a daily focal point for implementation in the field before leaving the ship for shore. Once on shore, the rule about ensuring that "wastes are managed in accordance with Annexes III and IV of the Protocol on Environmental Protection to the Antarctic Treaty" becomes very real—and includes human waste, which must be properly removed from the continent. This gives dull regulations new meaning—especially for those with weak bladders.[23]

Most of Antarctica's fragile flora and fauna are marine- rather than land-based; Antarctic tourism is largely sea-based and run through private companies, which means that most regulatory concerns about tourism surround ocean issues. Not only is there a great concern for preservation of the Southern Ocean, but also recognition that travel to south of 60 degrees south latitude, which defines the Antarctic region, poses potentially fatal hazards for tourists.

Safety and the Authorization Protocol

Mariano Memolli, director of the Human Biology and Medicine Section at the Dirección Nacional del Antártico and an executive committee member of the Council of Managers of National Antarctic Programs (COMNAP), shares his concern that while IAATO can be contacted for relevant information in an emergency, non-regulated tourism creates a dangerous situation. (He notes that in 2007 there was even a hot air balloon in the Antarctic area—although that is certainly more of an anomaly than the norm.) Memolli is adamant that Antarctica is a scientific location, yet he also reminds us that the Chilean state owns a hotel complete with shopping that is operated by the Chilean Air Force on King George Island.[24] Memolli is quick to point out the dangers posed by human error when piloting a ship in the Southern Ocean. Going too fast or relying on an inexperienced captain or crew can be a recipe for disaster, especially if there is pressure to please tourists by crossing uninteresting areas too fast.[25]

According to Memolli, a search and rescue (SAR) expert, the Antarctic Peninsula has capacity for no more than three hundred persons, and most bases can handle only sixty to eighty persons. On a cruise ship, one to two doctors with the same number of nurses and no blood supply pose a serious situation in an emergency. The high number of elderly tourists who are the main group that can afford the costly trip also complicates a rescue operation. Further complications arise, according to Memolli, simply because "a covered life boat would not matter if the passengers had wet clothes. They would die in subzero temperatures."[26] While most state-operated Antarctic programs require scientists to pass a rigorous physical in advance of participating in Antarctic research, tour operators have no such requirement.

If disaster strikes there are extremely limited SAR capabilities in the Antarctic with most SAR operations relegated to whoever is closest to the distressed vessel. Given the Antarctic Peninsula's proximity to South America, the Argentine and

Chilean navies often bear significant SAR responsibilities, including the financial burden.

Manfred Reineke, executive secretary for the Antarctic Treaty Secretariat, also maintains that SAR is a major issue, and uses the Norwegian yacht *Berserk*'s 2011 disappearance in the Ross Sea as an illustration. It is perhaps the best recent example of what can happen when a vessel's responsible party fails to complete the prescribed authorization protocol; in this case it was simply not followed by the yacht's owner and operator, Jarle Andhoy.[27] The yacht's owner should have received approval from the Norwegian Polar Institute (NPI) prior to its voyage, and that did not occur. Why approval was not obtained is unknown. In a press release IAATO stated that the NPI reported "the leader of the *Berserk* expedition to Norwegian prosecuting authorities for violations of Antarctic regulations, and we fully support that decision."[28] Since everyone perished aboard the *Berserk*, it remains to be seen whether Norwegian authorities will pursue a prosecution. Following the fateful distress call and unsuccessful rescue attempt in February 2011, IAATO adamantly sought to distinguish this incident by the unauthorized behavior involved, namely: "The Berserk . . . did not have proper authorization or permits for their Antarctica expedition. IAATO requires its members to secure all relevant authorization or permits from their national authorities, to provide advance notification of itineraries, contact information and expedition operating procedures, as well as contingency and safety plans."[29]

IAATO went on to explain that the *Berserk*'s organizers contacted some IAATO members for logistical support prior to its voyage, but the members declined because the yacht's owner failed to file the proper documents as required by national authorities. The *Berserk*'s documents were not in order, and IAATO members did not want their reputation tarnished by a yacht owner who failed to follow Antarctic regulations. This unfortunate series of actions hampered the possibility that a search and rescue team would find the yacht. Besides the tragic ending for the *Berserk*'s crew, this example illustrates the importance of following regulations that are aimed at preserving not only the environment but also the safety of Antarctic travelers.

Reineke noted that search and rescue also brings others into danger. The SAR team spent ten days looking for the *Berserk* and put its own vessels at risk.[30] While the Rescue Coordination Centre of New Zealand managed the operation, an IAATO-member ship operated by Heritage Expeditions, the *Professor Khromov* (also known as *Spirit of Enderby*) detoured from its own route to join the *Steve Irwin* and the *HMNZS Wellington* in the search for the *Berserk*, to no avail.

Linkage Politics: Oil Pollution and Large-Capacity Cruise Ships

One has only to think of the *Costa Concordia* disaster on 13 January 2012, when the cruise ship ran aground near an Italian island, and the environmental and safety benefits of keeping large cruise ships out of Antarctic waters become clear. In response to this disaster and the proliferation of megaships, Mark Dickinson, general secretary of the maritime union Nautilus International, reflected on a situation that many who deal with Antarctic tourism already knew—that "the sheer size of such ships presents massive challenges for emergency services, evacuation, rescue, and salvage—and we should not have to wait for a major disaster until these concerns are addressed."[31]

After the sinking of G.A.P. Adventures' *Explorer* in 2007, a rash of tourist vessel groundings, and the increase in mega-cruise ships to the area, Antarctic decision makers began to link two serious issues—oil spills and the large passenger capacity of immense cruise ships. To distinguish the *Explorer*'s ill-fated accident from that of the *Berserk*, one must emphasize that the Canadian tour operator, G.A.P. Adventures, received proper Canadian permits under the Canadian Antarctic Environmental Protection Act and Canada's Antarctic Environmental Protection Regulations.[32] Those concerned with environmental and safety concerns called for clearer and more comprehensive regulations.

Action became especially important in light of Princess Cruise Line's decision to sail the megaship *Star Princess*, with nearly 2,500 passengers, on two Antarctic cruises during the 2009–2010 cruise season.[33] The Antarctic Treaty parties had previously advocated for a regulatory structure; diplomats representing the AT parties and the International Maritime Organization joined forces. ATCM XXX Resolution 4 (2007) on Ship-based Tourism in the Antarctic Treaty Area called for Antarctic Treaty parties to "discourage or decline to authorize tour operators that use vessels carrying more than 500 passengers from making any landings in Antarctica; and . . . [to] restrict the number of passengers on shore at any one time to 100 or fewer."[34] The latter recommendation was not an issue, but the request to curb ships with more than five hundred passengers was without teeth, for the resolution to "discourage or decline to authorize" large-capacity ships' entrance in Antarctic waters gave parties a way out of actually imposing a ban and did nothing to substantively address the safety issue should a vessel experience an emergency. One party could decline authorization while another could merely discourage such travel; this rendered the resolution powerless to regulate safety concerns about large passenger ships. Vessels under non-AT country flags further complicate matters. The *Explorer*—a long-established tourist vessel that hit a growler (a small, low iceberg) and sank—was Liberian flagged. Liberia is not a party to the Antarctic Treaty and thus had no legal obligation to follow AT regulations.

How then does the international arena regulate environmental and safety concerns in the Antarctic, and take into account flag-states not party to the Antarctic Treaty? The answer lies, in part, beyond the boundaries of the AT, in other treaties and international governmental organizations with greater outreach, most of which are maritime by nature. One way to regulate vessel safety can be with increasing port state control over all ships bound for Antarctica. In a 2009 Antarctic Treaty Meeting of Experts, New Zealand reiterated the need for enhanced port state control to address the problem that some flag states may not adequately ensure that their flagged vessels meet accepted safety standards, increasing the risk of an oil spill or harm to passengers and crew.[35] This entailed a small step in the regulatory process; as many persons associated with the ATS explain, the ATCMs are diplomatic meetings with all the baggage that the term entails.[36] In short, diplomatic behavior often means slow and incremental actions intended to avoid alienating other states. While that political culture exists among AT members, the International Maritime Organization, which identifies itself heavily with science and the technical aspects of maritime affairs, does not suffer from the same diplomatic malaise. The AT includes fewer state parties than do other treaties, with only twenty-eight consultative parties while the MARPOL Protocol of 1978 Relating to the International Convention for the Prevention of Pollution from Ships has 151 contracting states.[37] While the Antarctic Treaty parties and their representatives did not effectively take up the charge to regulate large-ship tourism, they did advocate the back-door approach—and that door led to the International Maritime Organization.

IMO's Marine Environment Protection Committee (MEPC) designed and adopted new regulations pertaining to MARPOL that entered into force on 1 August 2011. The new MARPOL fuel oil ban on ships entering Antarctic waters aims to avoid heavy oil spills and subsequent environmental pollution. The spillover safety benefit to tourists on large ships that use heavy oil is obvious, because it means that large cruise ships can no longer sail in Antarctic waters. At issue is that existing search and rescue capability is unable to properly handle a disaster with over five hundred people in need of assistance. The solution: prohibit ships like those from the Princess Cruise Line with their two thousand–passenger capacity from sailing into Antarctic waters. Prior to the ban, Princess Cruise Lines' *Nordnorge* sailed the Antarctic route with its maximum capacity of 691 passengers and seventy-member crew, while the previously mentioned *Star Princess* had a maximum capacity of approximately 2,600.[38]

The 2011 regulation now appears as Regulation 43 in the Amendments to Annex I of the MARPOL Protocol of 1978, chapter 9, "Special Requirements for the Use or Carriage of Oils in the Antarctic Area."[39] The regulation stipulates:

> (1) With the exception of vessels engaged in securing the safety of ships or in search and rescue operation, the carriage in bulk as cargo or carriage and use as fuel of the following:
> 1. crude oils having a density at 15° C higher than 900 kg/m³;
> 2. oils, other than crude oils, having a density at 15° C higher than 900 kg/m³ or a kinematic viscosity at 50° C higher than 180 mm²/s; or
> 3. bitumen, tar and their emulsions, shall be prohibited in the Antarctic area, as defined in Annex I, regulation 1.11.7.
> (2) When prior operations have included the carriage or use of oils listed in paragraphs 1.1 to 1.3 of this regulation, the cleaning or flushing of tanks or pipelines is not required.[40]

With great simplicity, the regulation effectively eliminated large cruise ships from sailing into Antarctic waters. No longer does the Princess Cruise Lines' *Nordnorge*, for example, sail to Antarctica. While passenger and cargo ships could switch to another type of fuel while in Antarctic waters, the benefit apparently is not worth the extra cost for cruise lines. A perusal of post–August 2011 tour companies reveals that no large cruise ships advertise Antarctic cruises.

The IMO's Polar Code: Lessons Learned

Since most visitors to the Antarctic area go by ship, a technical approach aimed at specific ship requirements falls conveniently within the purview of the International Maritime Organization and explains why the Antarctic Treaty Secretariat is hopeful that the IMO-led Polar Code project will come to fruition. The IMO, the UN International Labor Organization (ILO), and the UN Food and Agriculture Organization (FAO) currently have created joint IMO-ILO and IMO-FAO guidelines related to labor and food issues, so joint ATS-IMO cooperation is not out of the question. During the XXVII ATCM (2004), the IMO's voluntary shipping guidelines were welcomed by the parties. The ATCM parties drafted a letter to the IMO secretary general recognizing that guidelines are a weak substitute for stronger regulatory standards; the parties recognized that the ATS was not in a position to accomplish the task, and the letter went on to state that the parties "recognize that a comprehensive approach towards setting standards for all vessels . . . can only be achieved through the IMO."[41] The ball was now clearly placed in the IMO's court to create a Polar Code with teeth that has two sections, one for the Arctic and another for the Antarctic.

Antarctic Treaty Secretariat executive secretary Reineke has emphasized that his office wants to cooperate with the IMO to create an Antarctic Polar Code.[42] As the tourism representative best positioned to voice private sector views and information, IAATO also actively participated at the Polar Code Workshop in Cambridge, England, in September 2011.

The current management trend for Antarctica is away from voluntary maritime guidelines and toward mandatory outputs by IGOs. The Antarctic Treaty Meeting of Experts Chairs' Report (2009) once again praised the IMO for approving the *Guidelines for Ships Operating in Polar Waters*, while the ATCM XXXII Resolution 8 (2009), *Mandatory Shipping Code for Vessels Operating in Antarctic Waters* was a stronger ATS call of support for the IMO to create mandatory requirements for ships.[43] Resolution 8 (2009) recommended that the chair of the ATCM XXXII "write to the International Maritime Organization to . . . express the desire of the Antarctic Treaty Parties that the IMO would commence work as soon as practicable to develop mandatory requirements for ships operating in Antarctic waters."[44] This was the formal approval by AT parties for the IMO to create a Polar Code and suggests a great willingness for joint ATS-IMO cooperation.

Participants at the 2011 Polar Code Workshop discussed environmental consequences of routine release of combustion gases, bilge water, ballast water, lubricants, and waste, and discussed the identification of all potential hazards as well as other risks associated with ships in polar waters. The Polar Code is not specifically aimed at tourism; rather it is intended to safeguard the polar area from ship-related environmental disasters, which also carry risk to a ship's passengers.

Environmental NGOs at the workshop took a strong stance in favor of accident mitigation and proposed several mandatory recommendations they felt should appear
in an "environmental chapter of the mandatory Polar Code." Such recommendations include more broad-based restrictions such as those on "oil and other harmful
substances," and the designation and protection of what they called "Particularly
Sensitive Sea Areas (PSSAs)."[45]

While various maritime conventions such as MARPOL and the International
Convention for the Safety of Life at Sea (SOLAS) of 1960 already exist, the Polar
Code would pull elements from existing mandatory regulations resulting from such
conventions and tailor them to polar waters. New regulations would be added where
needed, but the focus would recognize the unique aspects within each region stemming from factors such as geography, climate change, and ice conditions, and how
these impact activities in polar waters. The code would include approximately six
sections including certification, design, equipment and systems, operation, environmental protection, and personnel and training.[46]

Steady progress is being made toward the creation of a Polar Code. However,
Heike Deggim, head of the Marine Technology Section, Maritime Safety Division of
the IMO, reminds us not to expect the code to enter into force until 2017 at the earliest. The IMO Subcommittee on Ship Design and Equipment, the group in charge
of formulating the code, created a timetable that called for a final draft by the end of
2014.[47] While this may seem a rather slow process, the timetable is in pace with the
creation of most multilateral environmental agreements.

As this maritime Polar Code slowly progresses toward adoption and entry into
force, the creation of a comprehensive mandatory code specific to Antarctica is a
natural extension of the process. Mandatory land (or, more appropriately, ice) and
sea requirements already exist and could be brought together under one roof to
facilitate proper implementation of new and existing regulations. A comprehensive document duly categorized into appropriate sections and subsections could
pull together all mandatory Antarctic requirements and make compliance easier
to achieve. For instance, *maritime* and *land-based* might form two sample sections,
with relevant tourism or scientific subsections under each section. Much like the
US Code of Federal Regulations, an Antarctic Polar Code could be updated periodically and fall within the administrative duties of the Antarctic Treaty Secretariat,
which already compiles ATS-related documents in a repository or clearinghouse
manner that does not at present necessarily include regulations from the IMO or
other IGOs. The current clearinghouse system is organized as a library for ATS
documents—some mandatory and others recommendations—that does not initiate
or constitute legal documents itself. The ease of Internet postings to a website also
facilitates a code's maintenance, which could include hyperlinks to existing mandatory procedures and documents from other IGO websites.

An Antarctic Polar Code would represent a compilation of all mandatory requirements relating to Antarctica. It is difficult to surmise whether the *Berserk*'s owner
would have filed the proper documents if such a code existed, or whether the *Explorer* would not have sunk, but a code would certainly facilitate the work of those

advocating greater protection and the efforts of those who seek to abide by Antarctic regulations. Such a code could easily be posted online at the Antarctic Treaty Secretariat website, and its existence could be disseminated by IGOs and NGOs including IAATO. In the meantime, a maritime Polar Code will be a start toward comprehensive environmental and safety management of ships sailing the Antarctic waters, and this includes scientific, replenishment, tourist, and other vessels. Without ship safety, Antarctica's largely marine-based ecosystem could be compromised.

Notes

1. Richardson (2000: 71–72).
2. IAATO, Tourism Overview, 2007–2008; 2008–2009 (2012c).
3. IAATO, Information for Japanese Nationals planning a trip to Antarctica (2012e).
4. Zebich-Knos (2007: 167).
5. Oran Young (1994).
6. O. Young (2011: 287).
7. Antarctic Treaty Consultative Meeting XXXIV, *General Guidelines for Visitors to the Antarctic*. These guidelines are commonly referred to as the Antarctic Tourism Guidelines.
8. Mattli and Woods (2009: 45).
9. International Standards Organization, "About ISO," available at http://www.iso.org/iso/home/about.htm (2012).
10. Codex Alimentarius Commission, available at http://www.codexalimentarius.org/ (2012).
11. IAATO, "Who Is IAATO?" (2010); IAATO Membership Directory 2011–2012; Bylaws 2012.
12. IAATO, Bylaws (2012d).
13. Drezner (2007: 43).
14. Drezner (2007: 68).
15. Abbott and Snidal (2009: 49).
16. Abbott and Snidal (2009: 62–70).
17. Antarctic Treaty Consultative Meeting, Resolution 7, ATCM XXXII (2009: 284).
18. Antarctic Treaty, Article IX.2 (1959: 24–25).
19. See Antarctic Treaty Secretariat website.
20. See Antarctic Treaty Secretariat, Revised Rules of Procedure 2008 (2012: 14).
21. Antarctic Treaty Secretariat (2011a).
22. Antarctic Treaty Secretariat (2011b).
23. Antarctic Treaty Consultative Meeting, Resolution 3 ATCM XXXIV–CEP XIV (2011).
24. Memolli (2009, 26 June interview).
25. Memolli (2009, 26 June interview).
26. Memolli (2009, 26 June interview).
27. IAATO (2011, Press release, 3 March).
28. IAATO (2011, Press release, 3 March).
29. IAATO (2011, Press release, 3 March).
30. Reineke (2011, April interview).
31. Dickinson (2012: 1).
32. Antarctic Treaty Secretariat, Canadian Verbal Statement (2008: 643).
33. IAATO, Tourism Overview, 2009–2010 (2012c: 7).
34. Antarctic Treaty Consultative Meeting, Resolution 4 ATCM XXX (2007).
35. Antarctic Treaty Meeting of Experts, Chairs' Report (2009: 14).
36. Jan Huber (2009, 25 June interview).

37. International Maritime Organization (2012: 104)
38. Cruise Lines International Association (2012).
39. International Maritime Organization (2010: 2).
40. International Maritime Organization (2010: 2).
41. Antarctic Treaty Secretariat (2004: 442).
42. Reineke (2011, April interview).
43. Antarctic Treaty Consultative Meeting, Resolution 8 ATCM XXXII (2009: 286–287).
44. Antarctic Treaty Consultative Meeting, Resolution 8 ATCM XXXII (2009: 286).
45. Polar Code (2011: 38).
46. Deggim (2011: 18).
47. Deggim (2012, February correspondence).

PART TWO
Critical Actors
Power Dynamics and Driving Forces in Polar Regions

There must be, not a balance of power, but a community of power;
not organized rivalries, but an organized common peace.
—US PRESIDENT WOODROW WILSON

I N this section we turn to the major vectors of change in the polar regions, and
the driving forces that will shape the poles in the future. Of course, much attention is paid to the rich energy resources of the Arctic, which loom large in
the world's estimation. The geopolitical desirability of the Arctic is in large part tied
to its resources and strategic location, and therefore the globe's major powers are
redefining their Arctic policy to reflect strategic values. There is more to the story
than oil and gas reserves, however, as many of our authors point out.

To begin, chapter 6 tells a story of hope from Rasmus Bertelsen and Klaus Hansen, who describe the way Iceland used its abundant geothermal energy resources
to educate and train its population for high-skilled jobs, attract industry, and leap-
frog development stages while developing infrastructure. They offer this historical
lesson as a model for another Arctic "microstate," Greenland.

Next, the challenges that energy development holds for UNCLOS—the UN Convention on the Law of the Sea—are discussed. The authors of chapter 7 conclude that
UNCLOS will be inadequate for managing the complex interests of Arctic and non-
Arctic states, and that new approaches are needed. In chapter 8, Arthur Mason offers a unique and incisive look at the way in which discourse around energy shapes
its value and development, prodding us all to consider how language can affect the
field of policy options before us.

Turning to geopolitical trends in chapter 9, Damien Degeorges and Saleem H.
Ali examine the growing interest and influence of China in polar regions, and the
effects on Greenland and Australia. Finally, in chapter 10, coeditor Rebecca Pincus
offers a glimpse at US security policy in the Arctic, and how increasing activity by
Russia has affected American interests in the region.

Great tides are pulling at the poles today, and they are both environmental and
political. The warming temperatures herald enormous ecological change and offer
new levels of access to the Arctic region. However, globalization and the rise of a

multipolar world is another enormous driver of change. The global community has both expanded and fractured in the post–Cold War era, and forging international consensus has become significantly more challenging, particularly on contentious issues of resource access. The poles represent something close to new territory— regions that once were overlooked or considered to have value only for scientists and explorers are now hotspots of global interest. This new strategic value will make their protection, and the rights of their native communities, all the more difficult to defend.

6. From Energy to Knowledge?
Building Domestic Knowledge-Based Sectors around Hydro Energy in Iceland and Greenland

RASMUS GJEDSSØ BERTELSEN AND KLAUS GEORG HANSEN

Diversifying and Developing Very Small High North Atlantic Economies

Iceland and Greenland share significant social, economic, and political history and conditions. These shared circumstances make it possible to draw comparisons and learn possible lessons on the future course of Greenland's development based on the Icelandic experience.

Iceland and Greenland share a political history as overseas territories of the Kingdom of Denmark. Iceland became an overseas possession of the Kingdom of Denmark in the Middle Ages. It gained home rule (executive control of domestic issues) in 1904 and sovereignty in a union with Denmark in 1918, and became a republic in 1944. Greenland was a colony of Denmark until 1953, when it was integrated into the kingdom as an overseas county. Greenland gained home rule in 1979, and in 2009 gained self-rule, acknowledging its right to pursue independence. There is strong political desire to expand this self-government and eventually gain full independence, which is primarily a question of financial sustainability.

Economically, both Iceland and Greenland have historically been highly dependent on fisheries as a primary source of foreign currency. Iceland became financially independent from Denmark in 1918, and has, as a very small economy that is highly dependent on imports, been challenged to cover its foreign currency needs. Historically, the Icelandic economy was almost exclusively dependent on agricultural and fisheries exports and, after around 1900, fisheries products, to provide sources of foreign currency. There has always been a strong national desire to diversify the economy beyond overdependence on fisheries. Greenland is still highly dependent on financial transfers from the Danish government (about 3.5 billion DKK per year or about 640 million USD), but there is a strong desire to gain fiscal independency. Diversification and development of the economy is absolutely necessary for this goal.

The story of harnessing Iceland's powerful hydropower (and geothermal) energy resources for energy-intensive industry is the story of the attempt to diversify and develop this very small High North Atlantic economy. Iceland has succeeded in harnessing its energy resources, attracting very large foreign investments, creating jobs, diversifying its economy, and developing a globally connected knowledge-based sector creating highly skilled jobs for Icelanders, although the environmental trade-off is hotly disputed. Greenland is on the threshold of attempting to do the same. This chapter will trace the story of the Icelandic case and the Greenland case to see what can be learned from an analysis of the two.

In the historical and current debates about the diversification of these two very small High North Atlantic economies through harnessing energy resources for large-scale, energy-intensive industry, much attention has been directed to the creation of less-skilled jobs in construction and operation. However, what is striking about the Icelandic experience is the importance of knowledge for the development of energy resources, and the creation of a domestic, globally connected, knowledge-based sector. This observation points to both the importance of human capital for these energy megaprojects and the possibilities for human capital employment from these projects, subjects of great importance to Greenland as well.

This chapter employs the term "knowledge-based" economy or sector (Machlup 1962; Drucker 1969) in the double sense of both an "economy of knowledge" and a "knowledge-based economy." There is an energy-related "economy of knowledge" focused on the development and management of scientific, technological, legal, planning, and financial knowledge. There is also a "knowledge-based economy," since hydroelectrical power plants and energy-intensive industry are dependent on large amounts of knowledge in fields such as the ones mentioned.

The concepts of triple (Etzkowitz 2008) and quadruple helix (Carayannis and Campbell 2009; Afonso, Monteiro, and Thompson 2010) are useful to describe the interplay of domestic and foreign parties in the development of hydroelectrical power generation and large-scale energy-intensive industry in Iceland and Greenland. In Iceland, the triple helix can be seen in the creation of the knowledge at the basis of megaprojects forged by domestic government policy, together with government and university research, as well as construction and infrastructure companies. Initially, foreign advisors and contractors played a role, while Icelandic knowledge and skill developed. It is fair to speak of a quadruple helix due to the large role played by energy consumers, large and small, for this innovation. This quadruple helix has characterized Icelandic energy development since the earliest times. For example, the earliest small-scale hydroelectrical power plants in Iceland were installed by industrious farmers and local communities in the beginning of the 1900s. Since the 1950s, the energy-intensive industries, as energy consumers, have played a pivotal role in large-scale energy projects.

The challenge for Greenland as a significantly smaller society is to domesticate the quadruple helix as much as possible, which also creates new possibilities for Greenlandic human capital.

The research and innovation conducted in the triple or quadruple helix has interacted with very significant international technology transfer, historically and currently, to Iceland and Greenland. This international technology transfer is multifaceted (Hoekman, Maskus, and Saggi 2004), in the import of machinery for hydroelectrical power plants and energy-intensive industries, in foreign investments, and in the mobility of persons (Friðleifsson, Svanbjörnsson, and Thorsteinsson 1984). Domestic innovation has been evidenced in geoengineering (Jónsson 2005).

Iceland: From Raw Hydro Energy to a Globally Connected Knowledge-Based Sector

The story of hydro (and geothermal) energy in Iceland and the development of energy-intensive industry is the story of how one of Europe's smallest and poorest societies, with one of the narrowest economic bases, harnessed important energy resources, attracted very large foreign investment, diversified its economy and created a domestic, globally connected, knowledge-based sector.[1] It is thus a noteworthy story of economic development in the High North, which deserves close attention for its possible similarity with and differences from another small High North Atlantic economy, Greenland. This development has always been a trade-off with environmental concerns, which has been the cause for intense political debate since the early 1900s. This debate is covered in depth in the literature referenced herein and is outside the argument here concerning the role of knowledge in this sector for High North society.

The Earliest Attempts: "White Coal" to Bring Light, Heat, and Prosperity

At the end of the 1800s and in the early 1900s, Iceland was one of the poorest societies in Western Europe. Old Icelanders can tell of childhoods in subsistence households living off the land and sea for food and clothing, in abject poverty and suffering great losses of life to tuberculosis and other infectious diseases and to the sea. Iceland had an agricultural economy based on sheep herding, which had changed little for centuries. This sheep farming was often supplemented with winter fisheries in small open boats. Around 1900, the industrialization of Iceland started as motorization and mechanization of the fisheries brought the first engine-powered trawlers to the island. Iceland at the turn of the century was thus an agricultural society with sparse population, characterized by emerging fisheries and concentrations of settlement in coastal communities. The capital, Reykjavik, was a small town known for its darkness and limited street lighting (Kristjánsson 1997). Politically, Iceland pursued home rule within the Kingdom of Denmark, and subsequently, independence.

The question of hydro energy and energy-intensive industry was one of the greatest political, social, technological, and economic issues of the day, and crystallized questions about the future of the country (Ragnarsson 1975, 1976, 1977; Hálfda-narson and Karlsdóttir 2005; Kristinsson 2005; Karlsdóttir 2010). Thus arose the "waterfall question" (fossamálið), as it was known. The question of hydroelectric development laid out the key social, economic, political, and technological questions of a very small, underdeveloped economy in the High North politically dominated by a much larger state to the south, from which it was seeking greater political and economic independence.

Hydroelectricity generation was appearing rapidly in the late 1800s in countries such as Switzerland and Norway, gaining the name of "white coal." At the same time, the most advanced and talked-about energy-intensive industry was fertilizer manufacturing. Iceland followed the technological and cultural mores of the outside world closely, through reporting, for instance, from world expositions. There was, thus, great awareness from the last years of the 1800s of the hydro energy potential of Iceland. This awareness was displayed both in micro projects of the smallest power stations of individual farms and villages and ambitious plans for large power plants and energy-intensive industry in fertilizer manufacturing. The small-scale projects were often implemented by industries with brochures from abroad illustrating the importance of the consumer in innovation (the quadruple helix). Here we will focus on the large, ambitious schemes (Kristjánsson 1997, Sigurðsson 2002, Þórðarson 2004, Pálsdóttir 2005, Ísleifsson 2007, Karlsdóttir 2010).

As mentioned, Iceland faced great hardship and suffered from an economy limited to agriculture and emerging fisheries. There was, thus, among political leaders and entrepreneurs keen awareness of the potential of hydro energy for transforming Icelandic economy and society. Rivers and waterfalls had been dangerous obstacles to travel by foot and horseback between farms and towns; now they were to be "made to work" for Iceland. Hydroelectrical power stations were viewed as "taming" Iceland's waterfalls, providing power for fertilizer plants which would provide exports (and foreign currency) to help develop Icelandic agriculture. These ideas caused a flurry of political and commercial activity in Iceland and with the outside world. They also led to initial hydrological and geodetic surveys of major rivers carried out by the national engineer (landsverkfræðing) and the national engineer of roads (vegamálastjóri) (Jónsson 2005).

It was clear to the Icelandic entrepreneurs that poor and underdeveloped Iceland lacked both the technical know-how and especially the financial capital to harvest its hydro energy resources and develop industries. There was, therefore, close partnership between Icelandic entrepreneurs and foreign investors, which created the famous waterfall investment companies. Engineers and architects, Norwegian in particular, drew up plans for large-scale hydroelectrical power plants in Iceland (Ármannsson 2005). In the early years of the 1900s there was intense financial speculation in the ownership of waterfalls and rivers in Iceland, and the major rivers and waterfalls all came under the control of these investment companies (Pálsdóttir 2005; Karlsdóttir 2010).

This intense speculation caused great political controversy over foreign ownership of Icelandic energy resources. The Althingi legislated in 1907 to ensure that the investment companies should be based in Iceland. However, the capital was predominantly Norwegian or Danish or less commonly British, French, or German. Decades later when the first large hydroelectrical power stations rose, the Icelandic government had to buy back water rights from such foreign-owned investment companies. Those early years saw intense debates on the foreign ownership of natural resources and industry in Iceland (Pálsdóttir 2005; Karlsdóttir 2010). The first overview of the hydropower potential of Iceland was produced for the Althingi in 1919 by Jón Þorláksson, the national engineer (Jónsson 2005).

Social changes from creating industries in a formerly agrarian and fisheries society with the import of foreign workers were very controversial. Iceland also saw the first debates between positions advocating the harvesting of natural resources and conservationist positions. Both positions appealed to nationalism and national identity, whether development toward economic and political independence or the link between national identity and nature. However, nothing came of these ambitious schemes because of capital requirements, World War I, and later the Depression. Many years would pass before foreign capital and energy-intensive industry projects would push forward large-scale Icelandic hydroelectrical projects after World War II (Pálsdóttir 2005; Karlsdóttir 2010).

Local Activity, the Marshall Plan, and Domestic Energy-Intensive Industry

As mentioned, despite the early failure of the large projects to materialize, Iceland was electrified from the bottom up based on small-scale hydroelectrical power and generators. The city of Reykjavik got its first hydroelectrical power plant, Elliðaárvirkjun, in 1921, and farms and towns around the country established their own power plants early in the 1900s (Kristjánsson 1997; Ísleifsson 2007).

In 1946, the position of national director of electricity (*raforkumálastjóri*) was established to direct extensive hydrological and geodetic surveys of hydropower potential. These surveys continued until the early 1960s, conducted by Icelandic scientists assisted by the American engineering company Harza Engineering International and financed by the Icelandic government and the United Nations Special Fund. Later followed by extensive geological and glaciological surveys, this research and the water rights bought from the water investment company Titan were the capital contribution of the Icelandic government to the national power company Landsvirkjun when it was founded in 1965 (Jónsson 2005). The foundations of a domestic, energy-centered, knowledge-based sector were laid with this public research.

With the Marshall Plan–related loans after World War II, Iceland got funding for the completion of the Sogsvirkjun complex of hydroelectrical power plants, which powered the national fertilizer factory inaugurated in 1954 and the national cement factory from 1958 on. These factories were the first energy-intensive industries in the country. This time the seeds of large-scale hydroelectrical power plants and foreign-owned, energy-intensive industry were sown (Kristjánsson 1997; Sigurðsson 2002; Pálsdóttir 2005; Ísleifsson 2007).

The Early Initiatives: Búrfellsvirkjun Power Plant and
Straumsvík Aluminum Smelter

As University of Iceland professor of political science Svanur Kristjánsson used to say in class, Iceland was the only country where the end of the Depression could be dated to a specific day: 10 May 1940, when Britain occupied Iceland. The British—and from summer 1941, US—occupation of Iceland brought one of the greatest socioeconomic changes Iceland has ever lived through. The occupation forces hired large numbers of laborers in construction and other work. Iceland could also profitably export fish to Britain at the time, although the loss of life at sea to German torpedoes was massive. After the end of the war and occupation, Iceland was faced with the enormous economic policy challenge of how to maintain this economic growth and development.

This economic challenge reawakened the old ideas of large-scale hydroelectrical power generation and energy-intensive industry. Worldwide aluminum production and demand had expanded dramatically during the war. There were still serious domestic political objections, however, to industrializing Iceland with foreign technology and capital, rather than developing the traditional sectors of agriculture and fisheries. Much foreign currency collected during the war was invested in the modern and powerful "innovation trawlers" (nýsköpunartogarar), showing how Iceland was still limited to traditional agricultural and fisheries sectors (Pálsdóttir 2005; Karlsdóttir 2010).

American and European aluminum companies explored the possibilities for hydroelectrical power generation and aluminum smelting in Iceland in the late 1940s and 1950s. However, the challenges were too great; there was no tradition of large-scale foreign investment in Iceland, no legal framework for it, and certainly no political consensus about it with independence-conscious socialists strongly opposed. Iceland had politically responded to the Depression with one of the most state-regulated economies ever seen in the West, based on minimizing imports to save currency and a long range of subsidy programs for export and other sectors. This economic system was strongly opposed to large-scale foreign investments. The system gradually became unmanageable during the 1950s. In 1959, the Conservative–Social Democratic "Restoration Government" (Viðreisnarstjórn) took power, which introduced fundamental modernization and internationalization of the Icelandic economy. This government, which served until 1971, provided the political basis for engaging in large-scale hydroelectrical power projects funded by foreign loans supplying foreign-owned energy-intensive industry (Pálsdóttir 2005; Karlsdóttir 2010).

In the early 1960s, the government engaged in negotiations with a number of foreign aluminum companies. In parallel, Icelandic scientists continued and intensified hydrological, geodetic, geological, and glaciological research and surveys, which were the foundation for large-scale hydropower projects. The Icelandic government negotiated with the World Bank on funding, and the US engineering company Harza provided advice on the prospective power plant. It is important to note that Icelandic authorities had never engaged in such an exercise before. For the comparison with Greenland it is also important to note that this work was done by Icelandic civil servants, researchers, and engineers in collaboration with foreign partners and advisors (Jónsson 2005; Pálsdóttir 2005).

Around the mid-1960s, power sale negotiations focused on the Swiss aluminum producer Alusuisse, and negotiations on terms and prices for energy ensued. In these negotiations between an experienced aluminum producer (with hydroelectrical power purchasing agreements and aluminum production in, for instance, Norway) and Iceland (the latter with no previous experience), the World Bank provided assistance to Iceland. The World Bank was going to finance the Búrfellsvirkjun power station to power the aluminum smelter, so the bank was strongly interested in securing adequate revenues from power sales to Alusuisse. Based on these agreements, the Búrfellsvirkjun power station was built in the late 1960s by foreign construction companies but with Icelandic subcontractors and using mainly Icelandic labor. In parallel, the Alusuisse aluminum smelter was built in Straumsvík south of Reykjavik, foreign designed, but employing mainly Icelandic workers for the construction and later operation. The aluminum smelter started operation in 1969. There was a sense of urgency to get this project through; worldwide expectations were that cheap nuclear power would replace hydropower for aluminum smelting (Þjóðviljin 1969; Pálsdóttir 2005).

Gradual Expansion and the Long Time between New Projects

The Viðreisnarstjórn was replaced by a left-wing government in 1971, which was much more critical of large-scale direct foreign investments and was, therefore, much less interested in the model of large-scale power production funded by foreign loans to supply foreign-owned energy-intensive industry. As a result, there were no further attempts to attract power-intensive foreign industry in the coming years. In the late 1970s a new Conservative government reawakened an energy-intensive industry policy and sought to attract such industry. The government entered into negotiations with the US company Union Carbide about a ferrosilicon plant. This time, the foreign partner wanted the Icelandic government to take a majority stake. The US partner withdrew from the negotiations, but was replaced by the Norwegian company Elkem. The ferrosilicon plant opened in 1979 in Grundatangi, in western Iceland. The power was originally to be supplied by the new Sigalda hydropower plant, which was the last station financed by the World Bank, codesigned by the Swiss engineering company Electrowatt Engineering and the Icelandic firm Virkis Hlutafélag. The Hrauneyjarfoss power station was also built; Landsvirkjun now had creditworthiness that made World Bank funding unnecessary. Landsvirkjun could also now oversee the construction itself, which was subdivided so that the largest Icelandic contractors could bid successfully, which they did (Jónsson 2005; Pálsdóttir 2005).

After the ferrosilicon factory in Grundatangi, there was a long lull in attracting power-intensive industry to Iceland. In the meantime, the original aluminum

smelter in Straumsvík doubled its capacity, buying more power, and domestic electricity consumption grew by leaps and bounds. This led to a gradual expansion of
hydropower and, later on, to small-scale geothermal power capacity. What is interesting to note is how Icelandic know-how grew with these projects; the Blanda hydroelectrical power station inaugurated in 1991 was the first fully Icelandic-designed
hydroelectrical power station. The Icelandic Ministry of Industry and the national
power company Landsvirkjun founded a common marketing office to attract foreign power-intensive industry. There were continuous activities of planning and
research—including the idea of a subsea cable exporting electricity to the United
Kingdom or the European continent.

In the late 1990s, the American company Columbia Ventures approached Iceland about locating an aluminum smelter there after an aborted plan to do so in
Venezuela. This project led to the aluminum smelter in Hvalfjörður, which opened
in 1998, and also led to expansion of—this time—both hydro and geothermal power
generation capacity.

Reviving the East

Europe's biggest glacier is Vatnajökull, and a number of powerful glacial rivers
flow from it. Since the beginning of the twentieth century, people had dreamed of
harnessing those rivers. There were later, for decades, ideas and feasibility studies
about building enormous hydroelectrical power stations on the north and east coast
of Iceland to power energy-intensive industry there. Iceland had throughout the
twentieth century seen extensive urbanization around Reykjavik and depopulation
of the countryside. This development had hit the east coast very hard, and there
was strong political will and desire to revive the region through energy-intensive
industry.

In the late 1990s, the Icelandic government negotiated and reached agreement
with Norwegian Norsk Hydro for a massive hydroelectrical power station in the east
with an aluminum smelter. However, Norsk Hydro withdrew from that agreement
in 2002. The Icelandic government immediately entered into negotiations with
the American company Alcoa, and reached agreement (in the record time of nine
months) on a 360,000-ton-per-year aluminum smelter. To power this smelter, the
Kárahnjúkar dam and hydroelectrical power station was built, doubling the power
generation capacity of Iceland (Pálsdóttir 2005; Karlsdóttir 2010). This power station was the first to be codesigned by Icelandic and foreign engineers in a long time,
because of its size and complexity (Jónsson 2005). It was built by Portuguese and
Chinese workers.

Forty-five years before, at Búrfellsvirkjun, foreigners had provided the designs
and Icelanders had done the hard labor. Now, however, Icelanders held the high-skill
design jobs, while foreign labor was used for construction.

The enormous Kárahnjúkar project raises the question of timing and economic
policy. The early power station projects in the 1960s and 1970s coincided with
downturns in the business cycle and helped to stimulate the Icelandic economy and

created employment. Later projects were less well-timed and rather reinforced up-ticks in the business cycle (Sturluson 2005; see also Harðarson 1998). The Kárahn-júkar project contributed to the very unfortunate overstimulation of the Icelandic economy in the early 2000s, together with tax cuts and liberalizations. These de-velopments all worsened the severe Icelandic financial crisis from 2008 that was triggered by the international financial crisis.

In response to the severe economic downturn in Iceland since 2008 and the need to stimulate the economy and create new jobs, there have been loud calls for new energy-intensive industry projects. There are currently plans for aluminum smelters at Helguvík in southwest Iceland and at Húsavík in northeast Iceland. In addition, there are ideas of hosting energy-demanding server parks in Iceland and laying subsea power lines to Scotland. The idea of server parks brings us back to how technological advances developed the energy-intensive industries powered by the rivers. A hundred years ago, the energy-intensive industry to be powered was the fertilizer industry. Then for a long stretch it was aluminum; in the future it may serve European electricity consumers and others in a globally networked, knowledge-based technological society that was unimaginable in earlier times.

Future projects in aluminum or server parks are dependent on new power gen-eration either from hydro or geothermal resources. As mentioned, from the ear-liest days around 1900, there have been fierce debates in Iceland between those who want to harness the power of the rivers—and later the geothermal steam—and conservationists. This debate reached a crescendo with the Kárahnjúkar project in the east. Subsequently, there was intense opposition to new power station projects from—notably—the Left-Green government coalition junior partner in the left-wing government serving after the economic crisis from 2009 to 2013.

In order to manage the conflict between utilization and conservation and create greater transparency and predictability, Iceland has since the late 1990s worked on a national master plan for hydro and geothermal energy resources (Rammaáætlun), prioritizing conservation values and energy resources. This plan with its prioritiza-tions has been submitted to the Althingi for consideration. The plan defines around 13 tW as accessible, about 5 tW in a gray zone, and about 13 tW for conservation. The political future of this framework plan will heavily influence future hydro and geo-thermal power generation projects and the energy-intensive industries they would power (Rammaáætlun).

From Harnessing "White Coal" to a Globally Connected, Knowledge-Based Domestic Sector

When Iceland as a very small, poor society with a narrow agricultural and fisher-ies economy dreamed about harnessing "white coal," there was much attention to the creation of construction and manufacturing jobs to absorb agricultural workers and supplement work in agriculture and fisheries. What is striking, however, when trac-ing the history of large-scale hydroelectrical power generation and power-intensive industry in Iceland, is the amount of knowledge-intensive work surrounding these activities. Following this history, it becomes clear that power generation and energy-intensive industry in Iceland has created a globalized, knowledge-based domestic sector in Iceland staffed by Icelanders.

Besides creating construction and manufacturing jobs, power generation projects initially required extensive research efforts in hydrology, geodesy, geology, glaciology, and so on. With rising environmental consciousness, there has also been extensive scientific research on the ecological role, for instance, of wetlands, which may be flooded for reservoirs. This research activity has mainly been carried out by Icelandic scientists collaborating with foreign scholars and universities. Design of power stations and dams, and the industries they feed, as well as continuous studies and planning have demanded much engineering research. This research has been carried out by Icelandic engineering companies to an ever-increasing degree, which have then taken this knowledge overseas, exporting highly paid services (Friðleifsson, Svanbjörnsson, and Thorsteinsson 1984).

Looking at the often enormous tangibles of these projects, it is easy to forget the very large and complex intangible work behind such projects in fields such as finance, law, and planning. From the first negotiations between Alusuisse, the World Bank, and the Icelandic government in the early 1960s, Icelandic authorities and companies staffed by Icelanders have engaged in complex dealings of international finance and law. Studying and developing future projects have employed many Icelandic professionals. The ability of Icelanders to carry out these knowledge-intensive tasks naturally rests on strong human capital. This human capital builds on various factors, including a strong historical tradition of education, a strong tradition of studying abroad in leading higher education institutions and returning to Iceland with knowledge and ideas, and ever-developing domestic higher education opportunities.

Greenland: From Local Hydropower Stations to Mega-Industry Hydropower Stations?

Greenland was a Danish colony until 1953, when a change in the constitution formally changed the status of Greenland to an equal and integrated part of the Kingdom of Denmark. Technically, almost all legislation maintained a distinction between Greenland and the country of Denmark, and Greenland was still governed primarily by Denmark, from Copenhagen. The Ministry for Greenland was created in 1955 and existed until 1987.

The beginning of colonization in the eighteenth century introduced the first major economic changes in Greenland as a formal economy was introduced. Until the end of the nineteenth century, the economy was based on seal hunting and whaling. In the beginning of the twentieth century, fishing for cod was introduced. The first fish-processing plant was built in Sisimiut (at that time the town was called Holsteinsborg in Danish); it started production for export in 1921. Huge stocks of cod had invaded the waters around West Greenland in the beginning of the twentieth century, and by the end of the 1920s fishing was the main industry in Greenland.

The First Hydropower: Green Energy for Households

In spite of the rapidly growing fishing industry in the first part of the twentieth century, it was not until after World War II that the Danish authorities launched a massive modernization process for Greenlandic society. The first public power station started in Nuuk (Godthåb) in October 1949.

The Greenland Technological Organisation (GTO) was established in 1950 to orchestrate the modernization process. Managed from Copenhagen, the GTO created an almost entirely technical, economically driven development process with a rolling five-year planning model. The GTO decided in the early stages of the modernization process to create a one-string energy solution, and that was based on oil. The provision of energy for heating and electricity was thus based on oil-driven facilities. This 100 percent oil-based energy production was maintained for forty years. In 1979, home rule was introduced in Greenland. Fields within GTO responsibility were not transferred to the Greenland authorities until 1987; the political responsibility was transferred, but at first the same GTO employees were responsible for decisions and actions. It took some years to reorient the organization to the changed political reality.

The preliminary field studies for Greenland's first hydropower station started in 1981. Forty kilometers south of Nuuk, this first major hydropower station began to supply Nuuk with energy in 1993. During the following twenty years, Greenland has gradually increased its production of energy from hydropower stations.

Since 2012, when the Ilulissat hydropower station started, 70 percent of energy production for households in Greenland has come from hydropower. The potential for an even higher percentage of energy production coming from hydropower is documented. It only awaits a political decision to start new projects.

The Next Generation of Hydropower: Cheap Energy for the Mega-Industries

As early as the 1960s the GTO started survey projects to measure hydropower potential in a number of Greenland's inland lakes and connected rivers. Compared to Iceland the hydropower potential in Greenland is much more remote from the existing infrastructure, and access is much more challenging. The total hydropower potential in Greenland is less than what Iceland has, and there are no geothermal power potentials.

As shown in table 6.1, Greenland has already made use of the most obvious hydropower potentials closest to the major towns. Further inland, especially on the west coast of Greenland from the most southern parts to Disco Bay, there are some huge hydropower potentials. The rough terrain and climate, though, make it extremely expensive to utilize these potentials. The GTO-led survey projects in the last part of the twentieth century extended to users other than existing Greenland communities. In many of the reports, mega-industry such as aluminum smelters are mentioned as potential purchasers of hydropower resources. But at that time there were no formal contacts between international companies and any Greenlandic or

Table 6.1: Public hydropower stations in Greenland

Town	MW	GWh	Utilization rate[a]	Start year	Cumulated share[b]
Nuuk	45.0 MW	192 GWh	48.7 %	1993	39 %
Tasiilaq	1.2 MW	6 GWh	57.1 %	2005	41 %
Qaqortoq/Narsaq	7.2 MW	27 GWh	42.8 %	2007	46 %
Sisimiut	15.0 MW	52 GWh	39.6 %	2010	57 %
Ilulissat	22.5 MW	65 GWh	33.0 %	2013	70 %
Aasiaat/Qasigiannguit[c]	13.0 MW	*45 GWh	39.5 %	—	*88 %
Total	*103.9 MW*	*387 GWh*			

[a] The utilization rate is calculated on the basis of (X GWh × 100) / (Y MW × 8,760 hours) = Z %.
[b] The estimated cumulated share is the hydropower-generated energy share of the total consumption of energy in Greenland by domestic housing and smaller industries.
[c] The Aasiaat/Qasigiannguit hydropower station is not yet politically decided; the preparatory work began around 2010 (* = estimated).

Table 6.2: Milestones in the ongoing considerations about a first aluminum smelter in Greenland

Spring 2006	First inquiry by Alcoa
July 2006	Joint Action Plan between Greenland and Alcoa
April 2007	First open political decision in the Parliament regarding the project
May 2007	Memorandum of Understanding between Greenland and Alcoa
May 2008	Open political decision in Parliament on location (Maniitsoq chosen)
2014–15 (expected)	Open political decision in Parliament on ownership (partner/concession)
2015 (exp.)	Final political decision in Parliament on the project (start/not start)
2020 (exp.)	Earliest possible commencement of production (if project is approved)

Danish authorities. For Greenland, the first real contact with an international aluminum company had its genesis in the beginning of 2006. At that time the American aluminum company Alcoa contacted the Greenlandic authorities. Alcoa wished to initiate preliminary surveys whose object was to assess the potential for establishing an aluminum smelter in the central region of West Greenland in the area between Sisimiut to the north and Nuuk to the south. This aluminum project is potentially the most extensive of its type ever to be undertaken in Greenland. The most significant project milestones in this ongoing project are listed in table 6.2.

The projected aluminum smelter would be built twenty kilometers north of Maniitsoq, as a medium-sized facility with a full production capacity of around 400,000 tons per year, powered by two industrial hydropower stations located in the inland northeast and southeast of Maniitsoq, close to the ice cap. The projected total capacity for the two hydropower stations is 700 MW or 3,000 GWh, almost ten times the total capacity of all five existing hydropower stations in Greenland.

The potential production described here is an illustration of why places like Greenland and Iceland are of interest in a global market to international companies with energy-intensive operations. Almost everywhere in the world, these companies must compete with the surrounding societies on the consumption of energy. But in isolated places with huge unutilized energy potentials and a small population, these companies are not exposed to the same type of competition on the consumption of the energy.

Greenland has organized the aluminum project process in a limited company, Greenland Development, owned by the government of Greenland. The staff consists of local experts of different kinds; international expertise is hired on a consultant basis. For the process in Greenland, there has not been the same formal involvement by major players like the World Bank. It has not been possible for Greenland in the same way as it was for Iceland because Greenland still is an integrated part of the Kingdom of Denmark.

Mega-Industries and the Greenland Labor Market

In the public debate in Greenland over the aluminum project, several topics have been in focus. Culturalists are concerned about the destruction of unique cultural heritage sites around the lakes identified for one of the hydropower stations. The lake, Tasersuaq, for centuries has been one of the main sites for caribou hunting in West Greenland. Naturalists also have their concerns, for example about the disturbance of the fragile Arctic biotopes.

Among the central topics in the public debate are questions about jobs: What number of jobs can be expected in direct and indirect relation to a coming smelter, and what type of jobs will be needed? To what extent will these jobs be filled by people already living in Greenland, and to what extent will people come from outside of Greenland? The answer to the last question has been very difficult to estimate. Politically, the topic has been addressed with suitable vague phrases like "all qualified Greenlanders will be eligible for a job at the smelter." The joker clause then becomes the question: What will it take to be qualified for the jobs?

Almost no matter how these questions are addressed, some obvious answers are that these are extensive challenges for Greenland. One of the mantras on the political agenda in Greenland is "Education, education, and more education." Approximately one-quarter of the working force does not have a formal education higher than ten or eleven years of public school. Estimates suggest that less than half speak Danish as a working language, and only one-quarter are proficient in English. The possible establishment of an aluminum smelter in Greenland will mark the formal introduction of the Greenland job market to the global market. One of the challenges is that this kind of industrial employment requires a type of contemporary working culture that differs from the experience of the existing labor sector in Greenland.

Most significant, it will mean the end of "blue Mondays" and absence from work the days after payment. These elements in the existing working culture for the unskilled workers in Greenland today will be a tough challenge to overcome. We are not saying it is impossible; we are just pointing at the fact that socialization of the labor market of generations of unskilled has so far shown only limited success. Looking at the history in Iceland, a similar situation was in play in relation to the early industrialization in Iceland in the 1940s when former farm workers made their entry in the first industrial work. The same type of initial difficulties as we see in Greenland were overcome in Iceland. If and how Greenland can learn anything from Iceland in these matters is impossible to answer here. It will take thorough cultural and societal studies to get closer to a possible answer. It will not be during the first decades after the introduction of the global economy into Greenland that we will be facing the emergence of any kind of Greenlandic-initiated and managed, knowledge-based modern industries as a spin-off from mega-industries such as aluminum smelters.

Creating Domestic Energy-Centered, Globally Connected, Knowledge-Based Sectors in Very Small High North Atlantic Economies

As pointed out in the beginning of the chapter, Iceland and Greenland share important traits as very small Arctic societies highly dependent especially on fisheries. Politically, they share history as autonomous overseas territories of the Kingdom of Denmark that have pursued or are pursuing ever-greater independence from Denmark, raising questions of creating independent sustainable economies while managing foreign direct investment.

Iceland dreamed of harnessing "white coal" around 1900 as part of its pursuit of development, modernization, internationalization, and independence, with limited early results for internal and external reasons. The costs of those missed opportunities were well set out by then Central Bank governor and chairman of the national power company Landsvirkjun, Dr. Jóhannes Nordal, who in 1965 said that if Icelanders had harnessed Þjórsá in the 1920s, the nation would now have "a fully paid-for power station generating hundreds of millions in pure revenue annually and not least a class of specialists and scientists, who would place us [Iceland] on an equal footing with others in chemical industry" (quoted in Pálsdóttir 2005).

Thus, Dr. Nordal pointed out, as a side remark, how those early projects could have built up scientific and technological knowledge and expertise in Iceland. There, Dr. Nordal gave an early indication of what particularly strikes the authors of this chapter in their study of energy generation and energy-intensive industry in Iceland and Greenland: the development of a domestic, globalized, knowledge-based sector in Iceland and the challenges to and possibilities for creating such a sector in Greenland.

Iceland has created a globalized knowledge-based sector in energy generation and energy-intensive industry staffed by Icelanders. Preconditions for this development included human capital in Iceland based on domestic academic and vocational education, a strong tradition of studying abroad and returning, and rapidly developing higher education and research opportunities at home. Iceland has a very small population of about 318,000, which was even smaller, at about 200,000, at the time of the first major hydroelectrical power station of Búrfellsvirkjun in the late 1960s. Iceland still supplied most of the workforce, however, for construction until the megaproject of Kárahnjúkar in the 2000s.

Greenland faces a double challenge concerning benefiting from hydroelectrical power generation and energy-intensive industry. As was the case in Iceland, the benefit from such projects is in creating employment and—as pointed out in this chapter—the creation of a globalized knowledge-based sector. Greenland has a much smaller population than Iceland, making it harder to supply both specialized and general labor, and weaker human capital in terms of an educated workforce, both vocationally and academically. The planned hydroelectrical power plant near Maniitsoq would be designed by outside engineers and built by outside workers. However, that does not exclude the possibility of creating a globalized knowledge-based sector centered on hydroelectrical power and power-intensive industry in Greenland.

The Icelandic case tells of the development of a hydro- and geothermal-based power sector with dependent energy-intensive industry developed over decades. Of particular importance, the Icelandic case shows the importance of human capital developed through domestic academic and vocational education, education abroad, and development of domestic higher education and research. These lessons emphasize the importance for Greenland in succeeding in those aspects in order to develop over the long term a globalized, knowledge-based sector drawing on hydroelectrical power resources and energy-intensive industry. There are important environmental and cultural trade-offs in large-scale hydroelectrical projects, which are the subject of intense political debate in both societies. These trade-offs require careful democratic deliberation, which is yet another knowledge-intensive activity making demands on the human capital of a society.

Continued Arctic climate change will impact energy projects in Iceland and Greenland. For hydropower resources, climate change and glacial melt will have complex consequences in both countries, especially in Iceland, where smaller ice-caps will be greatly affected by climate change. Climate change will increase the complexity and risk surrounding these usually very large projects. Greater complexity and risk will call for greater human capital and knowledge in Icelandic and Greenlandic society to sustainably benefit from these hydropower resources.

Note

1. This section builds on interviews with Sigurður St. Arnalds, chairman of the board, Mannvit Engineering; Kristján Bjarnar Ólafsson, senior financial analyst, Reykjavik Energy Invest; Guðni A. Jóhannesson, director general, National Energy Authority; and Professor Sveinbjörn Björnsson, National Energy Authority.

7. Arctic Melting Tests the United Nations Convention on the Law of the Sea

ASIM ZIA, ILAN KELMAN, AND MICHAEL H. GLANTZ

> The Arctic future is THE NO. 1 priority issue for the Russian government, for both Putin and Medvedev; oil, gas, shipping, security and a return to . . . the empire status, dominance over much of the sea bed at the top of the planet are interlinked.
> —A Russian Policy Expert, 2011

> This isn't the fifteenth century. You can't go around the world and just plant flags and say "we're claiming this territory." There is no threat to Canadian sovereignty in the Arctic. We're not at all concerned about this mission—basically it is just a show by Russia.
> —PETER MACKAY, Canadian Foreign Minister, 2007

In a 2011 assessment, the Arctic Council's Arctic Monitoring and Assessment Program (AMAP) reported that 2005–2010 was the warmest period ever recorded in the Arctic. Further, the report, titled "Snow, water, ice and permafrost in the Arctic," found that there is evidence that two components of the Arctic cryosphere—snow and sea ice—are interacting with the climate system to accelerate warming. The assessment found that the extent and duration of snow cover and sea ice have decreased across the Arctic. Temperatures in the permafrost have risen by up to 2 degrees Celsius. The southern limit of permafrost has moved northward in Russia and Canada. The assessment also projected that the Arctic Ocean is expected to become nearly ice-free in summer within this century, likely within the next thirty to forty years. Perhaps rather startlingly, AMAP 2011 also found that the model projections reported by the Intergovernmental Panel on Climate Change (IPCC) in 2007 underestimated the rates of change now observed in sea ice. AMAP 2011 underscored that "there remains a great deal of uncertainty about how fast the Arctic cryosphere will change in the future and what the ultimate impacts of the changes will be. Interactions ('feedbacks') between elements of the cryosphere and climate system are particularly uncertain. Concerted monitoring and research is needed to reduce this uncertainty."

One of the key uncertainties in the speed and acceleration of Arctic melting concerns the global rate of greenhouse gas (GHG) emissions in the next fifty to one

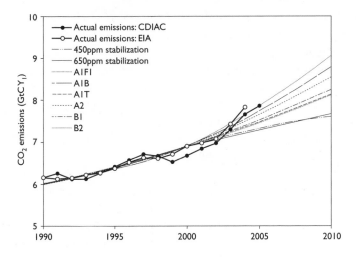

Figure 7.1: Actual versus projected CO_2 emissions (Source: Raupach et al., 2007)

hundred years. Recent studies have found that the IPCC's so-called A1F1 scenario that assumes a fossil fuel–intensive world economy unfolding in the twenty-first century appears to be panning out in economically nonrecessionary time periods. The study by Raupach et al. (2007), for example, compares IPCC projected scenarios with the observed CO_2 emissions (figure 7.1). Noticeably, the actual CO_2 emissions (shown as a dotted line between 1980 and 2007) are just above the so-called IPCC A1F1 scenario. There are two implications of this finding that pertain to polar diplomacy.

First, the developed and now increasingly the developing world is addicted to fossil fuels. This addiction is most prominent in the transportation and energy sectors. While the global financial crisis starting in 2008 temporarily dampened the demand for fossil fuels, the projections of long-term global demand for oil and natural gas are overwhelmingly strong (Energy Information Administration [EIA], 2011). Assuming current rates of growth, world use of petroleum and other liquid fossil fuels (e.g., ethanol, biodiesel, coal-to-liquids) is projected to grow from 85.7 million barrels per day in 2008 to 97.6 million barrels per day in 2020 and 112.2 million barrels per day in 2035 (EIA, 2011:1–2). Similarly, global consumption of natural gas is projected to increase by 52 percent, from 1.33 trillion gallons in 2008 to 2.02 trillion gallons in 2035 (assuming 100 cubic feet are equivalent to 1.2 gallons of natural gas).

Increasing consumption of fossil fuels will continue to contribute to anthropogenic global climate change, which in turn will augment Arctic melting. Under the IPCC's A1F1 scenario, for example, average temperatures are expected to increase by 4 degrees Celsius (2.4 to 6 degrees Celsius) at the global scale by 2090–2099 relative to 1980–1999. Due to so-called polar amplification processes, average winter temperature changes in the Arctic are projected to be almost twice the global average under the A1F1 scenario (Intergovernmental Panel on Climate Change,

2007). Researchers working to understand the effects of climate change are using the Arctic as the figurative canary in this warming coal mine because climate
change appears to be affecting the Arctic region, both the land and the sea, much
sooner and much more severely than most of the rest of the planet (AMAP, 2011;
IPCC, 2007). Such scenarios raise a fundamental diplomatic question about the
position of Arctic countries vis-à-vis global climate change mitigation policy. Would
Arctic countries make a sustained effort through diplomacy and international law
to impose mandatory restrictions on GHG emissions, both domestically and internationally, adequate to preempt worst-case Arctic melting?

The second implication of the rate of GHG emissions, in relation to polar diplomacy, is that the increased melting is expected not only to open up the Arctic for
shipping passageways, but also—especially promoted by media hype—to spur a
race among the surrounding Arctic states (particularly Russia, the United States,
Canada, Norway, Denmark, and Greenland) and incentivize many international oil
and gas conglomerates to maximize their property rights for mining oil and natural gas reserves. The United States Geological Survey (USGS) estimated that the
Arctic could contain approximately 90 billion barrels of oil, 20.02 trillion gallons
of natural gas, and 44 billion barrels of natural gas liquids (USGS, 2008). More
than 70 percent of the undiscovered oil resources were estimated to occur in Arctic
Alaska, the Amerasia Basin, East Greenland Rift Basins, East Barents Basins, and
West Greenland–East Canada. Approximately 84 percent of the oil and gas is estimated to occur offshore. Figure 7.2 shows more specific spatial information in the
Arctic region about prospective areas for oil and gas exploration, overlaid over existing oil, gas, and other mining sites.

If we compare USGS (2008) projections with EIA (2011) global projected demand for oil and natural gas in 2035, we estimate that the total recoverable oil in the
Arctic would be enough for approximately 2.19 years of global oil consumption (assuming 112.2 million barrels per day) and 9.87 years of global natural gas consumption (assuming 2.02 trillion gallons per year) in the 2030s. Increasing demand for
oil and natural gas is expected to raise prices, which coupled with the melting Arctic
will increase the feasibility and prospects for oil and natural gas extraction in two to
three decades' time, if not sooner. This raises fundamental sovereignty and property rights questions over the discovered recoverable oil and natural gas deposits in
the Arctic.

The UN Convention on the Law of the Sea (UNCLOS) is an internationally negotiated regime, which may or may not be able to resolve any sovereignty or property
rights conflicts that might arise in this contentious race for recoverable oil and natural gas among the Arctic states as well as non-Arctic states and global oil and mining corporations. On 2 August 2007, two Russian minisubmarines traveled below
the ice of the North Pole and planted a Russian flag on the seafloor, claiming the
territory for Moscow. The media played up this Russian flagging episode as being
a momentous event that brought this issue to global attention. In this chapter, we
explore the question of whether UNCLOS-driven policy in the Arctic is flexible and

Figure 7.2: Prospective areas for oil and gas exploration in the Arctic (Source: United Nations Environment Program, GRID-Arendal, http://maps.grida.no/library/files/storage/hydrocarbon_overview.jpg)

suitable for resolving any sovereignty and property rights questions that have arisen or are expected to arise in the melting Arctic.

In this context, in the next section we present key features of the current UNCLOS policy regime with respect to the Arctic. We then provide a sample of territorial disputes that have emerged in the melting Arctic, which are frequently linked to potential oil and natural gas exploration. Finally, we analyze the prospects and limits of the current UNCLOS policy regime in resolving potential oil and gas exploration conflicts and discuss two alternate options: modifications in UNCLOS to incorporate environmental security and indigenous rights concerns, and establishment of a transnational Arctic protected area or a biosphere reserve.

UNCLOS and the Arctic

Under UNCLOS, Arctic states are limited to an exclusive economic zone (EEZ) of two hundred nautical miles adjacent to their coasts. Upon ratification of UNCLOS, a country has a ten-year period to make claims to an extended continental shelf, which, if validated, give the country exclusive rights to resources on or below the seabed of that extended shelf area. Due to this, Norway, Russia, Canada, and Denmark, who ratified the convention in 1996, 1997, 2003, and 2004, respectively, have launched projects to provide a basis for seabed claims on extended continental shelves beyond their exclusive economic zones. The United States has signed, but not yet ratified this treaty. Since 1982, 158 countries have ratified and now abide by UNCLOS.

Article 76 of UNCLOS established the Commission on the Limits of the Continental Shelf (CLCS) to assess each Arctic nation's territorial claims.[1] The CLCS was established in 1982 by UNCLOS to: "[C]onsider the data and other material submitted by coastal States concerning the outer limits of the continental shelf in areas where those limits extend beyond two hundred nautical miles, and to make recommendations in accordance with Article 76 and the Statement of Understanding adopted on 29 August 1980 by the Third United Nations Conference on the Law of the Sea."

The CLCS panel comprises twenty-one members who serve five-year terms and are experts in geology, geophysics, or hydrography. This panel evaluates information submitted by a coastal state and recommends to the state whether or not a country may lay claim to a larger area of the Arctic. The process set forth by UNCLOS requires that, before making a claim to Arctic territory, a country must ratify the treaty itself. Up until July 2012, with respect to the ten-year period for a signatory Arctic nation to submit a proposal, Russia and Norway have submitted their proposals to CLCS in 2001 and 2006, respectively.[2] Note that the period of ten years for the Arctic states began to run in 1996 for Norway, 1997 for Russia, 2003 for Canada, and 2004 for Denmark. This implies that Canadian and Danish proposals were expected to come in 2013 and 2014, respectively.

The proposal itself may take many years to compose. Such proposals should contain scientific research and evidence that the Arctic seafloor's underwater ridges are not a separate feature from the country's continental shelf but, rather, are simply geological extensions of the shelf. This is determined according to geological findings concerning the composition of the shelf. Once the proposal has been submitted, it may take the CLCS a few more years to finalize their recommendations (Coston, 2008). Even though CLCS may make a recommendation, the commission has no actual jurisdiction or authority to decide continental shelf disputes.

Beyond the two-hundred-mile mark, however, countries may extend their sovereignty over a particular area only if they can prove that the continental shelf of their landmass is connected to the land in question. If proven, a country may claim jurisdiction up to 350 nautical miles from the coastal low-mark. According to CLCS, the term "continental shelf" is used to describe "submerged prolongation of the land territory of the coastal State—the seabed and subsoil of the submarine areas that extend beyond its territorial sea to the outer edge of the continental margin, or to a distance of two hundred nautical miles where the outer edge of the continental margin does not extend up to that distance."[3] And according to CLCS, the continental margin consists of the seabed and subsoil of the shelf, the slope, and the rise; it does not include the deep ocean floor with its oceanic ridges or the subsoil thereof. According to Article 76 of UNCLOS, the coastal state may establish the outer limits of its juridical continental shelf wherever the continental margin extends beyond two hundred nautical miles by establishing the foot of the continental slope, specifically by meeting the requirements of Article 76, paragraphs 4–7, of the convention.

Under Article 76 of UNCLOS, a state is thus allowed to express sovereignty over its continental shelf and any natural resources found therein. Such sovereignty, however, does not extend to the seawater above. According to Wagner (2010), in considering ratification, the United States is primarily concerned with these provisions because they restrict the freedom of seabed mining. When such regulations were not amended to the liking of the United States, it withdrew from the treaty negotiations and did not become a party to UNCLOS (Wagner, 2010).

Geographically, Article 76 provides two formulae, the so-called Gardiner Line and Hedberg Line, which coastal states can use to establish the basis of the Outer Continental Shelf (OCS) beyond the two-hundred-nautical-mile limit. They also help to establish the so-called cutoff points. Both of the formulae are based on the assumption that any extension is measured from the base of the continental slope (Dodds, 2010c). Article 76 also establishes certain outer limits to any OCS submission. The first involves 350 nautical miles from the baseline from which the territorial sea is measured. The second restraint is that the OCS cannot extend beyond 2500 meters in terms of water depth. These legal and geographical stipulations of Article 76 that establish OCS claims for a state have been subjected to varied interpretation by different Arctic countries, leading to territorial disputes; a small sample of these is discussed later in the chapter.

Territorial Conflict between Norway and Russia in the Barents Sea

In part due to the Cold War, Norway and Russia had a long-standing disagreement over maritime boundaries and the precise definition of limited maritime zones in the Barents Sea. The area is of particular interest in terms of fossil fuel resources, namely oil and gas. The USGS (2008) estimates recoverable deposits of 7.4 billion barrels of oil and 3.18 trillion gallons of natural gas in the eastern Barents Sea. The disputed region between Norway and Russia is shown in dashed lines in figure 7.3. This conflict emerges from the countries' joint land border as well as Norway's sovereignty over Svalbard, despite a unique treaty (Svalbard Treaty, 1920) giving signatory countries including Russia certain rights to natural resources:

- "fishing and hunting" (Article 2);
- "access and entry for any reason or object whatever to the waters, fjords and ports . . . subject to the observance of local laws and regulations, they may carry

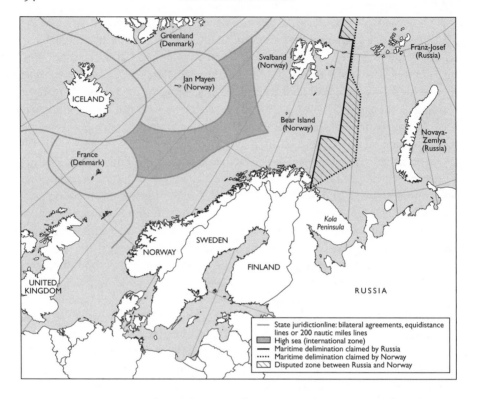

Figure 7.3: Norway–Russia disputed zones in the Barents Sea (Source: United Nations Environment Program, GRID-Arendal, http://maps.grida.no/go/graphic/northern_ atlantic_ocean_maritime_delimitation_and_disputes)

on there without impediment all maritime, industrial, mining and commercial operations" (Article 3);

- "methods of acquisition, enjoyment and exercise of the right of ownership of property, including mineral rights" (Article 7).

On 15 September 2010, Russia and Norway ostensibly resolved the conflict by signing the Treaty between the Kingdom of Norway and the Russian Federation concerning Maritime Delimitation and Cooperation in the Barents Sea and the Arctic Ocean. The treaty defines the "maritime delimitation line between the Parties in the Barents Sea and the Arctic Ocean" (Article 1), but the word "hydrocarbon" is mentioned thirty-three times in the eight-page treaty.

Neumann (2010) interpreted the ability of these two countries to resolve an Arctic conflict as an example of avoiding a race for the Arctic or a new Cold War, even suggesting it as a basis for resolving disagreements over interpreting the Svalbard Treaty. Hoel (2012) agrees, highlighting the cooperative nature of the negotiations seeking agreements and resolution on fishing and fossil fuels reserves.

Territorial Conflict between Canada (Yukon) and the United States (Alaska) in the Beaufort Sea

Another Arctic maritime dispute centered on fossil fuels but also linked to fishing is between Canada and the United States. The land boundary between the Yukon (Canada) and Alaska (USA) ends on the northern edge in the Beaufort Sea. For demarcating the Yukon-Alaska boundary in the sea, the Canadian position accepts a borderline that follows the meridian 141°W up to a distance of two hundred nautical miles directly north. The United States claims a line determined by the principle of equal length, based on the coastline's orientation, leading to a line that runs approximately north-northeast, thereby giving the United States more territory than Canada will permit. Baker and Byers (2012) trace the dispute back to the wording of an 1825 treaty between the United Kingdom and Russia, with Canada adopting rights from the United Kingdom following its 1867 independence and the United States adopting the rights from Russia following the Alaskan Purchase in the same year.

Although both countries have tended to agree to disagree on the Beaufort Sea, Canada's ratification of UNCLOS in 2003 meant that they needed to make a submission to the CLCS by 2013, bringing the dispute to a head. As Baker and Byers (2012) report, a further complication has arisen in that new data seem to extend the areas of the continental shelf in the Beaufort Sea, giving both countries much larger claims—which might spur both countries to a resolution so that they both win from the larger claims. Canada also faces some constraints due to a settlement with indigenous people that uses 141°W as the limit of indigenous access and rights (Baker and Byers, 2012). In the meantime, scientific cooperation and ecosystem management continue in the disputed area (Baker, *VLR* 2010).

On land, this region of the Beaufort Sea is adjacent to the Arctic National Wildlife Refuge (ANWR), which is a flashpoint in US politics regarding the environment, indigenous rights, and petroleum exploration and extraction. On the Canadian side sits the land included in their settlement with indigenous people. Although the Beaufort Sea is a maritime dispute between the two countries, conflicting uses might also spill over into the land area.

Territorial Conflict between Canada and Denmark (Greenland) in the Nares Strait

In 1973, Canada and Denmark agreed to delimit their continental shelf boundary, using the basis of a line equidistant from the opposite coastlines. In doing so, they did not take into account the uninhabited 1.3-square-kilometer Hans Island in the Nares Strait, just above 80°N at one of the narrower points between the two countries (Schofield et al., 2009). Kao et al. describe Hans Island as the only dispute "concerning land territory among the Arctic States" that does not preclude indigenous claims and rights to Arctic land (Kao et al., 2012: 834). They also point out, however, that both Canada and Denmark have been conducting intensive ocean mapping and that neither country has yet submitted to CLCS their extended continental shelf claims, so the assumption is that they will do so soon (Denmark ratified UNCLOS in 2004).

Stevenson (2007) analyzes possible outcomes of resolving the dispute through the International Court of Justice, pointing out that (at the time) there were no known natural resource deposits on the island, but that the seafloor around the island might be resource rich. He discusses that few precedents exist to award the island to either country. Instead, splitting the island between the two countries might be the result.

Of particular interest regarding the Hans Island dispute is that the area in question lies between two autonomous regions of the respective countries: Nunavut (Canada), created in 1999, and Greenland (Denmark), which attained full self-rule in 2009. Nonetheless, the dispute remains framed as Canada versus Denmark, and it is unclear how the disagreement would be affected if either or both regions increase their autonomy or achieve full independence.

Prospects and Limits of UNCLOS

Issues of territorial sovereignty have been broadly addressed by, among others, Blomley (1994); Agnew (2005); Elden (2007, 2009); and, in the specific context of Arctic melting, by Dodds (2010c) and Dittmer et al. (2011). These issues are closely aligned with the emergence of cooperative versus competitive policies by states under various legal and environmental conditions. Giddens, for example, argues, "Responding to climate change will intrinsically contribute to international collaboration. Yet the processes and interests promoting division are strong. The melting of the Arctic ice provides a good example. When the area was just an ice field, there was considerable international cooperation over the activities carried out there, which were mainly of a scientific nature. The fact that navigation across the Arctic is becoming increasingly possible, and that major new oil, gas and mineral resources might become available, has led to divisions of interest and to international friction, fortunately so far of a confined nature" (Giddens, 2009: 203).

The competitive nature of these divisions became apparent with the 2007 Russian flagging event. The controversy surrounding Russia's conduct gained international attention, particularly among countries such as Canada, Norway, and Denmark, whose territorial claims directly conflict with those asserted by Russia in terms of OCS and EEZs as per UNCLOS and other bilateral treaties. Ironically, under UNCLOS, if Russia's 2001 proposal is accepted by CLCS without any major amendments, this could extend its sovereignty over some of the EEZ and OCS territories that are also claimable by Norway, Denmark, and Greenland. While Russia and Norway have made some bilateral progress in resolving such disputes around EEZs (as discussed above), the disputes surrounding Russia's OCS and seabed claims are still outstanding, such as the Lomonosov Ridge controversy (Spielman, 2009). It remains to be seen whether Norway, Denmark, and Greenland will accept Russian claims if CLCS accepts the Russian OCS proposal.

In another example of defiance to the UNCLOS policy regime, the United States has rejected outright Canada's claim of sovereignty over the Northwest Passage and wishes to prevent Russia from acquiring its requested territory. Some authors (e.g., Wagner, 2010) have argued that the lack of teeth in UNCLOS and its failure to be ratified leaves the United States unhindered in doing what it wishes with the Arctic region, including allowing the state the necessary wiggle room to legally dismiss any other countries' formal assertions of sovereignty. In fact, Article 76 does not provide for any dispute settlements regarding territory claimed by more than one state, thereby essentially precluding CLCS from ruling in the event of such disputes.

Territorial disputes among the Arctic states, primarily between Russia, Canada, and the United States, are complicating an already difficult situation. To compound things further, UNCLOS, as the primary body of international law "governing" these territorial disputes, provides no insight as to how such competing claims should be resolved. The United States is in a unique situation, as it is the only country bordering the Arctic that has not ratified UNCLOS. A core group of senators and supporting lobbyists, for the most part responsible for UNCLOS remaining unratified, claimed that any limitations on national sovereignty would lead to the potential underexploitation of available resources. As an alternative, this faction is advocating for privatizing the seabed, which they believe will create economic incentives for owners to protect the long-term value of their property (Groves, 2007).

In general, where there are competing claims over a single territory in terms of EEZs or OCSs, UNCLOS is vague as to how the dispute should be resolved. Due to the lack of legal status, the CLCS possesses no power to decide such disputes. In fact, Article 76 does not provide for any dispute settlements regarding territory claimed by more than one state, thereby essentially precluding CLCS from ruling in the event of such disputes. As the Arctic melts and oil and natural gas exploration becomes more feasible, UNCLOS may be tested due to the lack of CLCS authority in dispute resolution. Further, the rejection of the UNCLOS system by a powerful country such as the United States raises other fundamental questions about the ability of the UNCLOS system to prevent the outbreak of major conflicts around the territorial settlement claims, including the demarcation of EEZs and OCSs. Some alternatives to the current policy regime therefore need to be considered, as discussed in the next section.

Alternatives to Consider

Here, we briefly introduce two policy regime options to deal with potential conflicts that might arise due to overlapping claims about OCS, EEZ, and seabed in the melting Arctic in the face of international interest in oil and natural gas. The first involves modifications to UNCLOS; the second alternative suggests establishment of a transnational Arctic protected area or biosphere reserve.

In response to the Russian flagging, Borgerson argued that "the situation is especially dangerous because there are currently no overarching political and legal structures that can provide for the orderly development of the region or mediate political disagreements over Arctic resources or sea-lanes" (Borgerson, 2008: 71). Despite such warnings, we have seen evolution of a cooperative regime amongst the Arctic states since 2007. In May 2008, five Arctic countries—Canada, Denmark, Norway, Russia, and the United States—issued the so-called Ilulissat Declaration, which noted that: "The Law of the Sea provides for important rights and obligations concerning the delimitation of the outer limits of the continental shelf, the protection of the marine environment, including ice covered seas, freedom of navigation, marine scientific research and other uses of the sea" (Ilulissat Declaration, 2008).

The five signatories also noted that they were committed to UNCLOS as a mechanism for resolving any "overlapping claims," despite the failure of the United States to ratify UNCLOS. As such the Ilulissat Declaration also announced that: "This framework provides a solid foundation for responsible management by the five coastal States and other users of this Ocean through national implementation and application of relevant provisions. We therefore see no need to develop a new comprehensive international legal regime to govern the Arctic Ocean. We will keep abreast of the developments in the Arctic Ocean and continue to implement appropriate measures" (Ilulissat Declaration, 2008).

Despite these collaborative statements by the five countries, many political and policy analysts express pessimism. For example, Berkman and Young (2009) claimed that the Arctic is on the threshold of a political and environmental state change. They warn that "the Arctic could slide into a new era featuring jurisdictional conflicts, increasingly severe clashes over the extraction of natural resources, and the emergence of a new 'great game' among the global powers." Similarly, the suggested likely rise of a "great game" in which global geopolitical forces try to control the fate of the Arctic, alongside the risk of a new Cold War breaking out in the Arctic, has been expressed as a "scramble for the Arctic" (Sale and Potapov, 2010); the prospect of "resource wars erupting in the Arctic" (Howard, 2009); the "Arctic as a battleground" (Emmerson, 2010); and the potential future occurrence of serious clashes over "who owns the Arctic" (Byers, 2009).

Other scholars, however, have argued that the race for Arctic oil and natural gas could also be construed as an opportunity for regional and international cooperation (Brosnan et al., 2011; Hong, 2012). Brosnan et al., for example, argued for the noninevitability of conflict in the Arctic: "A lack of cooperation regarding Arctic resource development and related environmental issues has been a source of public concern because the alternatives are believed to be conflict. But if incentives to cooperate are largely linked to developments that remain emergent, then a lack of cooperation should not be alarming. After all, cooperation is occurring on some important issues, including resource development in the Barents Sea, and creation of an Arctic-observing network. Additional cooperation is possible as issues become increasingly salient" (Brosnan et al., 2011: 203).

Despite these claims and counterclaims, there is widespread agreement that territorial dispute resolution mechanisms in UNCLOS need to be strengthened so that they could adequately deal with overlapping sovereignty claims from the states both within and outside of the UNCLOS system. The strengthening of dispute resolution mechanisms also needs to be accompanied by stronger environmental protections as well as explicit recognition of the rights of indigenous populations.

Another idea is to establish a transnational Arctic protected area or biosphere reserve, emulating such aspects of the Antarctic Treaty System, initiated by twelve states in 1959. The Antarctic Treaty System suspends all states' development rights to the Antarctic, holds that states could only use the continent for peaceful purposes including scientific research, and designates Antarctica as a "natural reserve," thereby halting all mining activities within the continent. The stark geopolitical and natural resource differences between the Arctic and Antarctic regions, however, mean that the feasibility of establishing the Arctic as a protected area or a biosphere remains unclear.

As compared with the Antarctic, isolated by cold, storms, and a wild sea, the Arctic includes a so-far ice-filled ocean, completely surrounded by industrialized states with significant indigenous populations, many with autonomy and many seeking increased autonomy. While some of these states agreed to preserve the Antarctic, they are currently planning to maximize their natural resource exploitation rights in the Arctic irrespective of territorial disputes.

As an alternative, establishing an Arctic-wide protected area or biosphere reserve could impact global GHG emissions as well as acknowledge indigenous rights in the Arctic.[4] Which way each of these issues goes is not certain. If tourism increases because the areas are protected, as often occurs, then GHG gas emissions might not be reduced, even without fossil fuel extraction. Indigenous peoples sometimes oppose formal protection of their lands because that can reduce their rights and inhibit their potential future autonomy, forcing on them external governance regimes with which they do not always agree. In some places, parks or other forms of protected areas have been used to exclude indigenous peoples from their traditional lands or to curtail their traditional activities such as hunting (Zia et al., 2011). Any governance regime implemented must consult indigenous peoples fully and fairly and must ensure that indigenous views and needs are fully accounted for in any decision.

The international community needs to broadly engage in evaluating current and alternate policy regimes that will govern the evolution of Arctic regions. The unfortunate reality is that economic and resource extraction considerations driven from capital cities are likely to dominate the debate over the Arctic. Considering other options and involving the people who live in the Arctic will, one hopes, somewhat balance such single-mindedness. Irrespective, it is clear that UNCLOS as it currently stands is inadequate for dealing with a warming Arctic, so further mechanisms and approaches are needed.

Notes

1. United Nations Convention on the Law of the Sea, Article 76(8), adopted 10 December 1982, entered into force 16 November 1994, http://www.un.org/Depts/los/clcs_new/clcs_home.htm [and] http://www.un.org/depts/los/convention_agreements/texts/unclos/unclos_e.pdf.

2. Commission on the Limits of the Continental Shelf, http://www.un.org/Depts/los/clcs_new/clcs_home.htm.

3. Commission on the Limits of the Continental Shelf, http://www.un.org/Depts/los/clcs_new/continental_shelf_description.htm#definition.

4. Note that areas currently protected under different regimes already exist within the Arctic, e.g., the Arctic National Wildlife Refuge, Denali, and Laponia. Political pressure may undermine protection of ANWR (and other protected areas).

8. Growth Imperative
Intermediaries, Discourse Frameworks, and the Arctic

ARTHUR MASON

The speed with which the future approaches the Arctic can be felt today in discussions on climate change, resource extraction, and sea transportation. Borrowing a phrase from Mabel Toolie, a Native elder of St. Lawrence Island, Alaska, the Arctic is a place "where the Earth is faster now" (Krupnik and Jolly, 2002: 7). But expert discussions taking place many miles from the North are also determining the speed with which the future is drawn into the Arctic present. The goal of these discussions is not directed toward the discursive shaping of the Arctic but toward exploiting the Arctic as a valuable energy extractive frontier. In particular, energy forecasts and scenarios created in office buildings and disseminated in hotel conference rooms are constructing the Arctic as hydrocarbon-rich and accessible landscapes.

The aim of this chapter is to improve the state of theory and knowledge in relation to forms of assembly and performance used by one group, intermediaries (consultants), to communicate economic forecasts of oil and natural gas development in the Arctic. I draw attention to conceptions of the Arctic energy future and the role played by expert formulations in elevating the interests of industry and government into actionable views thereby crystallizing an inner circle of participants with substantial powers. Unique access in unique social spaces contributes to a consultant expertise framework (Boyer, 2005; Mason and Stoilkova, 2012); this chapter expands the performativity thesis for a next generation of scholars involved in the anthropologies of finance, markets, futurity, and expertise, linked to science and technology studies–related genealogies.

The primary focus of this chapter bears on natural gas located at Prudhoe Bay on Alaska's North Slope, which, until recently, was regarded as an energy region capable of contributing significantly to North American energy security, representing nearly 10 percent of the resource base in the United States. In contrast to the drama of today's demand uncertainty, I employ a discursive characterization of the process by which intermediary knowledge shapes Alaska natural gas development through a period of volatility in supply. Examining intermediaries draws necessary attention to privatized knowledge systems in the Arctic that license the intervention of experts in debates about emerging infrastructures, contracting regimes, and community development plans that accompany concessions being newly put into place at this moment. Energy development is one of several industries reliant upon intermediaries, and understanding the results of this reliance sheds light on a more general phenomenon across society.

Since midcentury, publics underwriting research with substantial tax revenues acquired "a stake in what science produces, just as science acquired stakes in making its findings useful as a basis for continued public support" (Jasanoff, 2011: 132). As such, democratization efforts filtered into the processes of scientific discovery for purposes of shoring up the legitimacy of public funding for science—by seeking citizen acquiescence to research that purported to guarantee eventual widespread commercial applications. This pattern of democratization is apparent in the North American Arctic where redefinitions of local knowledge have created new partners in scientific inquiry and new publics to which science has become accountable.

By contrast, the rise of intermediary experts (consultants) suggests a trend toward greater control over access and production of Arctic knowledge that is privatized via commodification. Public accessibility exists but without authority to determine limits of access. It is not uncommon, for example, in the Alaska oil and gas sector to locate references to the products of intermediary knowledge, such as those found in government and corporate publications concerning forecasts, journalist accounts, briefings from think tanks, financial groups, or environmental NGOs, that offer assessments of project development and focus on supply-demand interactions as primary agents for determining events. While such references are widely available, public access to commodified analyses of Alaska oil and gas development tend to be sequestered by their circulation as client privilege reports or minutes of costly executive roundtable meetings. Such analyses, while not publicly available, may be shared within the intermediary community. Several consultant organizations are increasingly forthcoming about their methodologies, pointing to the collective nature of their research process whereby analysts critically scrutinize each others' work prior to publication.

Thus, the unabashed economic motivation behind the rise of intermediary knowledge reflects a postwar expansion of expert systems as part of a broader movement to a knowledge economy. The growth of this type of economy itself provides justification of an apparent contradiction, on the one hand, of increased democratization of academic expertise, and on the other, the privatization of expertise by intermediary consultants.

Rise of Consultants

Energy consultants can be considered "intermediary actors" because of their success in mobilizing expectations (Beunza and Garud, 2007). The visibility of these firms reflects a growing reliance on consultant advisory services that identify economic uncertainties and help industry actors have the capacity to be ready for them. By mediating an entire ensemble of relations about the energy industry, intermediaries may be seen as transnational agents who exert increasing control over economies once regulated in and through the national state (LiPuma and Lee, 2004). While interest in intermediaries is growing, there is little understanding of their specific type of expertise and how they create knowledge about Arctic energy development from specialized forms of study. Nor is there much information about the precise characteristics of knowledge produced or how their predictions exert complex forms of influence on Arctic oil and gas developments. These neglected areas suggest a need to characterize the role of intermediaries who create assessments and to develop analytical tools to allow researchers to carry out systematic study of these actors (Van Lente, 1993).

Figure 8.1 divides intermediary expertise into three practices for visualizing Arctic energy futures: assembling, mobilizing, and performing. *Assembling* refers to the process by which consultants build relationships with the Arctic largely by reference to practical understandings, but also through information technology (IT) systems such as Wood Mackenzie's Global Economic Model. For example, information-sifting is inherently selective and often depends upon high levels of embodied understandings usually developed through years of experience. By contrast, IT infrastructure such as Enterprise Resource Planning Systems employs a logic of conversion whereby the Arctic is abstracted and converted first into data, then into information, which is then mobilized as knowledge. While in the first instance, assembling renders (tacit) embodied knowledge explicit, in the second, technical systems redistribute calculative capacities from humans to machines.

Mobilizing refers to the presentability of the material and digital forms of consultant knowledge and their deployment. Specifically, consultant products (reports, memos, graphs, scenario narratives, PowerPoint slides) represent "integrated packages" (Knox et al., 2007) that capture a firm's activity of transforming information into knowledge that purports to have strategic decision-making value.

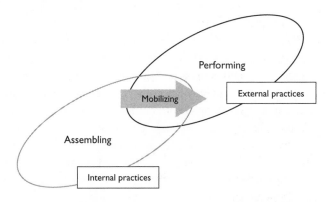

Figure 8.1: Assembling, mobilizing, performing

Finally, *performing* calls attention to forms of display, as in the specialized stance of intermediary expertise, such as its linguistic repertoire of technical terms, acronyms, and even nonverbal signs like facial expressions and gestures. Networking events are important performative locations. They entail spatiotemporal features such as the division of the given time into, on the one hand, plenary sessions that everyone can attend, and on the other, parallel sessions that participants must choose between. According to Wallace (2010: ch. 3), the allocation of individual and collective discussion through conferencing can represent "exemplary instances and instruments of future-management." At such events, consultants negotiate their ability to distribute assessments, which they hope will generate value, together with a simultaneous acknowledgment of the contingency of this aim. In these ways, intermediary expertise provides the possibility for industry actors to become conscious of an idea of futurity as singular and achievable. In doing so, consultants reduce complexity into knowledge that can form the basis of decisions that industry considers defensible and feasible.

Energy consultants emerged in North America in the mid-1980s during a period of energy market restructuring. Their initial duties included collecting, analyzing, and distributing information of relevance to buyers and sellers, including information about weather, demand patterns, and future prices of natural gas and other fuels. By the beginning of the twenty-first century, a much more elaborate system of advisory service had emerged, in which intermediaries rank future energy projects through combining technical prediction with new modes of communication, e.g., scenario planning and executive roundtables, making available what might be described as a "community of interpretation" on a commodified basis (Mason, 2007: 374). That is, through soliciting the opinions of a broad sector of industry, consultants begin to act as organizers of community knowledge for executives and government leaders about the future of energy systems and the viability of particular projects within these systems. Such knowledge begins forming the basis of strategic tools (Wood Mackenzie's Global Economic Model, for example) that are employed profitably by consultants through client fees for access. By enabling systematic and commodified access to community interpretations, consultants today provide the grounds for more formalized assessments of energy development projects. These have organizational significance for the way government and industry leaders stabilize future perspectives. Specialist organizations such as Cambridge Energy Research Associates (CERA) have taken center stage in global market forecasting. The growth of intermediaries is no doubt a response to deep uncertainties surrounding the future of supply and demand interactions but it is also an opportunity created by experts to enhance their own expansion and prestige (Brooks, 2002: 148).

The idea that the future has a significant role to play in the construction of the present is not new. Giddens writes that "under conditions of modernity, the future is continually drawn into the present by means of the reflexive organization of knowledge environments"; the discourse through which this occurs involves terminologies of risk (Giddens, 1991: 3). Beck characterizes late-modernity as a risk society, in which "we are caught up in defensive battles of various types, anticipating the hostile substances in one's manner of living" (Beck, 1994: 45). Calculating risk in the oil and natural gas industries is also an open-ended, future-oriented project, the goal of which is to anticipate all loci of uncertainty while increasing the chance of economic success. This has been especially the case since the 1980s, when market restructuring adopted institutions from the financial industry so that prices could be based on competition rather than regulation.

But the industry's competitive structure has raised problems for an older market segment of energy producers and pipeline companies that seek to develop new sources of Arctic oil and gas supply. In the natural gas industry, government deregulation effectively renounced control over price and dismantled an environment in which financial instruments like long-term contracts could diminish the high-stakes, high-costs uncertainty of investing in large energy systems. As such, market risk is critically privatized.

In the case of Alaska gas development, it is extremely difficult to synchronize the long-term horizon of Arctic energy production with the short-term volatility of markets because of uncertain policies around climate legislation and shale gas production. Indeed, the choice of market itself, whether the Asia-Pacific region or North America, is in part determined by expectations of how these uncertainties will be resolved. The tackling of these uncertainties is generating interest among industry and government leaders in the strategic research products created by consultants that formulate perspectives that are fundamental for social coordination surrounding issues of risk, i.e., for purposes of influencing policymakers and public opinion.

The Growth Imperative: Discourse Framework

Scholars examining intermediary expertise have become sensitive to the role that both technologies and theories play in constituting market development. Callon, Çaliskan, and MacKenzie argue that economic theories and financial tools are performative; that is, they not only describe but help produce the settings to which they are applied (Callon, 2007; Çaliskan and Callon, 2009; MacKenzie, 2006a–b). Through their application, theories and related tools change how people think about markets and enact the framing processes that serve to allow their operation (Mallard, 2007). This is an important insight that is worth transferring from the study of economic transactions to understanding the workings of energy consultants within Arctic energy development. Energy analysts are an ideal site to build on the performativity thesis because the subject matter deals with forms of influence as complicated as financial theories. Whereas Hardie and MacKenzie (2007) show how financial research can modify a price, it can be argued that consultant assessments can change the trajectory of energy transportation systems.

Perhaps the best case study in this regard concerns attempts to develop Alaska natural gas by, specifically, market design, beginning in 2000 with a formalized image of a "growth imperative" (CERA, 2000; Federal Energy Regulatory Commission, 2000). Details of the growth imperative appear in "The Long Ascent," a market report published in May 2000 by consultants for Cambridge Energy Research Associates (Robinson and Hoffman, 2000). "The Long Ascent" achieves significance in part by appearing within a sequence of studies. Months earlier, in January 2000, in association with the accounting firm Arthur Andersen, Cambridge Energy released "Natural Gas Trends" to a receptive audience of industry observers, as is visible in citations across the trade press. The *Oil and Gas Journal* (*OGJ*), for example, states, "[t]he North American natural gas sector will experience unprecedented growth over the coming decade [says] a joint study on North American natural gas trends by Arthur Andersen and Cambridge Energy Research Associates." The quote appears under the heading, "U.S. gas market to surge in coming decade" (*OGJ*, 2000).

Although details of "The Long Ascent" outlined data analyzed earlier that year, it presents itself also as a promissory note for pending research, as evidenced by an advertisement for future work within the report including "The Future of North American Gas Supply Study," 2001. Finally, "The Long Ascent" may be characterized as offering three discursive formations that can be attributed to similar types of reports produced from competing analysts during this period (Rasmussen, 2000). These three formations are: values, expectations, and limits.

Values of the Growth Imperative

Three values lie at the foundation of meaning in support of the growth imperative. First, the growth imperative is the product of a framework for evaluating investment decisions. Second, the growth imperative retains its own structuring principles through internal composition. Finally, the growth imperative places its entire coherence, both as a product of a framework and its internal composition, under a rubric best described as a dual-progressory.

As a product of a framework the growth imperative has a bounded quality. It represents the natural gas supply chain in North America as a continental system. Its technological status, therefore, is limited by its own self-enclosed (technical, economic, political) cultural self-sufficiency. The framework relies upon categories of data collection in which all qualities are translated into quantities that are measured against each other across incremental time periods. These quantities refer to a natural gas resource base and, in particular, activities that determine its production potential, including the possibility for increasing the availability of the resource and at what capacities and temporal rates, especially in those cases that relate to a response to expected demands from energy consumers. As a continentally self-enclosed system, the framework is partitioned or regionalized to create comparative values, as in comparative costs and economics of shipping, production, and so on. There is also a variety of categories that relate to external points of reference and projection, government regulation, economic growth, investments, and what might be referred to more generally as natural gas market fundamentals: demand, transportation, and pricing. Finally, there is constant attention to timing and sequencing of resource use.

To describe the growth imperative as expressing an internal composition refers to a series of internal logics that are imaginative. They include forms of causality such as "rippling effects" that are best described as underlying forces whose contact points with the surface of things can be missed even by the most careful of observers. They include "dramatic force-pressures" that are all too obvious to go unnoticed by the most casual of industry watchers. They include forms of temporality that relate a variety of suddenlys and unexpectednesses that cannot be accounted for in terms of evolution, progress, or navigation, but instead call to mind threshold, crisis, and potential. These suddenlys typically take place alongside descriptions of energy events that are isolated, single, and unique, and that can be described without any connection to an encompassing industry whole.

This form of duration, volatility time, can be contrasted to continuous forms of temporality where what is described instead are price paradigms, price environments, supply trends, and so on. It is this latter type of marked typicality that reflects a sigh of relief for the industry. It is a departure from the strange, unusual, and rare. But it can also threaten to create "treadmills" and thus impair the growth imperative. In addition to causality and temporality, there are prerequisites for rationalization, that is, contradictions that require smoothing out, such as "twists and turns," "booms and busts," "accelerations and downturns."

Finally, the growth imperative resides under a rubric best described as a dual-progressory. A dual-progressory, on the one hand, is a narrative description intending to be fully grasped as an empirical-based probability (with some yet unknown degree of certitude). Therefore, it has historical trajectory. On the other hand, it permits denial of responsibility upon its failure because, in fact, it retains an abstraction of plausibility. As such, it represents itself merely as a theoretically correct formulation (growth will happen; it is only a matter of how and when).

The dual-progressory is similar to what Marshall Sahlins and Elman Service in *Evolution and Culture* (1960), referring to an earlier period of anthropological theorizing, call specific and general evolution. According to their view, evolution describes a trend among all living organisms to move in the direction toward the maximization of energy efficiency, to utilize the earth's resources by some ratio of energy captured and used relative to the organism's own expenditure in the process of taking it. Sahlins clarifies the description of this trend by suggesting that evolution moves simultaneously in two directions. On the one side, evolution creates diversity through adaptive modification where new forms differentiate from old. On the other side, evolution generates progress: higher forms arise from, and surpass, lower forms. The first of these directions he calls specific evolution, and the second, general evolution.

Expectations of the Growth Imperative

For analysts, the year 2000 marked the beginning of a new millennium for the natural gas industry. This sense of expectation suggests analysts had become conscious of the industry in relation to new beginnings, but also in such ways as to be transfixed on a very ambitious growth target—building toward a 30 trillion cubic feet (Tcf) market in the United States by 2010. Analysts describe the target as driven by a surge of natural gas–fired electricity power generation, with underlying demand drivers in place to support a dramatic (35 percent) expansion in the gas market. They describe the path toward 30 Tcf as anything but smooth and perceive the industry as facing intensifying demand pressure from electric power markets at a moment when gas production in the United States is actually falling. Energy forecasters describe conflicting forces between new demands for natural gas fuel from increased electricity use and declining reserves that would require "rationalization," that is, coordinating the timing and sequencing of events for longer-term growth prospects.

Analysts compare their expectations of industry growth to present values. The market in 2000 was roughly 22 Tcf. Thus, they present the growth imperative as an item of significantly more annual growth (3.1 percent—significantly more than the 1.8 percent annual pace of growth during the 1990s). Moving forward therefore will require dramatic increases in investment in gas exploration and production as well as pipeline transmission infrastructure. The result of such investment will be a larger, more visible, and much changed industry compared to what existed in 2000.

Such pronouncements of growth were not new. What was telling, and what analysts seize upon in their descriptions, is how strongly they feel these pronouncements continue to resonate within the industry itself. But moving forward requires reconciling two conflicting forces. First, analysts argue that consumer demand pressure for electric power is intensifying. Second, the challenges for increasing gas supply are intensifying. Analysts describe in detail how electric power is the driver of growth. It is an anticipated power wave that had already begun. Natural gas use in electricity power generation rose during the 1990s, and the pace of growth was accelerating as 2000 began. In addition, natural gas continued to be the most cost-effective incremental generation technology that met increasingly stringent clean-air requirements. The combination of these forces had led to a surge in electricity power turbine orders and announcements of new gas-fired power plants. For energy analysts, the penetration of natural gas into the power sector had shifted from a widely discussed potential to a pervasive reality that would pressure the gas market—and gas supply—in the years ahead.

Limits of the Growth Imperative: Developing the New Frontier

What is clear from analyst descriptions is that during the first decade of the 2000s—whether the market actually grew to 30 Tcf or not—market forces were driving the industry. The growth imperative was likely to fundamentally alter the structure and functioning of the North American gas market. But reaching the goal would require connecting major new supply frontiers. Such a feat would require a price shock before the capital would be committed to bring such projects to completion. The interplay of the conflicting supply and demand forces was expected to accentuate a boom and bust cycle in the marketplace, making the road to 30 Tcf a "wild ride for the entire industry" (CERA, 2000: 3).

During this period, the supply frontiers included Alaska gas, Atlantic Canadian gas, and liquefied natural gas (LNG). These frontiers would be "economic" as understood in terms of falling below prices for natural gas in year 2000. These sources would also fall below the long-term future prices expected by major gas brokerages. The pattern demonstrated a shift in the underlying playing field for gas prices. That is, the price of natural gas had trended upward over the past decade. The institutionalization of this shift—coupled with the challenge of increasing production in traditional supply basins—would push industry into new supply frontiers.

Yet surmounting the economic threshold would only be the first step in tapping into Arctic frontiers. In most cases, these projects would require long-term capital commitments to develop the necessary infrastructure to connect them to the North American marketplace. Political challenges and competitive threats to existing supply regions and flows would follow. Through it all, investors would require confidence that once the capital commitment was made and these frontier projects were developed, they would become the low-cost suppliers to the North American marketplace.

Throughout the 1980s and 1990s, developing natural gas from Arctic Alaska and Canada was economically prohibitive. But its potential development emerged at the beginning of the new millennium. These projects would require large investments in infrastructure and in several cases would threaten to displace existing supplies into high value markets. Unlike existing supply sources, several of these frontier projects would require minimum scales (1.0 Bcf per day or more)—adding to the potential dislocating effects on the market as they come online. This concern with natural gas from Alaska linked the timing and sequencing of these supplies to regulation and politics.

Events

Across the United States, the winter of 2000 to 2001 was a period of natural gas market shock. A decline in productive capacity and low storage drove North American energy prices to record levels. By the end of January, natural gas prices were four times more than one year previously. State politicians and members of Congress reacted swiftly by publicizing concern for energy consumers while accusing energy traders and gas producers of price gouging. Some state leaders in Alaska found themselves stirring up public awareness over the winter gas shortfall, declaring the nation's energy crisis as a "window of opportunity" for commercializing Prudhoe Bay gas.

During this period, energy analysts arrived in Alaska with the idea that a large volume of Arctic natural gas had suddenly become valuable. Natural gas located under the earth's crust at Prudhoe Bay represents a vast amount indeed. But its extraordinary positioning far outside the continental energy market is a feature of extreme importance. The subsequent domestication of the growth imperative, with its hierarchy of meanings and sequence of events, in Alaska state and news media discourses suggests that the self-enclosed priorities of state officials were penetrated in a short time by their newly formed understandings of the US natural gas energy market. Working alongside consultants, state officials developed a new set of distinctions to critically reflect back onto the political event of the pipeline project. In the process of identifying multiple distinctions, a new recoding of the pipeline took place, transforming it from a political event into an economic event.

9. Connecting China through "Creative Diplomacy" Greenland, Australia, and Climate Cooperation in Polar Regions

DAMIEN DEGEORGES AND SALEEM H. ALI

Science was the unifying force behind the Antarctic Treaty, and many countries that were original signatories and collaborators on the southern pole have also had strategic interests in the northern pole. A clear shift occurred regarding the salience of polar regions beyond science and local community interests with the consequences of climate change, the melting of ice, and the growing demand for natural resources. Growing interest in Arctic natural resources may be considered by Antarctic countries as a potential difficulty when renegotiating the Protocol on Environmental Protection to the Antarctic Treaty, also known as the Madrid Protocol, at a time when global demand for natural resources may be even higher than it is today, particularly from economies that need economic growth to maintain financial viability. At the same time, the developments in the Arctic offer a unique opportunity to further engage these economies, also the largest CO_2-emitters, on climate research through international cooperation in order to get the best data to adapt to climate change and find a creative way to resolve the global climate challenge.

This chapter argues that Greenland and Australia, because of their particular geographical context and research strengths, can make a particular difference in moving the conversation from conflict to cooperation.[1] This can be accomplished by applying the concept of "creative diplomacy" to resolve global challenges such as climate change and energy security.[2] Both have the climate "laboratory" that is needed to conduct polar research in, respectively, the Arctic and the Antarctic, and further engage large CO_2-emitters and resource consumers into international cooperation. And they have the strategic resources—particularly rare earth elements (REE)—that are needed to secure global "green growth."[3]

Geological resources when framed within a scientific context have the potential for fostering collaboration, even among rivals and regional competitors. An example of such efforts in the context of Antarctica has been documented in detail by Howkins (2008) in his detailed review of "reluctant collaboration" between Chile and Argentina in 1957–1958 during the International Geophysical Year. Greenland and Australia have no preexisting regional rivalry but as suppliers of rare earth elements may be considered competitors. Appropriate framing around cooperation in the context of science, however, particularly with reference to climate change and its impacts on the full supply chain and consumption of minerals, can create an unusual locus for diplomatic initiatives.

Polar Regions: A Key for Action on Climate Change

While polar regions are most vulnerable to climate change, the best data to plan adaptation to climate change can be found in these regions. The Intergovernmental Panel on Climate Change (IPCC) provided in its Fourth Assessment Report data that estimated global sea level rise by 2100 to be between 0.18 and 0.59 meters. World leaders at the 2009 Copenhagen Climate Conference based their deliberations on such data. Two years later more alarming data was released: the SWIPA (Snow, Water, Ice, and Permafrost in the Arctic) project of the Arctic Monitoring and Assessment Program (AMAP) estimated global sea level rise to be at the same period (2100) between 0.9 and 1.6 meters.[4] More than a meter of difference in terms of climate adaptation makes scenarios and costs completely different, particularly for coastal populations and economies like China's, which are key to global financial and employment viability. Any impact to Chinese manufacturing along the coast, for instance, can have huge repercussions for the profitability of multinationals, but has potential for risk reduction through effective planning as became evident during the SARS epidemic.[5] It is therefore not only a domestic problem for China or other coastal countries, but a challenge of global concern. Polar regions have a unique potential to attract China and other large CO_2-emitters on further international cooperation on climate research in order to get the best data and develop strategies for adapting to climate change. Despite its protestations on coal emission reductions and its development imperative, China has been highly forthcoming in recent years on climate change policy and adaptation research and planning.[6]

Greenland and its icecap as well as Australia and its Antarctic territory—respectively the largest climate "laboratories" of the northern and southern hemispheres— offer this opportunity to China to bridge science and economic interests.[7] Greenland and Australia can thus be part of a creative way to resolve the global climate challenge and to provide a more inclusive pathway for China to engage on environmental diplomacy.[8] Their role is particularly important because neither are perceived as "hard powers" with agendas of regional domination. Australia's strong economic relationship with China still makes it far more credible as an interlocutor than other G20 countries.[9]

At the same time the role of Greenland was a key element of Denmark's climate diplomacy, which highlighted the quasi-sovereign land's prominence in this context. Prior to the Copenhagen Climate Change Summit (CoP15) in 2009, major policymakers from the United States and Europe—among them Nancy Pelosi, then

Speaker of the US House of Representatives; José Manuel Barroso, president of the European Commission; and Angela Merkel, German federal chancellor—as well as representatives from key countries of the international negotiations on climate change, visited Greenland and the Ilulissat Icefjord, a UNESCO World Heritage Site, to observe firsthand the effects of climate change and discuss climate negotiations in a creative and more effective way.

The whole G8 is either taking part or willing to be part of the Arctic Council, and almost the whole G20 is connected in some part to current Antarctic governance.[10] Polar regions have acquired prominence beyond just climate science cooperation and should be considered as a privileged platform for "creative diplomacy related to resource governance more broadly."[11]

A history of continuing human habitation differentiates the Arctic from the Antarctic, but more consequentially, unlike the Antarctic, there are no international agreements preventing resource exploitation in the Arctic. The potential opening of polar sea routes, which would reduce distances for shipping activities, gives the region an even stronger global dimension. The fact that major global actors like the United States and Russia are part of the region further highlights developments in the Arctic. The economic rise of China in the region and its appetite for extractive resources has, however, been a crucial issue of concern for Arctic stakeholders and has raised interest in the Arctic in countries as far as Australia, which sees itself as a major mineral resource provider.[12] The maritime route through the Arctic is also a major attraction for China as this could save as much as four thousand miles in transport distance from Chinese ports to European market centers. The Chinese interest in the Arctic can be seen positively if it leads to further international cooperation into polar research but can also be a source of regional conflict if there is a race for resource exploitation.[13]

As in the Arctic, climate research has been used by global powers to position themselves in the Antarctic, but the primacy of science through the Antarctic Treaty System has given these issues even more significance. The challenge of renegotiating the Protocol on Environmental Protection to the Antarctic Treaty will nevertheless need to be considered well in advance before its expiration to prevent resource conflicts in this pristine region.[14]

The Chinese Arctic and Antarctic Administration was established in 1981 and has two bases in Antarctica as well as an Arctic research station at Svalbard, Norway. China is a consultative signatory to the Antarctic Treaty and has ratified the Environmental Protocol of the treaty as well as the Convention on the Conservation of Antarctic Marine Living Resources (CCAMLR).[15] Given this degree of political investment in the Antarctic Treaty, China will no doubt want a voice on how any resource exploitation of the Antarctic would be balanced with a desire for ecological conservation and the use of the continent as a pristine laboratory for scientific research.[16] Due to the volume of the Antarctic ice sheet, the consequences of melting would be much more serious than in the Arctic. Resource exploitation could accelerate Antarctic melting in some areas. Even without any impending danger of expedited melting, however, mining or oil extraction activity could disrupt the sensitive ecological systems in the oceans around the continent with major impacts, such as on global fisheries. Therefore, even if natural resources are economically extractable on the continent, there remains a strong view among conservationists that Antarctica should remain a place for climate research and a reminder that our planet is not extensible.

Channeling Chinese Resource Power in the Polar Regions

The European Union—which has immediate geographic proximity to the Arctic through two of its member states, Finland and Sweden—has endeavored to be recognized by the Arctic Council.[17] In May 2013, China won permanent observer status at the Arctic Council after earlier rejections.[18] The significance of this win should be taken in context, however, since in the same session five other states (India, Italy, Japan, Singapore, and South Korea) also won membership, notably given their resource investment interests in the region.

Unlike the EU, China has a more united vision of its strategic priorities, and this may work to its advantage in terms of its influence on the Arctic Council as an observer. The rapidly increasing assertion of China in the polar regions poses a dilemma to smaller Arctic states as to whether to strengthen their relationship with a major power like China by leveraging their regional Arctic experience and access, or to potentially be intimidated by a stronger power that might opportunistically use them without full recognition and benefit. No military risk is at stake, but a strategic issue that could be a means of providing greater reciprocity between China and these regions is that of securing "global green growth." This is an emerging concept in economic development parlance specifying the incorporation of environmentally sound technologies for manufacturing and service provision in the development planning of an area.[19] Greenland and its enormous rare earth element deposits are seen to be crucial in this context since they are a pivotal component in many environmentally sound technologies such as hybrid cars and low-energy lighting. Noting that rare earth mining itself can be deleterious to the environment without proper mitigation measures, there is still potential for growth of this sector as a net "green investment." The Arctic territory could learn more from Australia on how to deal with China on natural resources, particularly in the rare earth sector. Chinese miners and processors have dominated the sector for the past twenty-five years; Australia has managed, nevertheless, to enter the market in both mining and processing without undermining its relations with the Asian giant.[20]

Greenland can be seen as a "hypermarket" of natural resources. Not only does the territory have large potential for hydrocarbons and enormous reserves of fresh water, but also a variety of minerals, including rare earth elements as well as antimony, barite, beryllium, celestite, chromium, coal, cobalt, copper, cryolite, diamond, gold, graphite, iron, lead, molybdenum, nickel, niobium, olivine, osmium, palladium, phosphorus, platinum, ruby, silver, tantalum, thorium, titanium, tungsten, uranium, vanadium, zinc, and zirconium.[21]

Greenland's state-building process becomes a major energy security issue, particularly given the territory's REE potential, and it will soon be in a position to economically assist China or other demand centers. The historic visit by then South Korean president Lee Myung-bak to Greenland in 2012, without his stopping off in Denmark and without the presence of the Danish prime minister, who is nevertheless responsible for Denmark's foreign and security policy, was another example of how resources are attracting Asian powers directly to Greenland. Such foreign engagement has come about because of the sovereignty Greenland acquired in 2010 in terms of managing its own raw materials.

The strength of a Greenlandic state, which is emerging beyond Danish dominion, is highly dependent on effective utilization of natural resources. Learning from China's involvement in Iceland, Greenland needs to develop an economic safety net in order that any foreign investment works to its advantage. As long as Greenland remains a self-ruled territory under the Kingdom of Denmark, the Danish yearly block grant to Greenland will ensure the autonomous territory this necessary economic safety net. It secures the possibility for Greenland to manage its natural resources as it wants. If Greenland decides to become independent, as is made possible by the Self Rule Act, a Greenlandic state will need to think about rejoining a partly supranational entity, either in North America or in Europe, to secure the country's economy in case of economic failure. As of 2013, the European Union would be the only option, as the North American Free Trade Agreement (NAFTA) is limited to trade protocols. A "secured" Greenlandic economy would benefit first and foremost Greenland but also its Arctic neighborhood and could provide securitization of global green growth.

China's political culture of long-term central planning gives it considerable endurance in developing relationships and thinking much further along timelines to reach certain economic goals than the short-term focused economic culture of the West.[22] The strengthened relationship between China and Iceland, following the economic crisis faced by the Arctic island in 2008, illustrates this tenacity and strategic planning. Some years at least may be needed before the Northern Sea Route (via the Northeast Passage) opens, but China has already invested in its future. Iceland is expected to become an Arctic hub for China's shipping activities—a strategic sector for the Chinese economy. The strengthened Chinese-Icelandic relationship went far beyond a bilateral currency swap agreement: the joint Chinese-Icelandic polar expedition, which reached the North Pole in April 2011, was one out of many examples. The Icelandic case demonstrates a long-term strategic approach for China, which has secured itself a privileged "entrance ticket" to the Arctic. In that regard, political developments during a coming Icelandic chairmanship of the Arctic Council will be interesting to follow. China has not only decided to invest in its relationship with Iceland—the impressive Chinese embassy in Reykjavik gives a clear signal of China's interest in the Arctic island—but also to apply what Joseph Nye (2004) has called "soft power." The Chinese embassy in Iceland hosted one of the dinners offered during an international Arctic conference in Iceland in 2011; the two others were hosted by the Icelandic Ministry of Foreign Affairs and the president of Iceland.[23] The fact that a non-Arctic state like China reaches that point of involvement in the Arctic through "soft power" clearly demonstrates that strategic issues are at stake in the region. What could be China's next stop in the Arctic?

Given its strategic Arctic coastal dimension and enormous potential for strategic natural resources, Greenland is highly attractive to China. Chinese interest in Greenland's natural resources has been confirmed on several occasions by Greenlandic ministers and notably by the visit to Greenland by China's then minister for land and resources Xu Shaoshi in 2012. If Greenland becomes independent and faces economic difficulties, Chinese economic assistance to a Greenlandic state could have substantial consequences for development in the Arctic as well as for global energy security, given the island's strategic assets. The possibility of Chinese investments in the Greenlandic REE sector, directly or indirectly, is highly consequential for global green growth, given that China controls more than 97 percent of global REE production. By some estimates Greenland could at least respond to 25 percent of the world's REE demand for fifty years—if not more, according to some.[24] This is expected to be more than what Australia can provide. In other words, should new mines open or be reopened in the United States or in Australia to face the Chinese quasi-monopoly position on rare earth elements, Chinese investment in Greenland could still give the country dominance in the sector. China could invest in Greenland, however, with a broader aim of developing an internationalized supply chain for renewable energy technologies, which could be viewed as a positive global undertaking within the paradigm of "green growth."

Taking the example of an Australian-Chinese joint venture named AusChina Energy, the possibility of having a "GreenChina Energy group" would illustrate the "green" potential that Greenland ironically has with its name to attract foreign investors in the renewable energy sector, particularly in the hydropower sector. China has "expressed an interest in pursuing scientific activities in Greenland," according to then Danish foreign minister Lene Espersen.[25] Such a research collaborative path gives Greenland an opportunity to further involve Chinese international cooperation in research and contribute in a creative way to engage China on adaptation and mitigation mechanisms for climate change.

Developments in polar regions are emerging as a new way of highlighting strategic national interests of powers such as China that see planetary exploration and reach as a mark of global political power, analogous to the "space race." Exploration and science are seen as natural pathways to also extract economic opportunities, as reflected by the presence of China's then minister for land and resources, Xu Shaoshi, in a delegation of Chinese dignitaries visiting Casey Station in the Australian Antarctic Territory in 2010. As noted by Jo Chandler in the *Sydney Morning Herald*: "Questioned about China's science and research priorities in its rapidly expanding Antarctic program, Mr Qu Tanzhou, director of the Chinese Arctic and Antarctic Administration, said: 'At this stage, we are paying attention to climate and environmental change . . . [looking at] oceanography, geography, [evidence of] meteorites. Also we are here about the potential of the resources and how to use these resources.' Asked if China had plans to mine in Antarctica, he said 'at this stage we just focus on the potential of the natural resources.'"[26]

Cooperation in the Antarctic poses different challenges and opportunities for creative diplomacy and sustainable cooperation. Unlike the Arctic, where nonregional actors need to comply with coastal states' sovereign rights, the Antarctic is replete with land claims. The uncertain future of the environmental protection framework offered by the Madrid Protocol may strengthen ambitions of resource consumers such as China. However, using creative diplomacy to highlight the importance of climate change research in Antarctica as a means of economically shielding coastal economies like China from adverse impacts can provide some respite to an Antarctic resource scramble. In the meantime, technology may catch up with finding reduced material usage or alternatives for particular commodities in products which countries like China need for economic development. Thus the opportunity for a more conservation-based approach to the Antarctic versus a measured and carefully regulated extractive future for the Arctic that benefits states like Greenland appears the most viable path toward Chinese engagement on polar diplomacy.

Synthesizing Creative Diplomacy: The Way Forward

In this chapter we have tried to provide some evidence for how relatively minor actors in the broader scheme of international relations can leverage their diplomatic influence. Thinking beyond the usual parameters of regional politics is essential to realize the otherwise abstract concept of "creative diplomacy." Climate change and its influence on the polar regions creates an unusual opportunity to test this concept. Scientific research, particularly in the Antarctic, provides clues to planning for climate change impacts in coastal regions for countries that might otherwise have minimal interest in such inquiry. Coupling scientific exploration with economic expediency of adaptation and mitigation strategies can provide a pathway for furthering a conservationist agenda that has sustained the Antarctic Treaty as a model of such international ecological cooperation. The Arctic, which will undoubtedly see a rush for resources in coming years from high demand centers like China, can leverage resource extraction with appropriate environmental and social performance standards to provide economic opportunity for its citizens.

Greenland and Australia, through their climate "laboratories"—in, respectively, the Arctic and the Antarctic—as well as their strategic REE deposits that are not Chinese-owned, are keys to ensure environmental diplomacy and security. While Australia remains a strong and economically healthy state, Greenland is in a statebuilding process facing enormous challenges. This process should be closely monitored in order to prevent economic difficulties. Greenland and Australia could learn from each other in order to mediate Chinese influence in polar regions by exercising "soft power." Greenland could learn from Australia's maturity in dealing with China on extractive natural resources while Australia could learn from Greenland's nascent scientific engagement with China in the Arctic as a means of moderating Chinese resource influence on the Antarctic Treaty System.

Our approach recognizes that there will always be voices of dissent regarding the extent and negotiability of resource extraction. However, with current challenges of economic development in the Arctic, there needs to be a pragmatic and truly global approach to harmonizing natural resource extraction and ecological conservation. A more absolute form of ecological conservation is far more likely to work for the Antarctic than for the Arctic, and we have offered a novel set of alliances that might negotiate a more sustainable grand bargain on polar engagement with China. We also suggest that the importance of strategic minerals for green technologies and the diversification of their source will improve global sustainability metrics through the paradigm of "green growth."

Operationalizing a process of lesson-drawing between Australia and Greenland on the one hand and working multilaterally with the Chinese on the other can be undertaken through an ad hoc working group of senior officials from Australia, China, Greenland, and Denmark. Research on multilateral environmental negotiating processes has shown that such small ad hoc working groups are a more effective way of reaching consensus among otherwise disparate and divergent national entities than larger institutional forums such as the G20 or United Nations entities.[27] It is important, however, that the parameters of discussions at such a forum at minimum follow existing commitments made under the international agreements of the United Nations Framework Convention on Climate Change (UNFCCC) as well as the Antarctic Treaty. As the Arctic Council gains further governance clout and is able to develop more tangible agreements, there may be further interface there as well.

As the world wrestles with mechanisms for effective polar governance, it is high time that we think "outside the box" of conventional political discourse on alliances. A planetary vision of environmental diplomacy necessitates such a view that transcends particular geographic regions as specters of geopolitical activity. Strategic alliances and bargains through "creative diplomacy" deserve to be tested further and developed with perseverance and patient persuasion.

Notes

Acknowledgments: The authors are grateful to the French Institute of Strategic Research (IRSEM) and to the Institute for Environmental Diplomacy and Security (IEDS) at the University of Vermont.

   1. Greenland, a self-ruled territory as large as half of the European Union and inhabited by about 57,000 persons, has increased its autonomy within the Kingdom of Denmark toward possible independence. The Self Rule Act of 2009 has generated growing interest from the international community and coincides with strengthened global attention on the Arctic region. For the latest information on Greenland government legislation, refer to the Government of Greenland site: http://www.nanoq.gl.

   2. "Creative diplomacy"—or more precisely "creative middle power diplomacy"—is a concept praised by former Australian prime minister and China expert Kevin Rudd for creatively resolving global challenges such as climate change and energy security. Without being a power, Greenland has the tools for such a "creative diplomacy." The Hon. Kevin Rudd, MP, "The Rise of the Asia Pacific and the role of creative middle power diplomacy," Professor Bernt Seminar

Series, Oslo University, 19 May 2011, accessed 4 October 2013, http://www.foreignminister.gov
.au/speeches/2011/kr_sp_110519.html.

3. Rare earth elements (REE) are a group of metals composed of fifteen lanthanide elements (atomic numbers 57 to 71) and yttrium (atomic number 39) to which scandium (atomic number 21) is commonly included. Rare earth elements are not "rare" but critical to many applications, mainly commercial but also military, due to their unique properties.

4. "Snow, Water, Ice and Permafrost in the Arctic," Oslo: Arctic Monitoring and Assessment Program (AMAP), 2011. Available online, accessed 5 March 2012, http://www.amap.no/
swipa/SWIPA2011ExecutiveSummaryV2.pdf.

5. For an excellent review of predictions and actual impacts of the SARS pandemic see
Keogh-Brown et al., 2008.

6. A rigorous empirical review of China's climate change adaptation strategy within development planning is provided in Li et al., 2011.

7. For the latest information on Australia's Antarctic program refer to http://www
.antarctica.gov.au.

8. Linda Jakobson, "China prepares for an ice-free Arctic," SIPRI Insights on Peace and Security No. 2010/2, Solna: Stockholm International Peace Research Institute (SIPRI), March 2010, accessed 5 March 2012, http://books.sipri.org/files/insight/SIPRIInsight1002.pdf.

9. A good review of Australia-China relations and the ways in which Australia has, to a large degree, effectively leveraged its resource economy status is provided in Wang, 2012.

10. Canada, Russia, and the United States are members of the Arctic Council; France, Germany, Italy, Japan, and the United Kingdom are permanent observers to the Arctic Council, while a final decision regarding the affirmatively received application of the European Union to become a permanent observer was still to be made as of March 2014. For the latest information on the Arctic Council refer to http://www.arctic-council.org.

11. For a discussion of G8+5 prospects for energy diplomacy see Lesage et al., 2010.

12. Reserve Bank of Australia, "Mining Industry: From Bust to Boom," 2011. Available online at: http://www.rba.gov.au/publications/rdp/2011/pdf/rdp2011–08.pdf.

13. Embassy of Iceland–Beijing, "China-Iceland Arctic Fox Mission on top of the world," 15 April 2011, accessed 5 March 2012, http://www.iceland.is/iceland-abroad/cn/english/news
-and-events/china-iceland-arctic-fox-mission-on-top-of-the-world/7716/.

14. For the latest information on the Antarctic Treaty System refer to http://www.ats.aq.

15. The Great Wall station was set up in 1985 and is located at the southern tip of Fildes Peninsula on King George Island in the Shetland Islands of West Antarctica at 62°12′59″S, 58°57′52″W. A second station, Zhongshan, was built in 1989 and is located at the Larsemann Hills of Princess Elizabeth Land, East Antarctica at 69°22′24″S, 76°22′40″E. Chinese Arctic Yellow River Station was founded in July 2004 at 78°55′N, 11°56′E in Ny-Alesund, Spitsbergen Archipelago of Norway. China also has one polar icebreaker, *Xuelong*, which was built in Ukraine in 1993 and strengthened to Class B1 (details from Chinese government site http://
www.chinare.gov.cn/en/index.html?pid=stations).

16. Jo Chandler (with John Garnaut), "China flags polar resource goals," *Sydney Morning Herald*, 7 January 2010, accessed 5 March 2012, http://www.smh.com.au/national/china-flags
-polar-resource-goals-20100106-luc2.html.

17. Greenland (Denmark) is not part of the European Union but remains linked to the EU as one of the Overseas Countries and Territories.

18. A good review of China's Arctic ambitions following the observer status win can be found in Blank, 2013.

19. There is an emerging genre of literature on "green growth" which has also been enshrined by the Organization for Economic Cooperation and Development (OECD) in a series of books, most notably *OECD Green Growth Studies: Towards Green Growth* (Paris: OECD Publishing, 2011). For a more academic review of the topic see Vasquez-Brust and Sarkis, 2012.

20. Australia's more nuanced approach to China's rare earth minerals policy is reflected in a good critical review by Hayes-Labruto et al., 2013.

21. Details on Greenland's geological potential from the Bureau of Minerals and Petroleum, Government of Greenland, http://www.bmp.gl.

22. A good introduction to Chinese political culture in this context can be found in Starr, 2010.

23. Sixth Northern Research Forum Open Assembly, 3–6 September 2011, Hveragerði (Iceland). Details accessed via http://www.nrf.is.

24. Meeting of the European Parliament's Intergroup on Climate Change, Biodiversity and Sustainable Development, "Why is the Arctic critical for European industry?," 13 April 2011, European Parliament, Brussels. Details accessed via http://www.ebcd.org/pdf/en/84-Agenda _Arctic.pdf.

25. "The Danish Minister of Foreign Affairs' Speech on the Arctic Strategy, 22 August 2011," accessed 7 October 2013, http://um.dk/da/~/media/UM/Danish-site/Documents/Politik-og -diplomati/Nyheder_udenrigspolitik/2011/UMerens%tale220811.ashx.

26. Jo Chandler, "China flags polar resource goals," n. 16 supra.

27. See Susskind et al., eds., 1999.

10. *Security in the Arctic*
A Receding Wall

REBECCA PINCUS

I have to-day hoisted the national ensign of the United States
of America at this place, which my observations indicate to be
the North Polar axis of the earth, and have formally taken possession
of the entire region, and adjacent, for and in the name of the
President of the United States of America.

I leave this record and United States flag in possession.
—ROBERT E. PEARY (US Navy), April 6, 1909

In 1938, well before the effects of increasing concentrations of carbon dioxide in the earth's atmosphere began to be noticed by humanity (most of whom were anxiously watching the European continent), Nicholas Spykman wrote that geography is "the most fundamentally conditioning factor in the formulation of national policy because it is the most permanent." He added: "George Washington defending thirteen states with a ragged army has been succeeded by Franklin Roosevelt with the resources of a continent at his command, but the Atlantic continues reassuringly to separate Europe from the United States and the ports of the Saint Lawrence are still blocked by winter ice" (Spykman, 29).

Now, however, that winter ice is retreating. The impenetrable Arctic icepack, which protected North America and frustrated Russia for so long, is weakening yearly. Sometime in the next twenty or thirty years, the Arctic Ocean will be ice-free throughout the summer months. Its frozen winters will grow steadily shorter, and its ice cover will be increasingly made up of thin, brittle, first-year ice rather than the harder multiyear pack ice. Once an impenetrable frozen ocean, a bulwark against invasion and a graveyard for sailors and adventurers, the Arctic Ocean is at risk of losing its climate-stabilizing role and transforming into a more conventional ocean, reshaping global geopolitics. Climate change is reshaping some of the fundamental geographic characteristics that have molded global geopolitics in the modern era. The national security implications of the warming Arctic are profound and will affect Arctic nations as well as non-Arctic states. This chapter will provide an introduction to the changes taking place as well as their context in the history of Arctic securitization, US Arctic policy, and the implications of Arctic warming for regional stability.

History of Arctic Securitization

The Arctic region, although ice-bound, has a history characterized by steadily increasing securitization throughout the twentieth century. Major developments pierced the ice shield: submarines, airplanes, and long-range missiles all compromised what had been an impenetrable border. The securitization of the twenty-first century will be fundamentally different. The change is of intent: melting ice means that humanity is increasingly seeking to establish a larger presence in the Arctic. During the twentieth century, as technology eroded the defensive value of polar ice, the Arctic was still seen as a frozen wasteland to be transited through (or over or under), with its only strategic value its geography. Although resource extraction remained a significant strategic interest, fishing was the primary activity. As ship traffic, mining, fishing, and tourism increase in coming decades, there will be more national assets to protect, and a greater need to assert sovereignty and defend territory through physical presence of armed forces. Surveillance and satellite imagery will no longer be adequate. Physical militarization will likely be a core element of the Arctic region in the twenty-first century.

The Arctic has always been a significant element of American grand strategy. As the geographic reality of the region changes, it will reshape the geopolitical balance among great powers. The ability to transit through the Arctic easily, albeit during the summer months, offers a rejuggling of global trade perhaps akin to the opening of the Panama Canal. In 1890, before the canal had sped up global shipping, naval theorist Alfred Mahan wrote of the potential consequences: "It is evident enough that this canal, by modifying the direction of trade routes, will induce a great increase of commercial activity and carrying trade through the Caribbean Sea; and that this now comparatively deserted nook of the ocean will become, like the Red Sea, a great thoroughfare of shipping, and will attract, as never before in our day, the interest and ambition of maritime nations. Every position in that sea will have enhanced commercial and military value . . . unless most carefully guarded by treaties, will belong wholly to the belligerent which controls the sea by its naval power" (Mahan, "The United States Looking Outward"). The opening of the Arctic, by similarly altering the basic geography of the world's oceans and shipping routes, may bring changes along the lines of the Panama Canal.

The writings of another military strategist, H. J. Mackinder, can be mined for potential insight into the geostrategic effects of Arctic sea access. He argued that Russia, as was previously the Mongol Empire, is located at the strategic pivot of the globe, or the heartland: "She can strike on all sides and be struck from all sides, save the north" (Mackinder, 313). This pivot state is bordered by an inner crescent, composed of India, China, Turkey, Germany, and other European states; beyond this lies an outer crescent, including the United States, Canada, Japan, the United Kingdom, Australia, and South Africa. Today, these crescents would include other powers, notably in South America and Southeast Asia. Mackinder's basic contention was that the resources and position of the vast interior area of Russia or Germany could potentially lead an empire centered in this area to world domination. This may sound far-fetched, but as Kurth noted, "It took the monumental events of the twentieth century—the First World War, the Second World War and the Cold War—to refute [Mackinder]. Each of these three wars was fought to prevent Mackinder's prediction from becoming true, and it took 75 years, 45 million lives and trillions of dollars to do so" (Kurth, 159). As the Arctic becomes increasingly accessible, the power dynamics of key states, notably the United States, Russia, China, Japan, Canada, Iceland, and others, will shift in as-yet unknown ways.

The significance of Arctic thawing for global geopolitics and American grand strategy therefore presents a challenge to US security planners. Grand strategy— the identification and pursuit of fundamental long-term national goals—must be revised in the twenty-first century to incorporate the new reality of a seasonally open Arctic Ocean. Activity by major US rivals underscores the urgency of this need.

Changing Security Needs

As nations begin to bump into each other in the Arctic, whether on naval patrols, fishing vessels, or drilling rigs, there will be greater room for both conflict and cooperation. A summertime ice-free Arctic will increasingly be like the rest of the world's oceans—most of which are shared peacefully, some of which regrettably are marked by tension. The changes taking place in the Arctic have drawn global attention, and some states are already positioning themselves to benefit. Russia, in particular, is eagerly anticipating the increased influence it expects will result from its dominance in the Arctic basin.

Russia has aggressively pursued extended continental shelf claims through the United Nations Convention on the Law of the Sea (UNCLOS), and has sent strategic bomber flights over the Arctic Ocean for the first time since the Cold War (Borgerson, 63). Although Russia is certainly interested in potential offshore energy reserves within its shelf claims, its offshore sector is underdeveloped. Baev argues that instead, Russia's bold Arctic strategy "appears also to be motivated by unquantifiable but irrationally powerful considerations related to international prestige, an urge to get ahead of geopolitical competitors, a desire to strengthen respect of the global peers, and an intention to build a particular northern identity stemming from Stalin's remarkably popular Arctic exploits in the late 1930s" (Baev, 303). Baev also notes that similar assertiveness has been demonstrated by the United States, Norway, Denmark, and Canada.

China recently launched a polar-class icebreaker, the *Snow Dragon* or *Xuelong*, and conducts Arctic scientific expeditions as well as maintains an Arctic station on Svalbard.[1] China is clearly interested in the Arctic region, and may recognize the strategic value of access, presence, and knowledge of both geography and players. China also requested permanent observer status on the Arctic Council (which it received in May 2013) and can therefore be described as pursuing a multipronged approach to establishing influence in the Arctic region.[2]

The relationship between China and Russia may give pause to US security planners, since the two states are fairly close partners and balance against the United

States and the European Union on occasion. Dmitri Trenin noted that Beijing is an indispensable partner in assuring security in Russia's "near abroad." Thus, Moscow has no alternative but to seek friendly and cooperative relations with Beijing (Trenin, 77). In addition, the Asia tilt of US policy as well as global focus has significant implications for Russia-China relations, as well as those of the United States to both states.

Other states are also closely interested in the future of the Arctic: Japan is dependent on energy supplies shipped through the Strait of Malacca, a global hotspot, and therefore may welcome alternative routes (Ebinger and Zambetakis, 1221). Arctic routes, either via the Northwest Passage or Northern Sea Route, offer significant savings of time and fuel over traditional routes like the Strait of Malacca, the Suez or Panama canals, or rounding Africa or South America—up to 40 percent (Ebinger and Zambetakis, 1221). Although these routes are beset by environmental hazards, mostly ice, they are free of pirates—perhaps offering a tempting alternative in the future.

The path forward is not yet clear. Lawson Brigham writes, "We are witnessing the cautious evolution of an Arctic region from a once-closed security bastion to a vast marine area more open for use and, potentially, integrated with the global economy" (Brigham, 54). Most states are, indeed, moving quite cautiously, as the time frame of the changes taking place is extended and the limited summer season places sharp boundaries on transit. Although many observers predict an impending Arctic "cold war" over energy resources, and point to tension between the United States and Russia as a source of conflict, Arctic nations are emphasizing the role of cooperation in the future management of the region. Although the United States has come relatively late to the table, it has picked up the pace of policymaking on the Arctic in recent years, although it remains to be seen if policy decisions will be adequately resourced.

US Discussion of Arctic Security

Within American national security institutions, awareness of how climate change is recalibrating geostrategic calculations is clear. In particular, the dramatic 2007 planting of a Russian flag at the North Pole by the Russian explorer and legislator Arthur Chilingarov sparked wide attention from US policymakers and Congressional representatives who had previously not paid much attention to the region. We are no longer in an era that attaches great import to flag-planting and claim-staking, but the showmanship associated with Chilingarov's submarine dive had the unintended benefit of drawing attention, which could then be redirected toward substantive issues. Strategists in the United States leaped at the opportunity, and policy emerged.

In January 2009, shortly before he left office, President Bush released National Security Presidential Directive/NSPD-66, on Arctic Region Policy. This document was the first presidential directive to update US policy in the Arctic region since 1994. It takes note of the effects of climate change and increasing human activity in the Arctic, and states US policy. Policy goals include protection of the environment, resource extraction, international cooperation, respect for indigenous populations, and scientific research. However, a focus of NSPD-66 is national security. National security interests are identified: "missile defense and early warning; deployment of sea and air systems for strategic sealift, strategic deterrence, maritime presence, and maritime security operations; and ensuring freedom of navigation and over-flight" (United States, Office of the President, NSPD-66, 2). The directive clearly states that the United States needs to "assert a more active and influential national presence to protect its Arctic interests and to project sea power throughout the region" (NSPD-66, 3).

With this directive in mind, and perhaps also encouraged by the sudden burst of Arctic interest, the US Navy in October 2009 released its Navy Arctic Roadmap, a production of the newly established Task Force on Climate Change. This plan outlined US Navy objectives and actions regarding the Arctic for the near future (FY10–14). It noted that the Arctic is warming rapidly and pointed to areas of concern: knowledge gaps of the interrelationships between atmosphere, ocean, and ice; unresolved maritime boundary disputes; conflicting overlap of US Navy operations with indigenous uses; lack of support infrastructure and logistics support; lack of bases and navigational and electronic aids; environmental hazards; lack of airfields; and lack of ice-capable vessels.[3] Taken together, these are significant challenges. The Arctic falls within the responsibility of the US Northern Command (USNORTHCOM); the USNORTHCOM commander is also responsible for NORAD, the North American Aerospace Defense Command, a binational national security command for aerospace and maritime control and warning for Canada, Alaska, and the continental United States.

The Pentagon's 2010 Quadrennial Defense Review Report (QDR) also identified climate change as a key issue shaping the future security environment. The Arctic was specifically addressed: "The effect of changing climate on the Department's operating environment is evident in the maritime commons of the Arctic. The opening of the Arctic waters in the decades ahead which will permit seasonal commerce and transit presents a unique opportunity to work collaboratively in multilateral forums to promote a balanced approach to improving human and environmental security" (United States Department of Defense, QDR 2010, 86). The very dovish language of this quote must be understood as the public message presented by the Department of Defense, and is only part of efforts to establish American security presence in the region.

The 2007 Cooperative Strategy for 21st Century Seapower, a joint strategy issued by the US Navy, Marine Corps, and Coast Guard, states, "Climate change is gradually opening up the waters of the Arctic, not only to new resource development, but also to new shipping routes that may reshape the global transport system. While these developments offer opportunities for growth, they are potential sources of competition and conflict for access and natural resources." The chief of naval operations (CNO) issued the Navy Strategic Objectives for the Arctic, a document to support the Roadmap, and summarized the navy's ultimate goal: "A safe, stable and secure Arctic region where US national and maritime interests are safeguarded and the homeland is protected."

However, the United States has not yet taken many steps to implement its Arctic policy. The CNO's Strategic Objectives noted that the immediate priorities in the Arctic are "Icebreaking, Search and Rescue, Marine Environmental Protection, Living Marine Resources/Law Enforcement, Marine Safety, and Waterways Management," and that these missions fall within the US Coast Guard's responsibility, but called for "close cooperation and collaboration" between the navy and coast guard (United States Navy, CNO, 2). The coast guard is an under-resourced agency and operates the significantly outdated US polar icebreaking fleet.[4] To date, neither the navy nor coast guard have adequate ice-capable assets, bases, or other critical Arctic infrastructure and platforms.

Most recently, in May 2013 President Obama released his National Strategy for the Arctic Region, prefaced by a cover letter stating, "The Arctic region is peaceful, stable, and free of conflict." In a reference perhaps to Russia's dramatic Arctic gestures, the document notes, "An undisciplined approach to exploring new opportunities in this frontier could result in significant harm to the region, to our national security interests, and to the global good" (United States, Office of the President, 2013, p. 4). The National Strategy for the Arctic Region summarizes American interests as follows: "the security of the United States; protecting the free flow of resources and commerce; protecting the environment; addressing the needs of indigenous communities; and enabling scientific research." The National Strategy, like almost all US security documents on the Arctic, reiterates the American commitment to freedom of the seas as an overarching international commitment: "We draw from our long-standing policy and approach to the global maritime spaces in the twentieth century, including freedom of navigation and overflight and other internationally lawful uses of the sea and airspace . . . ; security on the oceans; maintaining strong relationships with allies and partners; and peaceful resolution of disputes without coercion" (p. 4). The Strategy goes on to identify four lines of primary American security effort: "evolve Arctic infrastructure and strategic capabilities"; "enhance Arctic domain awareness"; "preserve Arctic region freedom of the seas"; and "provide for future United States energy security" (pp. 6–7).

However, little top-level American security language refers to the geopolitical and grand strategic consequences of a thawing Arctic. For example, although the National Strategy for the Arctic Region notes, "The melting of Arctic ice has the potential to transform global climate and ecosystems as well as global shipping, energy markets, and other commercial interests" (p. 11), it does not place these changes or the American response into a broader geopolitical or grand strategic discussion. In a very short document (under eleven pages), no explanation of the significance of the Arctic region is given, nor any broader discussion of the ways in which Arctic melting may reshape global strategy. This is an oversight. Although there is likely more attention to the topic in classified documents, the lack of discussion in what is publicly available fails to inform the American and global public of how US leadership views the Arctic as fitting into broader national and international goals and policies.

Conclusion

The major challenge for the United States will be the cost of securing the Arctic. At a time when the American military budget is facing large cuts, finding room for polar resources will be difficult. "Naval forces have always been expensive and relatively scarce," noted Rubel, concluding that their deployment must "be attended by clearheaded calculations of acceptable risk" (Rubel, 31). The US Navy's Roadmap lays clear the dilemma posed to strategic planners: "If the Navy acts too early it will waste resources, but acting too late will result in mission failure" (Titley and St. John, 44). The timelines of both navy planning and Arctic melt are very long, challenging planners to make decisions in the present that will not come to fruition for many years. The incentive to delay decisions, or "kick the can down the road," is significant, particularly in a contentious and difficult political situation such as currently prevails in the United States.

Cost awareness may be reflected in the emphasis on cooperation in US security discourse on the Arctic. Ice-capable assets are particularly expensive (for example, a polar-class icebreaker costs roughly $1 billion) and are of limited use—employed primarily in polar regions, during winter months. The combination of high cost and limited usefulness makes leaders, both political and military, loath to commit to polar acquisition programs. Recognizing the temporally and environmentally limited access that is emerging, policymakers within the military emphasize the low stakes: "Indeed, the likelihood of large-scale international conflict is small, and the Arctic environment will continue to be harsh and challenging for much of the year, making operations difficult and dangerous for the remainder of the twenty-first century" (Titley and St. John, 40). President Obama's National Strategy for the Arctic Region called for the United States to "pursue innovative arrangements"—in order to "more efficiently develop, resource, and manage capabilities, where appropriate and feasible, to better advance our strategic priorities in this austere fiscal environment" (United States, Office of the President, 2013, 3).

The muted nature of this security language, with its references to cooperation, efficiency, and timing, makes it clear that the Arctic is not a top security priority to American policymakers. This is partly positive—if US leaders believed there was a real danger of conflict or threats to US interests in the region, cost would not be so heavily emphasized in security language. However, the absence of thorough discussion of the connections between the Arctic and America's global grand strategy is noticeable. The Arctic is a remote region far from public attention, and we run the risk that Arctic policies may be pushed aside in favor of more visible interests. Even if, as is likely, Arctic security is getting much more attention in classified circles, the lack of public discussion is problematic. For US Arctic policy to succeed in defending American interests, as well as working to resolve transnational issues in a changing Arctic, the public needs to be better informed of how Arctic policy advances US global strategy. Deliberate discussion of American geostrategic goals and their relation to the Arctic region will help to gain public support and see Arctic policy goals through to their successful implementation.

Notes

Epigraph. The Peary quote that opens this chapter is taken from *The Ends of the Earth*, edited by Kolbert and Spufford, 2007 (p. 68).

1. For more information, see Petterson, *Barents Observer* 2012 articles on the subject.

2. Interestingly, the Arctic Council added China, India, Italy, Japan, Singapore, and South Korea, but delayed a decision on adding the EU. See the *New York Times* article by S. L. Myers, "Arctic Council Adds Six Nations as Observer States, Including China," 2013.

3. An informative discussion of the US Navy's Arctic Roadmap can be found in Titley and St. John. Rear Admiral Titley was Oceanographer of the Navy and director of the US Navy's Task Force Climate Change, both of which offices sponsored the Arctic Roadmap.

4. For further information on the state of the US Coast Guard's icebreakers, see R. Pincus, "'The US is an Arctic Nation': Policy, implementation and US icebreaking capabilities in a changing Arctic," *Polar Journal* 3(1) (2013).

PART THREE
Community
Human Rights, Indigenous Politics,
and Collective Learning

There is no comparison between that which is lost
by not succeeding and that which is lost by not trying.
—FRANCIS BACON

W ITH any emergent human activity, there is a need for community development to take root and gain ownership among the inhabitants of a region. Remote Arctic communities have a particular need to engage with global human rights discourse, not only because of the vulnerability of the communities but also because of what nascent Arctic governance processes can learn from the paradigm. This section of our volume begins with an exploration of how such an interface might occur. Would it be appropriate to consider the impact of climate change on such communities as a human rights issue? What might the application of a human rights framework in the context of such areas mean for international law?

The salience of such questions becomes particularly important since most communities in the Arctic identify themselves as indigenous and have a strong sense of sovereign decision making. Indigenous politics are strongly anchored in international human rights norms but are also keenly independent and assertive of tradition, which may at times counter those norms. Although development metrics such as health and education are important goals, the pace and texture of economic activity is questioned by communities. These communities would like to have the choice of being resource independent in terms of sustenance through traditional subsistence practice.

Food security is central to this narrative from Arctic communities, and the next chapter explores cooperative mechanisms that Innu and Inuit communities in Labrador, Canada, have developed to ensure such processes under changing climatic conditions. Quantitative methods and agent-based modeling techniques provide a prospective analysis of cooperative systems under development pressure. The results show convincingly that these communities have greater resilience through traditional cooperative mechanisms of food sharing, which should be considered as an important means of managing development with minimal conflict.

The power of comparative analysis is then used in the next chapter to consider how human rights discourse and economic development imperatives are being reconciled in Russia versus North America. Energy infrastructure development projects and their engagement processes with communities are analyzed in the shadow of legal and regulatory enforcement mechanisms. Market mechanisms of compensation and their impacts in these relatively subsistence-oriented communities is critically examined. Lesson drawing across the region to improve the application of "best practices" with infrastructure development that would provide incentives for these remote regions to remain populated beyond the resource boom are also explored.

The next chapter differentiates between meaningful cooperation and excessive collaboration with non-Arctic communities that might dilute tradition or hamper the development of indigenous capacity in Alaska. Given the dominance of the United States in world affairs and the unique history of Alaska and its connections across the Bering Strait to the greater Eurasian polar region, this case is particularly revealing as a prototype for understanding community tensions across the Arctic as larger organizations emerge to "manage" their interests.

The final chapter of the volume brings home the importance of education and the emergence of epistemic communities through the use of smart technologies and networks. The University of the Arctic and a constellation of other organizations have allowed for knowledge exchange to create a diplomatic safety net that is likely to prevent escalation of conflicts between informed citizens of this remote region.

The most acute dilemma of diplomacy in the Arctic is how best to reconcile global norms of institutional development with the assertion of sovereignty by indigenous communities. As the ice melts, diplomatic skills will be further tested as more stakeholders enter the spheres of interest within these distant lands. The role of research and adaptive strategies will become increasingly more important to reach consensus.

11. Using Human Rights to Improve Arctic Governance

REBECCA BRATSPIES

Each day brings new evidence that human activity is dramatically and irreversibly altering planet Earth, potentially unraveling the life support systems on which we and all other living creatures rely. Nowhere is that evidence more vivid than in the Arctic—where sea ice is retreating, and where in 2011 a record-breaking ozone hole was reported over Arctic skies.[1] Headlines about the Arctic with alarming phrases like "After the Ice" have become common fare.[2] As the ice melts, the once-remote Arctic becomes increasingly accessible to shipping, oil and gas extraction, fishing, and tourism. That accessibility, in turn, sparks further changes—potentially creating a self-reinforcing cascade of development and environmental degradation.

A complex series of feedback loops connect the Arctic to events unfolding in other parts of the world. As a result, decisions made elsewhere increasingly influence the Arctic's future. While it is clear that the Arctic is in the throes of profound changes driven by the twin pressures of climate change and globalization, it is not yet clear how those changes will be managed. Navigating these changes in a fashion that protects one of the world's most environmentally vulnerable regions while providing for the interests of the Arctic's 4 million inhabitants will require far more effective Arctic governance than we have had in the past.

The new Arctic activities made possible by a warming climate will ultimately be managed, coordinated, and regulated—the only questions are when, under what governance structures, and by whose rules. The international community faces a choice—governance initiatives must either get ahead of changing circumstances or will assuredly trail in their wake.

No country has sovereignty over the North Pole or the Arctic Ocean around it. Unlike Antarctica, the international community has not developed a specific treaty regime for the Arctic. Nevertheless, an extensive international legal framework already exists, and there is widespread agreement that governance in the Arctic should begin with implementing and enhancing the existing international agreements like the Framework Convention on Climate Change[3] and the United Nations Convention on the Law of the Sea,[4] as well as the host of other agreements, treaties, and institutions that limit and shape activities in the Arctic.[5] Implementation of these regimes in the Arctic must be done with careful attention to the region's unique ecosystems, and to the rights and needs of the Arctic's indigenous peoples. As such, the nascent human right to a healthy environment emerging at the intersection of human rights and environmental governance has a particular valence for Arctic governance. It is only by looking to these important emerging human rights norms that we get a clear sense of what full implementation of existing international agreements concerning the Arctic will entail.

This chapter makes the case that Arctic governance should draw on human rights norms in order to grapple more effectively with issues of participation, fairness, and transparency in managing Arctic resources.[6] In doing so, it draws on the emerging human rights norms associated with international environmental law, the jurisprudence of the Inter-American Human Rights System, and the UN Declaration on the Rights of Indigenous Peoples. Together, these important international law sources offer a new approach to Arctic governance. In particular, this chapter suggests that embrace of emerging human rights norms around participation, access to information, and prior informed consent will help decision makers exercise their discretion in a fashion that not only supports rather than undermines legitimacy but also leads to better, more sustainable decision making.

The Challenges of Arctic Governance in a Changing World

The region known as the Arctic (the area above 66.5 north latitude, or within the Arctic Circle) is roughly the size of Africa, encompassing approximately 6 percent of the earth's surface area. Eight countries have territory within the Arctic Circle—Canada, Denmark (through Greenland), Finland, Iceland, Norway, Russia, Sweden, and the United States. Of these, Sweden and Finland do not border the Arctic Ocean and thus have no jurisdictional claims to the Arctic Ocean or its continental shelf. The Arctic is home to forty different indigenous groups whose jurisdictional claims overlap those of the Arctic states.

The Arctic is widely believed to hold some of the earth's biggest untapped stores of hydrocarbons. Indeed, the United States Geological Survey recently estimated that the Arctic might hold as much as 412 billion barrels of conventional undiscovered oil and natural gas resources.[7] In the past, the challenges of infrastructure development in the harsh northern environment shielded the Arctic from the levels of resource exploitation seen in other oil-rich regions. Climatic conditions made drilling expensive and dangerous, and the narrow window of appropriate weather increased the costs and slowed the pace of developing Arctic oil fields. As a warming climate makes the Arctic more accessible, those cost differentials will decline. Melting sea ice also makes trans-Arctic shipping more attractive, both for tourism and to transport mineral resources—with both the Northern Sea Route and the Northwest

Passage now routinely clear of sea ice for part of the year.[8] These same changes are now increasing interest in commercial exploitation of Arctic fisheries.

Transportation, fisheries, tourism, and mineral resource extraction (including hydrocarbons) thus represent the primary points of intersection between Arctic governance and the global economy. Each activity poses its own hazards to the fragile Arctic environment, and offers a different set of risks and benefits to the Arctic's inhabitants. While the media frenzy over a "new gold rush" in the Arctic may be overstated, it is clear that states and private actors are moving expeditiously to exploit these newly accessible resources. Already, drilling is either taking place or planned off the coast of Greenland and in the Kara, Barents, and Chukchi seas, involving global oil giants Chevron, Royal Dutch Shell, and ExxonMobil as well as major regional players like Cairns, Rosneft, and Statoil. The Arctic is also home to massive extraction enterprises—to the world's largest zinc mine (Red Dog) and nickel mine (Norilsk). Not only do these extraction industries bring increased pollution to the Arctic, but the increased ship traffic associated with these activities also heightens the risk of spills and other disasters. As the twin forces of climate change and globalization weave the Arctic ever more firmly into the global economy, development will be increasingly driven by demands originating elsewhere—by global commodity prices, tourism, and the world's insatiable thirst for oil. Climate change thus poses new challenges, both for Arctic peoples and for their environment.

In contrast to this frenzied pace of change and development, the international organizations, regimes, and agreements that might temper governance choices in the Arctic tend to move slowly, if at all. This mismatch in reaction time is not unique to the Arctic but is part of a discernible global pattern. Around the world, the scramble for resources and mineral wealth has led to rapid social and economic changes, creating the possibility of enormous gains for those who succeed in claiming and extracting the resources. The institutions tasked with overseeing their activities cannot keep up, and the resulting legal vacuum makes it possible for important human rights and environmental considerations to be thrust aside in favor of short-term gains. Unless positive governance steps are taken, and soon, the Arctic might well suffer a similar fate. Indeed we are already seeing indications that this is occurring—for example, the United States moving ahead with drilling in the Chukchi Sea despite a record of extremely poor consultation, suggestions of tampering with scientific evidence, and an overall lack of transparent decision making.

Yet, history is not destiny. Just because mineral rushes have historically resulted in dispossession, destruction, and environmental devastation does not mean that this one has to do so as well. What is different now is the well-developed body of human rights law that gives states, civil society, and individuals new tools for managing the onslaught. This chapter takes up the question of what it would mean for the Arctic if both the problems and the solutions to managing the changing Arctic were analyzed through a human rights lens. As such, it offers human rights norms as an ordering principle for Arctic governance—a way to resolve issues of legal fragmentation, and to bridge the critical policy-setting gaps in participation and implementation.

The Arctic Council

Effective regional organization will be critical for ensuring a coherent and appropriate system of Arctic governance—one that is capable of managing rapid change as it occurs. One obvious candidate to take the lead in developing this kind of regional governance capacity would be the Arctic Council. The Arctic Council was formed in 1996 by the eight Arctic countries: Canada, Denmark (including Greenland and the Faroe Islands), Norway, Finland, Sweden, Iceland, the Russian Federation, and the United States, as a high-level intergovernmental forum for resolving Arctic issues.[9] Unlike most such intergovernmental organizations, the Arctic Council was built on a model of inclusion, with the Arctic states as voting members, representatives of the Arctic's six main indigenous groups as permanent members, and others, including non-Arctic states and civil society, eligible for observer status. Thus, from its very inception, the Arctic Council more closely embodied international human rights norms than do most international organizations. This innovative governance structure gives the Arctic Council a unique platform from which to embrace human rights as the decisional matrix for Arctic governance.

The Arctic Council, with its notable track record of successful policy shaping, might fill this role. But it is currently handicapped by a scope, mission, and structure that is not well-suited to the Arctic's changing needs. Indeed, in the context of oil and gas development, the Arctic Council has acknowledged that "the environmental and negative social effects of oil and gas development can only be minimized if existing regulations are effectively implemented and new regulations addressing current weaknesses are developed."[10] That means on both the international and domestic levels, there is a need for continual improvement of Arctic governance systems. Otherwise, changing conditions and technologies will outstrip regulatory capacities as new areas are explored and developed. By making some clear choices now, the international community can ensure that the norms and values embedded in whatever governance regimes emerge in the Arctic reflect core human rights principles of justice, equality, and participation.[11] Time will be of the essence because the governance choices made today will shape the Arctic for today and for the future. Improving and strengthening Arctic governance must be an urgent priority.

There is clear consensus that good governance in the Arctic must begin with implementing and enhancing existing international agreements, most notably the United Nations Convention on the Law of the Sea (UNCLOS) and the Framework Convention on Climate Change (UNFCC).[12] The Arctic Council has already begun doing some of this work. Indeed, the Council already recommends that oil and gas operations be conducted in accordance with various international law principles embedded in the UNFCC, including the precautionary approach[13] and the polluter-pays principle.[14] Given the many uncertainties and unknowns about oil and gas operations in the harsh Arctic environment, this emphasis on precaution is a prudent one, and the Arctic Council is wise to embrace the emerging substantive international environmental norm of precautionary decision making as a central tenet for oil and gas development in the Arctic. There is no question that a precautionary governance scheme, combined with strict enforcement of sound engineering practices, can greatly reduce emissions, discharges, and the risk of accidents.

Yet, precaution alone will not be enough. Physical impacts and disturbances are inevitable wherever industry operations occur. Spills, leaks, and other accidents are likely to occur even under the most stringent control systems. Moreover, even setting aside the prospect of accidents and mistakes, pollution from the extraction process itself will likely be significant. The Arctic Council recognizes that the risks associated with Arctic resource extraction "cannot be eliminated."[15] Human rights norms teach us that one consequence that should flow from this conclusion about unavoidable risk is that those most directly affected should have a major voice in making the decisions about these risky activities. As a result, a human rights approach to Arctic governance requires an emphasis on transparency, participation, and accessibility. These critical considerations are currently left to vagaries of national law—with very mixed results.[16]

Indeed one of the most striking aspects of current Arctic governance is the lack of engagement with human rights norms. In 2011, for example, the Arctic Council's Protection of the Arctic Marine Environment (PAME) Working Group prepared its Arctic Ocean Review, Phase I Report.[17] One of the key objectives of this report was to "compile information on global and regional measures that are relevant to the conservation and sustainable use of the Arctic marine environment and identify and highlight potential weaknesses."[18] Another was to "determine the adequacy of applicable international/regional commitments and to promote their implementation and compliance."[19] The bulk of the report, chapter 3, was dedicated to a review of global instruments and processes relevant to the Arctic marine environment. This otherwise detailed survey of the relevant international agreements, conventions, and soft-law instruments had one glaring omission—international human rights instruments were completely omitted.

Notably, neither in this report nor elsewhere has the Arctic Council fully embraced the UN Declaration on the Rights of Indigenous Peoples,[20] let alone the International Convention on Civil and Political Rights (ICCPR)[21] and the International Convention on Economic, Social and Cultural Rights (ICESCR)[22] as guiding principles for Arctic governance. This gap is particularly noticeable in the context of oil and gas development in the Arctic because these very important human rights documents complement the precautionary principle by announcing fundamental international principles for how governments should exercise their sovereign powers over territory in the face of uncertainty.

Climate Change as a Human Rights Issue

For all of these new governance challenges facing the Arctic, climate change acts as a "threat multiplier."[23] Indeed, climate change is at the core of these new activities (most notably resource extraction)—not only because it is climate change that makes them possible, but also because these activities will accelerate the pace of climate change. In general, international discussions tend to frame climate change as an environmental problem—and governance measures focus on environmental challenges posed by climate change, or on environmental measures intended to either prevent or delay destruction of sensitive ecosystems. While climate change is surely an environmental issue, it is much more than that as well. Climate change raises profound governance challenges precisely because it implicates every aspect of society—political, economic, and social.

Twenty years of global cooperation has produced voluminous documentation of the scope and scale of the climate change problem.[24] Yet, with over two decades of global attention, research, and negotiations, global society has failed to induce public and private actors to take meaningful steps to curb activities that contribute to climate change. If the problems are relatively clear, the solutions are far murkier. Part of the problem may be the framing of climate change as a conventional international law problem amenable to nation-based negotiations and technical resolution.

Existing institutions and agreements will have to adapt and innovate if they are to be resilient in the face of the multidimensional challenges of justice, development, and protection in a rapidly changing world. It is increasingly clear that navigating the effects associated with climate change is also the defining moral and social justice challenge of our times. The Arctic exemplifies this point—Arctic peoples have contributed very little to the climate change problem, yet are bearing the brunt of its effects. Moreover, they are not facing a speculative, future threat, but are bearing the costs of climate change now.

Indigenous groups have already sought to argue that their justiciable human rights are violated by activities that promote climate change. For example, the Inuit people of the Arctic filed a petition with the Inter-American Commission on Human Rights claiming that the acts and omissions of the United States with respect to climate change are violating their human rights.[25] Because human rights law is generally considered to define the bounds of universal morality and to be "the law's best response to profound, unthinkable, far-reaching moral transgression," we see it increasingly invoked as a way to frame responses to climate change in the Arctic and elsewhere.[26]

How a Human Rights Framework Might Change Arctic Governance

The Law of the Sea Convention is considered the fundamental instrument of international law concerning the world's seas and oceans, with the attendant consequence that other agreements are expected to be compatible with it.[27] Similarly, the Universal Declaration of Human Rights, and to a lesser extent the ICCPR and the ICESCR, are the definitive statements of the international human rights norms embedded in the United Nations' charter. The United Nations Declaration on the Rights of Indigenous Peoples will be of particular importance to Arctic governance. These documents embody a growing international consensus that the relationship between states and individuals vis-à-vis the environment must embody human rights norms.[28] Thus, human rights offer an organizing principle for "defining practices, assigning roles and guiding interactions" in order to address the collective problem of Arctic governance.[29] In particular, the emerging procedural human rights norms of transparency and access to information,[30] prior informed consent,[31] and participation in decision making[32] offer critical guidance for Arctic governance.

These participatory human rights norms also enrich our understanding of how to secure the substantive human rights articulated in the Universal Declaration and the major international human rights conventions such as the right to life,[33] health,[34] culture,[35] and property.[36] Justice Weeramantry, for one, has characterized protecting the environment as "a vital part of contemporary human rights doctrine, for it is a sine qua non for numerous human rights such as the right to health and the right to life itself."[37] Indeed, these procedural human rights also give content to the requirements of the Framework Convention on Climate Change for "the widest participation"[38] and "public access to information."[39]

Thus the emerging international consensus about the relationship between procedural human rights and substantive rights provides guidance for how to pursue Arctic governance through a human rights lens. These participatory human rights norms have clear resonance for Arctic governance in an era of climate change, particularly in the international framework for oil and gas activities. Viewed from this perspective, certain changes to the Arctic Council's mandate will be necessary in order to highlight human rights as a core organizing principle. These changes will, in turn, deepen the Council's policy-shaping capacity, while also strengthening its mission, scope, and structure.

Embracing an international human rights framework as a cornerstone of Arctic governance would ensure that full participation rights are accorded to indigenous groups and other affected local communities. Human rights, particularly the participatory rights that have emerged from the ongoing dialogue over environmental rights as human rights, can ensure that local and indigenous groups have the opportunity to participate meaningfully and early as key choices are made about resource exploitation—choices that will ultimately have important economic, social, and cultural ramifications for the lives of the Arctic's peoples.

Participation

Participation in decision making is a core tenet of a range of human rights, including the right to development[40] and the right to self-determination.[41] Principle 10 of the UN Draft Principles of Human Rights and the Environment specifically provided that: "Environmental issues are best handled with participation of all concerned citizens, at the relevant level."[42] This emphasis on participation reiterates almost verbatim the procedural rights endorsed by Principle 10 of the Rio Convention.[43] This commitment to participation was ratified, albeit on the state level, in the Espoo Convention,[44] then enshrined as an individual right in the Aarhus Convention.[45] The United Nations Framework Convention on Climate Change similarly requires public participation.[46]

Realizing the right to participation in the context of Arctic governance would, at a minimum, mean ensuring that the Arctic Council's permanent members are able to fully participate in the Council's decision-making processes. Merely creating the possibility of participation will not be enough—human rights teaches us that more affirmative steps are necessary, particularly when resources are a key limit to the capacity of permanent members to participate. Thus a pool of funds specifically earmarked for defraying the travel expenses associated with participating in the Council's meetings would make participation a meaningful possibility for more permanent members, enhancing their role in the decision-making process, and thereby building a model for more effective realization of the human rights embodied in the Declaration of Indigenous Rights and the draft Declaration of Human Rights to the Environment.[47] Indeed, such an approach, once adopted, could become a model for effective inclusion. For example, the Arctic Window policy that the EU is developing as part of its Northern Dimensions initiative could benefit from a model for effectively facilitating indigenous participation in decision making. The human rights benefits would redound, not only to indigenous groups, but also to other justice communities whose interests are at stake but whose voices are rarely heard in making decisions about resource management.

Access to Information

Effective participation in environmental decision making is necessarily tied to transparency and access to information. Indeed, Principle 10 of the Rio Declaration makes this link explicit, reiterating: "Environmental issues are best handled with participation of all concerned citizens, at the relevant level. At the national level, each individual shall have appropriate access to information concerning the environment that is held by public authorities, including information on hazardous materials and activities in their communities, and the opportunity to participate in decision-making processes. States shall facilitate and encourage public awareness and participation by making information widely available."[48]

The Council of Europe has interpreted the European Convention on Human Rights as requiring access to environmental information.[49] Similarly, the European Court of Human Rights has concluded that information about environmental risks must be made available to those likely to be affected.[50] This requirement includes an obligation for the state to provide access to studies and assessments carried out as part of the environmental and economic policy decision-making process.[51] The Aarhus Convention explicitly recognizes the critical role that access to information plays in the nexus between environmental protection and human rights, stating that; "in order to contribute to the protection of the right of every person of present and future generations to live in an environment adequate to his or her health and well-being, each Party shall guarantee the rights of access to information, public participation in decision making, and access to justice."[52]

While these legal developments are not binding on all the Arctic states, that fact alone does not end the conversation about their possible usefulness. Arctic governance will increasingly require decisions about resource extraction—decisions that will dramatically affect the lives, livelihood, and cultural practices of Arctic inhabitants. This well-developed governance theory about access of information rooted in human rights can provide useful guidance.

Prior Informed Consent

The opportunity to give or withhold free, prior, and informed consent is a cornerstone of the Declaration on the Rights of Indigenous Peoples.[53] Articles 29(2), 30(2), and 32(2) of the Declaration all explicitly require that states obtain free and informed prior consent before engaging in activities in the lands or territories of indigenous peoples. Initially, an unwillingness to recognize this right was the ground for United States and Canadian opposition to the Declaration. However, by 2010, both Arctic states had dropped their objection and had joined the overwhelming majority of states embracing the Declaration as a definitive statement of state responsibility under international law.[54] While the Declaration focuses specifically on the right of indigenous groups, this right to prior informed consent should be thought of more broadly—as one held by all local communities confronted with a major land use or resource use decision.

For the Arctic, the notion of prior informed consent embodied in the Declaration means that indigenous groups must have a more important and more formalized voice in resource extraction decisions. The Arctic Council currently recommends, "Prior to opening new areas to oil and gas exploration and development or constructing new infrastructure for transporting oil and gas, local residents, including indigenous communities, should be consulted to ensure that their interests are considered."[55] Thus, the Arctic Council already explicitly recognizes that indigenous groups are key participants in the decision making surrounding extractive activities.

However, this relatively weak recommendation for consultation falls short of state obligations under the Declaration, and therefore cannot satisfy the vision of human rights it embodies. First, consultation is not the same thing as consent. Indeed, prior informed consent encompasses far more than a bare right to be consulted, or even to participate in project design. Without a requirement of prior informed consent, this consultation can dwindle into a mere formality—sufficient perhaps to inform indigenous communities of the nature of, the likely impacts of, and the risks associated with proposed activities but without a way for those communities to refuse to accept those risks and impacts. Prior informed consent, by contrast, necessarily implies the power to withhold consent—the same power to make choices about what is or is not acceptable that any landowner or sovereign has with regard to resources under their control. Without a requirement of prior informed consent, Arctic governance decisions will trample on the indigenous right to make these choices.

Second, there is no requirement that even this watered-down consultation must occur prior to decisions being made. The persistent use of "should" rather than "must" or "shall" in describing consultation requirements clearly signals an inappropriate level of flexibility. Rather than a mandatory minimum that must occur in order for these decisions to be considered as comporting with international human rights, this framing allows prior consultation to dwindle into a token best practice. Even worse, the Arctic Council does not conduct follow-up to determine whether consultation has occurred. As a result, state practices vary widely.[56] Again, international human rights refines existing practices by guiding and informing states as they seek to implement their obligations in the Arctic.

Given the role that governments play as grantors of the right to develop—either through permitting schemes or as the owner of the underlying resources—the doctrine of prior informed consent embodied in the UN Declaration on the Rights of Indigenous Peoples is critical to protect indigenous communities.

Conclusion

Joseph Raz has persuasively argued that labeling something "a right" is in fact an assertion that the interest is sufficiently weighty to justify imposing obligations on others.[57] The claim that Arctic peoples have the human right to information, participation, and prior informed consent thus defines the boundaries of a rationale for governance and offers a normative framework for structuring and interpreting decisions. Human rights norms do this by prioritizing transparency, responsiveness, and consultation.

Embrace of human rights as a guiding principle for Arctic governance would transform the background assumptions that the Arctic Council brings to decision making. These assumptions play a particularly important role in resource extraction decisions in an era of climate change, where discretion is vast and scientific certainties are few.[58] Were officials making governance decisions about the Arctic to fully embrace human rights norms, we might well see a new, more participatory and transparent governance regime emerge. Thus, a human rights–based decision-making process will ultimately be more likely to enjoy the trust of the people affected by those decisions, and more likely to be perceived as legitimate.[59]

Notes

1. For reports on the first occurrence in the observational record of an Arctic ozone hole comparable to the Antarctic ozone hole, see: Gloria Manney et al., "Unprecedented Arctic Ozone Loss in 2011," *Nature* (2 October 2011); Michael Marshall, "Arctic Ozone Hole Breaks All Records," *New Scientist* (2 October 2011), http://www.newscientist.com/article/dn20988 -arctic-ozone-hole-breaks-all-records.html.

2. See, e.g., "Special Issue on the Arctic: After the Ice," *Nature* (12 October 2011), http:// www.nature.com/news/2011/111012/full/478171a.html.

3. United Nations Framework Convention on Climate Change, 9 May 1992, 1771 UNTS 107.

4. United Nations Convention on the Law of the Sea (UNCLOS), 10 December 1982 (entered into force 16 November 1994). The Arctic Governance Project identifies honoring, implementing, and enhancing existing Arctic governance systems as a key policy recommendation. Arctic Governance Project, *Arctic Governance in an Era of Transformative Change: Critical Questions, Governance Principles Ways Forward* (14 April 2010) (available in French, English, and

Russian at http://www.arcticgovernance.org/agp-report-and-action-agenda.156784.en.html). The Council of the European Union similarly identifies strengthening and implementing relevant agreements as a key basis for the EU's Arctic policy. Council of the European Union, "Council Conclusions on Arctic Issues" (Brussels, 8 December 2009), http://ec.europa.eu/maritimeaffairs/pdf/arctic_council_conclusions_09_en.pdf.

5. A selected and nonexhaustive list of the relevant international agreements would include: the Convention on Biological Diversity, 31 I.L.M. 818 (entered into force 23 December 1993); the London Convention on the Prevention of Marine Pollution by Dumping of Wastes, 22 March 1989, 1673 UNTS 57; the Basel Convention on the Control of Transboundary Movement of Hazardous Wastes, 22 March 1989, 1673 UNTS 57; the Convention for the Protection of the Marine Environment of the North-East Atlantic (OSPAR), 21 February 1974, 13 ILM 352 (1974); and the Convention on Long-range Transboundary Air Pollution, 13 November 1979, T.I.A.S. No. 10,541, 18 I.L.M. 1442 (entered into force 16 March 1983). In addition to these international treaties, there is also a host of International Maritime Organization (IMO) conventions on maritime safety and pollution from vessels. Information about these latter instruments is available at www.imo.org.

6. For a detailed analysis of these stages of the regulatory process, see Kenneth W. Abbott and Duncan Snidal, "The Governance Triangle: Regulatory Standards Institutions in the Shadow of the State," in *The Politics of Global Regulation* 1 (Walter Mattli and Ngaire Woods, eds., 2009). Human rights norms might be of value to regulators across all aspects of regulation, from agenda setting through negotiation and implementation to enforcement.

7. U.S. Geological Survey, "Circum-Arctic Resource Appraisal: Estimates of Undiscovered Oil and Gas North of the Arctic Circle," USGS Fact Sheet 2008, http://pubs.usgs.gov/fs/2008/3049/fs2008-3049.pdf. This would be roughly 22 percent of the world's total projected undiscovered oil and gas reserves. United States Energy Information Administration, Arctic Oil and Natural Gas Potential (19 October 2009), http://www.eia.gov/oiaf/analysispaper/arctic/index.html.

8. Arctic Climate Impact Assessment, "Key Finding 6," *Impacts of a Warming Arctic* (2004), available at http://www.amap.no/documents/doc/impacts-of-a-warming-arctic-2004/786.

9. Declaration on the Establishment of the Arctic Council, Art. 1(a) (19 September 1996), available at http://www.arctic-council.org/index.php/en/about/documents/category/4-founding-documents#.

10. Arctic Monitoring and Assessment Program, *Artic Oil and Gas 2007* (2007), at vii, available at http://www.amap.no/documents/doc/arctic-oil-and-gas-2007/71 (hereafter Arctic 2007 Oil and Gas Assessment).

11. While there is an ongoing debate about whether or not the Arctic Council needs mandatory governance authority, this chapter seeks instead to focus on how international human rights law can enhance Arctic governance regardless of the contours of any particular governance structure.

12. See, e.g., Arctic Governance Project Recommendations, *An Arctic Action Agenda* (14 April 2010); Communication from the Commission to the European Parliament and the Council, *The European Union and the Arctic Region*, COM (2008) 73, 22 November 2008, available at http://eur-lex.europa.eu/LexUriServ/LexUriServ.do?uri=CELEX:DKEY=483680:EN:NOT; Ilulissat Declaration, 28 May 2008.

13. Arctic 2007 Oil and Gas Assessment, supra note 10, at v (referencing Principle 15 of the Rio Declaration, and Art. 3(3) of the Framework Convention on Climate Change (UNFCC). It is indeed a positive indicator that the Arctic Council has embraced the precautionary principle as the decisional matrix for the Arctic. However, states act on multiple levels simultaneously. Embracing precaution at the international level is a good start, but Arctic states must also embrace precaution as their domestic decisional matrix.

14. Arctic 2007 Oil and Gas Assessment, supra note 10, at v (referencing Principle 16 of the Rio Declaration).

15. Arctic 2007 Oil and Gas Assessment, supra note 10, at v.

16. In perhaps the most famous case invoking human rights in the struggle between oil development and environmental protection, Shell Oil recently paid $15.5 million to settle allegations concerning the company's involvement in the torture and murder of Ogoni leader Ken Saro-Wiwa and other nonviolent activists in the Niger Delta. *Wiwa v. Royal Dutch Petroleum Co.,* 226 F.3d 88 (2d Cir. 2000). Brought under the U.S. Alien Tort Claims Act (ATCA), the case notably did not make an environmental human rights argument, in part because prior ATCA jurisprudence has refused to consider environmental claims under the statute. The complaint in *Wiwa v. Royal Dutch Petroleum Co.* is available at http://ccrjustice.org/files/11.8.96%20%20 Wiwa%20Complaint.pdf.

17. Arctic Council, 2011 Arctic Ocean Review, Phase I Report (2009–2011), available at http://www.aor.is/.

18. Ibid. at p. 3.

19. Ibid. at p. 4.

20. As of 16 December 2010, when the United States at last dropped its objections and became the last United Nations member state to join the UN Declaration on the Rights of Indigenous Peoples, all the Arctic states have adopted this Declaration and have committed themselves to recognizing indigenous rights under international law. The Declaration's implementation must therefore clearly be part of any Arctic governance plan.

21. International Convention on Civil and Political Rights, 19 December 1966, 999 UNTS 171.

22. International Convention on Economic, Social and Cultural Rights, 16 December 1966, 999 UNTS 3.

23. Communication from the Commission to the European Parliament and the Council, The European Union and the Arctic Region, COM (2008) 763 (20 November 2008), http:// eur-lex.europa.eu/LexUriServ/LexUriServ.do?uri=CELEX:DKEY=483680:EN:NOT.

24. The most recent reports from the Intergovernmental Panel on Climate Change can be found at http://www.ipcc.ch/. An extensive collection of climate change–related documents can be found through Columbia University Law School's Center for Climate Change Law, http:// www.law.columbia.edu/centers/climatechange/resources.

25. Inuit Circumpolar Conference, Petition to the Inter-American Commission on Human Rights Seeking Relief from Violations Resulting from Global Warming Caused by Acts and Omissions of the United States (7 December 2005) [hereinafter Inuit Petition], available at http://www.earthjustice.org/library/legal_docs/petition-to-the-inter-american-commission-on -human-rights-on-behalf-of-the-inuit-circumpolar-conference.pdf. For an in-depth discussion of the Inuit Petition, see Hari M. Osofsky, "The Inuit Petition as a Bridge? Beyond Dialectics of Climate Change and Indigenous People's Rights," 31 *American Indian Law Review* 675 (2007). The Inuit Petition was dismissed without prejudice in 2006 because the Commission was not convinced of the link between climate change and human rights. Andrew C. Revkin, "Inuit Climate Change Petition Rejected," *New York Times,* 16 December 2006. The Commission held hearings in early 2007 to explore this question. See Martin Wagner, "Testimony of Martin Wagner before the Inter-American Commission on Human Rights" (1 March 2007), available at http://www.earthjustice.org/library/legal_docs/testimony-before-iachr-on-global-warming -human-rights-by-martin-wagner.pdf; see also Sheila Watt-Cloutier, Earth Justice, and Center for International Environmental Law, "Global Warming and Human Rights," available at http:// www.earthjustice.org/library/references/Background-for-IAHRC.pdf (accessed 2 March 2012). The Commission has not issued any further findings or decisions on this topic.

26. Amy Sinden, "Climate Change and Human Rights," *Journal of Land Resources and Environmental Law* 27 (2007), 255, 257.

27. Arctic Council, 2011 Arctic Ocean Review, supra note 17, at p. 38, citing UNCLOS Art. 311.

28. There is a real question about the appropriate relationship between the individual human rights framework that developed in response to active and direct government abuses, and

the ravages of climate change, which is primarily the result of private economic activity. While government policies, particularly those involving exercise of governmental licensing, taxation, and police powers, obviously facilitate and channel private economic activity, there is at least arguably a difference between these activities and the kinds of direct government activities that human rights law has typically addressed. For this reason, the native Inupiat village of Kivalina, Alaska, proceeded under a nuisance theory when it recently sued nine oil companies, fourteen power companies, and one coal company for damages related to climate change. Complaint for Damages, *Native Village of Kivalina v. ExxonMobil Corp.*, 663 F. Supp. 2d 863 (N.D. Cal. 2008) (No. 08–1138), available at 2008 WL 594713. *Massachusetts v. EPA*, 549 U.S. 497 (2007), also proceeded on a nuisance theory.

29. This is Oran Young's very useful definition of institutions and the role they play in governance. Oran R. Young, *International Governance: Protecting the Environment in a Stateless Society* (Ithaca: Cornell University Press, 1994), 3, 15.

30. The Aarhus Convention is perhaps the most notable articulation of this right. Convention on Access to Information, Public Participation in Decision-Making and Access to Justice in Environmental Matters, Art. 1, 25 June 1998, 2161 UNTS 447 [hereinafter Aarhus Convention]. Other examples include the right of advanced informed consent in the Cartagena Protocol and the Declaration on the Rights of Indigenous Peoples. Cartagena Protocol on Biosafety to the Convention on Biological Diversity, 29 January 2000, 2226 UNTS 208; Declaration on the Rights of Indigenous Peoples, G.A. Res. 61/295, Annex, U.N. Doc. A/RES/61/295 (13 September 2007).

31. The Rotterdam Convention on the Prior Informed Consent Procedure for Certain Hazardous Chemicals in International Trade, the Basel Convention on Transboundary Movement of Hazardous Waste, and the Convention on Biological Diversity all embrace prior informed consent as a cornerstone of decision making, as does the United Nations Declaration on the Rights of Indigenous Peoples.

32. See United Nations Declaration on the Rights of Indigenous Peoples, Arts. 27, 32, 38.

33. Universal Declaration of Human Rights, G.A. Res. 217A, at 17, Art. 3, U.N. GAOR, 3d Sess., 1st plen. mtg., U.N. Doc. A/810 (12 December 1948).

34. Ibid., Art. 25.

35. Ibid., Art. 27.

36. Ibid., Art. 17.

37. International Court of Justice, Gabčíkovo-Nagymaros Project (*Hung. v. Slovk.*), 1997 I.C.J. 7, 91 (25 September 1997) (separate opinion of Vice-President Weeramantry).

38. UNFCC, Art. 4(1)(1).

39. Ibid. at Art. 6.

40. UN Declaration on the Rights of Indigenous Peoples, Art. 32, G.A. Res. 61/295, 13 September 2007; Vienna Declaration and Program of Action, Arts. 8, 20, 25, U.N. Doc. A/CONF.157/23 (1993); Declaration on the Right to Development, Art. 8. G.A. Res. 41/128, U.N. GAOR, 41st Sess., Supp. No. 53, at 186, U.N. Doc. A/41/53 (1986).

41. UN Declaration on the Rights of Indigenous Peoples, Art. 3, G.A. Res. 61/295, 13 September 2007; ICCPR, supra note 20, at Art. 1 (3).

42. Draft Principles on Human Rights and the Environment, U.N. Doc. E/CN.4/Sub.2/1994/9, Annex I (1994) at Principle 10.

43. Principle 10 of the Rio Declaration provides: Environmental issues are best handled with participation of all concerned citizens, at the relevant level. Rio Declaration on Environment and Development, A/Conf.151/26 (14 June 1992) available at http://www.unep.org/Documents.Multilingual/Default.asp?documentID=78&articleID=1163.

44. Convention on Environmental Impact Assessment in a Transboundary Context (Espoo Convention) (25 February 1991), Art. 3, available at http://www.unece.org/env/eia/documents/legaltexts/conventiontextenglish.pdf. The Espoo Convention guarantees nondiscriminatory public participation in environmental impact procedures. Art. 2(6) provides that "[t]he Party of origin shall provide an opportunity to the public in areas likely to be affected to participate

in relevant impact assessment procedures regarding proposed activities and shall ensure that the opportunity provided to the public of the affected party is equivalent to that provided to the public of the Party of origin."

45. The full name of the agreement commonly known as the Aarhus Convention is the Convention on Access to Information, Public Participation in Decision-Making and Access to Justice in Environmental Matters, adopted in Aarhus (Denmark) on 25 June 1998. The preamble to the Aarhus Convention "recognize[s] that adequate protection of the environment is essential to human well-being and the enjoyment of basic human rights, including the right to life itself."

46. United Nations Framework Convention on Climate Change, 9 May 1992, 1771 UNTS 107. In particular Article 4(1)(i) obliges states to "encourage the widest participation . . . including that of non-governmental organizations." Article 6 requires that parties promote and facilitate public access to information and public participation.

47. Such a plan would be in accord with Articles 39 and 41 of the Declaration, which require that financial assistance be provided to ensure that indigenous peoples can enjoy the other rights articulated in the Declaration.

48. Rio Declaration, supra note 43 at Principle 10.

49. European Parliament and the Council of Europe, Public Access to Environmental Information, Dir. 2003/4/EC, available at http://eurlex.europa.eu/LexUriServ/LexUriServ.do?uri =OJ:L:2003:041:0026:0032:EN:PDF. In particular, Article 1 of Directive 2003/4 requires, as a matter of course, that environmental information be "progressively made available and disseminated to the public in order to achieve the widest possible systematic availability and dissemination to the public of environmental information."

50. European Court of Human Rights, *Taskin and Others v. Turkey*, 2004-X 42 Eur. Ct. H.R. 50, 206 (2005) (citing the Aarhus Convention, Principle 10 of the Rio Declaration and the 2003 Council of Europe Recommendation); Oneryildiz 2004-XII 41 Eur. Ct. H.R. 20.

51. European Court of Human Rights, *Taskin*, supra note 50 at 206; see also *Giacomelli v. Italy*, App. No. 59909/00, at 17–18 (2008).

52. Aarhus Convention, Art. 1, supra note 45. See also U.N. Economic and Social Council [ECOSOC], Economic Commission for Europe, *The Aarhus Convention: An Implementation Guide*, 29, U.N. Doc. ECE/CEP/72 (2000). The Aarhus Convention operates under the assumption that access to information and participation improves environmental protection. See, generally, Jenny Steele, "Participation and Deliberation in Environmental Law: Exploring a Problem-Solving Approach," *O.J.L.S.* 21 (2001), 415 (arguing that enhanced participation may lead to better environmental protection while emphasizing the problem-solving benefits associated with this approach). But see Maria Lee and Carolyn Abbot, "The Usual Suspects? Public Participation under the Aarhus Convention," *Modern Law Review* 66 (2003), 80, 86 (questioning whether public access to information and participation improves environmental protection).

53. United Nations Declaration on the Rights of Indigenous Peoples, G.A. Res. 61/295, 13 September 2007.

54. Article 43 of the Declaration indicates that it provides "the minimum standards for the survival, dignity and well-being of indigenous people." James Anaya, the United Nations Special Rapporteur on the Rights of Indigenous People, characterized the Declaration as constituting "an authoritative common understanding, at the global level, of the minimum content of the rights of indigenous peoples." James Anaya, "The Human Rights of Indigenous Peoples in Light of the New Declaration, and the Challenges of Making Them Operable," Report of the Special Rapporteur, A/HRC/9/9 at para. 85 (5 August 2008), available at http://papers .ssrn.com/sol3/papers.cfm?abstract_id=1242451&rec=1&srcabs=1392569. This view has been adopted by the Inter-American Human Rights system. For example, the Inter-American Court of Human Rights cited Article 32(2) of the Declaration in its judgment in *Saramaka People v. Suriname*, Series C (No. 172) (28 November 2007), finding that there was an enforceable state duty to obtain indigenous peoples' free prior and informed consent with respect to any project affecting their lands and resources.

55. Arctic 2007 Oil and Gas Assessment, supra note 10, at vi.

56. See Betsy Baker, "Arctic Offshore Oil and Gas Guidelines White Paper No. 3: Northern Communities, Participation in Decision Making in the United States and Canada" (10 August 2010), http://www.vermontlaw.edu/Documents/IEE/20100812_bakerWP3.pdf.

57. Joseph Raz, *The Morality of Freedom* (Oxford: Oxford University Press, 1986), 166. Even without establishing specific environmental rights, domestic environmental law clearly follows this Razian formula—imposing obligations in order to protect the weighty environmental and health interests of both society as a whole and of its individual members. This parallelism between recognized interests and imposed obligations suggests that the ideas and concepts fleshed out in the human rights context about environmental decision making will provide useful models for fleshing out the contours of obligations in the context of Arctic governance.

58. For recognition of this point in the context of the United States Clean Air Act, see *Lead Industry Association v. EPA*, 647 F.2d 1130, 1147 (D.C. Cir. 1980) (noting the wide policy discretion agencies have when making decisions "at the frontiers of science").

59. For a discussion of what it takes to establish "regulatory trust," see Rebecca M. Bratspies, "Regulatory Trust," 51 *Arizona Law Review* 575 (2009).

12. Cooperative Food Sharing in Sheshatshiu Uncovering Scenarios to Support the Emergent Capacity of Northern Communities

DAMIÁN CASTRO, GLEN LESINS,

RACHEL HIRSCH, AND KAZ HIGUCHI

Circumpolar regions, including the Canadian Arctic, are facing accelerated warming due to climate change (Barber et al., 2008). Stroeve et al. (2007) report that from 1953 to 2006 there has been a steady decline in observable Arctic sea ice extent at the end of the summer melt season. Such evidence indicates that an ice-free summer is possible within this century (Intergovernmental Panel on Climate Change [IPCC], 2007). Young (2009) describes how large-scale ecological changes in the circumpolar north are paralleled by other more political "thaws" and "freezes." The end of the Cold War brought cooperative efforts (thaws) in polar diplomacy and resource development, evidenced by the establishment of the Arctic Council in 1996 (Arctic Council Secretariat, 1996; Young, 2009). Alternately, as changing climatic conditions open the Arctic to shipping and resource extraction, so have competitive forces (freezes) levied concerns about Arctic sovereignty and issues of military security (Borgerson, 2008).

Northern residents are faced most directly with the ramifications, both positive and negative, of these large-scale ecological, economic, and political changes (Duerden, 2004; Furgal and Seguin, 2006). Northern communities are not, however, defenseless against these changes. Indigenous and nonindigenous peoples living in the North are a driving force behind much of contemporary Arctic political change, such as efforts directed toward building community resiliency (Berkes and Jolly, 2001; Shadian, 2006).

Shadian (2006) recounts the long, hard battle Canadian Inuit have fought since the instantiation of the Inuit Tapirisat of Canada (ITC is now the Inuit Tapiriit Kanatami, or ITK) in 1971 to have their land claims recognized (see also Marecic, 1999/2000). A pivotal point in Canadian land-claims policymaking was the recognition of Nunavut as a separate, self-governed territory in 1999 (Marecic, 1999/2000). This was followed by the creation of the Nunatsiavut government in 2005, as a result of the land claim initiated by the Labrador Inuit Association. The

Labrador Innu settled their land claim by signing the Tshash Petapen Agreement in 2008 (Government of Newfoundland and Labrador, 2008). This agreement enabled the development of the Lower Churchill hydroelectric development, providing new sources of wage employment and funds available to community organizations. Even with the increasing recognition of land-claim rights and opportunities for wage labor, Innu, Inuit, and other Northern residents continue to be faced with the hardships (especially access to healthy food) of an isolated and delicate environment (Beaumier and Ford, 2010; Egeland et al., 2011; Shadian, 2006).

Our brief introduction to some of the political and ecological events experienced by Northern residents is meant to illustrate how acts of solidarity and cooperation regarding land-claim rights have been successful at a broad scale for Canadian Northern First Nations and Inuit (Marecic, 1999/2000; Shadian, 2006; Young, 2009). However, as Adger et al. (2005) argue, factors that influence success in responding to climate change vary across and within scales so that what works at the national level may not apply to the local (Salt, 1979). Northern communities, as is the case elsewhere (Cutter, 2006; Thomas and Twyman, 2005), have not experienced improvements, readaptations, or changes in food harvesting and distribution strategies in response to these large-scale changes to the same degree. For example, adaptation planners must not exclude non-Inuit Northern residents in their efforts; as Marecic states, "Many other peoples including Tlingit, Innu, Cree, Gwich'in, and Metis inhabit and claim aboriginal title to lands in the North" (Marecic, 1999/2000, p. 280).

Berkes explains how, according to complexity thinking, when multiple scales are at play, such as the network of behaviors between associations, households, and individuals in a community, there cannot be one "correct" perspective because "phenomenon at each level of the scale tends to have their own emergent properties" (Berkes, 2003, p. 623). We propose here that community resiliency can be viewed as an emergent property of a well-connected or cooperative community (Berkes, 2003; Gilchrist, 2000). We have built a prototype agent-based model (ABM) illustrating household-level and community-level rules of food sharing based on data obtained from a Northern community in Canada. A similar approach using an ABM (Berman et al., 2004) studied the economic sustainability of a small Arctic community under the stresses associated with climate and societal changes. In order to highlight a minority perspective in polar diplomacy, we base our model of cooperative behavior on data collected from the Innu community of Sheshatshiu, Labrador; but first, we provide additional background literature on cooperation and community resiliency.

Cooperation and Community Resilience

Efficient patterns of circulation and sharing characterize well-adapted cooperation systems and have been studied by many anthropologists during the twentieth century (e.g., Malinowski, 1984; 1922; Mauss, 1990; Polanyi, 2001; 1944; Sahlins, 1972). The ability to share locally acquired foods, such as caribou meat, is an important adaptive mechanism (Gurven 2006; Gurven et al., 2001; 2009; Hawkes et al., 1993; 2001; 2010) that helps promote community well-being in the face of growing ecological, economic, and social changes that are consequences of the global processes of climate change and large development projects. Cooperation is a traditional, locally based way to adapt and mitigate risks (Power, 2008). Authors such as Bodenhorn (2000) and Collings et al. (1998) suggest that hunter-gatherer cooperative livelihood strategies benefit communities even with the increasing advancement of the market economy into the North because they are thus less affected by the regional and global economy's instabilities and fluctuations.

In the 1990s, evolutionary ecologists developed models of cooperation among hunters based on the premise that motivation to cooperate is determined by the fitness produced either by providing food to the closest kin or acquiring different forms of social saliency, such as "signaling" (Hawkes et al., 1993; 2001). Saliency and signaling are associated with leadership and social prestige, since cooperation implies that individuals or groups of individuals with uneven resources and skills have two options. First, if they have insufficient resources they have to relinquish their autonomy to a leader or powerful person able to share resources. Second, if a person is a skilled provider, able to harvest more resources than the average, he or she shares his or her resources. Traditionally, among the Innu of Labrador, there was not a formal, established leadership but a circumstantial one based on forms of relinquishing autonomy and sharing in successful hunts (Henriksen, 1973). Hawkes et al. (1993) argue that a successful hunter signals his success by helping other, less successful hunters. This improves the status of particular harvesters in a community by providing, for example, options for mates and reception of care when sick. These authors define cooperation in terms of individual fitness, not limited to nutrition, but extended to different aspects that reinforce the chances of offspring survival (e.g., reciprocal care).

Gurven (2006) outlines a model of contingent sharing in which shared amount is inversely proportional to social distance, which can be applied to Innu sharing rules (i.e., closer friends share more). This model shows that the contingent expectations of reciprocal altruism (Trivers, 1971) are based on previous experiences with the cooperating partner (Axelrod and Hamilton, 1981). In this sense, cooperation as understood in evolutionary ecology depends on forms of score-keeping where value or utility (i.e., likelihood of being reimbursed) has to be tracked in order to make a decision to cooperate (Hawkes et al., 2001). However, the Innu sharing network shows an imbalance toward elders and those in need, who cannot compensate for what they are given in the usual way. Therefore, Innu cooperation is not only about the circulation of meat, but also about maintaining social relationships. In the nomadic past, this was of crucial importance when traveling to locate hunting places since individuals would join hunting camps based on their relationship with camp members (Mailhot, 1986).

Thus, by sharing, Innu not only cooperate among the participants of the hunt, but they also build and strengthen multiple types of "flow" circuits (e.g., meat, information, or shared wisdom) that make further cooperation possible and prepare the community for unforeseen events (Gilchrist, 2000). We postulate that the connectivity of the sharing network can be examined by identifying the level of social cohesion. Connectivity has been identified as an indicator of the social resiliency of a system (Janssen et al., 2006). We are interested in testing the resiliency of different cooperation strategies as indicated by the equal distribution of caribou.

As we discuss in the following section, the data on Innu sharing indicates that there are two main cooperation strategies that improve connectivity in different ways. One, the household-level, follows the social links of individuals, mostly kin related either by blood or marriage. The other strategy, the community-level, is planned by community organizations and is designed to distribute caribou evenly to all community members regardless of kinship links. The community-level strategy can be derived from the traditional "menikan" or corral hunting (Pasteen, 2011), and it is fueled today by the loss of hunting skills some families face so that, for whatever reason, household members cannot or do not spend the required time in the bush. Given that these two strategies appear to affect connectivity (our proxy for community resiliency) in different ways, we have chosen to represent them in an agent-based model.

Cooperation in Sheshatshiu: Household-Level and Community-Level Caribou Hunts

During the leading author's fieldwork, conducted in Sheshatshiu between October 2007 and December 2009, he participated in the two types of outings mentioned above, aimed to hunt caribou (*Rangifer tarandus*). The household-level hunt involved a small group of men who were interested in hunting cooperatively as part of informally organized trips that usually lasted a few days. The community-level hunts were organized and funded by either the Sheshatshiu Innu First Nation (SIFN is the Band Council) or the Labrador Innu Nation. These trips differ not only in the way that they were organized, but they also resulted in different distribution strategies. The yield of the household-level hunts was distributed among the participants, whereas the yield of the community-level was distributed among the whole community of Sheshatshiu.

Household-level hunts, however, are also promoted and supported in different ways by the Innu Nation and the SIFN. The Innu Nation, for example, allows for paid cultural leaves that employees can use to conduct livelihood activities in the country without risking their jobs. The SIFN, for its part, has a cabin where hunters can stay, located in Ossis Brook, at a short distance from Churchill Falls. This is a very good location to stay during hunting trips along the Trans-Labrador Highway (TLH). The SIFN also runs the Outpost Program that funds access to remote locations in the country. When the leading author participated in these trips, they were usually done using several private air carriers that chartered planes to the bush. These planes were equipped to land on water, ice, or dry land runways. The landing places were usually previously designated camps with cabins and tent frames, scaffolds, and other permanent structures. During the fieldwork, three of these sites were visited: Kamistastin, Tshipiskan, and Kapanien Lakes.

In addition, both the Innu Nation and the SIFN coordinated hunts during the fieldwork period. The SIFN hunts were planned to obtain caribou to be distributed among those unable to obtain their own, especially the elderly. Given the resources that SIFN possesses in order to perform its regular tasks, such as garbage collection and recreation, it is possible for them to organize affordable hunts relatively close to Sheshatshiu. As the organization responsible for a significant portion of the welfare of the local population, such as health and education, providing traditional meats could be seen as a natural community role for the SIFN.

The Innu Nation is the main political arm of the Innu of Labrador. The Environment Office is in a comanagement agreement of a vast portion of Labrador Forest and its resources with the provincial government, and has organized many activities to promote Innu knowledge and values, including those related to hunting. However, its main focus has been its role in the negotiation of the Innu land claim, and therefore it can be seen as a political department rather than technical. The hunting trips organized by the Innu Nation on their land were, therefore, an expression of political will and strength, and a way to express individual autonomy.

Distributing the Meat

Kinship-based linkages continue to be key to household-level food sharing even though innovations in technology and hunting strategies have changed since the nomadic days before settlement. This contrasts with the membership-based community-level distribution. Furthermore, the community-level hunts aim to evenly distribute the kill in an attempt to reach as many households as possible. To better understand these distribution strategies, a clustering algorithm (Girvan and Newman, 2002) based on the concept of betweenness (i.e., the number of nodes between receiver and sender) was applied to the distribution network (Freeman et al., 1991). In figure 12.1, the cluster indicated by the cross symbol has the most outgoing connections and represents community-level distribution. Clusters are more centralized in the community-level strategy. In other words, the centralized distribution of the community-level strategy yields a network in which many or most nodes are linked to a single node. In contrast, the household-level mode yields a topology with multiple distribution hubs so that connections are more evenly distributed across the network.

Because these clusters were calculated using the Girvan-Newman method, the level of centralization can also be appreciated in several flow measurements. Table 12.1 emphasizes the characteristic of having a limited number of nodes placed between other nodes. In a centralized distribution, most of the flow passes through the organization that coordinates the hunt. This difference increases relatively in the OutDegree measurement because it only includes the flow out of nodes. Conversely, the InDegree shows the concentration of receivers and the imbalance on the flow.

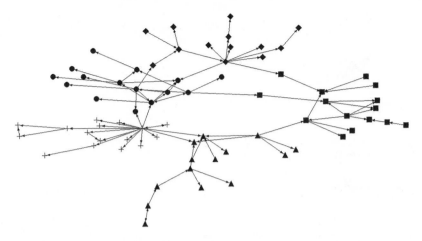

Figure 12.1: Distribution network divided in clusters using the Girvan-Newman algorithm

Table 12.1: Different values of betweenness

Group	Flow Betweenness	OutDegree	InDegree
Circle	1.550%	28.061%	12.755%
Square	0.476%	28.444%	21.333%
Triangle	0.592%	24.852%	16.568%
Cross	3.100%	75.510%	6.633%
Diamond	2.146%	45.833%	9.722%

The structural features of social networks, centrality and connectivity, are related to the network's resilience (Janssen et al., 2006) or the ability of the network to withstand system variations such as a decrease in the number of hunters or changes in the harvest yield. For example, the flow in a distribution network with a high level of centrality could be stopped if the gatekeeper nodes responsible for distribution are eliminated and there is no back-up strategy, whereas it would be easier for the household nodes in a well-connected network to create alternative paths for the meat to flow.

The differing network topologies denote different ways in which caribou meat circulates in the community. Thus, they affect the redundancy of meat sources and consequently the resiliency of the circulation system. Activities associated with this circulation, such as the stories that have to be told while hunting, butchering, or sharing, will also be affected by who is involved in sharing activities with whom. However, the impact is mitigated by the sharing rules, according to which those in need are the first to receive. Sharing rules are guarantors of proper distribution, and if a cluster is orphaned off of its source of meat, it could be incorporated into the closest cluster by demanding a share from a more distant relative. The topological distance might decrease but will never eliminate the chances of obtaining a portion of the kill because those who have been successful in their hunt will share

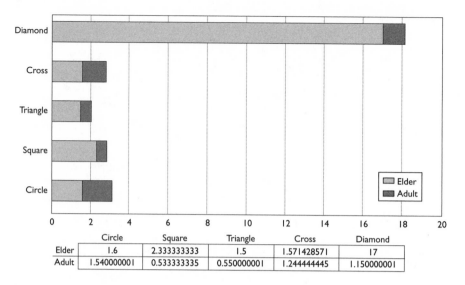

	Circle	Square	Triangle	Cross	Diamond
Elder	1.6	2.333333333	1.5	1.571428571	17
Adult	1.540000001	0.533333335	0.550000001	1.244444445	1.150000001

Figure 12.2: Distribution of caribou meat to households with elders

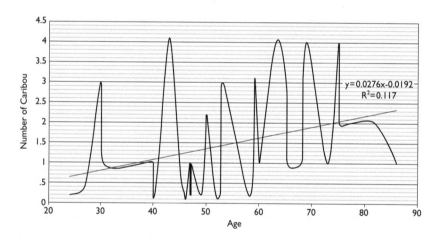

Figure 12.3: Correlation between caribou received and age of eldest household member

with everybody. The inclination to give to the elders seems to be respected across the clusters, as figure 12.2 shows, although the circle cluster shows a marginal difference. While there may not be elders in some households, the norm is to direct most of the meat to the elders wherever possible. In fact, the probability of receiving caribou meat increases with the age of the eldest person in the house, as can be appreciated in figure 12.3.

Different relationships are evident in the resulting network topologies with the community-level strategy indicating a centralized distribution and a less evenly distributed flow of meat indicated by the household-level strategy. However, if the sharing rules for both household and community-level network topologies are operating in parallel, a well-integrated network is possible and the two strategies can be considered complementary sets of practices. This leads us back to the importance of building and reinforcing network patterns in which cooperation is facilitated.

Each sharing cluster has a different level of centrality and connectivity, but because they coexist in an interconnected network the overall resiliency of the system is enhanced. The data indicates that the community uses multiple types of cooperation to achieve uniformity or equality of meat distribution. What is unclear is whether these findings can be generalized to other communities or scales of food sharing. These characteristics and salient features of the network configuration can be well represented by the ABM approach for analysis.

Representing Cooperation: An Agent-Based Model

Agent-based modeling is a relatively new computational method that enhances our understanding of the structure and interaction of various components that constitute a complex system. It has become popular and is being used in many fields of the social sciences, such as politics, economics, anthropology, or psychology. An agent in the ABM approach is an actor (for example, a person, family, company, school, or nation) that interacts as a unit with other agents in a specified environment. Unlike observational approaches that help build social theories or models, the characteristics or properties of each agent have to be explicitly specified in advance, and the interactions (or rules of engagement) with other agents need to be defined clearly in the computer program if the ABM model is to work (Gilbert, 2008; Wooldridge, 2005).

Furthermore, unlike the common equation-based models (EBM) in mathematics (such as statistical regression models, closed sets of partial or ordinary differential equations), agents (or "variables" in the EBM vernacular) can be heterogeneous in nature. In EBM models, the variables need to be homogeneous in order to obtain analytical solutions. In an advanced ABM, the agent-to-agent interaction can change with time as each agent "learns" from experience. In this context, the ABM approach continues to borrow from advancements made in artificial intelligence (AI) research.

An agent-based model is a bottom-up inferential or experimental approach to simulating a nonlinear, highly complex system composed of many agents interacting among themselves and with the environment in a nonequilibrium condition. The environment (for example, within the context of this study, the environment is represented by the size of the caribou herd) can also change with time. The characterization of the agents and the rules of interaction need to be as realistic as possible in order for the model results to be meaningful in the real world. These results represent the structural patterns of the social system that emerge at a macro-scale from the specification of the ABM, without any a priori constraint as to the structure of the resulting pattern.

A multiagent model was written using NetLogo (Wilensky, 1999) to track the distribution of caribou meat in a simulated community. Over 1300 individual

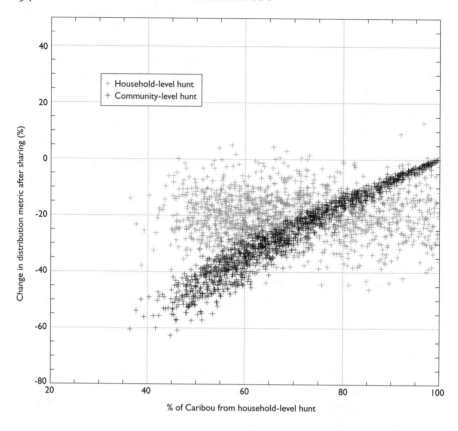

Figure 12.4: The characteristics of household-level versus community-level sharing of caribou are fundamentally different as shown by the decrease in the distribution metric as a function of the percentage of the total hunt coming from the household-level hunt.

simulations of an annual caribou hunt were run with community populations ranging from 127 to 257 people. The caribou hunt consists of two components: a kinship-based household-level hunt and a centralized community-level hunt. The total caribou killed in each hunt was randomized according to the number of hunters and their randomized skill levels. Sharing rules were applied for the distribution of the caribou meat based on kinship links for the household-level catch and on a need basis for the community-level catch. The model reported here does not include a cash or employment economy, but this will be developed in a future version.

The community and family links are built starting with twenty elder couples. Each generation has a maximum of five offspring for which marriage links and family links are determined randomly. The population is divided into households usually consisting of a married couple with offspring and perhaps elder parents. Each household with hunters engages in their own household-level hunt. The annual caribou hunt is shared one caribou per person in the following order: parent-in-laws, parents, offspring, and finally uncles and aunts. The community-level hunt kills a randomly determined number of caribou depending on the population of the community and distributes to people without caribou meat until the supply of meat is exhausted.

The preliminary objective of this study is to examine how the relative contributions of household-level versus community-level sharing of caribou affect the uniformity of caribou meat supply amongst the population. A distribution metric, M, which is a standard deviation, is defined as:

N is the total number of households, r_i is the number of caribou per person in household i, and R is the number of caribou per person averaged over the entire population. The distribution metric equals 0 if every household has a caribou-to-person ratio equal to the community average. As M increases from zero the inequities in caribou distribution become larger.

Figures 12.4 and 12.5 show how effective both the household-level and community-level sharing are in reducing the value of M. Each point on the scatter-plots represents one annual hunt for a different random community. Using our sharing

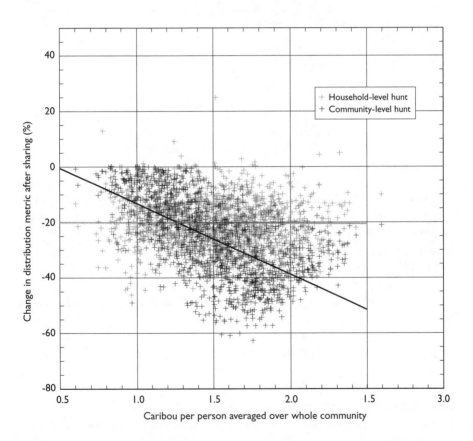

Figure 12.5: The same simulations are plotted here as in figure 12.4, but as a function of the caribou per person for the total annual hunt. The straight solid lines are linear regressions for the two sharing methods, showing that community-based sharing results in more equitable distribution when the hunt results in more than 1.3 caribou per person overall.

assumptions the household-level sharing is able to lower the distribution metric by about 20 percent regardless of the size of the hunt. This shows that the kinship rules and links impose limits on how evenly the caribou meat can be distributed amongst the population. On the other hand, the community-level sharing is more successful at evenly distributing the caribou meat when it accounts for more than 30 percent of the total hunt in a given year (figure 12.4). Furthermore, in years with an abundant hunt, community-level sharing results in lower M's when there are more than 1.3 caribou available per person (figure 12.5). This suggests that in bountiful years, much of the household-level sharing is limited to small family circles without necessarily benefiting the community at large.

The results presented here are preliminary, and many more tests are needed to vary the assumptions made about the kinship links and sharing rules. The agent-based model approach to understanding the consequences of different sharing regimes helps us explore the range of possible outcomes in evenly distributing caribou meat in Innu and other Northern communities with similar sharing patterns. Scaling up the results to a regional basis with multiple communities or even to a national basis with international trade and sharing are tantalizing prospects for this approach.

Reflections on Modeling Cooperation

Northern communities have faced political and ecological challenges in the framework of their local and regional environment, giving rise to various local scenarios. From the data collected in Sheshatshiu, it can be appreciated that both the household-level and community-level distributions enhance connectivity. Since connectivity through the equalization of the distribution of caribou meat is our measure of resiliency, then both strategies positively affect community resiliency. The ABM is able to represent connectivity in a controlled test environment indicating the giving and receiving actions of the agents. The preliminary results from the application of the ABM approach have shown that the agents operating at the higher scale of the community-level tend to distribute the meat more evenly: the community-level sharing tends to result in a more balanced, equal distribution that reaches those household clusters with less successful hunters or where hunting is practiced less often. The benefit of this more even distribution could, however, be offset by the higher centrality level that this distribution might have, which can affect connectivity in the event of the removal of the main distribution center (Janssen et al., 2006). Given the fact that some land claims and large-scale developments, such as Lower Churchill, have the potential to make more resources available to Labrador communities, various community-level cooperative projects could be implemented in these Labrador localities.

This study of the emergent properties of cooperation allows for the development of new questions about the impact of inter- and intracommunity cooperation policies. It is necessary to remember that cooperation, in most of the cases, can yield locally based configurations that are balanced or equalized in different ways. In the case analyzed here, the community-based cooperation produced a more uniform pattern of food sharing. Prospects for future scenarios that test for community resiliency include simulations that control for climate change, large development projects, cooperation at higher scales, or between communities.

Finally, the development of scenario-based case analyses such as this one allow for hypothesis testing across scales. We emphasize, in particular, the assumption that increasing the scale can enhance resiliency as measured in a balanced distribution of resources. Would that be true for different scenarios? Or perhaps combined approaches in which cooperation is supported at different scales could yield better outcomes, particularly when the circulation of resources of several types is considered at the same time. This certainly opens several doors with the promise to test other relevant scenarios among the Labrador Innu, Inuit, and other populations that live in close proximity to each other, sharing interests and resources, and for whom the stakes of developing better policies that promote cooperation at one or another scale are the highest.

13. Crossing the Land of Indigenous People in the Arctic
Comparison of Russian and North American Experiences of Economic Growth and Human Rights in Energy and Infrastructure Projects

NATALIA YAKOVLEVA AND RICHARD GROVER

Extractive projects and associated infrastructure are increasingly entering remote areas in the Arctic to access and transport natural resources, affecting the territories and activities of outlying communities, often of indigenous peoples, as rising prices of minerals and hydrocarbons cause companies to seek to exploit reserves in challenging locations.[1] These developments have a major impact on the environments on which indigenous peoples depend for their livelihoods. For example, studies of the breeding success of caribou, reindeer, elk, moose, wolves, and bear have shown declines with road density (United Nations Environment Program [UNEP], 2001). How indigenous communities interact with such projects is closely linked to the degree of recognition of their rights over the land and other natural resources, and of their rights to self-determination and ability to protect their culture. The livelihood of indigenous people relies on the use of natural resources, which tend to be adversely affected by industrial projects, posing questions about the impact of such development on the cultures, traditions, and well-being of the peoples living in the Arctic. At issue is whether they are forced to bear the costs of development that benefits others living in different regions or if they are able to share in the benefits and influence the mitigation of losses.

The minerals found in the Arctic are remote from the industry and populations that wish to consume them. In most cases it is not economically viable for the industry to migrate close to the source of the raw materials. Rather, alongside development associated with mineral extraction itself is the transport infrastructure needed to export the minerals from the region. For high-value low-bulk resources, such as diamonds and gold, existing transport infrastructure can be used. For low-value high-bulk resources, like oil and natural gas, extensive transport infrastructure is required in the form of pipelines, pumping stations, and ancillary facilities. These have an impact on the environment and communities in areas unaffected by the exploration and extraction of the resources themselves.

Before the 1920s there was limited European settlement in the Arctic regions of either North America or Asiatic Russia. The expansion of twentieth-century settlement and development was the result of the regions' increasing strategic importance and the rising importance of the regions' mineral resources. In recent years, the rising prices of minerals have made it economically viable to extract them in this hostile environment. The expansion of settlement and development has brought the indigenous peoples in the regions into conflict with peoples from other parts of the nation-states of which they are part. Central to this is the question of who should benefit from resource extraction in the Arctic. Should the peoples of the region have the right to prevent developments that have adverse impacts on their livelihoods or to insist on changes that mitigate these, and be compensated for any losses they may suffer? Should they share in the benefits of development?

Large-scale infrastructure developed alongside oil and gas extraction projects, such as pipelines that stretch over long distances, are an example for investigation of the interactions between industry and indigenous communities. This chapter analyzes and compares two pipeline projects that pass through territories traditionally inhabited by indigenous peoples: the Eastern Siberia–Pacific Ocean oil pipeline (ESPO) in Russia and the Mackenzie Valley oil and gas pipelines in Canada. The study investigates this interaction in the context of land relations. It examines how land relations influence outcomes for indigenous communities and how different configurations of land rights can address the interests of indigenous communities affected by pipeline projects.

The concerns of indigenous peoples about energy projects in the Arctic share certain similarities with those elsewhere about the impact of similar projects on their natural environmental, economic, and cultural activities and processes (Altamirano-Jiménez, 2004; Anderson et al., 2006; Dana et al., 2008; Stammler and Wilson, 2006). However, the way in which indigenous peoples' concerns are addressed by developers of industrial projects differs dramatically between countries, not only due to industrial and environmental policies, but also according to the degree of acceptance of land rights of indigenous peoples (Dana et al., 2008; Yakovleva, 2011a). The contrast between oil and gas pipeline projects in Russia and Canada is of particular interest because of the different histories of land rights in general and, specifically, those of indigenous peoples.

Fundamental Principles of Land Rights

Research on interactions between industrial projects and indigenous communities has mainly been conducted in the context of global mining industries. The critical areas of discussion are environmental conservation, sovereignty, cultural heritage, health, livelihoods, employment and training, and collective action (Hipwell et al., 2002; Mining, Minerals and Sustainable Development [MMSD], 2002; Ali, 2003; Anderson et al., 2006; O'Faircheallaigh, 2008; Kirsch, 2007). Issues about land, processes, and relations built around access to, use of, and ownership of land stand out as possible determinants of how interactions between indigenous peoples and other actors in the context of industrial projects are formed. Indigenous peoples often occupy or use land without having formal ownership rights over it, even though their use may be long-standing over many generations or centuries. In the Arctic these lands often appear empty, as the livelihoods earned from them do not require formal agriculture or continuous use. Rather, the use tends to be periodic or seasonal, for example, due to animal migrations. The lands may be designated as state lands or are held in trust for indigenous peoples by the state.

International policy on indigenous peoples calls for greater extension of ownership rights to indigenous peoples (International Labor Organization [ILO], Convention Concerning Indigenous and Tribal Peoples in Independent Countries, 1989; United Nations Declaration on the Rights of Indigenous Peoples, 2007). The regulation of land differs from country to country, and the settlement of indigenous peoples' land claims is uneven throughout the world (Sawyer and Gomez, 2008). In the context of extractive industry, land is central to many of the disputes and conflicts between private companies, national governments, and indigenous peoples, with the indigenous peoples frequently being in conflict with both private companies and their own national governments, often over consents granted to companies by national governments (Mercer, 1997; MMSD, 2002; Ali, 2003). Central to the issue of lands traditionally used by indigenous peoples is their relationship with the state and the extent to which the state is willing to concede to indigenous peoples the power to determine what happens on these lands.

Since the 1940s a body of international law and agreements voluntarily entered into by states has changed the basis on which indigenous peoples can seek to defend claims to land. These have recently been summarized by the United Nations Food and Agriculture Organization (FAO), in "Voluntary Guidelines on the Responsible Governance of Tenure of Land, Fisheries and Forests in the Context of National Food Security" (FAO, 2012). The guidelines argue that states should acknowledge the "social, cultural, spiritual, economic, environmental, and political value" of land to indigenous peoples with customary tenure systems. They should honor the obligations and voluntary commitments they have entered into to protect, promote, and implement human rights. States should recognize and protect the legitimate tenure rights of indigenous peoples to the ancestral lands on which they live, including those that they use exclusively and those that are shared. Those with customary tenure systems should not be forcibly evicted from their ancestral lands, and the state should protect their land from unauthorized use by others. States and other parties should not initiate any project affecting the resources for which indigenous peoples hold rights without holding consultations in good faith with them. The consultations should be aimed at obtaining the free, prior, and informed consent of indigenous peoples to a project, with the consultation being organized without intimidation and conducted in a climate of trust.

The International Labor Organization has adopted two conventions on indigenous and tribal peoples, C107 (1957) and C169 (1989). As the ILO (2007, p. 4) notes: "The main problem faced by indigenous peoples regarding their traditional occupations is the lack of recognition of their rights to lands, territories and resources. Many communities have been marginalized and alienated due to land grabbing, large-scale development projects, population transfer, [and] establishment of protected areas."

C169 revises C107 and came into force in 1991. Some of the language and implied attitudes in C107 are of their time. Not all the countries that ratified C107 have ratified C169.

C107 requires that the rights of ownership of indigenous peoples, whether individual or collective, over the land that they have traditionally occupied shall be recognized. They shall not be removed from their habitual territories without their free consent, except for national security, national economic development, or their health. Where removal is necessary as an exceptional measure, indigenous peoples shall be compensated with lands of equal quality or financially, with full compensation for any losses.

C169 reaffirms that governments shall recognize the rights of ownership and possession of indigenous people over their traditional lands and safeguard their rights over lands not exclusively occupied by them, but to which they have traditionally had access. Particular attention shall be paid to nomadic peoples and shifting cultivators. Handicrafts, rural industries, and traditional activities like hunting, fishing, trapping, and gathering shall be recognized as important for the maintenance of the culture of indigenous peoples and their economic self-reliance. Indigenous peoples have the right to decide their own priorities for development and the right to participate in the use, management, and conservation of their lands. Where the state retains the ownership of mineral or subsurface resources, governments shall consult with indigenous peoples to ascertain the extent to which their interests would be prejudiced before undertaking or permitting the exploration or exploitation of these resources. Indigenous peoples should participate in the benefits from these activities and receive fair compensation for any damages that they sustain as a result of these activities. Where the relocation of indigenous peoples is necessary as an exceptional measure, it shall take place only with their free and informed consent. There should be a right to return to traditional lands once the grounds for relocation cease. Persons relocated shall be fully compensated for any loss or injury. Rights to the natural resources in their lands, consultation about the use of subsurface resources and to participate in the benefits from these, and to receive fair compensation for damage from their exploitation and from relocation, with a right of return, had previously been set out in the 1958 ILO Convention on Discrimination in Employment and Occupation (C111, 1958).

In 2007 the United Nations General Assembly passed the Declaration on the Rights of Indigenous Peoples (UN, 2007). The Declaration had been debated for twenty-four years before finally being approved by the General Assembly. Even then there were a significant number of countries that either abstained or voted against it, including Australia, New Zealand, and the United States, who feared that the convention would reopen settlements they had reached with indigenous peoples in their countries. The motivation for the Declaration was the belief that indigenous peoples have suffered historical injustices as a result of the dispossession of their lands.

Only control over development affecting them and their lands could serve to maintain their cultures and determine development according to their own priorities. The Declaration states that indigenous peoples have the right to self-determination. Article 26 states that indigenous peoples have the right to the lands, territories, and resources that they have traditionally owned, occupied, used, or acquired and that states should give legal recognition and protection to these. Territories include waters and coastal seas. They have the right to the conservation of the environment and productive capacity of their lands and for their lands not to be destroyed or degraded. They also have the right to the recognition of treaties concluded with states or their successors and to have these honored. The Declaration reiterates many of the principles set out in the ILO conventions, including that indigenous peoples shall not be forcibly removed from their lands or be relocated without their free prior and informed consent and with fair compensation and, where possible, the option to return. If deprived of their means of subsistence, they are entitled to just and fair redress.

The World Bank has adopted principles in its operational policy on involuntary settlement similar to those set out in the ILO conventions; these apply to any scheme funded directly or indirectly by the World Bank (World Bank, 1998). While not having the same force as an ILO convention or a UN declaration, they are a clear statement of the international investment community's expectations. Although Canada is a World Bank contributor country, the Russian Federation is a borrower from the World Bank for a variety of projects, including ones associated with land titling and cadastres. There are two fundamental principles: that every effort will be made to avoid or minimize the need for involuntary resettlement, and that when displacement is deemed unavoidable, a resettlement plan must be prepared to ensure that those affected receive fair and adequate compensation and rehabilitation. Where large numbers of people or a significant proportion of the affected community will have to be relocated or the impacts of a project on assets and values are difficult to quantify and compensate, the option of not going ahead with the project should be given "serious consideration." Compensation can be considered fair and adequate if within the shortest period of time both the host and resettled population are able to achieve a minimum standard of living and access to land, water, sanitation, community infrastructure, and land titling at least equivalent to presettlement levels; recover all losses caused by transitional hardships; experience as little disruption as possible to social networks, opportunities for production and employment, and access to natural resources and public facilities; and have access to opportunities for social and economic development. There are special considerations that the World Bank applies to projects that involve the displacement of indigenous peoples, because of their identity being based on the territory they have traditionally occupied; their lack of formal property rights to the areas on which they depend for their livelihoods and the consequential problems they have in pressing claims for compensation; and because of the impoverishing effect on them of resettlement. The conditions are that the resettlement will directly benefit the community, customary rights will be fully recognized and compensated, compensation will include land-based resettlement, and that the indigenous people have given their informed consent to the resettlement and compensation. The research undertaken by the World Bank before the adoption of this policy showed that energy projects had a particular tendency to result in displacement and inadequate resettlement programs.

The Inter-American Development Bank (2006), in its indigenous peoples' policy, develops operational policies to support the World Bank's principles. It requires consideration of the potential benefits and losses for indigenous peoples. Potential benefits could include socioculturally appropriate opportunities for development, including health and education benefits; opportunities to implement indigenous peoples' rights; support for the culture, language, arts, and intellectual property of indigenous peoples; the strengthening of titling and resource management; the sharing of benefits from natural resource management; improved access to labor, production, and financial markets; strengthening capacity in governance; and the participation of indigenous peoples in supplying services for the project. The potential losses include a reduction in physical or food security; threats to way of life and cultural identity; threats to legal status, possession, or management of land and natural resources they have traditionally occupied or used; exclusion from the benefits of the project on grounds of ethnicity; and commercial development of their culture or knowledge resources without the participation of indigenous peoples in the benefits. Emphasis is placed on due diligence to discover the potential benefits or losses to the indigenous peoples themselves and monitoring the consequences of the project.

The implications of the ILO conventions and the UN Declaration on the Rights of Indigenous Peoples, together with the protection of property rights and rights of fair access to justice provided by the UN Universal Declaration of Human Rights, are that the claims of indigenous peoples to the land they have traditionally occupied should not be dismissed as customary or informal use rights. Rather they should be entitled to fair compensation for any losses or damage from resource exploitation and a share of the benefits from development. The freedom of action for the state is constrained by the need to secure the free and informed consent of the indigenous population to its plans if these involve their removal or the degradation of the environment that supports their livelihoods.

Eastern Siberia–Pacific Ocean Oil Pipeline

Russia is one of the world's leading oil and gas producers, predominantly exporting oil and natural gas to Europe. The recent development of oil and gas resources in the eastern part of the country and expansion of infrastructure offers Russia the opportunity to export oil to Asia (Milov et al., 2006). The recent large-scale oil pipeline project in Russia is the Eastern Siberia–Pacific Ocean oil pipeline, operated by Transneft, the state-owned pipeline monopoly (and largest Russian oil pipeline infrastructure company), which manages the majority of Russian oil traffic (Makarov, 2005; Stammler and Wilson, 2006; Yakovleva, 2011a).

The idea of exploiting the oil reserves of Eastern Siberia and transporting oil from the landlocked Siberian plains to eastern energy markets was contemplated by the USSR in the 1970s. After the collapse of the Soviet Union, the idea was revived in 1999, when the Russian government signed an agreement with the Chinese government in the sphere of energy, which implied the construction of an oil pipeline between the countries. The initial plan was put forward in July 2001. A pipeline was proposed from Angarsk in Russia to Daqing in northwestern China (2,400 km) with the capacity to carry 20 million metric tons of oil per annum, then 12 percent of China's oil consumption. In 2003, another proposal emerged to extend the eastern pipeline to Nakhodka on the Russian Pacific coast to enable exports to Japan and beyond.[2] The Russian government started to favor the Pacific route for the pipeline, developed by Transneft (Buszynski, 2006; Polivanov, 2007).

In December 2004, the Russian government issued a decree to build the oil pipeline extending to the Pacific Ocean. The proposed route was from Taishet in Irkutsk Oblast to Skovorodino in Amur Oblast and Perevoznaya Bay in Primorskii Krai. The total capacity of the pipeline was to be 80 million tons of oil per annum, of which 24 million tons would be sourced from Western Siberia and the remaining 56 million tons from Eastern Siberia (Government of the Russian Federation, 2004). In 2004, the initial cost of the project was estimated at US$11.5 billion. The first phase from Taishet to Skovorodino, near the Chinese border, was estimated to cost US$6.5 billion, to be constructed between 2006 and 2008. The pipeline was supposed to recover its costs in eight to ten years. The second phase, from Skovorodino to the Pacific Coast, was planned to be completed between 2008 and 2015 (Belova and Mel'nikova, 2005; Sagers, 2006).

Planning Decision Making

The route set out in the 2004 government decree has since been altered. In 2005, the first wave of public concern emerged about the government-approved route, specifically environmental risks posed to the pristine Perevoznaya Bay, the initial location of the final terminal.[3] In November 2006, the head of Transneft declared that the final point of the Eastern Siberia–Pacific Ocean oil pipeline will be Koz'mino near Nakhodka, pending environmental approval.[4] The route of the middle section of the pipeline was challenged on the grounds of the environmental risks posed to Lake Baikal, the world's deepest freshwater lake, and the endangered Amur leopard. The ESPO pipeline was to pass within 800 meters of the northern shore of Lake Baikal. The environmental movement to save Lake Baikal from potential oil spill risks was backed by Greenpeace Russia, World Wildlife Fund for Nature–Russia, the Baikal Regional Union, and the Baikal Environmental Wave.[5]

Shortly before construction was to begin, in April 2006, Russian president Vladimir Putin proposed that Transneft shift the pipeline route forty kilometers to the north of Baikal in order to minimize the possible risk from accidents.[6] This suggestion was put into action, and due to various considerations such as terrain and the closeness of the Yakutian oil fields, the route was shifted 400 km north from Lake Baikal, adding an additional 1,600 km to the overall length—and including another region, the Republic of Sakha (Yakutia), in the project. The "ESPO expansion" (as the change of route was titled) added the equivalent of US$3.5 billion to the cost of the first phase of the pipeline (between Taishet and Skovorodino), according to official estimates (Sagers, 2006).

The Republic of Sakha (Yakutia) thus became in 2006 the last region to be involved in the project, although the pipeline had been under discussion since 1999. The pipeline aimed to embrace the Talakan oil field, Verkhnechonskoe, Chayandinskoe, and the Srednebotuobinskoe oil deposits, which should reduce the development costs of these deposits. The present ESPO project spans 4,400 km and has two phases: the first phase from Taishet to Skovorodino (2,770 km in length) crosses through Irkutsk Oblast, the Republic of Sakha (Yakutia), and Amur Oblast; and the second phase from Skovorodino to Koz'mino near Nakhodka (1,670 km in length) passes through Amur Oblast, Khabarovskii Krai, and Primorskii Krai. Transneft set up a subsidiary company, the Center for Project Management of the Eastern Siberia–Pacific Ocean Oil Pipeline, which commenced the construction of ESPO from its starting point at Taishet in April 2006.

Decision making over the route of the oil pipeline has not been transparent. Indeed, as Milov et al. pointed out, "the system governing access to the state's crude oil pipeline monopoly Transneft is non-transparent. At one time such access was controlled by an inter-ministerial government committee that allowed pipeline capacity without transparent criteria. Today, the government still controls how much crude oil can be exported by any one company, and access to pipelines remains in the hands of Transneft" (Milov et al., 2006, p. 286).

The eastern oil pipeline project has been negotiated only between two parties— the Russian government and the state pipeline monopoly Transneft, while private oil producers have not been invited to participate in the implementation of the pipeline project. Moreover, the route has been decided by the Russian government and Transneft, with the regions through which the oil pipeline passes not being consulted.

ESPO: Land and Indigenous People

In Sakha, ESPO crosses the territories inhabited by the Evenki, an indigenous nation that traditionally resided in the vast area stretching from Irkutsk Oblast to Primorskii Krai (Fondahl and Sirina, 2006).[7] Sakha itself is an autonomous republic within the Russian Federation in which the ethnic Russian population is now a minority, with the Sakha being the largest ethnic group. The Evenki are recognized as an indigenous nation by the Russian government and are protected by the state under the regulations on indigenous minorities of the North, Siberia, and Far East.[8] Politically they are a minority within a republic dominated by another ethnic minority. There is some evidence that the Evenki were displaced by the migration northwards of the Sakha, probably during the Middle Ages, sometime before Russian contact. The ESPO passes through the Aldan, Olekminsk, and Neryungri districts of Yakutia, where an estimated three hundred Evenki people pasture nineteen thousand reindeer. The ESPO descended on Evenki communities in Aldan in 2006, when the project started to organize public hearings about the approval of an environmental impact assessment of the pipeline.[9] The Evenki communities, along with other communities of ethnic groups such as Sakha, Russian, and Ukrainian who reside in the area of proposed construction, were asked to comment on the environmental impacts assessment prepared by the pipeline developer, Transneft. They had not been consulted on the overall decision about the pipeline since its planning in the 1990s, which largely involved the Russian government and Transneft. In the course of these late public hearings, several concerns emerged about potential impacts of ESPO on traditional economic activities of Evenki communities (Yakovleva and Munday, 2010). Environmental and Evenki organizations in Yakutia stated that the pipeline could negatively affect traditional trades, practices, and livelihoods of the Evenki through its potential impact on animal migration, vegetation and water resources, and increased risk of poaching, fires, and disturbance from the introduction of access roads and construction (Yakovleva, 2011a). Mechanisms for compensation for compulsory purchase and disturbance are poorly developed in the Russian Federation with a significant gap between legislative provisions and reality (Grover et al., 2008). No long-term plans for improving socioeconomic conditions of Evenki communities, employment and training programs, or social investment were planned for the Evenki communities in Aldan affected by the pipeline project (Yakovleva, 2011a).

A review of participation of the Evenki in the planning process shows that the Evenki do not have formal land rights over the area in which they lead their traditional economic activities of hunting, fishing, and reindeer herding. The Evenki have engaged in these activities on the basis of changing legal entitlements; the land legally belongs to the state. Since the end of the 1990s, when Russia launched new land reform policies, the processes of land allocation and registration have been changing, but the land still belongs to the state and not to indigenous nations such as Evenki. The state can withdraw, resume, or reallocate occupancy or use rights as it has the power to determine the uses to which state land is put. In Soviet times the withdrawal of land occupancy could result in compensation for losses (Vondracek, 1975). This could include compensation for the value of expropriated buildings and crops and damage to other buildings as a result of expropriation, the costs of tillage and improvements for which revenue had not been received, and the costs of reinstatement at another location, but not for the value of the land taken. A similar approach has been taken in current regulations.[10] These provide a complex algorithm for the calculation of losses on land that is used by defined indigenous juridical bodies (Grover et al., 2013). These include losses to thirteen listed traditional activities of indigenous peoples, such as animal husbandry (reindeer breeding, horse breeding, and so on), processing of animal-husbandry products, fur farming, dog breeding, fur trading, sea and river fishing, local market gardening, and medicinal herb collecting.[11] What they do not do is provide a way in which indigenous peoples can share in the benefits of development. Clearly, the absence of formal land ownership rights for the territories of their traditional natural resource use and the absence of recognition for their customary rights prevents Evenki communities from actively influencing project planning and benefiting from projects on these territories by, for example, selling the right of access to their land. This makes their social and cultural status and overall economic development largely dependent on the state.

Russian legislation is extensive on the subject of protection of indigenous minorities of the North, Siberia, and Far East in that it provides support for education, exemption from military service, support for setting up and maintaining the traditional economic activities of hunting and reindeer herding, and the protection of cultural heritage, language, and cultural traditions. It fails to promote adequately the participation of indigenous nations in planning projects and in negotiation of compensation for the negative impacts of projects conducted in the territories of traditional natural resource use (Yakovleva, 2011b). Nor does it provide protection for customary land rights over the areas that have traditionally been used by the Evenki.

Mackenzie Valley Gas Pipeline

Although the Klondike is seen as the archetypal model for the exploitation of mineral resources in the North American Arctic, the development of most of these has been a long, slow, drawn-out affair. In the USSR, mineral resources, including hydrocarbons, could be developed under a central planning system that placed strategic objectives ahead of commercial ones and which, until the 1950s, had access to gulag labor to develop them. In Canada, the United States, and Greenland, the development of Arctic mineral resources has taken place in a market economy. Therefore, the expected financial payoff has had to be sufficient to justify the heavy costs and risks of the projects. While one might argue that the three countries involved in Arctic mineral exploitation in the region of North America, the United States (Alaska), Canada, and Denmark (Greenland), have in the past displayed a colonial attitude to their far-flung lands and the indigenous peoples, since the 1970s policies have been influenced by both a human rights approach toward indigenous peoples and recognition of the need to balance environmental considerations against purely economic ones. The sociopolitical context in which hydrocarbon exploration and exploitation and the construction of pipeline and transportation infrastructure have taken place has been very different from that of the USSR and the modern Russian Federation.

The existence of oil was reported by Alexander Mackenzie in northern Canada in 1789; the geology of the Mackenzie Basin and parts of Alaska were known to be favorable for oil in the last quarter of the nineteenth century. In 1920 a wildcat strike found oil at Fort Norman on the Mackenzie River, leading to some commercial production in the 1930s and 1940s (Emmerson, 2011). The oilfield played a strategic role during World War II by offering a secure supply route once the Japanese had seized two of the Aleutian Islands. Aside from this, the oilfield only supplied a limited local market. The Prudhoe Bay oilfield in Alaska did not start production until 1968, and was followed by the exploitation of the North Slope. The stimulus was the rising price of oil brought about by the creation of the OPEC cartel of leading oil-producing countries. This made oil production in these expensive and inhospitable areas and its removal to areas of demand economically feasible.

Prudhoe Bay, the Alaska North Slope, and the Mackenzie Basin are remote from centers of population and industry. The problems of railway construction in permafrost conditions, of shipping through the ice-bound Northwest Passage, and liquification of natural gas in the Arctic make a pipeline the only feasible solution to the problem of exporting hydrocarbons. Even this presents huge technical issues, such as frost heave if the pipeline is buried and ice scouring in rivers if not. Initially, a Mackenzie Valley pipeline was proposed as a means of exporting oil from Alaskan oilfields, but in 1973 the oil companies secured their preferred solution, the Trans-Alaska Pipeline to an ice-free tanker port at Valdez (Emmerson, 2011). This separated the questions of how to export Alaskan and Canadian hydrocarbons. If the Canadian oil and natural gas deposits were to be exploited commercially, a pipeline would be needed along the Mackenzie Valley to Alberta. Aside from the environmental considerations the construction of the pipeline would pose, there were many public concerns about the impact of such a project on aboriginal land (Ironside, 2000; Dana et al., 2008).

The political problem in the Arctic countries is that the majority of indigenous populations live far away from the region to the south. Governments are faced with balancing immediate benefits from exploiting the resources of the Arctic region, which affect all of their population, against impacts on the natural environment and on the communities that live in the Arctic. These impacts take place a long way from the majority of the population and occur in areas with relatively few people (Sale and Potapov, 2010). Many in the aboriginal population earn a significant part of their living from natural resources through hunting or fishing. Mineral extraction and the construction of pipelines can degrade the natural habitats on which these activities depend. It can bring rapid social changes that can be disruptive to communities. Many of the jobs created through mineral extraction go to outsiders as companies import labor. Indigenous peoples throughout the world have problems in asserting their claims to land and natural resources. Their traditional lands have often come to be regarded as "public" land. Governments capture the rising values of these lands, depriving the indigenous populations of a capital base with which to escape poverty or to cope with social transformation (Wily, 2006). Development rights in what is seen as public land can be allocated by governments to outsiders and investors in the interests of generating revenue or economic development for the country as a whole.

The Canadian government had a poor record in relation to human rights, in relocating aboriginal groups in order to permit commercial or urban development of their land with minimal compensation or assistance in relocation (Royal Commission on Aboriginal Peoples, 1996, vol. 1, ch. 11; York, 1990). Starting in the 1970s, however, a series of watershed legal decisions brought about the reversal of this trend. The Canadian Supreme Court in *Calder v. the Attorney General of British Columbia* (1973) ruled that Indian title was a legal right independent of any form of enactment. It had not been extinguished by colonization, irrespective of whether it was recognized by Europeans. It did not depend upon a sovereign grant, but on occupancy (Hurley, 1998, revised 2000). The 1982 Constitution Act recognized and affirmed the existing aboriginal and treaty rights of indigenous peoples in Canada.

The economic and social distress caused to aboriginal communities by relocation and the pollution from development of the lands from which they earned their livelihoods led to a Canadian government inquiry into the Mackenzie Valley pipeline proposals under then justice Thomas Berger, at the time a member of the Supreme Court of British Columbia (Berger, 1977). The inquiry lasted for three years (1975–1977), during which time Berger carefully examined and tested the evidence of the costs and benefits of the pipeline, including holding many meetings in the areas likely to be affected. He identified that there was a conflict of opposing interests between businesses, including local business leaders as well as the oil and gas companies, who favored the pipeline, and the aboriginal groups in the region, who strongly opposed it and feared its impact on their communities, livelihoods, and culture. Berger identified that the project would have a huge impact as the corridor through the Mackenzie Valley would have both oil and natural gas pipelines and associated infrastructure; he concluded that it was impossible for the conditions imposed on their construction to protect the environment. Development was therefore bound to have a major impact on the lives and livelihoods of the communities along the route. Unlike the transitory European populations of the region, aboriginal communities could not easily migrate to other parts of Canada. He argued that the future of the north should not just reflect the views of those living in the south but also those whose homeland would be affected. Berger proposed a moratorium on development until the native land claims in the area affected had been resolved. In effect, Berger recognized that if the property rights of the aboriginal peoples were recognized, the outcome would be different than if, as in previous developments, they were disregarded. The businesses seeking to develop the oil and gas reserves and build the pipeline would be obliged to negotiate with the aboriginal communities living in the areas and some of the benefits from development would have to be shared with them. The delay also allowed more research to be conducted (Ironside, 2000).

In the 2000s, following the increase in natural gas prices, the project has been revived. The National Energy Board approved the Mackenzie pipeline in 2010.[12] The project has the support of the Northwest Territories Legislative Assembly and government.[13] During the intervening period the issues of aboriginal land claims and land rights in the area have to some extent been resolved. The Inuvialuit reached a final agreement in 1984 with amendments in 1987 (Inuvialuit R.C., 1987). The Gwich'in reached a comprehensive land agreement with the Canadian government in 1992 (Siddon, 1992) and the Sahtu in 1993 (Rwin, 1993), which resolved disputes about Treaty 11 made in 1921. The Dehcho, over whose land approximately 40 percent of the pipeline would pass, approved a framework agreement with the governments of Canada and the Northwest Territories in 2001, with an agreement in principle in 2007 (Dehcho First Nations, 2001; 2007; 2012). Negotiation of a final agreement is still ongoing. There have been litigation and judicial reviews since the initial agreement. The Dehcho negotiations concern disputes over Treaty 8 made in 1900 and Treaty 11.

The precise details vary between agreements, such as whether the claim concerned land that had been surrendered under an earlier treaty over which there were disputes about whether the treaty had been fully honored, or land that had never been subject to treaty because it lay north of the area of European settlement. In essence, the aboriginal groups surrendered their claims to land to the Canadian government and any future rights arising from these; in return, they secured self-governing agreements, financial payments, the protection of wildlife harvesting, and habitat management agreements; the receipt of lands in fee simple includes water and lakebeds, with and without oil, gas, and mineral rights. The agreements give the aboriginal groups the right to determine who has access to their land and the terms and conditions on which this takes place, controls over land use in the areas, control over the use of water, protection from the expropriation of their land without fair compensation, and the ability to influence environmental protection programs and policies for the maintenance of public order in the event of development. The tenure over aboriginal lands is collective though vested in a juridical person in which each person in the community has a share. Those seeking to exploit the mineral wealth of the region typically have to negotiate access agreements with the aboriginal communities, may have to purchase the mineral rights themselves, and seek the agreement of the communities for the environmental and community protection policies they propose to undertake. The land claims settlements give aboriginal communities considerable leverage in their dealings with commercial interests both in terms of protection of the environment and culture and in securing a share of the benefits from development. The leverage comes through property rights and also permits for land use and water.

In 2001 the Mackenzie Valley Aboriginal Pipeline Corporation entered into a memorandum of understanding with the four producing companies, Imperial Oil, Conoco Phillips, Shell, and Exxon, and in 2003 became a full participant in the project. The production companies own interests in the Niglintgak, Taglu, and Parsons Lake natural gas fields, which were discovered during the 1970s, but the value of these is limited unless the gas can be transported to users. The Mackenzie Valley Aboriginal Pipeline Corporation is owned by the Aboriginal Pipeline Group (APG), which was formed in 2000 to represent the interests of the indigenous peoples of the area. The Mackenzie Valley Aboriginal Pipeline Limited Partnership holds the APG's financial interest in the Mackenzie Valley Pipeline and is owned by organizations under the direction of the Dehcho, Sahtu, Gwich'in, and Inuvialuit. Other aboriginal groups in the Northwest Territories can join at the discretion of the four founding members. The Aboriginal Pipeline Group owns a 33.3 percent share in the consortium. Its share of the development costs have to be raised through conventional debt markets with backstop finance being provided by the fields' owners. The project's goals include providing benefits to aboriginal and northern communities, and its priorities include fostering the development of aboriginal and other northern suppliers of goods and services and consulting with and involving the communities in the area (Imperial Oil Resources Ventures, 2004). The impacts considered included those on aboriginal culture, language, and traditional means of sustaining livelihoods. In addition to the share of the pipeline, applications have to be made for development permissions in the settlement areas, which provides the aboriginal groups with some important regulatory powers over land use and water resources. In this way, the indigenous people have a degree of control over the details of the development but also stand to benefit financially from the pipeline.

Conclusions

The examination of the Russian pipeline shows that consideration of indigenous peoples' interests and the extent to which they can influence the project as well as benefit from it is closely linked to state recognition of their land rights. Indigenous peoples in Russia do not have ownership rights to land, but are regulated land users under the conditions of "traditional natural resource use." However, the setup of land use in the current legislation does not provide sufficient means for indigenous peoples to be included in consultation over pipeline planning. While regulations provide for compensation for the impacts caused, they do not enable indigenous peoples to have a share in benefits from development of hydrocarbons. Development is likely to destroy the natural environments on which traditional livelihoods depend, and the process of compensation does not provide for the construction of alternative livelihoods. The extent to which the interests of indigenous peoples as established in international law and agreements are being respected is therefore open to question.

In the case of the Mackenzie Valley pipeline, many aboriginal groups that originally opposed the gas pipeline, after having their land claims settled and following a series of consultations, have given support to the project and expect to benefit from it through job creation and community development. The change in policy in Canada toward the recognition of the land rights of aboriginal peoples since the 1970s has given these communities considerably more power to determine the development of their traditional lands and to share in the benefits from development. Through the Aboriginal Pipeline Group, aboriginal communities are also incorporated as ultimate beneficiaries and partners in the project (Altamirano-Jiménez, 2004; Anderson et al., 2006; Dana et al., 2008) and through the devolution of government have valuable powers to regulate land use and water access and to influence environmental and community protection policies. This power has ultimately come from the recognition of collective property rights in a society in which governments respect the rule of law. This model of aboriginal equity as participants in development of natural resources has been followed elsewhere. In essence, the model proposes that aboriginal groups accept and embrace change and development and suggests that they can use the rewards to preserve and enhance their cultures. It also requires governments to recognize that, although they have the power to force through these projects, those who will experience losses from projects should be fairly compensated and share in the benefits.

Notes

1. The term "indigenous peoples" is used throughout this chapter because of its wide acceptance, although in Canada there tends to be the use of the term "First Nations," or "Aboriginal peoples" following the practice of the 1991 Royal Commission.

2. "Japan fights for Russian pipeline." BBC News 24. 30 June 2003. http://news.bbc.co.uk/1/hi/business/3031566.stm (accessed 17 October 2007).

3. "Pipeline risk to Siberia wildlife." BBC News 24. 15 July 2005. http://news.bbc.co.uk/1/hi/world/europe/4685753.stm (accessed 17 October 2007).

4. Nikolai Chekhovsky, "Transneft has adopted ESPO financing." *Expert Online*, 10 November 2006. http://www.expert.ru/news/2006/11/10/baikal_vsto/ (accessed 27 September 2007).

5. "Nezavisimye eksperty otvergli project VSTO." *Regnum*, 21 December 2005. http://www.regnum.ru/news/569611.html (accessed 27 September 2007).

6. "Putin orders oil pipeline shifted." BBC News 24, 26 April 2006. http://news.bbc.co.uk/1/hi/world/europe/4945998.stm (accessed 17 October 2007).

7. The total number of Evenki living in Russia is approximately 35,500; of these about 18,200 Evenki reside in Yakutia.

8. The Indigenous Minorities of the North, Siberia, and Far East is a group of different nations protected by the state. Each nation has a population of not more than thirty thousand people; they lead a traditional lifestyle, predominantly engaging in traditional economic activities such as fishing, hunting, and reindeer herding. These activities form the base of their economic livelihoods and are supported by the state.

9. In Russia, developers present environmental impact assessments for public hearing and later seek approval from government departments.

10. "Approved procedures for calculating the amount of losses caused to Associations of Indigenous Peoples of the Russian Federation as a result of economic and other activities of enterprises of all ownership and individuals in places of traditional economic activities of indigenous minorities of the Russian Federation," Russian Federation Ministry for Regional Development, N565, 9 December 2009. "Methodic recommendations for valuation of the indigenous peoples of the Russian Federation North, Siberia, and Far East immemorial land sites, approved by the Russian Federation, 'Roszemcadastre,'" 2 March 2004.

11. See the official list of traditional economic activities of the small indigenous populations in the Russian Federation, approved by Russian Federation Government Act, N631-p, 8 May 2009.

12. National Energy Board, *Mackenzie Gas Projects—Reasons for Decision*, vols. 1 and 2 (2010).

13. Seventeenth Legislative Assembly, Caucus Priorities (2014), www.assembly.govt.nt.ca/sites/default/files/17th_assembly_caucus_priorities.pdf.

14. Emergent Cooperation, or, Checkmate by Overwhelming Collaboration
Linear Feet of Reports, Endless Meetings

GLENN W. SHEEHAN AND ANNE M. JENSEN

Too much to read, too much to hear, just too much to allow a normal life. That's a reasonable reaction of someone living in the American Arctic who is tasked with or feels responsible for knowing and responding to the largely political elements from outside that impact every aspect of life on Alaska's North Slope. More than a decade ago the residents of the small village of Nuiqsut, adjacent to the Prudhoe Bay oilfields, considered hiring an outsider to move to Nuiqsut and attend meetings on their behalf. They wanted time to go about their own lives.

Inupiat people on the North Slope have transitioned in living memory from a primarily subsistence hunting economy to a Western cash economy. Remarkably, in this transition the people's cultural focus has remained sharp. Social ties, social activities, and wholehearted attention are directed toward hunting of the bowhead whale in the coastal communities and caribou in interior communities. Secondary prey species include most of the creatures that thrive in abundance in the Arctic. More precisely, attention is upon preparations for hunting, upon the hunt, and upon sharing the harvest of the hunt. Everything else is organized around this age-old annual rhythm.

Traditional life allowed and demanded great attention to detail. The failure of a waterproof stitch in an umiaq (skin boat) could be the difference between life and death on the ocean. An inability to convey exact information about geography, topography, or other physical conditions could lead to missed opportunities or worse. Today, young people who need to learn how to be successful subsistence hunters and who need to learn how to work as a team do not have the time available to them that was available a generation ago to their parents. Schools demand a huge time commitment. Televisions, video games, and Facebook inevitably draw more hours out of the day. Adults who formerly would have been shadowed by young people now mostly have jobs. In the American Arctic, many of these jobs require significant travel, and attendance at evening meetings when home. Between daily work, meetings, and travel, managing to hunt and otherwise remain familiar with the natural world becomes a scheduling tangle.

It was only a few decades ago that this change took off. Changes are documented in the North Slope Borough publication *Taking Control: The Story of Self Determination in the Arctic* (Hess, 1993). In the 1950s and 1960s, "Life had few comforts, children had to go far to attend school, and, out in the country, people from distant places were coming in to do whatever they wanted, and to claim the ancient wealth of the Inupiat homeland for themselves" (Hess, 1993, p. 6).

The environment tends to be classified differently by the Native Inupiat Eskimo people of Alaska's North Slope and Western people, and the groups interact with and value its aspects differently. Understanding these varying epistemologies is useful. Westerners tend to identify three classes of resources in the North and Inupiat are more likely to see two. Both identify offshore commercial nonrenewable resources (e.g., oil and gas). Subsistence resources (that support diet and cultural lifestyle) and natural resources (most of which are renewable) are seen as the same thing by Inupiat. Westerners' views tend to divide subsistence resources and natural resources, excluding people from the matrix of natural resources (sea ice, whales), seeing hunting people as separate from and impinging upon natural resources. This difference in viewpoints complicates discussions and dispute resolution, since it can lead to the parties talking past each other.

Some Westerners want to preserve their version of natural resources, often to the extent of excluding traditional human impacts or interactions. Some Westerners want to exploit natural resources while excluding people or other resource values that might limit exploitation. Westerners have the upper hand in numbers, rule-making ability, and finances. Yet the Inupiat culture thrives today not in isolation, but by successfully interacting with these outside forces.

The subsistence bowhead whale hunt is the organizing focus of today's Inupiat coastal communities, and has been for many generations (Sheehan, 1997). Westerners who see nature as stopping short of including Inupiat people pose a threat to the culture by their active efforts to ban the hunt. Westerners who value extreme commercial exploitation of offshore oil and gas pose a threat by their apparent willingness to disrupt migrations and endanger whales. Adaptation today for Inupiat culture means limiting damage from these disparate groups of Westerners, and that means integrating into the Western world to a significant extent, in order to understand and effectively react to it. And this must be accomplished with limited resources.

Too Many Meetings and Too Much Paper

Much of the land in the North Slope Borough (NSB) is owned by or at least regulated by various federal agencies, and much of what remains is under the control of the state of Alaska. The state controls the oceans out to the three-mile limit, after which the US government has jurisdiction out to two hundred miles. Almost all of this area is important to subsistence hunters. All of the animals on which people depend for subsistence, some of them endangered or threatened, are regulated by one or more agencies. Regulation of animals extends to regulating the land and water on and in which the animals live, which then leads to "regulating" people by restricting their activities. For instance, environmental groups sued the federal government and successfully forced the listing of polar bears as a threatened species. One result: in 2010 the US Fish and Wildlife Service designated 187,000 square miles of coastal waters and lands as critical habitat. Access to most of the area listed is crucial to the cultural survival of the Inupiat people, but the area (and therefore the people) are now subject to additional layers of remotely situated bureaucratic and legal control.

Additional controls that deeply impact US Arctic residents include international treaties that can stymie subsistence hunting, such as one affecting the primary subsistence animal and cultural pivot point, the bowhead whale—the International Convention for the Regulation of Whaling, administered by the International Whaling Commission (IWC)—as well as treaties to protect migratory birds (the Migratory Bird Treaty Act of 1918) or other game. The US Department of State is a link between these treaty regimes and the domestic groups that are impacted.

The federal government and the state of Alaska have different interpretations of subsistence hunting. For people who just want to continue their traditional ways, conflict on these levels is not necessarily helpful. The federal agencies and their various components whose decisions, rule making, and activities affect the lives of people in the North include the National Oceanic and Atmospheric Administration (NOAA), and its National Marine Fisheries Service (NMFS) and National Ocean Service (NOS).

Also federally, the Marine Mammal Protection Act (MMPA, administered by the Marine Mammal Commission, or MMC) might hinder some local activities while also giving local people a place to be heard and to direct enforcement activity toward groups that are seen as interfering with subsistence activities or with the game upon which subsistence depends. The same applies to the Environmental Protection Agency (EPA). The Department of the Interior (DOI) and its components also significantly impact local people, especially the Bureau of Indian Affairs (BIA); the Bureau of Land Management (BLM); the Bureau of Ocean Energy Management (BOEM); the Bureau of Safety and Environmental Enforcement (BSEE); the National Park Service (NPS); the Office of Surface Mining (OSM); the US Fish and Wildlife Service (USFWS); and the US Geological Survey (USGS). The Army Corps of Engineers (ACE) and the Federal Aviation Administration (FAA) also are part of the mix.

The Alaska state legislature periodically attempts to diminish the local taxing authority of the North Slope Borough. Diminished financial resources would greatly diminish local ability to respond effectively to the many rule-making and enforcement authorities already listed. For instance, the borough has spent tens of millions of dollars conducting studies mandated by the International Whaling Commission and critical to preventing the IWC from reducing or eliminating the subsistence bowhead whale quota, as the IWC did one time previously. If the borough's income through changes to taxing authority is sufficiently diminished, that line of cultural defense will be impeded. State agencies that directly impact subsistence and other activities in the North include the Alaska Department of Fish and Game (ADF&G), the Department of Natural Resources (DNR), the Alaska Oil and Gas Conservation Commission (AOGCC), and the Department of Transportation and Public Facilities (DOT).

Rules require that agencies and corporations undertaking actions on these lands or in adjoining waters, or affecting various species, hold meetings with stakeholders. In some cases, several agencies may be involved in a single undertaking, and each agency holds multiple meetings during the planning and execution of a project. Add on the many other gatherings (city council meetings, church services, tribal government meetings, corporation board meetings, school advisory council meetings, Elders' council meetings, sporting events, and so forth) that are held in each of the eight North Slope villages. A community and its residents' capacity for dealing with meetings are easily oversaturated in this political and social environment. A resident of a remote village with significant oil development told one of the authors that seventeen public meetings, not counting church services and games, were to be held in the village in a two-week period.

Travel to meetings elsewhere in the state may take more than a day each way, not counting the time spent at the meeting. Travel for meetings in the Lower Forty-eight often takes two days each way, meaning that a person will be away from home for a week for a two-day meeting. From a local perspective, any one of the meetings could be "the" critical meeting, or they all could be pro forma and useless. Or the same meeting could be critical and useless, in the sense that local input will never be heard, no matter how cogently or loudly the local position is put forward. "MMS has no ears," read a picket sign in one of the region's rare public demonstrations a number of years ago, referring to the former US Minerals Management Service.

Meetings are only one aspect of the time sinks confronting residents. Studies that extend, when printed, to inches and linear feet cascade into the North Slope Borough. Many relate to federal documents such as Environmental Impact Statements (EIS), which are issued in draft (DEIS) for comments, sometimes repeatedly. Failure to respond in an effective way may allow activities or projects to proceed that could be devastating to the Inupiat way of life.

An EIS is triggered based on a preliminary assessment that a proposed project's effects on the environment will be nontrivial. This can range from potentially harming flora and fauna to obstructing aesthetic views or practically any other harm that could be imagined. Even field investigations performed in support of an EIS are fraught, in that a poorly conceived or poorly interpreted investigation can form the basis for harmful rulings and be cited as precedent for decisions far removed from the original project that triggered the EIS. This means that subsistence hunters must worry not just about each particular project and its associated EIS, they must also take one step back and worry about the potential impact of the associated reports and rulings on other undertakings. For any given project, the importance of the EIS is that, once finalized, there are few ways short of lawsuits to affect the course of a project.

An undertaking is potentially required to develop an EIS if it is a federally financed project or if it requires one or more federal permits in order to proceed. If the federal government has ceded its authority for authorizing certain types of projects to the state, the projects remain subject to the federal EIS process.

The former MMS (Minerals Management Service, which became the Bureau of Ocean Energy Management, Regulation, and Enforcement and is now two agencies, BOEM and BSEE) once hired the authors to write an Inupiat epistemology. When a prime conclusion of the draft said that officials would have to understand that Western science itself represents a worldview, the draft was rejected with scathing comments that of course Natives have a worldview, but basically scientists and bureaucrats have only the truth to live by.

This attitude from outsiders and officials presents challenges, particularly in small rural communities. Comments on a DEIS can be very important, but if not written in the "EIS style" they may have little impact. Understanding the EIS process, including the various stages of the process and the points at which stakeholders have the opportunity to provide input, as well as the vital importance of keeping to deadlines, is complicated. It takes time and experience to become adept. This level of expertise comes to a few people who stay in the same job for years at a time, but many jobs in Arctic Alaska have high rates of turnover. A few exceptional individuals manage to participate at this level as community members through their own personal dedication.

Subsistence hunting is tied to patterns of migration, and migrations don't follow a calendar or clock. When caribou are near, or when beluga pass by, chairs empty out as people move to take advantage of the passing opportunity. The culturally central bowhead whale hunt is time consuming, with crews out for days and weeks at a time. When the requirements of a job or governmental process interfere with the requirements of providing culturally and nutritionally vital food for family and community, the work can be left behind; another job will be sought later. Not surprisingly, the depth of knowledge brought to bear on any given Western subject area often is broad but not deep, which can allow outside voices to gain more ground not on merit but by a sort of superiority in Western data presentation.

Lack of Job Tenancy, Lack of Financial and Western-Style Human Capital

Frequently, individuals leave their jobs before their successor is identified, let alone hired. If there is a need for review and response to a document, it may fall through the cracks, effectively leaving the entity without a voice. Every regional and local organization in the American Arctic confronts this problem. Subsistence hunters leave with the expectation of finding another job when needed, and with the intention of hunting or preparing for the hunt in the meantime, or they leave because another organization offers them a new job. People who are not originally from the community often leave because they have family commitments elsewhere, or because they cannot adjust to life in the North, or because they have been offered new jobs. Since specialized medical care is a seven-hundred-mile jet ride away, many job holders must abandon jobs to provide support and care for family members at specialized service locations.

These are small, isolated communities. Even Barrow, administrative center of the North Slope Borough, has a population of less than 4,500. Except for occasional seasonal ice roads, all travel to the outside takes place by air. Everything that functions in such a community does so because it is run locally.

Adding further complexity, the majority of Alaska Native villages have numerous interlocking and overlapping governmental and quasi-governmental entities. These usually include a municipal government, a village-level tribal government, and a village corporation formed under the Alaska Native Claims Settlement Act (ANCSA). Village residents also are associated with regional-level tribal governments and regional ANCSA corporations and their associated nonprofits. A not unheard-of tactic employed by outside organizations is to play these groups off by consulting with the one least likely to respond, or by consulting serially with different groups, or by consulting for months and years until there is a local job turnover that limits or stops any ability to respond effectively. Bureaucracies live forever and villagers don't.

Historically, it has been difficult for residents of American Arctic communities to obtain extensive education. Elders, and other older residents, often grew up in families that had to move seasonally for subsistence or trapping opportunities, so that many people were able to complete only a few years of formal schooling. Until after the Molly Hootch case was settled, most communities in Alaska did not have a high school.[1] Even children of families who settled in villages could only finish high school if they were selected to be sent to one of the Bureau of Indian Affairs schools located in faraway cities, like Sitka, or even farther, such as Chemawa, Oregon. Once high schools were available in rural communities, their small size limited the education they could offer.

A further complicating factor has been the natural desire of the North Slope Borough and ANCSA corporations to hire local residents. In many cases, people were hired after they completed one or two years of college. The initial idea may have been to support people in their studies by providing an opportunity to earn enough to go back for additional education, but the practical effect often has been that these individuals acquire homes, families, and the associated recurring bills. This can make returning to the impoverished student life unattractive, if not impossible. No good solution has been found to promote widespread North Slope Native completion of college and higher degrees. Those who complete degrees often have a difficult time during their initial college experience, and as a result may choose to live elsewhere during the years their own children attend school, in order to provide them the opportunity for better school education. This then interferes with the children's learning of cultural and subsistence knowledge, and can weaken their ties to their communities of origin.

Remoteness has other effects. People sometimes tend to see themselves in unique situations and cast about for unique responses and solutions, when in fact they may be encountering widespread policies that affect both them and many rural disadvantaged people in other locations. This insularity, based on history and the reality of living at the tail end of the logistics and communications pipeline, means that tried and true means of coping with intrusive or destructive initiatives and policies can be unavailable when needed. A terrestrial example is the landlocked North Slope village of Anaktuvuk Pass. The people of Anaktuvuk Pass are only one of many groups, mostly composed of rural residents with limited education, often but not always minorities, who live in areas which a federal or state government has decided to turn into a park or similar protected area (e.g., Hughes, 1996; Knott, 1998). Anaktuvuk folk are subsistence caribou hunters, so enforcing areas of restricted activity and travel can dramatically impact people's ability to eat. Remote groups can suddenly find their lives turned upside down, at the whim of a well-funded regulatory agency that is often located at a considerable distance and is made up of well-educated, well-connected people who have never lived in the area, although they may use it for recreation. Any one of these local groups has little power. Even if their elected representatives find their position convincing, those representatives are a small minority. In the case of Anaktuvuk Pass, a solution eventually was found that involved land exchanges to provide travel corridors.

In the case of public comment meetings or hearings, community members may be able to attend formal meetings, but the meetings often fail to accomplish their intended purpose. This can be due to poor planning by those convening the meeting. They may have an idea about the format of the meeting that is appropriate and culturally relevant in an urban, primarily Western setting, where it might lead to the desired outcome in terms of stakeholder input. For instance, in Washington, D.C., or Anchorage, other than a few invitees at meetings, it is first come, first served to speak at a public forum. Individual speaker time limits tend to be closely observed, and conveners generally can stay longer if there are more potential speakers. If not, many attendees are comfortable with commenting in written form or via e-mail or website. This is impossible in the bush setting.

In rural Alaska, conveners frequently start packing before the scheduled time is up, and many leave their own meetings early to catch the evening plane, while testimony is still in progress. The culture regularly thwarts the concept that anyone can speak, mainly because elders and leaders (primarily whaling captains in the Alaskan Arctic) get to speak first and they get to speak as long as they wish, on or off topic, because that is the traditional way to "do a meeting." Traditional meetings do not have deadlines for finishing. The conveners give up and leave, even if they don't have a plane waiting, with many people who wish to contribute unheard. Given such experiences, community members realize that the conveners generally don't have the stamina or will to hear everyone, so many don't bother to attend the meetings. This in turn leads agencies to mistakenly imagine that there is little or no concern in the community.

There have been a number of attempts to develop helping organizations. Notable among these are the Inuit Circumpolar Council (ICC) and the Alaska Federation of Natives (AFN). The ICC is a pan-Arctic organization that includes Inuit peoples and that cooperates with other Arctic indigenous groups. AFN is composed of Alaska

Natives from all parts of the state and can serve as a powerful voice. To date, there do not seem to be effective organizations that incorporate both Native and nonnative groups and that can address issues connected to remote regulators.

One option is to hire outside experts with requisite credentials, and, it is hoped, the necessary experience in the regulatory process. This is not a panacea. For example, the North Slope Borough Department of Wildlife Management (DWM) has several biologists who each have been with the department for over twenty years. But the department also has had some short-tenure scientists in recent years. One borough official who prefers to remain anonymous said, regarding some hired experts, "It's all about 'Look how many meetings I've had' with honchos, but what is come of it?"

Another complication is "Arctic experts" who attempt to mediate, usually for the benefit of the environment and, they believe, the community. But often they don't know how their answers fit into the community. As a result, sometimes they can push to "trade off" something of value that creates a worse, if different, problem than the one they were assigned to address. Their tactical knowledge, the kind that can help defend people and their culture, is limited, and their lack of on-the-ground knowledge limits their ability to think of "novel" adaptive responses to strategic challenges. A novel response might be one grounded in traditional knowledge. How many experts on the Arctic sit on panels, write articles, and give advice, and have never experienced the Arctic or its communities? We host these first timers frequently in Barrow, and they invariably state that the experience has refined and sometimes changed their understanding of the issues.

Experts with little local knowledge are not just confined to giving advice to or affecting the activities of organizations within the Arctic. In 2011 the new head of the Coast Guard's Alaska District visited Barrow for the first time. Rear Admiral Ostebo remarked, "There's a lot of people that think they know the Arctic and have never been there and have never really seen the challenges that we face" (DeMarban, 2011, p. 8).

Coping with the Onslaught: How Do Choices Get Made?

The genius of traditional knowledge includes peoples' ability to state facts with nuanced but clear degrees of certitude, and the ability to patiently state them over and over again. It includes the ability to teach by example and to conduct the same activities over and over, with the willingness to extend that teaching to other adults. The public demonstration against the former Minerals Management Service was all the more remarkable in this context. MMS indeed "had no ears," but Inupiat people are patient teachers. They pointed out that their words had been recorded for over a generation from multiple individuals, always with the same points and the same facts and desires, and those words had dutifully been boxed and set in the margins of the MMS reports. But the words were never included in the text, while the agency proceeded as if the boxed words had never been said, much less heard.

An issue that remains important today is that of cumulative impacts. Federal studies and rule interpretations consistently treat each project as a unique effort whose impacts relate only to the immediate boundaries or vicinity of the project. The residents of the North Slope (current authors included) repeatedly point out at federally sponsored meetings that a piecemeal square mile by square mile approach to understanding the impacts of projects sidesteps visualizing or managing many of these impacts, which may only be apparent after numerous similar or small projects have run to completion. If an impact is not recognized, its effect cannot be mitigated.

The traditional ability to get the facts straight and keep teaching from year to year and generation to generation does pay off as a means of engaging the West. Dr. Tom Albert, one of the expert scientists who worked for many years with the people of the North Slope, always emphasized the lack of baseline data in every aspect of the decision making that is imposed on the American Arctic. What we see now is that the years of testimony have themselves provided, and continue to provide, some of the temporally controlled and consistent baseline data that otherwise is still lacking. For instance, eyewitness accounts of an oil spill near Point Barrow in 1944 are preserved in public testimony, but the eyewitnesses are now all gone.

Cultural resiliency is exemplified in a variety of institutions created or supported by the local home rule government, the North Slope Borough. The creation of the NSB itself was a heroic example of resiliency in the face of seemingly overwhelming outside forces (e.g., Anon., 1972; Hess, 1993). Much of the organizing experience that led to the NSB was gained in fighting the federal effort to blow up Point Hope with "our friend the atom," which itself led to the modern Environmental Impact Statement (O'Neill, 2007). Countering the reams of "scientific" proof that the Project Chariot "bombs to harbors" project was safe and sane provided an early lesson in coping with deliberate distortions, hidden in masses of reports, which made incorrect conclusions—and were then used to justify policy.

The federal government was moving toward an atmospheric test ban on nuclear weapons. Those who wanted to keep on testing conceived of dropping bombs as tools instead of weapons, getting the same scientific results but avoiding the onus of testing weapons. In 1958 the Atomic Energy Commission (AEC) determined that a series of atmospheric blasts would make a nice harbor at Point Hope. That they failed in their mission to employ nuclear bombs is thanks mainly to the Inupiat people of the region. Project Chariot was cancelled in 1962. The AEC was dissolved in 1975.

The Alaska Eskimo Whaling Commission (AEWC) was created by coastal hunters in 1977 "in response to [a] marked increase in outsiders' involvement with their bowhead subsistence harvest" (Albert, 2001, p. 267). The International Whaling Commission (IWC) had justified an attempt to eliminate the subsistence whaling quota on alleged scientific grounds. The AEWC created the Science Advisory Committee (SAC) in 1980 in response to the IWC's interference and also to have the wherewithal to review agency and oil industry reports that claimed to use "scientific

data" to reach administrative decisions of sometimes drastic local and regional import. The SAC's value was obvious to the North Slope Borough, and in 1982 the NSB
Mayor's Office took on the SAC as the North Slope Borough Science Advisory Committee (Kelley and Brower, 2001). Since the SAC's creation it has been emulated
around the world by other governments.

Decades of community members' experience working with scientists at Barrow's
Naval Arctic Research Laboratory (NARL) helped provide support for the creation of
the Barrow Environmental Observatory by the village corporation in 1992. Rather
than isolate scientists or keep them away, the intent has been to bring in more
of them, as long as they are willing to work with local people and students while
gathering and reporting on their data. To help in the process of broadening residents' knowledge base, the North Slope community created the nonprofit Barrow
Arctic Science Consortium (BASC), a science advocacy, education, and outreach
organization.

While much research has been facilitated by BASC and other entities, the research most critical to residents is conducted by or in conjunction with the NSB's
own research arm, its Department of Wildlife Management. DWM works with
the agencies and organizations whose findings and rulings impact the subsistence
hunting at the core of Inupiat culture. DWM also provides the Western scientific
research data that enables the Alaska Eskimo Whaling Commission to defend its
bowhead whale quota under the international treaty that is administered by the less
than friendly International Whaling Commission.

Taqulik Hepa, director of the North Slope Borough DWM, states, "We really pay
attention [to these meetings and reports]. It's cultural survival to make sure we still
have access to marine resources. It happened to Nuiqsut first and now it's happen-
ing to us. And now we depend on our technical people to attend meetings along
with Harry [Brower, deputy director and a whaling captain] and me, and maybe
that's too bad. That's not the way it was, with whaling captains attending in force,
meeting after meeting. But we can have three or four meetings a week, week after
week" (personal comment, 2011). In fact, it was reported recently that Royal Dutch
Shell alone "has had more than 450 meetings with borough citizens and local governments over the years as it tried to gain support for its controversial offshore oil
program" (Coyne, 2012).

How do people and their organizations make choices between endless Western-
style demands on their time and the traditional and culturally critical time requirements of a subsistence way of life? It is a difficult balancing act, requiring repeated
adjustments on the part of individuals and organizations. It has been possible in
part due to the hard work and sacrifice of many North Slope residents, and in part
due to their ability to hire specialists to provide specific expertise that is not available
within the small North Slope workforce.

Coping mechanisms employed by the people of the North Slope operate externally, allowing both defense from and collaboration with outside forces from the
state and national level to the international stage. Maintaining a seat at the table in
high-stakes proceedings is an ongoing effort. Walking out of meetings is unusual

enough to garner headlines (Adams and Farrington, *Arctic Sounder*, 19 July 2012). Coping mechanisms also operate within the communities, helping compensate for limited numbers of people, limited depths of specialized experience, and limited finances compared to state or national government agencies or multinational oil companies.

Inupiat culture remains thriving and viable. As the pace of development increases and the number of players grows, it will be a real challenge to ensure that this continues to be true. The experiences of the past decades will be critical in maintaining that viability through the oncoming waves of impacts from offshore development, increased and unprecedented shipping, climate change, and all of the entailed governmental regulatory reactions and restrictions.

Note

1. Order Approving Amended Consent Decree, *Toboluk v. Reynolds*, C.A. No. 72–2450 (Alaska Super. Ct., 3rd Dist., order entered 1 June 1983).

15. *From Northern Studies to Circumpolar Studies In the Field and in the Ether*

KATHLEEN OSGOOD AND STEVEN B. YOUNG

To the North! Humans and the Arctic World

From the moment of their arrival in the postglacial North at the end of the Pleistocene epoch twelve thousand years ago, humans have used ingenious adaptations to the challenges of a frigid environment. However, it was not until the twentieth century that the North became a subject of study in its own right, and not until the twenty-first century that the entire circumpolar world has been considered as a singular region, critical in world development. From the earliest days, when humans traveled light across the snow and ice carrying the knowledge to survive in their minds, to this postmodern era when technology makes it possible to share knowledge and information about the circumpolar world, the North has been a frontier of human potential and capacity. The way we describe and visit and use the North is the product of centuries of inquiry and speculation and exploration, both systematic and unsystematic.

As Barry Lopez says so well in his investigation of Arctic realities, human dreams of the northern landscape have been shaped by desire and imagination (*Arctic Dreams: Imagination and Desire in a Northern Landscape*), but the North has also been shaped sometimes by indigenous adaptation, sometimes by colonial exploitation, sometimes by missionary fervor, sometimes by economic imperatives, and sometimes by military necessities. And, now, it is shaped by national policies of the eight nations with territories in the North.

In the more than half-century since the end of World War II, we have gone from the creation of academic and scientific disciplines around the Arctic to issues-based circumpolar studies in the twenty-first century. This chapter seeks to show the roots of northern studies following World War II and their evolution into circumpolar studies following the fall of the Soviet Union and the establishment of the Arctic Council. As will be seen, each disciplinary focus yields a different kind of understanding of the Far North, and all the disciplines lend themselves to an appreciation of a circumpolar world.

Humanistic: The first descriptions of Ultima Thule reach back to classical times. The North, or perceptions of legendary hyperborean regions and their divine or semi-divine denizens, played an additional role in the artistic traditions of the Western world. Perhaps the strongest example of this is the Wagnerian Ring cycle, which built upon ancient sources from northern cultures and which tapped into a mythical layer of northern European society. C. S. Lewis is explicit in the role that "northernness" played in his development as an artist, and much of Tolkien's writing is close to being an adaptation, or reimagining, of the mythic traditions of northern Europe. In this, he followed in the footsteps, although in a different medium, of Grieg and Sibelius.

The arts, from a Western perspective, played a relatively minor role in the Far North until the twentieth century. Painters, such as the Luminist artist Frederic Church, romanticized polar exploration, but the indigenous arts of northerners were appreciated more as ethnographic material than as true art. This was partially dispelled by the strange and evocative artifacts, often carved of walrus ivory, unearthed by archaeologists in such places as St. Lawrence Island and the Point Hope area of Alaska. Indigenous art came into its own only in the mid-twentieth century, with the commercial success of ivory and soapstone carving and, later, prints. While arts and letters have had a significant role in describing and depicting the North, they have had a minor role in its study or exploration.

Commercial: The Hudson Bay Company and its Eurasian counterparts were mainly a single resource effort, based on furs from the terrestrial environment or, in the case of fur seals and sea otters, in coastal and inshore waters. The marine resources of the North had already been exploited for centuries. European fishermen were working the Grand Banks by the end of the fifteenth century, and whalers were going as far afield as Svalbard and the coast of Labrador within a few decades. Many of these early commercial expeditions are poorly documented. It is often suggested that this is not the result of disinterest or illiteracy, but to maintain secrecy: to avoid sharing the resources and interference by various representatives of national interests such as the navies of European powers. It is noteworthy that Newfoundland became the first British overseas colony in 1607. This was based on the protection of the cod fishing industry, especially the onshore processing of the catch, which, before refrigeration, needed to be salted and dried before being shipped.

Political: European exploration of the North reached its peak in the nineteenth century with the quest for the Northwest Passage through the Canadian Arctic Archipelago. Although exploratory expeditions figure prominently in the northern literature, it should not be ignored that the underlying principle of these expeditions was generally commercial and (or) political. While the members of the Franklin expedition were perishing to a man, the same area of the Canadian Arctic was regularly traversed in safety, if not comfort, by Hudson Bay employees such as Scotsman John Rae, often with the assistance of indigenous colleagues.

Evangelical-Missionary: Issues of international relations and diplomacy were thus obviously of major importance in northern regions from the earliest days of Western

civilization's penetration of the northern lands and seas. These issues were not always based on commerce. The recolonization of Greenland, begun by the Danes
in 1721, was mainly evangelical, with a strong substrate, at least initially, of the re-
discovery, and re-Christianization, of long-lost countrymen. Missionaries from the
Anglican, Roman, Greek Orthodox, and Moravian churches established themselves
in northern regions soon after—sometimes before—commercial interests arrived.
The missionaries were often, in a sense, the first Europeans to take a scholarly, not
explicitly exploitive, approach to northern peoples, cultures, and the environment
in which they lived.

Scientific: Various nineteenth-century expeditions to the North were usually
charged with making at least minimal scientific observations, but Arctic physical
science was mostly launched in the early twentieth century by explorers such as
Amundsen and Sverdrup, and popularized by Vilhjálmur Stefánsson. Meanwhile,
many Russian scientists were working in the intensely cold, forested regions of
Siberia and making major advances in the study of such features as polar soils and
permafrost.

Ethnographic: A Western fascination with northern peoples was well established
by the early twentieth century. Ethnographic collections at major museums expanded rapidly, anthropologists and ethnographers such as Boas and Rasmussen
became well known, and northern archaeology was spearheaded by Collins, Knuth,
Geist, and Rainey.

Strategic and Military: During World War II, with the rise in the importance of
air power, interest in the North became more strongly focused. With the German
occupation of Denmark, the United States temporarily took over the administration of Greenland and established military bases, refueling stations, and weather
observatories there, largely in support of aircraft being ferried to Europe. Alaska,
whose Aleutian Islands were actually invaded by Japan, also became heavily militarized and a way station for aircraft going to Russia and the Far East. This military
activity resulted in a substantial group of engineers, resource geologists, military
strategists, and many more "pure" scientists with expertise, fascination, and commitment to the North and its issues.

With the beginning of the Cold War immediately after World War II, the perceived importance of the North increased dramatically. The threat of long-range
bombers approaching either North America or Russia "over the Pole" resulted in the
placement of Distant Early Warning (DEW line) sites from Western Alaska across
Canada to Greenland, and Ice Islands—large, and rare, tabular icebergs broken off
from an ice shelf on Ellesmere Island—were manned by both Americans and Sovi-
ets. Absurd proposals such as "Project Chariot"—a plan to blast a useless harbor in
northwestern Alaska with multiple hydrogen bombs—also proliferated.

Academic: Actors like those involved in the militarization of the North, many of
whom had no commitment to respecting academic disciplinary boundaries, were
instrumental in setting up new organizations such as the Arctic Institute of North
America, established by a Canadian Act of Parliament in 1945, with its journal,
Arctic.

The concept of circumpolarity—the idea that northern regions around the globe were similar in terms of plants, animals, glacial history, permafrost, and other ecological factors, became important in the scientific community at about this time. It was recognized, for example, that caribou and reindeer are the same species, as are grizzly bears and Eurasian brown bears. (One definition of the terrestrial Circumpolar North is the historical range of caribou and reindeer, *Rangifer tarandus*.) This circumpolar perception led to an awareness of common ground among northerners in terms of not only the natural and social sciences but also common interests in politics and development. One result was some significant breaching of the Iron Curtain through interchanges between Western and Soviet scientists. By the time of the breakdown of the Soviet Union, there was a long and fertile tradition of cooperation between East and West in the northern scholarly community.

Development of Area Studies, Interdisciplinarity, and Northern Studies

It is fair to say that the elements of Northern Studies coalesced into a recognizable constellation in the immediate aftermath of World War II. Interdisciplinary programs sometimes arise from a shared conviction that the traditional disciplines are unable or unwilling to address an important problem. In the aftermath of World War II, area studies became increasingly popular in North America, fueled by the Cold War and an increasing need to bring interdisciplinary knowledge to bear on regions of national security and interest (Moseley, 2009).

As Ludger Müller-Wille points out in his article about the role of Northern Studies in intercultural and transnational education, area studies emerged in the era after World War II, partly to reflect changes in intellectual paradigms, but also to promote national interests. Furthermore, the study of regions rather than nations became an important part of academic endeavors. Northern Studies emerged in the 1970s to focus attention on and to deepen knowledge of the Circumpolar North, as well as to shed light on the status of indigenous peoples (Müller-Wille, 1998, 63–64).

While these threads were being picked up in various ways in many northern countries, Northern Studies as an academic subject that transcended disciplinary boundaries really came into its own only in the last three decades of the twentieth century. One of the early efforts in this connection was the formation of the Center for Northern Studies in Wolcott, Vermont, in 1971.

At the time, there was little awareness in the United States of the potential for including Northern Studies within an academic program. The University of Alaska Fairbanks (UAF) had a few courses with a specific northern focus, as well as programs in fields such as anthropology and biology that dealt with characteristic features of the Alaskan region. The Stefánsson program at Dartmouth College, which had emerged around the Canadian explorations of Vilhjálmur Stefánsson, was in eclipse. The Institute of Polar Studies at Ohio State University specialized in research in Antarctica, especially in the fields of glaciology and geology.

Although regional studies encompassing such areas as Africa, Latin America, and the Soviet Union were becoming well established in many colleges and universities, there were few if any counterparts in northern, polar, or circumpolar studies. Especially at the undergraduate level, the few opportunities for developing broad concepts regarding northern issues were mainly confined to working with individual professors with northern interests. This was especially true with respect to fieldwork.

The Center for Northern Studies (CNS) was founded in 1971 with the express purpose of redressing these shortcomings. CNS was physically located in Wolcott, Vermont, at the southernmost fringe of the boreal forest. (In the chilly 1970s, Wolcott was climatically within the subarctic, since the mean monthly temperatures exceeded 10 degrees C for only four months of the year.) With its long, snowy winters, spruce-fir forests, abundant wildlife such as moose and ravens, and comparative isolation, Wolcott had many of the features of a true boreal environment, and effective fieldwork could be carried out literally in our own backyard. CNS was also within comfortable traveling distance of Newfoundland, Labrador, and northern Quebec, so that fieldwork within the continuous northern environment, and in isolated northern communities, could easily be supported.

At the founding of CNS, it was decided that there should be a research component to the overall program. This gained impetus in 1973, when CNS contracted with the National Park Service to carry out an interdisciplinary survey of the Noatak River Valley, in the Brooks Range of Arctic Alaska. As well as providing essential baseline data on this remote and unspoiled Arctic region, the Noatak project set the tone for research and field educational projects of CNS for the next decade. Graduate and undergraduate students became important participants, and researchers from a variety of disciplines worked together closely for weeks at a time in the field. The Noatak project was followed by several similar efforts in interior and Arctic Alaska.

By 1974, the Center for Northern Studies had developed intensive summer and winter courses housed at the new headquarters building in Wolcott. The Winter Ecology course, developed largely by Dr. Peter Marchand, was the epitome of a fieldwork and laboratory course that utilized the special features of the Wolcott environment—deep, long-lasting snow, extreme low temperatures, and a variety of specialized adaptations and behaviors of northern organisms. One additional benefit of this course was the production of Marchand's book, *Life in the Cold*, which has gone through several editions and is still widely utilized as a textbook in university Winter Ecology courses.

A major advance for CNS came about through a developing relationship with Middlebury College. By 1978, Middlebury was the only college in the United States to offer an undergraduate major in Northern Studies. The introductory Northern Studies course regularly enrolled over one hundred students, and ten or more students graduated annually in Northern Studies for several years. The program was supported by a National Science Foundation FIPSE grant, and courses in the social sciences were created to supplement the earlier predominately natural sciences orientation. It involved a semester-long residence at Wolcott, as well as a field component, usually in Newfoundland and Labrador, later including northern Scotland and Scandinavia.

Another initiative of this time was the development of a program to provide support and impetus for people from indigenous communities in the north to participate as full members of the student body at CNS. Over several years about ten native students from Alaska and Canada joined the CNS student body and added immeasurably to the experience of more "traditional" students, as well as broadening their own academic experiences.

The Northern Studies program at Middlebury began to decline in the later 1980s. The social science component proved to be less popular than the natural sciences, administrative changes in the college reduced support, and the program ultimately became a subsidiary of the Geography Department, where its key personnel were lost through tenure decisions. Although the program continued at a diminished level for several more years, reduced enrollments made it necessary to recruit students from other colleges. Enrollment uncertainties plagued the program for the remaining years of its existence.

Ultimately, in 2003, a decision was made to merge the Center for Northern Studies with Sterling College, a local institution which had recently become a four-year college, and which specialized in outdoor education and conservation biology. It turned out that Sterling did not have the resources or the vision to support or provide leadership for the program. Northern Studies was dismantled, its personnel left or were dismissed, and its major facilities sold.

Establishment of the University of the Arctic

Meanwhile, significant political changes in the North, particularly the dissolution of the Soviet Union in 1991, made it possible to establish the Arctic Council following the Ottawa Declaration of 1996, "as a high level intergovernmental forum to provide a means for promoting cooperation, coordination and interaction among the Arctic States, with the involvement of the Arctic Indigenous communities and other Arctic inhabitants on common Arctic issues, in particular issues of sustainable development and environmental protection in the Arctic" (Arctic Council, 2007: "About Arctic Council").

The Arctic Council comprises the eight sovereign nations in the North (the United States, Canada, Denmark with Greenland and the Faeroe Islands, Iceland, Norway, Sweden, Finland, and the Russian Federation). The Arctic Council also intentionally included indigenous communities whose territories transcend international boundaries, such as the Inuit, whose distribution ranges from Chukotka in the Russian Federation, across the Alaska coast, spanning all of the Canadian Arctic and on across Greenland.

Soon after the formation of the Arctic Council, a presentation was made to the Senior Arctic Officials (SAO) of the Arctic Council on the concept of a circumpolar university. The SAO invited Professor Bill Heal to form a task force to undertake the initial planning for an Arctic university. The rationale for establishing a systematic study of the circumpolar world for undergraduate students in the Far North is eloquently described in the introductory module to the entire curriculum, penned by Aron Senkpiel:

> Some years ago, at a conference of northern specialists held in Rovaniemi, the regional capital of Finnish Lapland, several northern researchers and educators met over dinner. As they relaxed, they began to talk about the conference and how, good as it was, many of the participants seemed to form little cliques or "pockets," based on their nationalities or areas of expertise. At one level this was understandable—it is quite human to seek the company of those with whom we share common backgrounds or interests—but at another level, it was frustrating. After all, one of the fundamental purposes of the conference was to get people to share important information across national and disciplinary boundaries.
>
> Why was this so difficult to "do," the group wanted to know. It was then that they began to talk not about what they knew as "northern experts" about this or that northern subject, but to admit to what they didn't know.
>
> One person admitted that he knew very little about the peoples of the Russian North or their re/settlement during the Communist Era. Another admitted that she knew no history, about any "North"—Russian, European or North American—but did know about some of the psychological strains of living in environments characterized by prolonged periods of cold and isolation. An educator admitted that he'd heard so many references to Svalbard that he was just going to have to look it up on a map. And so it went, each "northern specialist" admitting that outside of her limited area of expertise, her knowledge of the North, of its peoples, of its flora and fauna, its political organization and so on was, as one of them said, "spotty at best."
>
> Novaya Zemlya? Nope.
> Rangifer? Nope.
> The Even? Nope.
> Thule? Nope.
> Pingos? Nope.
>
> Since there were no students around and since the dinner was good, everyone at the table agreed that if they were given a "basic" test about the peoples and places of the Circumpolar North, they'd probably fail. That is, though considered "northern experts," they weren't broadly knowledgeable—literate—about the North.
>
> The group's tentative thesis about the state of northern knowledge—at least their northern knowledge—was that it was like patterns of transportation or patterns of historical development in the region: that it did much to separate people, not bring them together. In a sense, it was as though their academic training had not prepared them to talk broadly with spe-

cialists from other fields about major northern problems or with other northerners.

This begged a question. Surely, if, as the conference organizers intended, northern people were to meet and converse about common concerns and issues they needed to share some basic knowledge about the region. Wasn't one of the prerequisites of informed or "literate" discussion something called common or shared knowledge?

The fundamental premise of this course, then, is that now, more than ever before, northerners need to know a great deal about the Circumpolar North, they need to know more about the other peoples with whom they share the region, and, thirdly, they need to know something about the issues that northerners face as they interact with each other and the land on which they live. Thus, BCS [Bachelor of Circumpolar Studies] 100 is meant to help students begin to build a comprehensive, accurate knowledge base about the Circumpolar North. (Senkpiel, 2003, 2–4)

As in the program at the Center for Northern Studies, such basic knowledge about the Circumpolar North is a fundamental principle behind educational initiatives of the University of the Arctic, which was officially launched in June 2001. Its motto, *In the North, For the North, By the North—Towards a Sustainable World*, continues to inform its collaborative network of institutions with a commitment to higher education, research, and sustainability in the North.

By promoting education that is *"circumpolar, interdisciplinary, and diverse in nature"* and by engaging the perspectives of northerners in all its activities, the University of the Arctic has consolidated the many facets of human endeavor in the North into an educational program that is truly circumpolar in its breadth. UArctic uses technology to its fullest to implement these programs and sustain networks among students, faculty, researchers, and institutions. Hosted by Iceland, the Arctic Portal (www.arcticportal.org) serves as the publisher of most Arctic Council reports and provides a base for its working groups. At the student level, shared online circumpolar courses will often have students enrolled from all eight of the Arctic nations. Friendships fostered online often continue by way of social networking, and are renewed in person with student mobility among institutions.

Establishment of the Center for Circumpolar Studies

The fundamental changes occurring in higher education are nowhere more obvious and important than in the Circumpolar North. Modern communications technology has made it possible for people in the remotest Arctic villages to have real-time participation in basic and advanced coursework at the university level, including the kind of personal interactions that, until recently, could take place only on college campuses. Students also have access to research articles as soon as they are published; library material that could only be available in a major research institution is now accessible to community colleges in small northern villages.

This technological shift occurs at a time when the political barriers that formerly isolated Russia from the rest of the North have largely dissolved, and indigenous peoples throughout the North have learned to operate effectively as respected and empowered members of the global community. Simultaneously, there is a rapid expansion in the awareness of the potential for resource development in the North, and an increasing influx of business and political interests to northern locations. The importance of first-quality higher education opportunities for people who live in the North, or who are planning careers that will take them northward, cannot be overemphasized.

Hard on the heels of the establishment of the University of the Arctic, a group of American scholars with deep connections to the Arctic and Boreal regions of the world incorporated the Center for Circumpolar Studies in the state of Vermont in 2011, building on past accomplishments in Northern Studies and drawing on the experience of many faculty involved previously with the Center for Northern Studies. The Center seeks to implement a fully circumpolar and interdisciplinary program at the undergraduate and graduate level, using the best in immersion learning and experiential practice. The Center is intended as a gateway for American students to study the circumpolar world in a vibrant community of scholars, using the best of collective knowledge and exploiting to the fullest technological resources that increasingly connect all corners of a globalizing world.

The Internet puts valuable teaching and learning tools directly in the hands of teachers and students, at no or very low cost. Sharing knowledge about a circumpolar world is less a problem of distances than it is a problem of logistics. "For Arctic peoples, engagement with print, video, commercial art and, of late, digital media has served different functions: enabling people to feed their families . . . promoting forms of cultural continuity, and, finally demonstrating their sovereignty and cultural autonomy to greater political constituencies" (Wachowich, 2010, 15). The realities of a circumpolar world, issues, and the capacity of technology make it possible for the Center for Circumpolar Studies to be situated in the Northern Forest of Vermont, but to do real work in the circumpolar world.

At the same time, northern education contains challenges that are different than those of the better known and more densely populated temperate regions. Perhaps most important, in our view, should be the continued need to ignore or break down traditional disciplinary boundaries. An executive in the extractive industries without a working knowledge of issues ranging from fisheries to indigenous traditions to climatic change trends is likely to be both ineffective as a businessperson and a danger to the respect and protection of values that are fundamental to northerners, both indigenous and adopted, and to the integrity of the environment itself. We cannot afford to leave the future of the North in the hands of narrowly trained specialists, and northern education must reflect this need for a transdisciplinary approach.

The field of circumpolar studies is increasingly important to the world. Climate change has been especially evident in the North, with consequent loss of sea ice, the endangerment of fauna such as polar bears and walrus, and the opening up of new sea routes and potential for energy development. Issues regarding indigenous peoples, wildlands protection, fisheries, and international sovereignty have become prominent on the national and international scene. The United States has lagged behind the other circumpolar nations in its concern for polar regions: the presence of polar expertise in the "Lower Forty-eight" is critical for a change in our attitudes and policies. With the focused and collaborative efforts of the University of the Arctic and the Center for Circumpolar Studies, knowledge about the northern dimension of the globe is within the reach of anyone.

Epilogue

REBECCA PINCUS

There is a tide in the affairs of men,
Which, taken at the flood, leads on to fortune;
Omitted, all the voyage of their life
Is bound in shallows and in miseries.
On such a full sea are we now afloat,
And we must take the current when it serves,
Or lose our ventures.

—WILLIAM SHAKESPEARE, *JULIUS CAESAR*

The earth's two poles have always been seen by outsiders as fascinating, other-worldly zones of adventure, exploration, and exploitation. Outsiders first penetrated Arctic and Antarctic waters in search of resources to remove, specifically fish, whales, and the hides and tusks of smaller marine mammals. Earlier eras of polar exploration proved enormously popular with publics across the globe.

We appear to now be entering another era of polar fascination. Evidence of this can be seen in the recent explosion of media coverage linked to climate change. A simple Google search for "Arctic warming" reveals a sharp spike in mentions from 2010 to 2011 (see figure 16.1).

This clear bump can be attributed to increased scientific awareness of climate change and to the public's enduring fascination with the poles, but also to the atten-tion-grabbing specter of conflict produced by a sudden rush North. The "Arctic cold war" trend piece was replicated across a variety of major popular news outlets. The *New York Times* opined on "Preventing an Arctic Cold War."[1] The *Guardian* warned, "Arctic military rivalry could herald a twenty-first-century cold war."[2] The question was asked in *Time*, "Is the Arctic Headed for Another Cold War?"[3] And an Associ-ated Press story entitled "The New Cold War: Militaries Eying Arctic Resources" was carried by CBS and Fox News.[4] The plateau indicates that the issue of Arctic warm-ing appears to have staying power, and perhaps has entered the public conscious-ness to a broader degree. But if the general public is only exposed to alarming and dramatic stories, public and policy discourse may be distorted. Increasing public awareness offers the opportunity to shape public opinion about the likely course of Arctic (and Antarctic) development under current warming projections, and to counter the hype around potential conflict.

In an excellent history of the Arctic, Robert McGhee notes that the modern era of epic polar exploration was primarily in pursuit of adventure, fame, and enter-tainment: "The polar quest added little to human knowledge, but considerably

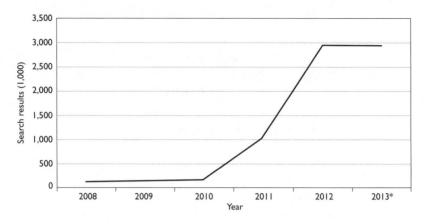

Figure 16.1: Google search results: Arctic warming
*Data for 2013 was projected from search results taken in August 2013.

embellished the fantastical vision of the Arctic painted in the minds of southern-
ers" (McGhee, 2005, p. 234). Today's era of polar fascination is largely due to over-
wrought tall tales of energy riches, easy access, and impending wars—stories that
generally contain a small kernel of truth within a puff of cotton candy.

There are indeed enormous deposits of oil and gas at both poles, and probably
many minerals as well. Harvesting these resources will, however, be terribly difficult, dangerous, and expensive for the foreseeable future, and the Arctic Ocean
will not be dotted with derricks, Gulf Coast–style, anytime soon. Oil and gas, as
well as other minerals, are extracted only when their market price is higher than the
costs of extraction. The relatively low cost of natural gas, and to some degree oil, as
a result of modern hydraulic fracturing (fracking) techniques will likely delay major
development of Arctic energy resources, which are very expensive. Of course, fracking has its own problems, as yet not fully understood, so our current energy boom
may prove short-lived. However, it has delayed the offshore energy rush that once
seemed nearly headlong, and may give policymakers some room to plan carefully
for the future of energy extraction in the Arctic.

Warming truly is occurring faster at the poles than any other parts of the globe,
and the effects of climate change can already be seen. The Arctic and Antarctic are,
however, and will remain, the extreme ends of the earth, and whatever moderation
in climate occurs must be seen in the context of the absolute cold and darkness that
is their birthright. Although the Arctic Ocean is predicted to be ice-free sometime in
the early to middle twenty-first century, as I often remind audiences, this is just in
the summertime. During winter, ice will still dominate and darkness will prevail. It
will not be an easy jaunt to either pole, and this realization must temper the enthusiasm of any optimistic polar investor.

And finally, there is some potential for conflict, particularly in the Arctic. As presence increases, longstanding tensions will have a greater chance of simmering over.
But the notion that major powers such as the United States, Russia, and China will

rush into war over energy resources buried below a frozen ocean is pure hysteria. The chance of conflict must be balanced against the desire for peace, and from this perspective the odds are quite small. Once again, the Antarctic example may prove a timely reminder. That continent, which once drove major nations much closer to open conflict in the tense years following World War II, ultimately found resolution in cooperation and the shared desire to avoid war.

It is not a foregone conclusion, nor will it be easy to manage the multiple pressures on these regions, but the likelihood of preserving the peace will be far higher if we can tone down the rhetoric and remind ourselves of what is at stake. And the truth is that much of the excitement is due to myth and symbol. Much of our fascination with the poles is based on myth and the symbolic values we have long attached to polar regions. Barry Lopez sums up the situation well: "The literature of arctic exploration is frequently offered as a record of resolute will before the menacing fortifications of the landscape. It is more profitable I think to disregard this notion—that the land is an adversary bent on human defeat, that the people who came and went were heroes or failures in this. It is better to contemplate the record of human longing to achieve something significant, to be free of some of the grim weight of life. That weight was ignorance, poverty of spirit, indolence, and the threat of anonymity and destitution. This harsh landscape became the focus of a desire to separate oneself from those things and to overcome them. In these arctic narratives, then, are the threads of dreams that serve us all" (Lopez, 1986, 310).

Despite our fascination, there is a dangerous undercurrent of ambivalence and even hostility—coupled, among some players, with disdain for Arctic peoples. In a discussion of the overwhelming burden of indigenous peoples' managing their role in Arctic governance, Sheehan and Jensen (chapter 14) note that even today, federal officials still discount the Native worldview and the unique perspective of indigenous communities.

This ambivalence and disdain have contributed to a history of ineradicable damage: extraction of natural resources to their limits with concurrent environmental damage, including generations of whaling, trapping, mining, and drilling; the toxic legacy of unbridled nuclear testing and dumping (by Russia); and trampling of the rights and dignity of Native peoples.

In the twentieth century, growing awareness of the fragility of these frigid areas led to international efforts toward their protection. But these efforts came only at the end of one round of the gluttony, when whales had been essentially fished out of the seas, and before humanity's addiction to carbon fuels had led prospectors to the water's edge.

There are clear paths for further research and understanding; this volume was assembled in hopes of paving the way for future work. The pursuit of human rights in the Arctic must be accompanied by an understanding of the reality of what that means for Arctic communities. The complex interfaces among forces such as energy development, environmental protection, tourism, safety, and invasive species make policy and rule making quite complex. Further study of the linkages between regulatory regimes is necessary. In addition, more must be done to elucidate the complex relationships between major global powers, international bodies, and local communities.

Today, as an energy-hungry world exhausts readily available deposits of oil and gas, there is increasing pressure to look north for buried energy treasure, aided by a rapidly expanding Arctic summer. Other pressures are mounting, north and south: ship traffic, fishing, mineral exploration, military patrols, and tourism. These pressures come at a time when the fabric of the polar ecosystems is fraying at the seams from rapid warming. The impacts of increased carbon dioxide in the earth's atmosphere are especially concentrated at the poles, where warming is occurring the fastest. As native species disappear, and invaders from warmer latitudes increasingly appear in polar regions, these remote zones will lose the uniqueness that has for so long made them regions of fascination to outsiders, and treasured homes for their native communities.

It remains to be seen whether the new era of polar development will continue to be characterized by the same blinkered perspectives that marked the past. The world is now confronted with an urgent question: How should we manage the final frontiers? Will we repeat history, and do lasting damage to these fragile ecosystems and traditional ways of life? Or can we create new, durable governance structures that can protect these irreplaceable zones of discovery and awe, and usher in a new era of cooperation at the ends of the earth?

Notes

1. Paul Arthur Berkman, "Preventing an Arctic Cold War," *New York Times*. Opinion, March 12, 2013.

2. Terry Macalister, "Arctic military rivalry could herald a twenty-first-century cold war," *The Guardian*. World News, June 5, 2012.

3. Krista Mahr, "Is the Arctic Headed for Another Cold War?" *Time*, Science and Space, October 12, 2010.

4. The Associated Press, "The New Cold War: Militaries Eying Arctic Resources," April 16, 2012; the Associated Press, "As Arctic Ice Cap Melts, a New Cold War," April 16, 2012.

Selected Resources

Abbott, Kenneth W., and Duncan Snidal. "The Governance Triangle: Regulatory Standards Institutions in the Shadow of the State." In *The Politics of Global Regulation*, edited by Walter Mattli and Ngaire Woods. Princeton: Princeton University Press, 2009.

Adams, Duncan, and Aaron Farrington. "15 Years Ago in the *Arctic Sounder*: Whaling captains boycott hearing." 17 July 1997. *Arctic Sounder* 26(29) (19 July 2012): 2.

Adger, W. N., N. W. Arnell, and E. L. Tompkins. "Successful adaptation to climate change across scales." *Global Environmental Change* 15 (2005): 77–86.

Afonso, O., S. Monteiro, and M. Thompson. *A Growth Model for the Quadruple Helix Innovation Theory*. Núcleo de Investigação em Políticas Económicas. Universidade do Minho, 2010.

Agnew, J. "Sovereign regimes: Territoriality and state authority in contemporary world politics." *Annals of the Association of American Geographers* 95 (2005): 437–461.

Agreement Concerning Cooperation in the Quarantine of Plants and Their Protection Against Pests and Diseases. Sofia, 14 December 1959. http://sedac.ciesin.org/entri/texts/quarantine.of.plants.1959.html.

Albert, Thomas F. "The Influence of Harry Brower, Sr." In *Fifty More Years Below Zero: Tributes and Meditations for the Naval Arctic Research Laboratory's First Half Century at Barrow, Alaska*, edited by David W. Norton. Calgary and Fairbanks: Arctic Institute of North America, 2001.

Ali, S. H. *Mining, the Environment and Indigenous Development Conflicts*. Tucson: University of Arizona Press, 2003.

Allen, Craig R., Alan R. Johnson, and Leslie Parris. "A framework for spatial risk assessments: Potential impacts of non-indigenous invasive species on native species." *Ecology and Society* 11(1) (2006): 39.

Altamirano-Jiménez, I. "Northern American First Peoples: Slipping up into market citizenship?" *Citizenship Studies* 8(4) (2004): 349–365.

Anaya, James. "The Human Rights of Indigenous Peoples in Light of the New Declaration, and the Challenges of Making Them Operable." *Report of the Special Rapporteur*,

A/HRC/9/9, para. 85. 5 August 2008. United Nations, Office of the High Commissioner for Human Rights.

Anderson, R. B., L. P. Dana, and T. E. Dana. "Indigenous land rights, entrepreneurship, and economic development in Canada: 'Opting-in' to the global economy." *Journal of World Business* 41(1) (2006): 45–55.

Anonymous. "Oil Suit on North Slope: Suit Against Creation of Slope Borough Filed by Seven Major Oil Companies." *Tundra Times* 9(29) (29 March 1972): 1, 6.

Antarctic Treaty Consultative Meeting XXX. Resolution 4 ATCM XXX–CEP X. *Ship-Based Tourism in the Antarctic Treaty Area.* Adopted 11 May 2007, New Delhi (2007).

Antarctic Treaty Consultative Meeting XXXII. Resolution 7 ATCM XXXII—CEP XII. *General Principles of Antarctic Tourism* (2009).

———. Resolution 8 ATCM XXXII—CEP XII. *Mandatory Shipping Code for Vessels Operating in Antarctic Waters.* Adopted 17 April 2009, Baltimore (2009).

Antarctic Treaty Consultative Meeting XXXIV. Resolution 3 ATCM XXXIV–CEP XIV. *General Guidelines for Visitors to the Antarctic.* Adopted 1 July 2011, Buenos Aires (2011).

Antarctic Treaty Meeting of Experts, Chair Report. Antarctic Treaty Meeting of Experts on the Management of Ship-borne Tourism in the Antarctic Treaty Area, 9–11 December 2009, Wellington, New Zealand (2009).

Antarctic Treaty Secretariat. "Shipping Guidelines: Antarctica." In *Final Report of the Twenty-Seventh Antarctic Treaty Consultative Meeting, May 24–June 4, 2004, Cape Town, South Africa.* Buenos Aires: Secretariat of the Antarctic Treaty (2004).

———. Canadian Verbal Statement Regarding Incident of M/S Explorer. In *Final Report of the Thirty-first Consultative Meeting, June 2–13, 2008, Kiev, Ukraine.* Additional Documents from ATCM XXXI, Part IV, Annex H. Buenos Aires: Secretariat of the Antarctic Treaty (2008).

———. *Final Report of the Thirty-fourth Consultative Meeting, June 20–July 1, 2011, Buenos Aires, Argentina.* Buenos Aires: Secretariat of the Antarctic Treaty (2011a).

———. Report of the International Association of Antarctica Tour Operators 2001–2011. In *Final Report of the Thirty-fourth Consultative Meeting, June 20–July 1, 2011, Buenos Aires, Argentina.* Buenos Aires: Secretariat of the Antarctic Treaty (2011b).

———. Revised Rules of Procedure 2008, *Compilation of Key Documents of the Antarctic Treaty System* 2, Buenos Aires: Secretariat of the Antarctic Treaty (2012).

Arctic Council. Declaration on the Establishment of the Arctic Council 1996–Ottawa Declaration. Arctic Council Secretariat. 19 September 1996. http://www.arctic-council.org/index.php/en/about/documents/category/4-founding-documents#.

———. *Arctic Climate Impact Assessment* (ACIA). ACIA Secretariat. Cambridge: Cambridge University Press, 2005. Also available at http://www.acia.uaf.edu/pages/scientific.html.

———. "Impacts of a Warming Arctic." *Arctic Climate Impact Assessment* (2006). ACIA Secretariat. http://amap.no/acia/.

———. "About Arctic Council." 22 October 2007. http://arctic-council.org/article/about.

———. "Environmental Considerations and Impacts." *Arctic Marine Shipping Assessment* (AMSA) (2009), 134–153. http://www.arctic.gov/publications/AMSA/environmental.pdf.

———. *Arctic Biodiversity Trends 2010: Selected indicators of change report* (2010). http://abt.arcticportal.org/images/stories/report/pdf/Key_Findings.pdf.

_____. *Arctic Ocean Review*, Phase I Report (2009–2011). http://www.aor.is/.

_____. Kiruna Declaration on the Occasion of the Eighth Ministerial Meeting of the Arctic Council Arctic Council Secretariat. MM08, 15 May 2013. www.ArcticCouncil.is.

_____. "Working Groups." Arctic Council. http://www.arctic-council.org/.

Arctic Council, Arctic Monitoring and Assessment Program (AMAP). Arctic 2007 Oil and Gas Assessment. http://www.amap.no/oga/.

_____. "Snow, water, ice and permafrost in the Arctic" (AMAP 2011). Oslo: AMAP Secretariat, 2011. http://www.amap.no/swipa/SWIPA2011ExecutiveSummaryV2.pdf (accessed 5 March 2012).

Arctic Council, Protection of the Arctic Marine Environment (PAME) Secretariat. Arctic Council Arctic Marine Strategic Plan, Akureyri (2004).

_____. Arctic Offshore Oil and Gas Guidelines, Akureyri (2009).

_____. The Arctic Ocean Review Project, Final Report (Phase II 2011–2013), Kiruna (May 2013).

_____. "Arctic Marine Shipping Assessment Recommendations." http://www.pame.is/amsa/on-focus/81-the-arctic-marine-shipping-assessment-recommendations.

Arctic Environmental Protection Strategy (AEPS). The Declaration on the Protection of the Arctic Environment (Rovaniemi Declaration). Rovaniemi, Finland. 14 January 1991.

Arctic Governance Project. *Arctic Governance in an Era of Transformative Change: Critical Questions, Governance Principles, Ways Forward* (14 April 2010). http://www.arctic governance.org/agp-report-and-action-agenda.156784.en.html).

_____. *Recommendations, An Arctic Action Agenda* (14 April 2010).

Arctic Institute of North America (AINA). http://www.arctic.ucalgary.ca/index.php (accessed 30 September 2011).

Ármannsson, P. H. "Orkuver og arkitektúr [Power plants and architecture]." In *Landsvirkjun 1965–2005: Fyrirtækið og umhverfi þess [Landsvirkjun 1965–2005: The company and its environment]*, edited by S. Pálsdóttir. Reykjavík: Hið íslenska bókmenntafélag, 2005.

Art, Robert J., and Robert Jervis, eds. *International Politics: Enduring Concepts and Contemporary Issues*. 8th ed. New York: Pearson, 2007.

Associated Press. "As Arctic Ice Cap Melts, a New Cold War." 16 April 2012. From CBS News.com (http://www.cbsnews.com/8301-202_162-57414522/as-arctic-ice-cap-melts-a-new-cold-war/), accessed 21 August 2013.

_____. "The New Cold War: Militaries Eying Arctic Resources." 16 April 2012. From Fox News.com (http://www.foxnews.com/scitech/2012/04/16/new-cold-war-as-ice-cap-melts-militaries-vie-for-arctic-edge/), accessed 21 August 2013.

Association of Canadian Universities for Northern Studies (ACUNS). http://acuns.ca/website/ (accessed 27 September 2011).

Baev, Pavel K. "From West to South to North: Russia Engages and Challenges Its Neighbors." *International Journal* 63 (2008): 2.

Baker, Betsy. Arctic Offshore Oil and Gas Guidelines White Paper No. 3: Northern Communities, Participation in Decision Making in the United States and Canada (10 August 2010). http://www.vermontlaw.edu/Documents/IEE/20100812_baker WP3.pdf.

_____. "Filling an Arctic Gap: Legal and Regulatory Possibilities for Canadian–U.S. Cooperation in the Beaufort Sea." *Vermont Law Review* 34 (2010): 57–120.

_____. "Marine Biodiversity, Ecosystem Services and Better Use of Science Information."
In *Securing the Ocean for the Next Generation*, edited by H. Scheiber and M. Kwon.
Papers from the Law of the Sea Institute–Korea Institute of Ocean Science and Technology Conference, Seoul, Korea, May 2012. Published at http://www.law.berkeley
.edu/15589.htm (2013).

Baker, James S., and Michael Byers. "Crossed Lines: The Curious Case of the Beaufort
Sea Maritime Boundary Dispute." *Ocean Development and International Law* 43(1)
(2012): 70–95.

Barber, D. G., et al. "The changing climate of the Arctic." *Arctic* 61(1) (2008): 7–26.

Barcott, Bruce. "Grolar Bears and Narlugas: Rise of the Arctic Hybrid." *On Earth*, December 2010. http://www.onearth.org/article/grolar-bears-and-narlugas-rise-of-the
-arctic-hybrids.

Barnes, J. N. "Environmental protection and the future of the Antarctic: New approaches
and perspectives are necessary." In *The Antarctic Treaty Regime: Law, Environment and
Resources*, edited by Gillian D. Triggs. Cambridge: Cambridge University Press, 1989.

Barnett, Jon. *The Meaning of Environmental Security: Ecological Politics and Policy in the
New Security Era*. New York: Zed Books, 2001.

Bastmeijer, Kees, and Machiel Lamers. "Reaching Consensus on Antarctic Tourism
Regulation: Calibrating the Human-Nature Relationship?" In *New Issues in Polar Tourism*, edited by D. Mueller, L. Lundmark, and H. Lemelin. Heidelberg: Springer, 2012.

Bastmeijer, Kees, and Ricardo Roura. "Regulating Antarctic Tourism and the Precautionary Principle." *American Journal of International Law* 98 (2004): 4.

Beaumier, M. C., and J. D. Ford. "Food insecurity among Inuit women exacerbated by
socio-economic stresses and climate change." *Canadian Journal of Public Health* 101(3)
(2010): 196–201.

Beck, P. J. "Regulating one of the last tourism frontiers: Antarctica." *Applied Geography*
10(4) (1990): 243–356.

_____. "Fifty years on: Putting the Antarctic Treaty into the history books." *Polar Record*
46(236) (2010): 4–7.

Beck, U. "The Reinvention of Politics." In *Reflexive Modernization*, edited by U. Beck,
A. Giddens, and S. Lash. Cambridge: Polity, 1994.

Belova, M. and E. Mel'nikova. "Truba nalevo, truba napravo [Pipeline left, pipeline
right]." *Politicheskii zhurnal* [*Political Journal*] 5(56) (14 February 2005). http://www
.politjournal.ru/ (accessed 27 September 2007).

Berg, Eiki, and Ene Kuusk. "What Makes Sovereignty a Relative Concept? Empirical Approaches to International Society." *Political Geography* 29:1 (January 2010): 40–49.

Berger, T. R. "Northern Frontier, Northern Homeland: The Report of the Mackenzie Valley Pipeline Inquiry," 2 vols. Ottawa: Minister of Supplies and Services Canada, 1977.

Bergin, Anthony. "Recent Developments in Australia's Antarctic Policy." *Marine Policy*
9:3 (July 1985): 180–191.

Berkes, F. "Rethinking community-based conservation." *Conservation Biology* 18:3 (2003):
621–630.

Berkes, F., and D. Jolly. "Adapting to climate change: Social-ecological resilience in a
Canadian western Arctic community." *Conservation Ecology* 5(2) (2001) [online].

Berkman, P. A. "Common interests in the international space of Antarctica." *Polar Record*
46(236) (2010): 7–9.

Berkman, Paul Arthur. "Preventing an Arctic Cold War." *New York Times*. Opinion. 12 March 2013.

Berkman, P., and O. Young. "Governance and environmental change in the Arctic Ocean." *Science* 324 (2009): 339–340.

Berman, M., C. Nicolson, G. Kofinas, J. Tetlichi, and S. Martin. "Adaptation and sustainability in a small Arctic community: Results of an agent-based simulation model." *Arctic* 57 (4) (2004): 401–414.

Bernstein, Steven, and Benjamin Cashore. "Nonstate Global Governance: Is Forest Certification a Legitimate Alternative to a Global Forest Convention?" In *Hard Choices, Soft Law: Voluntary Standards in Global Trade, Environment, and Social Governance*, edited by John J. Kirton and M. J. Trebilcock. Hants: Ashgate, 2004.

Beunza, D., and R. Garud. "The Intermediary Role of Securities Analysts." *The Sociological Review* 55 (2007): 13–39.

Biermann, Frank, and Philipp Pattberg. "Global Environmental Governance: Taking Stock, Moving Forward." *Annual Review of Environment and Resources* 33 (2008).

Blank, Steven. "China's Arctic Strategy." *The Diplomat*, 30 June 2013.

Blank, Yishai. "Localism in the New Global Legal Order." *Harvard International Law Journal* 47(1) (2006).

Blomley, N. *Law, Space and the Geographies of Power*. New York: Guildford, 1994.

Bloom, Evan. "Establishment of the Arctic Council." *American Journal of International Law* 98(712) (July 1999).

Bodansky, Daniel M. "The Legitimacy of International Governance: A Coming Challenge for International Environmental Law?" *American Journal of International Law* 7:1 (1999).

Bodenhorn, B. "It's good to know who your relatives are but we were thought to share with everybody: Shares and sharing among the Inupiaq households." In *The Social Economy of Sharing: Resource Allocation and Modern Hunter-Gatherers*, edited by G. W. Wenzel, G. Hovelsrud-Broda, N. Kishigami, and Kokuritsu Minzokugaku Hakubutsukan. Osaka: National Museum of Ethnology, 2000, 27–60.

Borgerson, S. "Arctic meltdown: The economic and security implications of global warming." *Foreign Affairs*. March–April 2008. http://www.foreignaffairs.com/articles/63222/scott-g-borgerson/arctic-meltdown.

Boyer, D. "The Corporeality of Expertise." *Ethnos* 70:2 (2005): 243–266.

Bratspies, Rebecca M. "Regulatory Trust. " *Arizona Law Review* 51 (2009): 575.

——. "Human Rights and Environmental Regulation." *NYU Journal of Environmental Law* 19:225 (2012).

Brigham, Lawson, Capt., Ret., USCG. "Russia Opens Its Maritime Arctic." *Proceedings*, US Naval Institute, 2011.

Brooks, David. *Bobos in Paradise: Bourgeois Bohemians, the New Upper Class and How They Got There*. New York: Simon and Schuster, 2000.

Brosnan, Ian G., Thomas M. Leschine, and Edward L. Miles. "Cooperation or Conflict in a Changing Arctic?" *Ocean Development and International Law* 42(1–2) (2011): 173–210.

Buck, S. J. *The Global Commons: An Introduction*. Washington, D.C.: Island Press, 1998.

Bulkeley, R. "The political origins of the Antarctic Treaty." *Polar Record* 46(236) (2010): 9–11.

Burgiel, S., Greg Foote, et al. *Invasive Alien Species and Trade: Integrating Prevention Measures and International Trade Rules.* Washington, D.C.: Center for International Environmental Law (CIEL), 2006.

Burgiel, Stanley W., and Adrianna A. Muir. *Invasive Species, Climate Change and Ecosystem-Based Adaptation: Addressing Multiple Drivers of Global Change.* Washington, D.C.: Global Invasive Species Program (2010). http://data.iucn.org/dbtw-wpd/edocs/2010-054.pdf.

Burke, R. C. "Land, resource and discourses of development in central Labrador." Master's thesis, Memorial University of Newfoundland, 2003. Available at Theses Canada, http://www.collectionscanada.gc.ca/obj/thesescanada/vol2/002/mr09916.pdf (accessed 5 September 2013).

Buszynski, L. "Oil and territory in Putin's relations with China and Japan." *The Pacific Review*, 19(3) (2006): 287–303.

Byers, Michael. *Who Owns the Arctic? Understanding Sovereignty Disputes in the North.* Vancouver: Douglas and McIntyre, 2009.

Çaliskan, K., and M. Callon. "Economization I." *Economy and Society*, 38(3) (2009): 369–398.

Callon, M. "What Does It Mean to Say that Economics Is Performative?" In *On the Performativity of Economics: Do Economists Make Markets?*, edited by D. MacKenzie, F. Muniesa, and L. Siu. Princeton: Princeton University Press, 2007.

Cambridge Energy Research Associates (CERA). "Long-term Outlook." Decision Brief, December 2000.

Carayannis, E. G., and D. F. J. Campbell. "'Mode 3' and 'Quadruple Helix': Toward a 21st-century fractal innovation ecosystem." *International Journal of Technology Management*, 46(3–4) (2009): 201–223.

Carlson, J. M., and J. Doyle. "Complexity and Robustness." *Proceedings of the National Academy of Sciences* 9 (suppl. 1) (2002): 2538-2545.

Center for Circumpolar Studies. Press release. 7 October 2011.

Chambers, W. Bradnee. *Interlinkages and the Effectiveness of Multilateral Environmental Agreements.* Tokyo: United Nations University Press, 2008.

Charters, Claire, and Rodolfo Stavenhagen. International Working Group for Indigenous Affairs (IWGIA), *Making Declarations Work: The United Nations Declaration on the Rights of Indigenous Peoples*, Doc. 127. IWGIA: Copenhagen, 2009.

Clark, Margaret. "The Antarctic Environmental Protocol: NGOs in the protection of Antarctica." In *Environmental NGOs in World Politics*, edited by Thomas Princen and Matthias Finger. London: Routledge, 1994.

Clark, Gen. Wesley A. *Winning Modern Wars.* New York: Public Affairs, 2003.

Codex Alimentarius Commission (2012). http://www.codexalimentarius.net/web/index_en.jsp.

Collings, P., R. G. Condon, and G. Wenzel. "Modern food sharing networks and community integration in the central Canadian Arctic." *Arctic* 51(4) (1998): 301.

Collins, Alan, ed. *Contemporary Security Studies*, 2nd ed. Oxford: Oxford University Press, 2010.

Commission of Europe (COM). Communication from the Commission to the European Parliament and the Council. "The European Union and the Arctic Region" (2008). http://eur-lex.europa.eu/LexUriServ/LexUriServ.do?uri=CELEX:DKEY=483680:EN:NOT.

Conservation of Arctic Flora and Fauna (CAFF). Arctic Biodiversity Assessment: Report for Policy Makers. Akureyri, Iceland. www.arcticbiodiversity.is (2013).

Convention on the Conservation of Antarctic Marine Living Resources (CCAMLR) (1980). http://www.ccamlr.org/.

Convention on International Trade in Endangered Species of Wild Fauna and Flora (CITES). Resolution Conf. 13.10 (Rev. CoP14)–1. "Trade in alien invasive species." http://www.cites.org/eng/res/all/13/E13-10R14.pdf.

Convention on the Protection of the Marine Environment of the Baltic Sea Area. Adopted 1992 (entered into force 17 January 2000). http://www.helcom.fi/stc/files/Convention/Conv1108.pdf.

Convention for the Protection of the Marine Environment of the North-East Atlantic (OSPAR). OSPAR Commission. 21 February 1974. *International Legal Materials* 13 (1974).

Convention for the Protection of the Marine Environment of the North-East Atlantic (OSPAR). OSPAR Commission. "Winning the war on invasive species." http://www.ospar.org/content/news_detail.asp?menu=00600725000000_000004_000000.

Convention on the Regulation of Antarctic Mineral Resource Activities, *International Legal Materials* 27 (1988): 868.

Convention on Wetlands of International Importance, especially as Waterfowl Habitat (RAMSAR). Adopted 2 February 1971 (entered into force 21 December 1975). http://www.ramsar.org/cda/en/ramsar-documents-texts-convention-on/main/ramsar/1-31-38%5E20671_4000_0_.

Convention on Wetlands of International Importance (RAMSAR). Resolution VIII.18. Resolutions of the 8th meeting of the Conference of the Parties. "Invasive species and wetlands." Valencia, Spain, 18–26 November 2002. http://www.ramsar.org/pdf/res/key_res_viii_18_e.pdf.

Coston, Jacqulyn. "Recent Development: What Lies Beneath: The CLCS and the Race to Lay Claim over the Arctic Seabed." *Environmental and Energy Law and Policy Journal* 3 (2008): 149.

Council of the European Union. Council Conclusions on Arctic Issues. Brussels, 8 December 2009. http://ec.europa.eu/maritimeaffairs/pdf/arctic_council_conclusions_09_en.pdf.

Coyne, Amanda. "Shell Oil top contributor in campaign to stop Alaska coastal initiative." *Alaska Dispatch* (31 July 2012). http://www.alaskadispatch.com/article/shell-oil-top-contributor-campaign-stop-alaska-coastal-initiative.

Cruise Lines International Association. *Ship Information–Nordnorge*, 2012. http://www.cruising.org/vacation/cruiseline/hurtigruten/ships/nordnorge-0.

Cutter, S. "Issues in environmental justice research." In *Hazards, Vulnerability and Environmental Justice*, edited by S. L. Cutter. London: Earthscan, 2006.

Dana, L. P., A. Meis-Mason, and R. B. Anderson. "Oil and gas and the Inuvialuit people of the Western Arctic." *Journal of Enterprising Communities: People and Places in Global Economy* 2(2) (2008): 151–167.

Dawkins, R. *The Selfish Gene.* New York: Oxford University Press, 1976.

Degeorges, Damien. "The Arctic—A region of the future for the European Union and the world economy." *European Issues* no. 263. Paris: Fondation Robert Schuman, 8 January 2013.

Deggim, H. *Development of a Mandatory Polar Code–Update on Progress.* International Maritime Organization, Marine Technology Section, Maritime Safety Division, 2011.

_____. Head, International Maritime Organization, Marine Technology Section, Maritime Safety Division. E-mail correspondence, 21 February 2012.

Dehcho First Nations. Dehcho First Nations Framework Agreement among the Dehcho First Nations, the Government of Canada and the Government of the Northwest Territories (2001). http://www.dehcho.org/documents/agreements/Dehcho%20First%20Nations%20Framework%20Agreement.pdf (accessed 29 July 2012).

_____. General Agreement-in-Principle between the Dehcho First Nations and the Government of Canada and the Government of Northwest Territories (2007). http://www.dehcho.org/documents/negotiations/07_03_05_general_agreement_in_principle.pdf (accessed 29 July 2012).

_____. General Agreement-in-Principle between the Dehcho First Nations and the Government of Canada and the Government of Northwest Territories Rolling Draft 8 May 2012. http://www.dehcho.org/documents/negotiations/negotiations_session_may_23_2012_video_conference/08%20ROLLING%20DRAFT%20AIP%20VERSION%20DATED%20MAY%2018,%202012.pdf (accessed 29 July 2012).

DeMarban, Alex. "Arctic openings get Coast Guard's attention." *Arctic Sounder* (6 June 2011).

Desch, Michael C. "Culture Clash: Assessing the Importance of Ideas in Security Studies." *International Security* 23(1) (1998).

Dickinson, M. "A wake-up call for shipping." *Telegraph: Nautilus International Newsletter* 45(2) (2012): 1, 3.

Didham, Raphael K., et al., "Interactive effects of habitat modification and species invasion on native species decline." *Trends in Ecology and Evolution* 22(9) (2007).

Dittmer, Jason, Alan Ingram, Sami Moisio, and Klaus Dodds. "Have you heard the one about the disappearing ice? Recasting Arctic geopolitics." *Political Geography* 30 (2011): 202–214.

Dodds, K. "Governing Antarctica: Contemporary Challenges and the Enduring Legacy of the 1959 Antarctic Treaty." *Global Policy* 1(1) (2010a): 108–115.

Dodds, K. J. "Amongst the palm trees: Ruminations on the 1959 Antarctic Treaty." *Polar Record* 46(236) (2010b): 1–2.

Dodds, Klaus. "Flag planting and finger pointing: The Law of the Sea, the Arctic and the political geographies of the outer continental shelf." *Political Geography* 29 (2010): 63–73.

Drezner, Daniel. *All Politics Is Global: Explaining International Regulatory Regimes.* Princeton: Princeton University Press, 2007.

Drucker, P. F. *The Age of Discontinuity: Guidelines to Our Changing Society.* New York: Harper and Row, 1969.

Duerden, F. "Translating climate change impacts at the community level." *Arctic* 57(2) (2004): 204–212.

Duyck, Sébastien. "Participation of non-state actors in Arctic environmental governance." *Nordia Geographical Publications* 40 (2012): 4.

Ebbert, S. E., and G. V. Byrd. "Eradication of invasive species to restore natural biological diversity on the Alaska Maritime National Refuge." In *Turning the Tide: The Eradication of Invasive Species,* edited by C. R. Veitch and M. N. Clout. Gland, Switzerland, and Cambridge: International Conservation Union (IUCN), 2004, 102–109.

Ebinger, Charles K., and Evie Zambetakis. "The Geopolitics of Arctic Melt." *International Affairs* 85 (2009): 6.

Egland, G. M., L. Johnson-Down, Z. R. Cao, N. Sheikh, and H. Weiler. "Food insecurity and nutrition transition combine to affect intakes in Canadian Arctic communities." *The Journal of Nutrition* 141 (2011): 1746–1753.

Elden, S. "Governmentality, calculation, territory." *Environment and Planning D: Society and Space* 25 (2007): 562–580.

_____. *Terror and Territory: The Spatial Extent of Sovereignty*. Minneapolis: University of Minnesota Press, 2009.

Emmerson, C. *The Future History of the Arctic*. London: Vintage, 2011.

Energy Information Administration (EIA). "International Energy Outlook 2011." http://205.254.135.7/forecasts/ieo/pdf/0484(2011).pdf. (2011).

Esty, Daniel C. "Good governance at the supranational scale: Globalizing administrative law." *Yale Law Journal* 115(7) (2006).

Etzkowitz, H. *The Triple Helix: University-Industry-Government Innovation in Action*. New York: Routledge, 2008.

European Court of Human Rights. *Giacomelli v. Italy*, 2006-XII Eur. Ct. H. R. 345 (2006).

_____. *Oneryildiz v. Turkey*, 2004-XII 41 Eur. Ct. H. R. 20 (2004).

_____. *Taskin and Others v. Turkey*, 2004-X 42 Eur. Ct. H.R. 50, 206 (2005).

European Parliament and the Council of Europe. "Public Access to Environmental Information," Dir. 2003/4/EC. http://eur-lex.europa.eu/LexUriServ/LexUriServ.do?uri=OJ:L:2003:041:0026:0032:EN:PDF.

Evengard, Birgitta, and Rainer Sauerborn. "Climate change influences infectious diseases both in the Arctic and the tropics: Joining the dots." *Global Health Action* 2 eISSN 1654–9880 (2009).

Falkner, Robert. "Private Environmental Governance and International Relations: Exploring the Links." *Global Environmental Politics* 3(2) (2003).

Federal Energy Regulatory Commission (FERC). "State of the Markets 2000: Measuring Performance in Energy Market Regulation" (2000).

Field, Michael H., Brian Huntley, and Helmut Muller. "Eemian Climate Fluctuations Observed in a European Pollen Record." *Nature* 371(6500) (October 1994).

Fifield, Richard. *International Research in the Antarctic*. Oxford: Oxford University Press, 1987.

Florini, Ann, and Benjamin K. Sovacool. "Who Governs Energy? The Challenges Facing Global Energy Governance." *Energy Policy* 37, no. 12 (December 2009): 5239–5248.

Freeman, L. C., S. P. Borgatti, and D. R. White. "Centrality in valued graphs: A measure of betweenness based on network flow." *Social Networks* 13(2) (1991): 141–154.

French, D., and K. Scott. "International Legal Implications of Climate Change for the Polar Regions: Too Much, Too Little, Too Late?" In *Melbourne Journal of International Law* 10(2) (2009): 631–654.

Friðleifsson, I. B., A. Svanbjörnsson, and L. Thorsteinsson. "Icelandic experience in transfer of energy technology." In *Tímarit Verkfræðingafélags Íslands* 69 (1984): 6–10.

Frug, Gerald, and David Barron. "International Local Government Law." *The Urban Lawyer* 38(1) (2006).

Furgal, C., and J. Seguin. "Climate change, health, and vulnerability in Canadian northern aboriginal communities." In *Environmental Health Perspectives* 114(12) (2006): 1964–1970.

Genovesi, P., and C. Shine. *European Strategy on Invasive Alien Species. Nature and Environment.* Strasbourg: Council of Europe, 2004.

Genovesi, Piero, and Riccardo Scalera. *Toward a Blacklist of Invasive Alien Species Entering Europe through Trade, and Proposed Responses.* Strasbourg: Council of Europe, 2007. https://wcd.coe.int/wcd/com.instranet.InstraServlet?command=com.instranet.Cmd BlobGet&InstranetImage=1298206&SecMode=1&DocId=1438902&Usage=2.

Gerhardt, Hannes, Philip E. Steinberg, Jeremy Tasch, Sandra J. Fabiano, and Rob Shields. "Contested Sovereignty in a Changing Arctic." *Annals of the Association of American Geographers* 100(4) (2010): 992–1002.

Giddens, A. *Modernity and Self-Identity.* Stanford: Stanford University Press, 1991.

Giddens, Anthony. *The Politics of Climate Change.* Cambridge, UK: Polity Press, 2009.

Gilbert, N. *Agent-Based Models.* London: SAGE Publications, 2008.

Gilchrist, A. "The well-connected community: Networking to the 'edge of chaos.'" *Community Development Journal* 35 (3) (2000): 264–275.

Girvan, M., and M. E. J. Newman. "Community structure in social and biological networks." *Proceedings of the National Academy of Sciences of the United States of America* 99(12) (2002): 7821–7826.

Global Invasive Species Programme (GISP). "Global Strategy on Invasive Alien Species." http://www.cites.org/common/com/AC/16/E16-Inf-12.pdf.

Goldthau, Andreas. "Governing Global Energy: Existing Approaches and Discourses." *Current Opinion in Environmental Sustainability* 3(4) (September 2011): 213–217.

Government of Newfoundland and Labrador. The Tshash Petapen Agreement (2008). http://www.releases.gov.nl.ca/releases/2008/exec/0926n07agreement.pdf (accessed 5 September 2013).

Graczyk, Piotr, and Timo Koivurova. "A new era in the Arctic Council's external relations? Broader consequences of the Nuuk observer rules for Arctic governance." *Polar Record* (2013).

Grainey, Michael W. "Recent Federal Energy Legislation: Towards a National Energy Policy at Last?" *Lewis and Clark Law School Journal of Environmental Law* 12 (1981): 29.

Grover, R., I. Anghel, B. Berdar, M. Soloviev, and A. Zavyalov. "Compulsory Purchase in the Transitional Countries of Central and Eastern Europe." *Theoretical and Applied Economics* 4 (2008): 3–18.

Grover, R., G. Ledkov, and M. M. Soloviev. "Indigenous Peoples' Interests and the Oil-Gas Industry." Paper presented at the European Real Estate Society Conference, Vienna, 4–6 June 2013. http://library.eres.org/eres2013/paperupload/143.pdf (accessed 16 August 2013).

Groves, S. "LOST in the Arctic: The US need not ratify the Law of the Sea Treaty to get a seat at the table." Heritage Foundation (2007). http://www.heritage.org.

Gurven, M. "The evolution of contingent cooperation." *Current Anthropology* 47(1) (2006): 185–192.

Hálfdanarson, G., and U. B. Karlsdóttir. "Náttúrusýn og nýting fallvatna [View of nature and utilization of waterfalls]." In *Landsvirkjun 1965–2005: Fyrirtækið og umhverfi þess [Landsvirkjun 1965–2005: The company and its environment]*, edited by S. Pálsdóttir. Reykjavík: Hið íslenska bókmenntafélag, 2005, 165–199.

Hall, C. Michael, and Stephen J. Page. *The Geography of Tourism and Recreation: Environment, Place and Space*. London: Routledge, 2003.

Hamelin, Louis-Edmond. *Canadian Nordicity: It's Your North, Too*, translated by William Barr from *Nordicité Canadienne*. Montreal: Harvest House, 1978.

Hamilton, W. D. "The genetical evolution of social behaviour." *Journal of Theoretical Biology* 7(1) (1964): 1–16.

Hansen, Klaus Georg. "Alcoa aluminium coming to Greenland." *Journal of Nordregio* 11(2) (June 2011): 20–21.

Hansen, Klaus Georg, and Rasmus Ole Rasmussen. "New Economic Activities and Urbanization: Individual reasons for moving and for staying–Case Greenland." In *Proceedings from the First International Conference on Urbanization in the Arctic, 28–30 August 2012, Ilimmarfik, Nuuk, Greenland*, edited by Klaus Georg Hansen, Rasmus Ole Rasmussen, and Ryan Weber. Nordregio, Stockholm, Nordregio Working Paper 2013:6 (2013): 157–182.

Hansen, Klaus Georg, Freia Lund Sørensen, and Steen R. Jeppson. "Decision processes, communication and democracy: The aluminium smelter project in Greenland." In Janne Hukkinen, Klaus Georg Hansen, et al., *Knowledge-based tools for sustainable governance of energy and climate adaptation in the Nordic periphery*. Nordic Research Programme 2005–2008, Report No. 7. Nordregio, Stockholm (2009), 57–84.

Hardie, I., and D. MacKenzie. "Assembling an Economic Actor." *The Sociological Review* 55(1) (2007): 57–80.

Harðarson, P. "Mat á þjóðhagslegum áhrifum stóriðju á Íslandi 1966–1997 [Assessment of national economic effects of large-scale industry in Iceland 1966–1997]." *Fjármálatíðindi* 45(2) (1998), 153–167.

Hasanat, Waliul. "Cooperation in the Barents Euro-Arctic Region in the Light of International Law." *Yearbook of Polar Law* 2 (2010).

———. "A unique arrangement of soft-law cooperation in the Barents Region." In *Politics of Development in the Barents Region*, edited by Monica Tennberg. Rovaniemi: Lapland University Press, 2012.

Hawkes, K., Jon Altman, S. Beckerman, R. R. Grinker, H. Harpending, R. J. Jeske, N. Peterson, E. A. Smith, G. W. Wenzel, and J. E. Yellen. "Why hunter-gatherers work: An ancient version of the problem of public goods" [and comments and reply]. *Current Anthropology*, 34(4) (1993): 341–361.

Hawkes, K., J. F. O'Connell, and N. G. Blurton Jones. "Hadza meat sharing." *Evolution and Human Behavior*, 22(2) (2001): 113–142.

Hayes-Labruto, Leslie, Simon J. D. Schillebeeckx, Mark Workman, and Nilay Shah. "Contrasting Perspectives on China's Rare Earths Policies: Reframing the Debate through a Stakeholder Lens." *Energy Policy* 63 (December 2013).

Heal, O. W., Richard Langlais, and Outi Snellman, eds. *A University of the Arctic: Turning Concept into Reality. Phase 1: A Development Plan*. Rovaniemi: International Relations, University of Lapland, 1997.

Heap, J. A. "Antarctic Treaty System." In *Encyclopedia of the Antarctic*, edited by B. Riffenburgh. New York: Routledge, 2007, 82–86.

Heinämäki, Leena. "Rethinking the Status of Indigenous Peoples in International Environmental Decision Making: Pondering the Role of Arctic Indigenous Peoples and the

Challenge of Climate Change." In *Climate Governance in the Arctic*, edited by T. Koivurova et al. Berlin: Springer, 2009.

——. "Towards an Equal Partnership between Indigenous Peoples and States: Learning
from Arctic Experiences?" *Yearbook of Polar Law* 3 (2009).

Hemmings, A. D. "Beyond Claims: Towards a Non-Territorial Antarctic Security Prism
for Australia and New Zealand." *New Zealand Yearbook of International Law* 6 (2008):
76–91.

——. "From the New Geopolitics of Resources to Nanotechnology: Emerging Challenges
of Globalism in Antarctica." *Yearbook of Polar Law* 1 (2009): 55–72.

——. "Environmental Law—Antarctica." In *Berkshire Encyclopedia of Sustainability: The
Law and Politics of Sustainability* 3, edited by K. Bosselmann, D. Fogel, and J. B. Ruh.
Great Barrington, MA: Berkshire, 2010, 188–194.

Henriksen, G. *Hunters in the Barrens: The Naskapi on the Edge of the White Man's
World*. Memorial University of Newfoundland, Institute of Social and Economic
Research, 1973.

Herber, B. P. *Protecting the Antarctic Commons: Problems of Economic Efficiency*. Tucson:
Udall Center for Studies in Public Policy, University of Arizona, 2007.

Herr, Richard A. "The changing roles of non-governmental organizations in the Ant-
arctic Treaty System." In *Governing the Antarctic: The effectiveness and legitimacy of the
Antarctic Treaty System*, edited by Olav Schram Stokke and Vidas Davor. Cambridge:
Cambridge University Press, 1996.

Hess, Bill. *Taking Control: The North Slope Borough, the Story of Self Determination in the
Arctic*. North Slope Borough, Barrow, Alaska, 1993.

Hill, K., H. Kaplan, and K. Hawkes. "On why male foragers hunt and share food." *Current Anthropology* 34(5) (1993): 701–710.

Hipwell, W., K. Mamen, V. Weitzner, and G. Whiteman. "Aboriginal peoples and mining
in Canada: consultation, participation and prospects for change." Working Discussion Paper, The North–South Institute (2002). http://www.nsiins.ca/english/pdf/
syncanadareport.pdf (accessed 3 October 2010).

Hoekman, B. M., K. E. Maskus, and K. Saggi. "Transfer of technology to developing
countries: Unilateral and multilateral policy options." Working Paper, Institute of
Behavioral Science, University of Colorado at Boulder, Research Program on Political
and Economic Change, 2004.

Hoel, A. H. "The 2010 Norway–Russia Marine Boundary Agreement and Bilateral Cooperation on Integrated Oceans Management." *Nordlit* 29 (2012): 15–27.

Hong, Nong. "The energy factor in the Arctic dispute: A pathway to conflict or cooperation?" *Journal of World Energy Law and Business* 5(1) (2012): 13–26.

Hossain, Kamrul. "The EU ban on the import of seal products and the WTO regulations:
Neglected human rights of the Arctic indigenous peoples?" *Polar Record* (2013).

Howard, Matthew. "The Convention on the Conservation of Antarctic Marine Living Resources: A five-year review." *International and Comparative Law Quarterly*
38(104) (1989).

Howard, Roger. *The Arctic Gold Rush: The New Race for Tomorrow's Natural Resources*.
London and New York: Continuum, 2009.

Howkins, Adrian. "Reluctant Collaborators: Argentina and Chile in Antarctica during
the International Geophysical Year, 1957–58." *Journal of Historical Geography* 34(4)
(October 2008): 596–617.

Huber, J. "The Antarctic Treaty: Toward a New Partnership." In *Science Diplomacy: Antarctica, Science, and the Governance of International Spaces*, edited by P. A. Berkman, M. A. Lang, D. W. H. Walton, and O. R. Young. Washington, D.C.: Smithsonian Institution Scholarly Press, 2011, 89–95.

———. "Notes on the ATCM Recommendations and Their Approval Process." In *The Antarctic Legal System and Environmental Issues*, edited by G. Tamburelli. Milan: Giuffrè, 2006, 17–31.

Huber, Jan. Interview with Mr. Jan Huber, past executive secretary of the Antarctic Treaty Secretariat in Buenos Aires, Argentina, 25 June 2009.

Huebert, R., H. Exner-Pirot, A. Lajeunesse, J. Gulledge. "Climate change and international security: The Arctic as a Bellwether." Arlington, Virginia: Center for Climate and Energy Solutions. http://www.c2es.org/publications/climate-change-international-arctic-security/ (2012).

Hughes, D. M. "When Parks Encroach upon People: Expanding National Parks in the Rusitu Valley, Zimbabwe." *Cultural Survival Quarterly* 20(1) (1996): 36–40.

Huntington, Samuel P. *The Common Defense: Strategic Programs in National Politics*. New York: Columbia University Press, 1961.

Hurley, M. C. *Aboriginal Title: The Supreme Court of Canada Decision in Delgamuukw v. British Columbia*, Library of Parliament, Parliamentary Information and Research Service (1998, revised 2008). www.parl.gc.ca/information/library/PRBpubs/bp459-e.htm (accessed 29 October 2005).

Ilulissat Declaration. Adopted 28 May 2008. http://www.oceanlaw.org/downloads/arctic/Ilulissat_Declaration.pdf.

Imperial Oil Resources. "Mackenzie Gas Project" (2003). http://www.mackenziegasproject.com/ (accessed 19 January 2010).

———. "Application for the Approval of the Mackenzie Valley Pipeline." Submitted to the National Energy Board, August 2004.

Inter-American Court of Human Rights. *Saramaka People v. Suriname*. Series C (No. 172) (28 November 2007).

Inter-American Development Bank. "Operating Guidelines: Indigenous People's Policy." Washington, D.C., 6 October 2006.

Intergovernmental Panel on Climate Change (IPCC). *Climate Change 2007: Working Group I: The Physical Science Basis*. Cambridge: Cambridge University Press, 2007.

International Agreement for the Creation at Paris of an International Office for Dealing with Contagious Diseases of Animals, and Annex 1924. ATS. No. 15. Adopted 25 January 1924 (entered into force 12 January 1925).

International Association of Antarctica Tour Operators (IAATO). "Statement from IAATO regarding *Berserk* Antarctic Expedition." Press release, 3 March 2011.

———. IAATO "Membership Directory 2011–2012." (2012a). http://apps.iaato.org/iaato/directory/list.jsf.

———. "Who is IAATO?" (2012b). http://iaato.org/who-is-iaato;jsessionid=308B203BE6C2CBCA0A3D7A1BF2ABB1D8.

———. "Tourism Overview." *Summary of Seaborne, Airborne, and Land-Based Antarctic Tourism* (2012c). http://iaato.org/tourism-overview.

———. "Bylaws." 12 May 2011 (2012d). http://iaato.org/bylaws.

———. "Information for Japanese Nationals planning a trip to Antarctica." (2012e). http://iaato.org/info-for-japanese-nationals.

International Conservation Union (IUCN). Invasive Species Specialist Group. "IUCN Guidelines for the Prevention of Biodiversity Loss Caused by Alien Invasive Species." Approved by the 51st Meeting of the IUCN Council. Gland, Switzerland, February 2000. http://intranet.iucn.org/webfiles/doc/SSC/SSCwebsite/Policy_statements/IUCN_Guidelines_for_the_Prevention_of_Biodiversity_Loss_caused_by_Alien_Invasive_Species.pdf.

International Convention for the Control and Management of Ships' Ballast Water and Sediments. Concluded 13 February 2004 (not in force). IMO Doc. BWM/CONF/36. http://water.epa.gov/type/oceb/habitat/upload/2004_10_29_invasive_species_BWM-Treaty_36.pdf.

International Court of Justice. Gabçíkovo-Nagymaros Project (*Hung. v. Slovk.*), 1997 I.C.J. 7, 91 (25 September 1997) (separate opinion of Vice-President Weeramantry).

International Labor Organization (ILO). Convention Concerning the Protection and Integration of Indigenous and Other Tribal and Semi-Tribal Populations in Independent Countries, C107, Geneva (1957).

_____. Convention Concerning Discrimination in Respect of Employment and Occupation, C111, Geneva (1958).

_____. Convention Concerning Indigenous and Tribal Peoples in Independent Countries, C169, Geneva (1989).

_____. *Eliminating discrimination against Indigenous and Tribal peoples in employment and occupation—A guide to ILO Convention 111*, Geneva (2007).

International Maritime Organization (IMO). Assembly of the International Maritime Organization, Resolution A. 868 (20). Adopted 27 November 1997. IMO-661E. http://www.krs.co.kr/kor/dn/Tec/pdf/BWMP-INTERTANKO.doc.pdf.

_____. Amendments to MARPOL Annex I to Add Chapter 9—Special Requirements for the Use or Carriage of Oils in the Antarctic Area. MEPC 60/22 Annex 10, Resolution MEPC.189(60). Adopted 26 March 2010.

_____. "Status of Multilateral Conventions and Instruments in Respect of Which the International Maritime Organization or Its Secretary-General Performs Depositary or Other Functions," 31 January 2012. London: International Maritime Organization, 2012. http://www.imo.org/About/Conventions/StatusOfConventions/Pages/Default.aspx.

International Plant Protection Convention, ATS No. 23. Adopted 17 November 1997 (entered into force 2 October 2005). http://www.opbw.org/int_inst/env_docs/1997IPPC-TEXT.pdf.

International Standards Organization. "About ISO." (2012). http://www.iso.org/iso/about.htm/www.iso.org/iso/about.htm.

Inuit Circumpolar Conference. Petition to the Inter-American Commission on Human Rights Seeking Relief from Violations Resulting from Global Warming Caused by Acts and Omissions of the United States (7 December 2005).

Inuit Circumpolar Council. "A Circumpolar Inuit Declaration on Resource Development in Inuit Nunaat." 2011. http://inuit.org/en/about-icc/icc-declarations.html.

_____. "A Circumpolar Inuit Declaration on Sovereignty in the Arctic." http://inuitcircumpolar.com/files/uploads/icc-files/declaration12x18vicechairssigned.pdf (2009).

Inuvialuit Regional Corporation. *The Western Arctic Claim: Inuvialuit Final Agreement as amended.* Reprinted by Inuvialuit Regional Corporation, Inuik, Northern Territories (1987).

Ironside, R. G. "Canadian Northern settlements: Top-down and bottom-up influences." *Geographical Analysis* 82B(2) (2000): 103–114.

Irwin, R. A. "Sahtu Dene and Metis Comprehensive Land Agreement." Published under the authority of the Hon. Ronald A. Irwin PC MP, Minister of Indian Affairs and Northern Development. Ottawa, 1993.

Ísleifsson, S. R. *Saga Rafmagnsveitu Reykjavíkur 1921–1998* [*The history of Reykjavik Electricity 1921–1998*]. Reykjavík: Orkuveita Reykjavíkur, 2007.

Jabour, J., and M. Weber. "Is It Time to Cut the Gordian Knot of Polar Sovereignty?" *RECIEL* 17(1) (2008), 27–40.

Jacobsson, M. "Building the International Legal Framework for Antarctica." In *Science Diplomacy: Antarctica, Science, and the Governance of International Spaces*, edited by P. A. Berkman, M. A. Lang, D. W. H. Walton, and O. R. Young. Washington, D.C.: Smithsonian Institution Scholarly Press, 2011, 1–15.

Janssen, M. A., Ö. Bodin, J. M. Anderies, T. Elmqvist, H. Ernstson, R. R. J. McAllister, P. Olsson, and P. Ryan. "Toward a network perspective of the study of resilience in social-ecological systems." *Ecology and Society* 11(1) (2006): 15.

Jasanoff, S. "Cosmopolitan Knowledge." In *The Oxford Handbook of Climate Change and Society*, edited by J. Dryzek, R. Norgaard, and D. Schlosberg. New York: Oxford University Press, 2011.

Johnsen, Kathrine I., Bjorn Alfthan, Lawrence Hislop, and Janet F. Skaalvik, eds. *Protecting Arctic Biodiversity: Limitations and Strengths of Environmental Agreements*. United Nations Environment Program. Arendal, Norway: GRID-Arendal, 2010. http://www.grida.no/_res/site/file/publications/arctic-biodiv/arcticMEAreport _screen.pdf.

Johnson, Mona. "How Circumpolar Mobility Contributes New Arctic Knowledge." Presentation at Sixth Northern Research Forum Open Assembly. Akureyri, Iceland. 15 September 2011.

Johnston, Alastair Iain. "Thinking about Strategic Culture." *International Security* 19(4) (1995).

Jónsson, B. "Þróun tækniþekkingar og fagvinnu við virkjunarframkvæmdir Landsvirkjunar [Technological development and the power projects of Landsvirkjun]." In *Landsvirkjun 1965–2005: Fyrirtækið og umhverfi þess* [*Landsvirkjun 1965–2005: The company and its environment*], edited by S. Pálsdóttir. Reykjavík: Hið íslenska bókmenntafélag, 2005, 243–266.

Joyner, C. C. "Challenges to the Antarctic Treaty: Looking Back to See Ahead." *New Zealand Yearbook of International Law* 6 (2008): 25–62.

——. "Potential Challenges to the Antarctic Treaty." In *Science Diplomacy: Antarctica, Science, and the Governance of International Spaces*, edited by P. A. Berkman, M. A. Lang, D. W. H. Walton, and O. R. Young. Washington, D.C.: Smithsonian Institution Scholarly Press, 2011, 97–102.

Kalicki, Jan H., and David L. Goldwyn, eds. *Energy and Security: Toward a New Foreign Policy Strategy*. Washington, D.C.: Woodrow Wilson Center Press, 2005.

Kankaanpää, Paula, and Oran R. Young. "The effectiveness of the Arctic Council." *Polar Research* 31 (2012).

Kao, Shih-Ming, Nathaniel S. Pearre, and Jeremy Firestone. "Adoption of the Arctic search and rescue agreement: A shift of the Arctic regime toward a hard law basis?" *Marine Policy* 36 (2012): 832–838.

Karkkainen, Bradley C. "Post-Sovereign Environmental Governance." *Global Environmental Politics* 4(1) (2004).

Karlsdóttir, U. B. *Þar sem fossarnir falla: Náttúrusýn og nýting fallvatna á Íslandi 1900–2008* [*Where the water falls: Views of nature and use of waterfalls in Iceland 1900–2008*]. Reykjavík: Hið íslenska bókmenntafélag, 2010.

Katzenstein, Peter J., ed. *The Culture of National Security*. New York: Columbia University Press, 1996.

Kawagley, A. Oscar. *A Yupiaq World View—A Pathway to Ecology and Spirit*. Prospect Heights: Waveland, 1995.

Kelley, John J., and Arnold Brower, Sr. *The NARL and Its Transition to the Local Community. Fifty More Years Below Zero: Tributes and Meditations for the Naval Arctic Research Laboratory's First Half Century at Barrow, Alaska*, edited by David W. Norton. Calgary and Fairbanks: Arctic Institute of North America, 2001.

Keogh-Brown, Marcus Richard, and Richard David Smith. "The Economic Impact of SARS: How Does the Reality Match the Predictions?" *Health Policy* 88(1) (October 2008): 110–120.

Keskitalo, Eva C. H. *Negotiating the Arctic: The Construction of an International Region*. New York: Routledge, 2004.

Khalilian, Setareh. *The WTO and Environmental Provisions: Three Categories of Trade and Environmental Linkage*. Kiel Working Papers, No. 1485. Kiel, Germany: Kiel Institute for the World Economy, 2009.

Kimball, Lee. "The role of non-governmental organizations in Antarctic affairs." In Christopher Joyner and Sudhir Chopra, *The Antarctic Legal Regime*. Dordrecht: Martinus Nijhoff, 1988.

King, Alexander D. *Living with Koryak Traditions: Playing with Culture in Siberia*. Lincoln and London: University of Nebraska Press, 2011.

Kingsbury, Benedict, Nico Krisch, and Richard Stewart. "The Emergence of Global Administrative Law." *Law and Contemporary Problems* 68 (2005).

Kirsch, S. "Indigenous movements and the risks of counterglobalization: Tracking the campaign against Papua New Guinea's Ok Tedi mine." *American Ethnologist* 34(2) (2007): 303–321.

Knott, Catherine. *Living with the Adirondack Forest: Local Perspectives on Land Use Conflicts*. Ithaca: Cornell University Press, 1998.

Knox, H., D. O'Doherty, T. Vurdubakis, and C. Westrup. "Transformative Capacity, Information Technology, and the Making of Business 'Experts.'" *The Sociological Review* 55(1) (2007).

Koivurova, Timo. "Alternatives for an Arctic Treaty—Evaluation and a New Proposal." *Review of European Community and International Environmental Law* 17(1) (2008).

———. "The Status and Role of Indigenous Peoples in Arctic International Governance." *Yearbook of Polar Law* 3 (2011).

Koivurova, Timo, and Leena Heinämäki. "The Participation of Indigenous Peoples in International Norm-Making in the Arctic." *Polar Record* 42(221) (2006).

Koivurova, Timo, and E. Molenaar. "International Governance and Regulation of the Marine Arctic (Part III: A Proposal for a Legally Binding Instrument)." Oslo: World Wide Fund for Nature (WWF)—International Arctic Program (2010).

Koivurova, Timo, and David VanderZwaag. "The Arctic Council at 10 Years: Retrospect and Prospects." *University of British Columbia Law Review* 40 (2007), 121–194.

Kolbert, Elizabeth, and Francis Spufford, eds. *The Ends of the Earth: An Anthology of the Finest Writing on the Arctic and the Antarctic.* New York: Bloomsbury, 2007.

Kristinsson, G. H. "Raforka, efnishyggja og stjórnmálaátök [Electricity, materialism and political strife]." In *Landsvirkjun 1965–2005: Fyrirtækið og umhverfi þess [Landsvirkjun 1965–2005: The company and its environment],* edited by S. Pálsdóttir. Reykjavík: Hið íslenska bókmenntafélag, 2005, 137–163.

Kristjánsson, H. Birta. *Saga Rafmagnsveita Ríkisins í 50 ár 1947–1997 [Light, power and heat: The history of Iceland State Electricity for 50 years 1947–1997].* Reykjavík: Rafmagnsveitur Ríkisins, 1997.

Krupnik, I., and D. Jolly, eds. *The Earth Is Faster Now.* Fairbanks: Arctic Research Consortium, 2002.

Kurth, James. "The Decline and Fall of Almost Everything: Paul Kennedy Peers into the 21st Century." *Foreign Affairs* 72(2) (1993).

Lassuy, Dennis R., and Patrick N. Lewis. "Invasive Species (Human Induced)." In *Arctic Biodiversity Assessment.* Arctic Council (2011). http://www.arcus.org/files/page/documents/1622/invasivespecies.pdf.

Lead Industry Association v. Environmental Protection Agency, 647 F.2d 1130, 1147 (D.C. Cir. 1980).

Leary, D. "Looking Beyond the International Polar Year: What Are the Emerging and Re-emerging Issues in International Law and Policy in the Polar Regions?" *Yearbook of Polar Law* 1 (2009): 1–19.

Lee, Maria, and Carolyn Abbot. "The Usual Suspects? Public Participation under the Aarhus Convention." *Modern Law Review* 66 (2003): 80.

Leffler, Melvyn P. "The American Conception of National Security and the Beginnings of the Cold War, 1945–48." *American Historical Review* 89 (1984): 2.

Leland, Sigve R., and Alf Håkon Hoel. "Learning by doing: The Barents cooperation and development of regional collaboration in the north." In *The New Northern Dimension of the European Neighborhood,* edited by Pami Aalto, Helge Blakkisrud, and Hanna Smith. Brussels: Centre for European Policy Studies, 2008.

Lesage, Dries, Thijs Van de Graaf, and Kirsten Westphal. "G8+5 Collaboration on Energy Efficiency and IPEEC: Shortcut to a Sustainable Future?" *Energy Policy* 38(11) (November 2010): 6419–6427.

Li, Yangfan, et al. "Integrating Climate Change Factors into China's Development Policy: Adaptation Strategies and Mitigation to Environmental Change." *Ecological Complexity* 8(4) (December 2011): 294–298.

LiPuma, E., and B. Lee. *Financial Derivatives and the Globalization of Risk.* Durham: Duke University Press, 2004.

Long, Andrew. "Developing Linkages to Preserve Biodiversity." *Yearbook of International Environmental Law* 21(1) (2010): 41–80.

Lopez, Barry. *Arctic Dreams: Imagination and Desire in a Northern Landscape.* New York: Charles Scribner's Sons, 1986.

Low, Tim. *Climate Change and Invasive Species: A Review of Interaction.* Biological Diversity Advisory Committee, 2005–2007, Commonwealth of Australia (2008). http://www.environment.gov.au/biodiversity/publications/pubs/interactions-cc-invasive.pdf.

Lui, K., B. Cudmore, and L. D. Bouvier. *Monitoring of Aquatic Invasive Species in the Central and Arctic Zone.* Canadian Manuscript Report of Fisheries and Aquatic Sciences 2806, Fisheries and Ocean Canada (2007).

Macalister, Terry. "Arctic military rivalry could herald a 21st-century cold war." *The Guardian*. World News, 5 June 2012.

Machlup, F. *The Production and Distribution of Knowledge in the United States*. Princeton: Princeton University Press, 1962.

MacKenzie, D. *An Engine, Not a Camera: How Financial Models Shape Markets*. Cambridge, MA: MIT Press, 2006a.

＿＿＿. "Is Economics Performative?" *Journal of the History of Economic Thought* 28(1) (2006b): 29–55.

Mackinder, H. J. "The Geographical Pivot of History." *The Geographical Journal* 170(4) (2004). Reprint from *The Geographical Journal* XXIII 4, 1904.

Mahan, Alfred T. "The United States Looking Outward." In *The Interest of America in Sea Power, Present and Future* (1890). Project Gutenberg e-book #15749 (2005).

Mahr, Krista. "Is the Arctic Headed for Another Cold War?" TIME. Science and Space, 12 October 2010.

Mailhot, J. *The People of Sheshatshiu : In the Land of the Innu* [Au pays des Innus]. University of Newfoundland, Institute of Social and Economic Research, 1977.

＿＿＿."Territorial mobility among the Montagnais-Naskapi of Labrador." In "À qui appartient le castor? Les régimes fonciers algonquins du nord remis en cause" [Who Owns the Beaver? Northern Algonquian Land Tenure Reconsidered], ed. Charles A. Bishop and Tony Morantz, special issue, *Anthropologica* 28/(1/2) (1986): 92–107.

Makarov, A. "Energy relations between the European Union and Russia in the global context." Russian policy for energy markets, Conference MIEC-CGEMP, 18–19 April 2005, Paris, France. www.dauphine.fr/cgemp/Manifestations/MIEC/MAKAROV.pdf (accessed 14 February 2008).

Malinowski, B. *Argonauts of the Western Pacific: An Account of Native Enterprise and Adventure in the Archipelagoes of Melanesian New Guinea*. Chicago: Waveland Press, 1984; 1922.

Mallard, A. "Performance Testing." In *Market Devices*, edited by M. Callon, Y. Millo, and F. Muniesa. Boston: Blackwell, 2007.

Manney, Gloria, et al. "Unprecedented Arctic Ozone Loss in 2011." *Nature*, 2 October 2011.

Marauhn, Thilo. "The Potential of the Convention on Biological Diversity to Address the Effects of Climate Change in the Arctic." In *Climate Governance in the Arctic*, edited by T. Koivurova et al. Berlin: Springer, 2009.

Marchand, Peter. *Life in the Cold: An Introduction to Winter Ecology*, 3rd ed. Hanover: University Press of New England, 1996.

Marecic, C. J. "Nunavut Territory: Aboriginal governing in the Canadian regime of governance." *American Indian Law Review* 24(2) (1999–2000): 275–295.

Margolis, Michael, and Jason F. Shogren. *How Trade Politics Affect Invasive Species Control*. Discussion Paper 04–07. Washington, D.C.: Resources for the Future, 2004. http://www.rff.org/documents/RFF-DP-04-07.pdf.

Marshall, Michael. "Arctic Ozone Hole Breaks All Records." *New Scientist* (2 October 2011). http://www.newscientist.com/article/dn20988-arctic-ozone-hole-breaks-all -records.html.

Mason, A. "Rise of Consultant Forecasting in Liberalized Natural Gas Markets." *Public Culture* 19(2) (2007): 367–379.

Mason, A., and M. Stoilkova. "Corporeality of Consultant Expertise." *Journal of Northern Studies* 6(2) (2012): 85–98.

Massachusetts v. Environmental Protection Agency, 549 U.S. 497 (2007).

Mattli, Walter, and Ngaire Woods, eds. *The Politics of Global Regulation*. Princeton: Princeton University Press, 2009.

Mauss, M. *The Gift: The Form and Reason for Exchange in Archaic Societies*. New York: W. W. Norton, 1990.

May, John. *The Greenpeace Book of Antarctica: A New View of the Seventh Continent*, 2nd ed. New York: Doubleday, 1989.

McGhee, Robert. *The Last Imaginary Place: A Human History of the Arctic World*. New York: Oxford University Press, 2005.

McNeely, Jeff. "Invasive Species: A Costly Catastrophe for Native Biodiversity." *Land Use and Water Resources Research* 1 (2001): 1–10.

Memolli, Mariano. Interview with Dr. Mariano Memolli at the Dirección Nacional del Antártico. Buenos Aires, Argentina, 26 June 2009.

Mercer, D. "Aboriginal self-determination and indigenous land title in post-Mabo Australia." *Political Geography* 16(3) (1997): 189–212.

Milne, Richard. "China Wins Observer Status in Arctic Council." *Financial Times*, 15 May 2013.

Milov, V., L. L. Coburn, and I. Danchenko. "Russian energy policy, 1992–2005." *Eurasian Geography and Economics* 47(3) (2006): 285–313.

Mining, Minerals and Sustainable Development (MMSD). "Breaking New Ground: Mining, Minerals, and Sustainable Development: The Report of the MMSD Project." London: Earthscan Publications, 2002.

Molenaar, E. J. "Sea-Borne Tourism in Antarctica: Avenues for Further Intergovernmental Regulation." *International Journal for Marine and Coastal Law* 20(2) (2005): 247–295.

Molenaar, Erik Jaap. "Current and Prospective Roles of the Arctic Council System within the Context of the Law of the Sea." *International Journal of Marine and Coastal Law* 27 (2012): 553–595.

Moore, P. D. "Favoured aliens for the future." *Nature* 427 (2004): 594.

Moseley, W. G. "Area Studies in a Global Context." *Chronicle of Higher Education*. 29 November 2009. http://chronicle.com/article/Area-Studies-in-a-Global-Co/49284/ (accessed 27 September 2011).

Muir, Adrianna A. "Managing Coastal Aquatic Invasive Species in California: Existing Policies and Policy Gaps." California Research Bureau, 2011.

Müller-Wille, Ludger. "Northern environments and peoples. Reflections on intercultural and transnational education." In *Learning to Be Circumpolar. Experiences in Arctic Academic Cooperation*, edited by Richard Langlais and Outi Snellman. Publications in the University of the Arctic Process 5. Rovaniemi: University of Lapland, 1998, 63–68.

Mulvaney, Kieran. *At the Ends of the Earth: A History of the Polar Regions*. Washington, D.C.: Island Press / Shearwater Books, 2001.

Myers, Steve Lee. "Arctic Council Adds 6 Nations as Observer States, including China." *New York Times* (Europe), 15 May 2013. http://www.nytimes.com/2013/05/16/world/europe/arctic-council-adds-six-members-including-china.html.

National Oceanic and Atmospheric Administration (NOAA). "Arctic Report Card: Update for 2012." http://www.arctic.noaa.gov/reportcard.

Native Village of Kivalina v. ExxonMobil Corp., 663 F. Supp. 2d 863 (N.D. Cal. 2008) (No. 08–1138).

Neumann, Thilo. "Norway and Russia Agree on Maritime Boundary in the Barents Sea and the Arctic Ocean." *The American Society of International Law Insights* 14(34) (2010): 1–4.

Norman, Howard, ed. *Northern Tales: Traditional Stories of Eskimo and Indian Peoples.* New York: Pantheon Books, 1990.

Nye, Joseph S., Jr. *Soft Power: The Means to Success in World Politics.* New York: Public Affairs, 2004.

Oceans North Canada. "The Future of Marine Mammals in a Changing Arctic." Oceans North Canada. http://oceansnorth.org/future-marine-mammals-changing-arctic.

O'Faircheallaigh, C. "Negotiating Cultural Heritage? Aboriginal–Mining Company Agreements in Australia." *Development and Change* 39(1) (2008): 25–51.

Oil and Gas Journal (OGJ). "U.S. Gas Market to Surge in Coming Decade." 31 January 2000.

Olsen, Panêraq, and Ane-Birgithe Pedersen. *Projektering af vandkraft i Grønland* [*The projection of hydropower in Greenland*]. Center for Arktisk Teknologi, BYG DTU, 2010.

O'Neill, Dan. *The Firecracker Boys: H-Bombs, Inupiat Eskimos, and the Roots of the Environmental Movement.* New York: Basic Books, 2007.

Ontario's Invading Species Awareness Program. "Zebra Mussel (Dreissena polymorpha)." http://www.invadingspecies.com/Invaders.cfm?A=page&PID=1.

Orheim, O., A. Press, and N. Gilbert. "Managing the Antarctic Environment: The Evolving Role of the Committee for Environmental Protection." In *Science Diplomacy: Antarctica, Science, and the Governance of International Spaces,* edited by P. A. Berkman, M. A. Lang, D. W. H. Walton, and O. R. Young. Washington, D.C.: Smithsonian Institution Scholarly Press, 2011, 209–221.

Osgood, Kathleen. "Uralic Imaginations on Film: Markku Lehmuskallio and Anastasia Lapsui in Siberia and the Circumpolar World." *Sibirica* 11(1) (Spring 2012): 70–83.

Osofsky, Hari M. "The Inuit Petition as a Bridge? Beyond Dialectics of Climate Change and Indigenous People's Rights." *American Indian Law Review* 31 (2007): 675.

Ostrom, E. *Understanding Institutional Diversity.* Oxford: Princeton University Press, 2005.

Pálsdóttir, S. "Landsvirkjun: Fyrirtækið, framkvæmdir þess og hlutverk [Landsvirkjun: The company, its constructions and its role]." In *Landsvirkjun 1965–2005: Fyrirtækið og umhverfi þess* [*Landsvirkjun 1965–2005: The company and its environment*], edited by S. Pálsdóttir. Reykjavík: Hið íslenska bókmenntafélag, 2005, 13–110.

Papa, Mihaela, and Nancy W. Gleason. "Major Emerging Powers in Sustainable Development Diplomacy: Assessing Their Leadership Potential." *Global Environmental Change* 22(4) (October 2012): 915–924.

Pappal, Adrienne. *Marine Invasive Species: State of the Gulf of Maine Report.* Boston: Marine Life/Gulf of Maine Area Program, 2010.

Pascual, Carlos, and Jonathan Elkind, eds. *Energy Security.* Washington, D.C.: Brookings Institution Press, 2010.

Pasteen, T. "Corral description." In *Tipatshimuna.* http://www.tipatshimuna.ca (accessed 7 July 2011).

Petrov, Nahaar. "Just one step to great happiness." Student forum. BCS 100 (2010).

Petterson, Trude. "Chinese icebreaker bound for North Pole." *Barents Observer*, Arctic, 23 August 2012. http://barentsobserver.com/en/arctic/chinese-icebreaker-bound -north-pole-23-08.

_____. "China's icebreaker 'Snow Dragon' docked Thursday in Shanghai after becoming the first vessel from China to cross the Arctic Ocean." *Barents Observer*, Arctic, 27 September 2012. http://barentsobserver.com/en/arctic/chinese-icebreaker -concludes-arctic-voyage-27-09.

Pimentel, David, et al. "Economic and environmental threats of alien plant, animal, and microbe invasions, Agriculture." *Ecosystems and Environment* 84 (2001): 1–20.

Pincus, Rebecca. "'The US is an Arctic Nation': Policy, implementation and US icebreaking capabilities in a changing Arctic." *The Polar Journal* 31 (2013).

Plunz, Glenys. Personal interview. University of the Arctic Council Meeting. Rovaniemi, Finland: 9 June 2011.

Polanyi, K. *The Great Transformation*, 2nd ed. Boston: Beacon Press, 2001.

Polar, Perry, and Ulrike Krauss. "Status of International Legislative Framework for the Management of Invasive Alien Species in the Wider Caribbean Region." CABI. www .cabi.org.

Polar Code Hazard Identification Workshop Report. *Report for International Maritime Organization*, 24 November 2011, DE 56/INF.3, Annex 3. Prepared by Det Norske Veritas. London: 2011.

Polivanov, A. "Yukos ushel v istoriyu [Yukos is gone in history]." *Lenta.ru* (online newspaper), 29 October 2007. http://www.lenta.ru/articles/2007/10/29/yukos (accessed 2 November 2007).

Polk, W. A. "Welcome to the Hotel Antarctica: The EPA's Interim Rule on Environmental Impact Assessment of Tourism in Antarctica." *Emory International Law Review* 12 (1998): 1395–1442.

Porras, Ileana M. "The city and international law: In pursuit of sustainable development." *Fordham Urban Law Journal* 36 (2009).

Power, E. M. "Conceptualizing food security for aboriginal people in Canada." *Canadian Journal of Public Health* 99(2) (2008): 95–97.

Ragnarsson, S. "Innilokun eða opingátt: Þættir úr sögu fossamálsins [Closure or openness: Elements of the history of the waterfall question]." *Saga* 13 (1975): 5–105.

_____. "Fossakaup og framkvæmdaáform: þættir úr sögu fossamálsins. Fyrri hluti [Waterfall investments and planning: Elements of the history of the 'waterfall question.' First part]." *Saga* 14 (1976): 125–182.

_____. "Fossakaup og framkvæmdaáform: þættir úr sögu fossamálsins. Siðari hluti [Waterfall investments and planning: Elements of the history of the 'waterfall question.' Second part]." *Saga* 15 (1977): 125–222.

Rammaáætlun. "Rammaáætlun um vernd og nýtingu náttúrusvæða með áherslu á vatnsafl og jarðhitasvæði [Master plan for hydro and geothermal energy resources in Iceland]." Homepage of Rammaáætlun at http://www.rammaaaetlun.is/ (accessed 26 October 2011).

Rasmussen, J. "The Majors' Shift to Natural Gas." Office of Energy Markets and End Use, Energy Information Administration (2000).

Raupach, Michael R., Philippe Ciais, Gregg Marland, Corinne Le Quéré, Josep G. Canadell, Gernot Klepper, and Christopher B. Field. "Global and regional drivers of accelerating CO_2 emissions." *Proceedings of the National Academy of Sciences* (PNAS) 104(24) (2007): 10288–10293.

Raustiala, Kal. "States, NGOs, and International Environmental Institutions." *International Studies Quarterly* 41 (1997).

Rayfuse, Rosemary. "Melting Moments: The Future of Polar Oceans Governance in a Warming World." *Review of European Community and International Environmental Law* 16(2) (2007).

———. "Protecting Marine Biodiversity in Polar Areas Beyond National Jurisdiction." *Review of European Community and International Environmental Law* 17(1) (2008): 3–13.

Raz, Joseph. *The Morality of Freedom.* Oxford: Oxford University Press, 1986.

Reaveley, Alice, Karen Bettink, and Leonie Valentine. "Impacts of Introduced Species on Biodiversity." In *Biodiversity Values and Threatening Processes of the Gnangara Groundwater System*, edited by Barbara A. Wilson and Leonie E. Valentine. Government of Western Australia, Department of Environment and Conservation, 2009. http://www.water.wa.gov.au/sites/gss/Content/reports/Chapter%208%20Impacts%20of%20Introduced%20Species%20on%20Biodiversity.pdf.

Reineke, Manfred. Interview with Dr. Manfred Reineke, Executive Secretary of the Antarctic Treaty Secretariat in Buenos Aires, Argentina, April 2011.

Revkin, Andrew C. "Inuit Climate Change Petition Rejected." *New York Times*, 16 December 2006.

Richardson, Mike G. "Regulating Tourism in the Antarctic: Issues of Environment and Jurisdiction." In *Implementing the Environmental Protection Regime for the Antarctic*, edited by Davor Vidas. Boston: Kluwer Academic Publishers, 2000, 71–90.

Robinson, T., and P. Hoffman. "The Long Ascent: The Challenge of Climbing to a 30 Tcf Market." Advisory report to Cambridge Energy Research Associates (CERA) (2000).

Rodriguez, Laura F. "Can invasive species facilitate native species? Evidence of how, when, and why these impacts occur." *Biological Invasions* 8 (2006): 927–939.

Rosenau, James N., and Ernst Otto Czempiel. *Governance without Government: Order and Change in World Politics.* Cambridge: Cambridge University Press, 1992.

Rothkopf, David J. *Running the World: The Inside Story of the National Security Council and the Architects of American Power.* New York: Public Affairs, 2005.

Rothwell, D. R. *The Polar Regions and the Development of International Law.* Cambridge: Cambridge University Press, 1996.

———. "Sovereignty and the Antarctic Treaty." *Polar Record* 46(236) (2010): 17–20.

Rothwell, D. R., and H. Nasu. "Antarctica and International Security Discourse: A Primer." *New Zealand Yearbook of International Law* 6 (2008): 3–23.

Rowe, J. S., and W. E. D. Halliday. *Forest regions of Canada.* Ottawa: Information Canada, 1977.

Royal Commission on Aboriginal Peoples. "Rapport de la Commission royale sur les Peuples autochtones." Government of Canada (1996).

Rubel, Robert C. "Command of the Sea: An Old Concept Resurfaces in a New Form." *Naval War College Review* 65 (2012).

Sagers, M. J. "The regional dimension of Russian oil production: Is a sustained recovery in prospect?" *Eurasian Geography and Economics* 47(5) (2006): 505–545.

Sahlins, M., and E. Service. *Evolution and Culture.* Ann Arbor: University of Michigan Press, 1960.

Sahlins, M. D. *Stone Age Economics.* Chicago: Aldine-Atherton, 1972.

Sale, R., and E. Potapov. *The Scramble for the Arctic: Ownership, Exploitation and Conflict in the Far North*. London: Francis Lincoln, 2010.

Salt, G. W. "A comment on the use of the term emergent properties." *The American Naturalist* 113(1) (1979): 145–148.

Sawyer, S., and E. T. Gomez. "Transnational governmentality and resource extraction: Indigenous peoples, multinational corporations, multilateral institutions and the state." Identities, Conflict and Cohesion Programme Paper Number 13, United Nations Research Institute for Social Development, 2008.

Schofield, Clive, Tavis Potts, and Ian Townsend-Gault. "Boundaries, Biodiversity, Resources, and Increasing Maritime Activities: Emerging Oceans Governance Challenges for Canada in the Arctic Ocean." *Vermont Law Review* 34 (2009): 35–56.

Scott, K. N. "Managing Sovereignty and Jurisdictional Disputes in the Antarctic: The Next Fifty Years." *Yearbook of International Environmental Law* 20(1) (2010): 3–40.

Scrivener, David. "Arctic Environmental Cooperation in Transition." *Polar Record* 35(192) (1999).

Sellheim, Nikolas. SKYPE conference for the establishment of a University of the Arctic Student Council. 26 August 2011.

_____. "The Establishment of a Permanent Arctic Council Secretariat: Challenges and Opportunities." In *The Arctic Council: Its Place in the Future of Arctic Governance*, edited by Thomas Axworthy, Timo Koivurova, and Waliul Hasanat. Walter and Duncan Gordon Foundation, 2012.

Senkpiel, Aron. "Introduction to the Circumpolar World." BCS 100, University of the Arctic. Archived original curricula (2003).

Shadian, J. "Remaking Arctic governance: The construction of an Arctic Inuit polity." *Polar Record* 42(222) (2006): 249–259.

Sheehan, Glenn W. "In the Belly of the Whale: Trade and War in Eskimo Society." *Aurora*. Alaska Anthropological Association Monograph Series–VI. Anchorage (1997).

Siddon, T. "Comprehensive Land Claim Agreement between Her Majesty the Queen in Right of Canada and the Gwich'in as represented by the Gwich'in Tribal Council." Published under the authority of the Hon. Tom Siddon PC MP, Minister of Indian Affairs and Northern Development, Ottawa (1992).

Sigurðsson, H. M. *Vatnsaflsvirkjanir á Íslandi [Hydro power stations in Iceland]*. Reykjavík: Verkfræðistofa Sigurðar Thoroddsen, 2002.

Sinden, Amy. "Climate Change and Human Rights." *Journal of Land, Resources and Environmental Law* 27 (2007): 255.

Sivek, Martin, Pavel Kavina, and Jakub Jirásek. "European Union and the Formation of Its Initiative in Energy Minerals." *Energy Policy* 39(9) (September 2011): 5535–5540.

Snow, Donald M. *National Security for a New Era*. 3rd ed. New York: Pearson Education, 2008.

Solomon, S., D. Qin, M. Manning, Z. Chen, et al. *Contribution of Working Group I to the Fourth Assessment Report of the Intergovernmental Panel on Climate Change*. Cambridge: Cambridge University Press, 2007.

"Special Issue on the Arctic: After the Ice." *Nature* (12 October 2011). http://www.nature.com/news/2011/111012/full/478171a.html.

Spectar, J. M. "Saving the Ice Princess: NGOs, Antarctica and International Law in the New Millenium." *Suffolk Transnational Law Review* 23 (1999).

Spielman, Brian. "An Evaluation of Russia's Impending Claim for Continental Shelf Expansion: Why Rule 5 Will Shelve Russia's Submission." *Emory International Law Review* 23 (2009): 309–349.

Spykman, Nicholas J. "Geography and Foreign Policy I." *The American Political Science Review* 32(1) (1938).

Sreejith, S. G. "Subjective Environmentalism: The Barents Euro-Arctic Council and Its Climate Change Policy." In *Climate Governance in the Arctic*, edited by Timo Koivurova, Carina Keskitalo, and Nigel Bankes. Berlin: Springer, 2009.

Stammler, F., and E. Wilson. "Dialogue for development: An exploration of relations between oil and gas companies, communities, and the state." *Sibirica* 5(2) (2006): 1–42.

Starr, John Bryan. *Understanding China: A Guide to China's Economy, History, and Political Culture.* New York: Hill and Wang, 2010.

Steele, Jenny. "Participation and Deliberation in Environmental Law: Exploring a Problem-Solving Approach." *Oxford Journal of Legal Studies* 21 (2001): 415.

Stevenson, Christopher. "Hans Off! The Struggle for Hans Island and the Potential Ramifications for International Border Dispute Resolution." *Boston College International and Comparative Law Review* 30(1) (2007): 16.

Stokke, Olav Schram, and Geir Hønneland. *International Cooperation and Arctic Governance: Regime Effectiveness and Northern Region Building.* New York: Routledge, 2007.

Stroeve, J., et al. "Arctic sea ice decline: Faster than forecast." *Geophysical Research Letters* 34 (2007): 1–5.

Struzik, Ed. "Warming Arctic brings invasion of southern species." *The Guardian.* 14 February 2011. http://www.guardian.co.uk/environment/2011/feb/14/warming-arctic-southern-species.

Studer, Isabel, and Carol Wise, eds. *Requiem or Revival? The Promise of North American Integration.* Washington, D.C.: Brookings Institution Press, 2007.

Sturluson, J. Þ. "Afkoma Landsvirkjunar og þjóðhagsleg áhrif stóriðju [Revenue of Landsvirkjun and national economic effect of large-scale industry]." In *Landsvirkjun 1965–2005: Fyrirtækið og umhverfi þess [Landsvirkjun 1965–2005: The company and its environment]*, edited by S. Pálsdóttir. Reykjavík: Hið íslenska bókmenntafélag, 2005.

Summerhayes, C., and P. Beeching. "Hitler's Antarctic base: The myth and the reality." *Polar Record* 43 (2007): 1–21.

Summerhayes, C. P. "International collaboration in Antarctica: The International Polar Years, the International Geophysical Year, and the Scientific Committee on Antarctic Research." *Polar Record* 44(231) (2008): 321–334.

Susskind, Lawrence E., Sarah McKearnen, and Jennifer Thomas-Lamar, eds. *The Consensus Building Handbook: A Comprehensive Guide to Reaching Agreement.* SAGE, 1999.

Svalbard Treaty. "Treaty between Norway, The United States of America, Denmark, France, Italy, Japan, the Netherlands, Great Britain and Ireland and the British Overseas Dominions and Sweden Concerning Spitsbergen. Signed in Paris 9th February 1920."

Thomas, D. S. G., and C. Twyman. "Equity and justice in climate change adaptation amongst natural-resource-dependent societies." *Global Environmental Change* 15 (2005): 115–124.

Titley, Rear Adm. David W., and Courtney St. John. "Arctic Security Considerations and the US Navy's Roadmap for the Arctic." *Naval War College Review* 63(2) (2010).

Tracey, P. J. "Managing Antarctic Tourism." PhD thesis, University of Tasmania, Hobart, Australia, 2001.

Trenin, Dmitri. "Russia Reborn: Reimagining Moscow's Foreign Policy." *Foreign Affairs* 88(6) (2009).

Triggs, G. "The Antarctic Treaty System: A Model of Legal Creativity and Cooperation." In *Science Diplomacy: Antarctica, Science, and the Governance of International Spaces*, edited by P. A. Berkman, M. A. Lang, D. W. H. Walton, and O. R. Young. Washington, D.C.: Smithsonian Institution Scholarly Press, 2011.

Trivers, R. L. "The evolution of reciprocal altruism." *The Quarterly Review of Biology* 46(1) (1971): 35–57.

United Nations. Basel Convention on the Control of Transboundary Movement of Hazardous Wastes. United Nations Treaty Series: 1673 UNTS 57. 22 March 1989.

———. Cartagena Protocol on Biosafety to the Convention on Biological Diversity. 2226 UNTS 208. 29 January 2000.

———. Conference on Environment and Development, "Agenda 21." Rio de Janeiro, Brazil, 3–14 June 1992. http://sustainabledevelopment.un.org/content/documents/Agenda21.pdf.

———. Conference on Environment and Development. Rio Declaration on Environment and Development. U.N. Doc. A/Conf.151/26. 14 June 1992. http://www.unep.org/Documents.Multilingual/Default.asp?documentID=78&articleID=1163.

———. Convention on Biological Diversity. *International Legal Materials* 31:818. Entered into force 23 December 1993.

———. Convention on the Law of the Non-navigational Uses of International Watercourses. U.N. Doc. A/51/49. Adopted 21 May 1997. http://untreaty.un.org/ilc/texts/instruments/english/conventions/8_3_1997.pdf.

———. Convention on the Law of the Sea (UNCLOS; LOS Convention), preamble. Adopted 10 December 1982 (entered into force 16 November 1994). http://www.un.org/depts/los/convention_agreements/texts/unclos/unclos_e.pdf.

———. Convention on Long-range Transboundary Air Pollution. T.I.A.S. No. 10,541. 13 November 1979. *International Legal Materials* 18:1442.

———. Declaration on the Right to Development. Art. 8. G.A. Res. 41/128, U.N. GAOR, 41st Session, Supp. No. 53, at 186, U.N. Doc. A/41/53. 1986.

———. Declaration on the Rights of Indigenous Peoples. U.N. Doc. A/Res/61/295. Adopted by the General Assembly 13 September 2007.
http://www.un.org/esa/socdev/unpfii/en/declaration.html.

———. Draft Principles on Human Rights and the Environment. U.N. Doc. E/CN.4/Sub.2/1994/9, Annex I. 1994.

———. Framework Convention on Climate Change. 1771 UNTS 107. 9 May 1992.

———. International Covenant on Civil and Political Rights. 999 UNTS 171. 19 December 1966.

———. International Covenant on Economic, Social and Cultural Rights. 999 UNTS 3. 16 December 1966.

———. London Convention on the Prevention of Marine Pollution by Dumping of Wastes. 1673 UNTS 57. 22 March 1989.

———. Oceans and the Law of the Sea. U.N. Doc. A/Res/59/24. 2004.

———. Office of the High Commissioner for Human Rights. Vienna Declaration and Program of Action, Arts. 8, 20, 25, U.N. Doc. A/CONF.157/23. 1993.

_____. Rio Declaration on Sustainable Development (Rio Plus 20) (2012).

_____. Universal Declaration of Human Rights. General Assembly (G.A.) Res. 217A, at 17, art. 3, U.N. GAOR, 3rd Session, 1st plenary meeting, U.N. Doc. A/810. 12 December 1948.

United Nations. Office of the High Commissioner for Human Rights. "The Human Rights of Indigenous Peoples in Light of the New Declaration, and the Challenges of Making Them Operable." *Report of the Special Rapporteur*, U.N. Doc. A/HRC/9/9, para. 85. 5 August 2008.

United Nations. Alta Outcome Document. Global Indigenous Preparatory Conference for the United Nations High Level Plenary Meeting of the General Assembly to be known as the World Conference on Indigenous Peoples, 10–12 June 2013, Alta. http://wcip2014.org/1530.

United Nations Economic and Social Council [ECOSOC], United Nations Economic Commission for Europe. Convention on Environmental Impact Assessment in a Transboundary Context (Espoo Convention). 25 February 1991.

_____. Convention on Access to Information, Public Participation in Decision-Making and Access to Justice in Environmental Matters. 2161 U.N.T.S. 447. 25 June 1998.

_____. *The Aarhus Convention: An Implementation Guide* 29, U.N. Doc. ECE/CEP/72. 2000.

United Nations Environment Program (UNEP). CBD/COP/2/19, Report of the Second Meeting of the Conference of the Parties to the Convention on Biological Diversity. 30 November 1995. http://www.cbd.int/doc/meetings/cop/cop-02/official/cop-02-19-en.pdf.

_____. "Alien Species: Guiding Principles for the Prevention, Introduction and Mitigation of Impacts, Subsidiary Body of Scientific, Technical and Technological Advice." Montreal: UNEP, 2000. http://www.cbd.int/doc/meetings/sbstta/sbstta-05/official/sbstta-05-05-en.pdf.

_____. "The Arctic 2050 Scenario and Global Application: Global Methodology for Mapping Human Impacts on the Biosphere." Nairobi, 2001.

_____. World Conservation Monitoring Center, Workshop Report, "Towards the harmonization of national reporting to biodiversity-related treaties." A workshop convened by UNEP-WCMC in cooperation with the governments of Belgium and the UK, Haasrode, Belgium, 22–23 September 2004. Doc: AEWA/StC Inf. 2.5. 11 November 2004.

_____. "Global International Waters Assessment, Challenges to International Waters–Regional Assessments in a Global Perspective." GIWA Final Report. Nairobi, 2006.

_____. Decisions Adopted by the Conference of the Parties to the Convention on Biological Diversity at Its Ninth Meeting. CBD/COP/9/29, Decision IX/13. Article 8(J) and Related Provisions. Bonn, 19–30 May 2008.

_____. "New and emerging issues." CBD/SBSTTA 14. Recommendation XIV/16, http://www.cbd.int/recommendations/sbstta/?m=sbstta-14. 2010.

United Nations Food and Agriculture Organization (FAO). *Code of conduct for the import and release of exotic biological control agents.* Rome: FAO, 1996. http://www.fao.org/docrep/x5585e/x5585e0i.htm.

_____. "Voluntary Guidelines on the Responsible Governance of Tenure of Land, Fisheries and Forests in the Context of National Food Security, Food and Agriculture Organization of the United Nations." Rome: FAO, 2012.

United Nations General Assembly. A/66/119, Letter dated 30 June 2011 from the co-chairs of the Ad Hoc Open-ended Informal Working Group to the President of the General Assembly (2011).

United States Department of Defense. Quadrennial Defense Review Report (2010).

United States Department of the Interior. Invasive Species Advisory Committee. *Invasive Species and Climate Change.* Washington, D.C., 2010. http://www.invasivespecies.gov/ISAC/White%20Papers/Climate_Change_White_Paper_FINAL_VERSION.pdf.

United States Energy Information Administration. Arctic Oil and Natural Gas Potential (19 October 2009). http://www.eia.gov/oiaf/analysispaper/arctic/index.html.

United States Geological Survey. Circum-Arctic Resource Appraisal: Estimates of Undiscovered Oil and Gas North of the Arctic Circle. *USGS Fact Sheet 2008.* http://pubs.usgs.gov/fs/2008/3049/fs2008-3049.pdf.

United States Navy. US Navy Arctic Roadmap (2009).

———. Chief of Naval Operations (CNO). Navy Strategic Objectives for the Arctic (2010).

United States Navy, United States Marine Corps, United States Coast Guard. A Cooperative Strategy for 21st Century Seapower (2007).

United States Northern Command (USNORTHCOM). "About USNORTHCOM." http://www.northcom.mil/AboutUSNORTHCOM.aspx.

United States. Office of the President. National Security Presidential Directive and Homeland Security Presidential Directive (NSPD-66/HSPD-25) (2009).

———. National Strategy for the Arctic Region (2013).

University of the Arctic web site. http://uarctic.org/Frontpage.aspx?m=3 (accessed 30 September 2011).

Van Lente, H. *Promising Technology: Dynamics of Expectations in Technological Developments.* PhD thesis, University of Twente, Enschede, Netherlands, 1993.

Vazquez-Brust, Diego A., and Joseph Sarkis. *Green Growth: Managing the Transition to a Sustainable Economy: Learning by Doing in East Asia and Europe.* Heidelberg: Springer, 2012.

Vicuna, Francisco. *Antarctic Mineral Exploitation: The Emerging Legal Framework.* Cambridge: Cambridge University Press, 1988.

Vidas, Davor. "The Protocol on Environmental Protection to the Antarctic Treaty: A Ten-Year Review." *Yearbook of International Cooperation on Environment and Development* 3 (2002).

Vondracek, T. J. "Compensation for losses resulting from acts of public policy in Soviet law." In *Compensation for Compulsory Purchase,* edited by J. F. Garner. United Kingdom National Committee of Comparative Law, UK Comparative Law Series no. 2. London, 1975.

Wachowich, Nancy. "Creative Technologies: Experimentation and Social Practice in Arctic Societies." *Études/Inuit/Studies* 34(2) (2010), 13–19.

Wagner, Andrew Van. "It's Getting Hot in Here, So Take Away All the Arctic's Resources: A Look at a Melting Arctic and the Hot Competition for Its Resources." *Villanova Environmental Law Journal* 21 (2010): 189.

Wagner, Martin. Testimony of Martin Wagner before the Inter-American Commission on Human Rights (1 March 2007). http://www.earthjustice.org/library/legal_docs/testimony-before-iachr-on-global-warming-human-rights-by-martin-wagner.pdf.

Wallace, D. *Governing the Future.* Champaign, IL: Common Ground Publishing, 2011.

Wang, Yi. *Australia-China Relations Post 1949: Sixty Years of Trade and Politics.* Farnham and Burlington, VT: Ashgate, 2012.

Watt-Cloutier, Sheila. "Global Warming and Human Rights." Earth Justice and Center for International Environmental Law (undated).

Weber, M. "The Strength to Continue: A Case Study Approach to Examining the Robustness of Polar Governance in the Era of Environmental and Energy Security." PhD thesis, University of Tasmania, Hobart, Australia, 2011.

Wilensky, U. *NetLogo.* Center for Connected Learning and Computer-Based Modeling, Northwestern University, Evanston, IL, 1999. http://ccl.northwestern.edu/netlogo/ (accessed 5 September 2013).

Willetts, Peter. "Transnational Actors and International Organizations in Global Politics." In *The Globalization of World Politics,* edited by J. B. Baylis and S. Smith. 2nd ed. Oxford: Oxford University Press, 2001.

Wily, L. A. "Land Rights Reform and Governance in Africa." United National Development Program Discussion Paper. New York: UNDP, 2006.

Wiwa v. Royal Dutch Petroleum Co., 226 F.3d 88 (2d Cir. 2000).

———. Complaint. http://ccrjustice.org/files/11.8.96%20%20Wiwa%20Complaint.pdf.

Wolfrum, Rüdiger, and Nele Matz. *Conflicts in International Environmental Law.* Berlin: Springer, 2003.

Wooldridge, M. *Multiagent Systems.* Chichester: John Wiley and Sons, 2005.

World Bank. "Involuntary Resettlement: Operational Policy and Background Paper." Washington, D.C. (October 1998).

World Commission on Environment and Development. *Our Common Future.* Oxford: Oxford University Press, 1987.

World Trade Organization (WTO). "Accessions. Russian Federation." http://www.wto .org/english/thewto_e/acc_e/a1_russie_e.htm.

———. Trade and Environmental Ministerial Decision, 14 April 1994, GATT Doc. MTN. TNC/MIN (94)/Rev.1. *International Legal Materials* 33:1267 (1994).

———. Agreement on Technical Barriers to Trade (entered into force 1995). http://www .wto.org/english/docs_e/legal_e/17-tbt_e.htm.

———. The WTO Agreement on the Application of Sanitary and Phytosanitary Measures (entered into force 1995). http://www.wto.org/english/tratop_e/sps_e/spsagr_e.htm.

Yakovleva, N. "Oil pipeline construction in Eastern Siberia: Implications for indigenous people." *Geoforum* 42 (2011a): 708–719.

———. "Oil sector developments in Russia and indigenous people." *OGEL: Oil, Gas and Energy Law Intelligence* 9(4), Special Issue: *Indigenous People and Resource Development* (2011b): 1–28.

Yakovleva, N., and Munday, M. "Pipeline development and community participation." BRASS Research Report, BRASS Research Centre, 2010. http://www.brass.cf.ac .uk/uploads/Pipeline_Development_and_Community_Participation.pdf (accessed 2 February 2012).

York, G. *The Dispossessed: Life and Death in Native Canada.* Toronto: McArthur, 1990.

Young O. "Governing International Spaces: Antarctica and Beyond." In *Science Diplomacy: Antarctica, Science, and the Governance of International Spaces,* edited by P. Berkman, M. Lang, D. Walton, and O. Young. Washington, D.C.: Smithsonian Institution Scholarly Press, 2011.

Young, O. R. "The effectiveness of international environmental regimes: A mid-term report." *International Environmental Affairs* 10(4) (1998): 267–289.

———. "Whither the Arctic? Conflict or cooperation in the circumpolar north." *Polar Record* 45(1) (2009): 73–82.

Young, Oran R. *International Governance: Protecting the Environment in a Stateless Society.* Ithaca: Cornell University Press, 1994.

Young, Oran, and Gail Osherenko, eds. *Polar Politics: Creating International Environmental Regimes.* Ithaca: Cornell University Press, 1993.

Young, Steven B. *To the Arctic: An Introduction to the Far Northern World.* New York: John Wiley and Sons, 1989.

Zebich-Knos, Michele. "Conflict Avoidance and Environmental Protection: The Antarctic Paradigm." In *Peace Parks: Conservation and Conflict Resolution,* edited by S. Ali. Cambridge: MIT Press, 2007.

Zia, Asim, Paul Hirsch, Alexander N. Songorwa, et al. "Cross-Scale Value Trade-Offs in Managing Social-Ecological Systems: The Politics of Scale in Ruaha National Park, Tanzania." *Ecology and Society* 16(4) (2011): 7. http://dx.doi.org/10.5751/ES -04375-160407.

Zimmerbauer, Kaj. "Unusual Regionalism in Northern Europe: The Barents Region in the Making." *Regional Studies* 47 (2013): 1.

Þjóðviljin. "Lærdomsríkar andstæður [Instructive opposites]." 10 May 1969.

Þórðarson, S. *Afl í segulæðum: Saga rafmagns á Íslandi í 100 ár [Power in magnetic veins: The story of electricity in Iceland in 100 years].* Reykjavík: Verkfræðingafélag Íslands, 2004.

Contributors

Saleem H. Ali is professor of politics and international studies and director of the Centre for Social Responsibility in Mining at the University of Queensland, Australia. He is also adjunct professor of Environmental Planning at the University of Vermont's Rubenstein School of Environment and Natural Resources. Among his numerous publications is the critically acclaimed book *Treasures of the Earth: Need, Greed and a Sustainable Future* (Yale University Press, 2010). Dr. Ali was selected as a Young Global Leader by the World Economic Forum and an Emerging Explorer by the National Geographic Society for his applied research on environmental conflict and cooperation. He serves on the board of governors of the Pakistan chapter for Leadership in Environment and Development (LEAD).

Betsy Baker is professor of law at Vermont Law School and a senior fellow. She has also served as a visiting scholar with the interagency Extended Continental Shelf Task Force in Washington, D.C., at the US State Department, Office of Ocean and Polar Affairs, Bureau of Oceans and International Environmental and Scientific Affairs. Professor Baker was co–lead author on the Arctic Council "Arctic Ocean Review Phase II Report," a survey of all international agreements relevant to the Arctic Ocean, which the Arctic Council ministers adopted at their May 2013 meeting in Kiruna, Sweden. Before returning to the United States to oversee the graduate program for international students at Harvard Law School from 2003 to 2007, Professor Baker spent more than a decade in Germany, where she obtained her doctorate in law, worked as legal historian at the Heidelberg Academy of Sciences, and was affiliated with the Max Planck Institute for Comparative Public Law and International Law.

Rasmus Gjedssø Bertelsen is assistant professor in the Department of Culture and Global Studies at Aalborg University, Denmark. He has studied political science in Copenhagen, Reykjavik, Geneva, Lausanne, and Amsterdam and earned a PhD in international relations from Cambridge, during which he spent time at Sciences Po. He has held postdoctoral fellowships at Harvard Kennedy School of Government, Tokyo

Institute of Technology with United Nations University–Institute of Advanced Studies, and Aalborg University. His field of research is transnational flows of knowledge and talent, where he works on socioeconomic-political development and the interplay of natural resources and human capital in Iceland, the Faroe Islands, and Greenland. He also works on US–European–Middle East–East Asian academic relations. His Arctic work has appeared in proceedings from the Northern Research Forum, *Strategic Insights*, *The Fast Changing Arctic* (University of Calgary Press, 2013), and in the *Handbook of the Politics of the Arctic* and *Arctic Yearbook*.

Rebecca Bratspies is professor of law at the City University of New York (CUNY). Her teaching and scholarly research focus on environmental and public international law, with a particular emphasis on how legal systems govern the global commons and how law can further sustainable development. She has published widely on the topics of environmental liability, regulatory uncertainty, regulation of international fisheries, and regulation of genetically modified food crops. Before entering academia, Professor Bratspies served as a judicial law clerk to the Honorable C. Arlen Beam of the United States Court of Appeals for the Eighth Circuit. In 1994, she was selected to be a Henry Luce Foundation Scholar. Professor Bratspies spent a year appointed to the Republic of China (Taiwan) Environmental Protection Administration. She earned her B.A. in biology from Wesleyan University and her J.D., cum laude, from the University of Pennsylvania.

Damián Castro is a PhD candidate at Memorial University of Newfoundland. He was born in Buenos Aires, Argentina. He has a licenciatura in anthropology from the University of Buenos Aires. Upon completing his degree he worked in the software industry. For his graduate research he conducted fieldwork in Labrador between 2007 and 2010. His research focus is the convergence between software tools and social sciences, building models to simulate or represent social processes.

Damien Degeorges is head of international business diplomacy at Paris School of Business (France). He graduated in Nordic studies (Danish) from Sorbonne University and wrote a doctoral thesis in political science, "The Role of Greenland in the Arctic," at Descartes University in Paris. After a first visit to Greenland in 1998, he has worked extensively with Greenland issues for more than ten years and is a former freelance foreign correspondent for the Greenlandic newspaper *AG/Grønlandsposten*. In 2010, he lectured on Greenland in Australia and followed closely the Australian debate on climate change, as well as Australian-Chinese relations. He is the founder of the Arctic Policy and Economic Forum.

Sébastien Duyck is a PhD candidate and a researcher at the Northern Institute for Environmental and Minority Law, Arctic Center, University of Lapland. The focus of his dissertation is on the procedural rights of nonstate actors in the international climate change regime. His main areas of research include climate governance, human rights and the environment, and Arctic governance. He has participated in numerous environmental governance processes in recent years and has written most recently about climate governance in the Arctic and about the protection of the rights of climate-vulnerable communities through international environmental governance. He is an Earth System Governance research fellow.

Michael H. Glantz is director of the Consortium for Capacity Building at the University of Colorado at Boulder. He was a senior scientist at the National Center for Atmospheric Research (NCAR) and served as the head of the Environmental and Societal Impacts Group (ESIG). His research and applications activities center on how climate, water, and weather affect society as well as how society affects climate. He has also coordinated joint research in the Central Asian Republics of Uzbekistan and Turkmenistan. Glantz was honored with UNEP's Global 500 Award in 1990. He has authored or edited over thirty multidisciplinary books on climate and development-related issues. His most recent publication is "Heads Up: Early Warning Systems for Climate, Water and Weather-Related Hazards" (United Nations University Press, April 2009).

Richard Grover is a chartered surveyor and economist. He is particularly interested in property rights. He has undertaken a number of projects in transition economies in areas such as land registration, valuation, and property taxation for national governments, the World Bank, and the Food and Agriculture Organization of the United Nations. He has recently completed twenty-five years working for Oxford Brookes University. Before retiring he was assistant dean of the School of Built Environment and now teaches property economics and valuations on a part-time basis. He represents the Royal Institution of Chartered Surveyors on Commission 7 of the International Federation of Surveyors (FIG).

Klaus Georg Hansen directs the Ilimmarfik Institute, University of Greenland. Klaus has studied anthropology and Greenlandic language and culture at Aarhus University, Denmark. Former positions include head of Groenlandica (the National Library of Greenland), head of Sisimiut Museum, head of department in the government of Greenland in charge of national spatial planning for Greenland, and deputy director and senior research fellow at Nordregio in Sweden. He has a special interest in research on societal development in Greenland, in the North Atlantic, and in the Arctic, and the colonial history of Greenland with a focus on the question of legality. Since 2007 he has primarily focused his research on large-scale industries, demography, and urbanization in Greenland and in the Arctic.

Kaz Higuchi retired from conducting research in various aspects of climate science as a research scientist in Environment Canada, and now teaches climate change science and adaptation as an adjunct professor in the Faculty of Environmental Studies, Graduate Program in Geography at York University, Toronto, Canada. With a few graduate students, Dr. Higuchi is pursuing his new research interests in complex systems dynamics and agent-based modeling, as well as in the climatology of extreme weather events. He also participates actively in promoting interdisciplinary research as an executive member of IRIS (Institute for Research and Innovation in Sustainability) at York University.

Rachel A. Hirsch is an adjunct research professor with the Faculty of Environmental Studies at York University, Toronto, and a Health, Environment, and Indigenous Communities Research Group postdoctoral fellow at Trent University. She is a researcher advocate with over three years of experience working collaboratively with government, academic, and indigenous stakeholders to evaluate success in local knowledge translation and almost ten years of experience conducting environmental health policy research. Dr. Hirsch completed her award-winning doctoral work on residential pesticide policy preferences at the University of Western Ontario. Since then she has developed a collaborative research program focused on building research and evaluation capacity on the topic of knowledge translation and food security in Iqaluit, Nunavut, and Nain, Nunatsiavut (Labrador). She is also affiliated, as a postdoctoral associate, with the Arctic Network of Centres of Excellence of Canada (ArcticNet).

Kamrul Hossain is a senior researcher at the Northern Institute for Environmental and Minority Law (NIEM) in the Arctic Center of the University of Lapland, acting as director (ad interim) of the institute in 2011. In 2010, he was invited as a visiting professor to the School of Law of the Harbin Institute of Technology in China. He has attended visiting scholar fellowships at the Muroran Institute of Technology in Japan, as well as at the Walter and Duncan Gordon Foundation within its Munk-Gordon Arctic Security Program in Canada in 2011 and 2013, respectively. His research interests lie in the field of international environmental law as applied in the Arctic with special focus on energy and mineral development, marine pollution, continental shelf development and law of the sea, and indigenous peoples' human rights. He has extensively published his works in a number of internationally acclaimed journals including *Polar Record*, published by Cambridge University Press. He was the special editor of the *Yearbook of Polar Law* published in 2011.

Anne M. Jensen is senior scientist for UIC Science LLC, an Alaska Native corporation. She has thirty years' experience in anthropology in Alaska, including archaeological and ethnographic research. Dr. Jensen has been principal investigator for several major projects on the North Slope. She is a longtime resident of Barrow, Alaska. She has published on various aspects of coastal North Alaska archaeology as well as cultural resource management in bush Alaska; the material correlates indigenous and Western science traditions, resource use, and evidence for climate change in North Alaska. Her current research focuses on sustainable human adaptation in the Arctic and subarctic environments, coastal adaptations in the North, global change effects on the archaeological and paleoecological record, and digital archaeology.

Ilan Kelman is a reader in risk, resilience, and global health at University College, London. His main research relates to two areas: creating and maintaining safer and healthier communities on islands and in other isolated areas such as Arctic communities; and disaster diplomacy, examining how and why disaster-related activities do and do not reduce conflict and create peace. Other areas include school safety, disaster-related education, disaster deaths, refugee settlement and shelter, and connecting research and practice. He has lived and worked in Barbados, Canada, Ireland, New Zealand, Norway, the United Kingdom, and the United States.

Glen Lesins is a professor in the Department of Physics and Atmospheric Science at Dalhousie University in Halifax, Nova Scotia, Canada. His research activities examine connected Arctic climate change, and include the Arctic amplification warming phenomenon, the role of clouds and radiation during the Arctic night, and multiagent modeling of Inuit dependence on the caribou.

Daniela Liggett is a lecturer in Antarctic environmental management at Gateway Antarctica, the University of Canterbury's Centre for Antarctic Studies and Research in New Zealand. She has made important contributions to Antarctic tourism and environmental management research. Dr. Liggett is a leader of interdisciplinary exchange: she cochairs the Social Sciences Action Group of the Scientific Committee on Antarctic Research (SCAR); is an active member of SCAR's Capacity Building, Education and Training Committee; has co-organized several conferences and conference sessions; and is on the editorial board of *The Polar Journal.* Her publications include journal articles "Antarctic Futures: Human Engagement with the Antarctic Environment," "Tourism in the Antarctic," and "Exploring Antarctic Values."

Arthur Mason is an adjunct associate professor in the Department of Anthropology at Rice University. He is currently on extended professional leave at the University of California, Berkeley, where he is the Ciriacy-Wantrup Fellow in the Department of Geography and in the Energy and Resources Group. His publications include the coedited volume *Oil Talk: The Material and Political Worlds of the Global Petroleum and Natural Gas Industry* (Cornell University Press, forthcoming). Dr. Mason was selected as an energy research chair by the International Fulbright Commission on two occasions, for Canada (2006–2007) and for Norway (2012–2013), for his applied research on Arctic hydrocarbon development. His energy policy leadership positions include serving as associate director of energy and natural resources for the state of Alaska.

Kathleen Osgood has a doctorate in comparative literature; her primary research focus is the literary ecology of northern native peoples. She studied at the Giellegas Institute at the University of Oulu, Finland, and is collaborating on a series of online courses with Sakha State University in Yakutsk, Siberia. She is active with the University of the Arctic, a consortium of institutions involved with the circumpolar world. A long-term Vermonter, Kathleen Osgood lives in the same house where she grew up. While the stone walls and sugarbush of her farmlands look much as they did in the nineteenth century, twenty-first-century reality has shifted from hardscrabble farming to locavore economies, from mutual aid to development covenants, from rural isolation to global connection.

Rebecca Pincus is associate director of the Institute for Environmental Diplomacy and Security at the University of Vermont, where she is also a lecturer and postdoctoral researcher. Her research focuses on the relationship between national security and natural resources, primarily energy and water, with theoretical interests in organizational behavior, military culture, and networks. She earned a PhD and a master's degree from the University of Vermont, and a second master's degree in environmental law from the Vermont Law School, as well as a BS from the Walsh School of Foreign Service at Georgetown University. Her longstanding interest in the Arctic began in childhood, with an early fascination with polar bears and Norse mythology.

Glenn W. Sheehan lives in a Quonset hut at the former Naval Arctic Research Laboratory near Point Barrow, Alaska. He helped found and run the Barrow Arctic Science Consortium from 1995 to the present. Dr. Sheehan started his research in the American Arctic in 1981 and has secured grants for Arctic research totaling about $30 million since then. He also works for the North Slope Borough Department of Health and Social Services.

Natalia Yakovleva is a reader in sustainable development at the University of Winchester, Winchester Business School. She has a degree in economics and a PhD in environmental studies. Prior to joining Winchester University, she worked at the Research Centre for Business Relationships, Accountability, Sustainability and Society (BRASS) at Cardiff University. Natalia specializes in corporate social responsibility, sustainable production and consumption, and business and community relations. She has conducted research on social conflicts in the extractive sector in Argentina, interaction between large- and small-scale miners in Ghana, community engagement and oil pipeline development in Russia, and sustainability of food supply chains in the United Kingdom. She is an author of *Corporate Social Responsibility in the Mining Industries* (Ashgate, 2005) and is on the editorial board of the journal *Extractive Industries and Society* (Elsevier).

Steven Young is a botanist and paleoecologist who has worked in the Arctic, Antarctic, and boreal regions since 1963. His major interest has been the changes in northern ecosystems since the height of the last Ice Age, and the processes involved. He is especially interested in how these factors have been related to human migrations and the development of modern human cultures in the North. His work has recently extended into the Russian Arctic and Central Asia, areas that seem to be keys to our understanding of the formation of modern Arctic ecosystems. Most recently, he has resumed work in northern and western Alaska in efforts to understand the physical (especially permafrost) and biotic factors influencing local plant distribution.

Michele Zebich-Knos is professor emerita of political science and international affairs and was founding director of the Master of Science in International Policy Management program at Kennesaw State University, Georgia (USA). Dr. Zebich-Knos's research focuses on global environmental policy and multilateral environmental agreements and regulation, with a focus on polar issues. She is author of numerous publications, and coauthored a chapter with Lassi Heinenen (University of Lapland, Finland), "Polar Regions—Comparing Arctic and Antarctic Border Debates," in Doris Wastl-Walter, ed., *Ashgate Research Companion to Border Studies* (2011). She currently serves on the External Advisory Board, Institute for Environmental Diplomacy and Security, University of Vermont.

Asim Zia is director of the Institute for Environmental Diplomacy and Security at the University of Vermont, where he is also an associate professor in the Department of Community Development and Applied Economics and the Department of Computer Science. He received his PhD in public policy from the Georgia Institute for Technology and has studied in Germany and his native Pakistan. Dr. Zia's research is focused on the development of computational and complex systems–based approaches for policy analysis, governance informatics, and adaptive management and decision making; as well as transportation, air quality, land-use planning, climate change mitigation, international development, and environmental sustainability.

Index

Page numbers in *italics* indicate figures and tables.

Aarhus Convention, 16, 178, 183n30, 184n45
ABA (Arctic Biodiversity Assessment), 49, 76, 86
Abbott, Kenneth W., 98
ABDS (Arctic Biodiversity Data Service), 50
ABNJ Working Group, 48
Aboriginal peoples. *See* Indigenous peoples
Aboriginal Pipeline Group (APG), 210, 211
ACIA (Arctic Climate Impact Assessment), 44–45, 72, 73, 76–77
Adams, Duncan, 223
Adger, W.N., 187
Ad Hoc Technical Expert Group on Biodiversity (AHTEG), 50
AEPS (Arctic Environmental Protection Strategy), 23, 25, 43
AEWC (Alaska Eskimo Whaling Commission), 221–222
AFN (Alaska Federation of Natives), 219–220
Afonso, O., 114
Agenda *21*, 15–16, *16*, 17, 30, 45, 90n67
Agent-based model (ABM), 187, 193–196
Agnew, J., 136
Agreement Concerning Cooperation in the Quarantine of Plants and Their Protection Against Pests and Diseases, 81
Agreement on the Conservation of Polar Bears, 85–86

Agreement on Sanitary and Phytosanitary Measures (STP), invasive species regulation under, 82–83
AHTEG (Ad Hoc Technical Expert Group on Biodiversity), 50
Air temperatures, rise in, 1, 72, 74, 76, 128
Alaska: and Beaufort Sea dispute, 135; indigenous communities in North Slope, 213–214, 217–223; natural gas development in, 141–142, 145; oil deposits in, 207–208; regulation of North Slope Borough, 214–217, 221; Trans-Alaska Pipeline, 208
Alaska Eskimo Whaling Commission (AEWC), 221–222
Alaska Federation of Natives (AFN), 219–220
Alaska Native Claims Settlement Act (ANCSA), 218
Albert, Thomas F., 221
Alcoa, 120, 124
Ali, Saleem H., 1–9, 111, 158–160, 199, 200
Almaty Guidelines of 2005, 16
Altamirano-Jiménez, I., 199, 211
Alta Outcome Document, 52
Aluminum production: in Greenland, 124, 124–125; in Iceland, 118–120, 121
Alusuisse, 119
AMAP (Arctic Monitoring and Assessment Program), 86, 128, 152

AMSA (Arctic Marine Shipping Assessment), 26, 86

AMSP (Arctic Marine Strategic Plan), 44, 45

Anaktuvuk Pass (Alaska), 219

Anderson, R.B., 199, 211

Andhoy, Jarle, 104

Animal species, Antarctic, 95, 198

Animal species, Arctic: breeding decline for, 198; and climate change, 88; contagious diseases, 79; endangered migratory, 81; migratory birds, 86; nonnative invasive, 76–77, 81; U.S. regulations for, 214–215

Antarctic: exploration of, 235; geographical characteristics of, 14; governance of (See Antarctic Treaty of 1959; Antarctic Treaty System); historical background of, 62–63; ice mass, 95; invasive species regulations, 81; sovereignty claims in, 61, 62, 65, 69–70, 70n2; sovereignty concept in, 14–15, 33. See also Climate change, Antarctic; Fisheries, Antarctic; Tourism, Antarctic

Antarctic and Southern Ocean Coalition (ASOC), 20–21, 36n52, 96, 101, 102

Antarctic Treaty Conference of Parties, 96

Antarctic Treaty Consultative Meeting (ATCM), 21, 61, 99, 100

Antarctic Treaty Consultative Parties (ATCPs), 61–62

Antarctic Treaty Meeting of Experts Chairs' Report, 107

Antarctic Treaty of 1959, 1, 95, 100; consensus-based decision making under, 61, 68; and environmental protection protocol (Madrid Protocol), 63–64, 65, 70n2, 71n5, 100, 151; nationality-based jurisdiction under, 67; and NGO status, 21; objective of, 19; political security and scientific activity as focus of, 63

Antarctic Treaty on Environmental Protection, 81

Antarctic Treaty Secretariat, 64, 97, 100, 102

Antarctic Treaty System (ATS), 11–12, 95; and Chinese influence, 156–157; criticism/challenges to, 61–62, 64–69, 66–67; defined, 100; future of, 69–70; historical context for, 14; and Madrid Protocol, 63–64; meetings under, 100–101; and nongovernmental organizations (NGOs), 20–22, 31–32, 64; and private sector, 22–23, 32; science/policy interface, 19–20, 32–33, 139; success of, 61, 64, 68; and tourism regulation, 100–103

Aquatic Animal Health Code, 79

Arctic: countries of, 27, 46, 172, 174; exploration of, 225, 235–236; geographical characteristics of, 14, 111, 172; governance of (See Arctic Council; Arctic governance); missionaries in, 225–226; resource extraction in (See Oil and gas deposits; Oil and gas pipelines; Resource extraction); and sovereignty claims (See Sovereignty claims, Arctic); and sovereignty concept, 14–15, 33; treaties relevant to, 41, 44; wildlife (See Animal species, Arctic; Fisheries, Arctic). See also Climate change, Arctic; Greenland; Iceland; Indigenous peoples; Invasive species, Arctic

Arctic Biodiversity Assessment (ABA), 49, 76, 86

Arctic Biodiversity Data Service (ABDS), 50

Arctic Climate Impact Assessment (ACIA), 44–45, 72, 73, 76–77

Arctic Council, 23; and biodiversity issues, 49–50; China in, 154; and circumpolar business forum, 31; and circumpolar studies, 229–230; and climate change, 50–51; establishment of, 24, 25, 43, 45, 94–95n123, 174, 229; indigenous participation in, 24, 25, 43, 178, 229; and information exchange, 53–54; institutional developments in, 29–30; and invasive species, 86–87; nations of, 44–45, 93n123, 229; observer status in, 24–25, 28–29, 30, 44, 55n8, 55n13; permanent participants status in, 25–26, 28, 29, 30, 33, 43, 44, 52, 55n8; permanent secretariat of, 25, 29, 43–44, 53; private sector role in, 30–31; purpose of, 42; and resource extraction decision making, 174–175, 179, 180; working groups of, 86, 93n123

Arctic Council Observer Manual for Subsidiary Bodies, 24

Arctic Dreams (Lopez), 224

Arctic Economic Council, 31

Arctic Environmental Protection Strategy (AEPS), 23, 25, 43

Arctic governance: Alaska North Slope Bureau, 214–217, 221; in Barents Euro-Arctic Region, 23–24, 26–27, 31; and economic development, 172–173, 179; future of, 138–139; historical context for, 14; human rights framework for, 176–177, 180, 237; and invasive species problem, 84–85; legal framework for, 171–172; and ocean management, 27–28. *See also* Arctic Council

Arctic Marine Shipping Assessment (AMSA), 26, 86

Arctic Marine Strategic Plan (AMSP), 44, 45

Arctic Monitoring and Assessment Program (AMAP), 86, 128, 152

Arctic National Wildlife Refuge (ANWR), 135

Arctic Ocean: governance of, 27–28; and melting, 128, 130, 161, 186, 236; seabed claims, *66*, 132–133; as strategic asset, 27

Arctic Roadmap, U.S. Navy, 2, 165, 167

Arctic Search and Rescue Agreement, 45

Arctic studies. *See* Circumpolar studies

Argentina: Antarctic territorial claims, 62; collaboration with Chile, 151–152; Falklands conflict, 67

Ármannsson, P.H., 116

Art, indigenous, 225

Art, Robert J., 3–4

Arthur Andersen company, 146

ASOC (Antarctic and Southern Ocean Coalition), 20–21, 36n52, 96, *102*

ATCM (Antarctic Treaty Consultative Meeting), 21, 61, 100

ATCP (Antarctic Treaty Consultative Parties), 61–62

Atomic Energy Commission (AEC), 221

ATS. *See* Antarctic Treaty System

AusChina Energy, 156

Australia, 21, 62, 70, 201; -China relations, 156, 157, 159n9

Australian Antarctic Division (AAD), 98

Axelrod, 188

Bacon, Francis, 169

Baev, Pavel K., 163

Baker, Betsy, 11, 41–60

Baker, James S., 135

Ballast water management, 78, 79, 84, 85, 86–87

Baltic Sea Convention, 86

Barber, D.G., 186

Barents Euro-Arctic Council (BEAC), 26

Barents Euro-Arctic Region (BEAR), 23–24, 26–27, 31, 130

Barents Regional Council (BRC), 26

Barents Sea, territorial conflict in, 133–134, *134*, 138

Barnett, Jon, 6

Barroso, José Manuel, 153

Barrow (Alaska), 218

Barrow Arctic Science Consortium (BASC), 222

Barrow Environmental Observatory, 222

BEAC (Barents Euro-Arctic Council), 26

BEAR (Barents Euro-Arctic Region), 23–24, 26–27, 31, 130

Bears: breeding decline, 198; "grolar bear" hybrid, 77; nonnative species, 76

Beaufort Sea dispute (Canada-U.S.), 135

Beaumier, M.C., 187

Beck, P.J., 62, 63, 65

Beck, U., 144–145

Beeching, P., 62

Belova, M., 204

Berger, Thomas, 209

Berkes, F., 186, 187

Berkman, P.A., 63, 138

Berman, M., 187

Berserk, disappearance of, 104, 105, 108

Bertelsen, Rasmus Gjedssø, 111, 113–127

Beunza, D., 142

Biodiversity Clearing House Mechanism (CHM), 48

Biodiversity treaties, 47–48

Biological Diversity Convention. *See* Convention on Biological Diversity

Biological prospecting, Antarctic, *66*

Biological Weapons Convention (BWC), 81

Biosafety Clearing House, 80

Biosphere reserve plan, Arctic, 139

Blanda power station, Iceland, 120

Blomley, N., 136

Bodenhorn, B., 188

BOEM (Bureau of Ocean Energy Management), 215, 217

Borgerson, S., 137–138, 163, 186

Boyer, D., 141

Bratspies, Rebecca, 171–185

BRC (Barents Regional Council), 26

Brigham, Lawson, 164

Brooks, David, 144

Brosnan, Ian G., 138

Brower, Arnold, Sr., 222

Brower, Harry, 222

Brundtland Report of *1987*, 16

BSEE (Bureau of Safety and Environmental Enforcement), 215, 217
Buck, S.J., 64
Bulkeley, R., 70
Bureau of Indian Affairs (BIA), 215, 218
Bureau of Land Management (BLM), 215
Bureau of Ocean Energy Management (BOEM), 215, 217
Bureau of Safety and Environmental Enforcement (BSEE), 215, 217
Búrfellsvirkjun power station, Iceland, 119, 120, 126
Bush, George W., 164–165
Buszynski, L., 204
BWC (Biological Weapons Convention), 81
Byers, Michael, 135, 138

CAB International (CABI), 84
CAFF (Conservation of Arctic Flora and Fauna), 49, 50, 86
Calder v. the Attorney General of British Columbia, 208–209
Çaliskan, K., 145
Callon, M., 145
Cambridge Energy Research Associates (CERA), 144, 146
Campbell, D.F.J., 114
Canada, 44, 172, 174; Arctic activity and development of, 2; in Beaufort Sea dispute, 135; in Hans Island dispute, 135–136; Ilulissat Declaration, 138; indigenous peoples' cooperative strategies, 189–197; indigenous peoples' land-claim rights, 186–187, 208–209, 211–212; Mackenzie Valley gas pipeline, 199, 208–212; and observer status, 28; oil deposits of, 130, 207–208; resource extraction policies of, 207; seabed claims of, 132; sinking of *Explorer*, 105
Carayannis, E.G., 114
Carbon dioxide (CO2) emissions, 74, 129, 129, 238
Caribou: breeding decline, 198; food sharing, 189–197; and hunting regulation, 219
Carlson, J.M., 68
Cartagena Protocol on Biosafety, 79, 80
Castro, Damián, 186–197
CBD. *See* Convention on Biological Diversity
CBMP (Circumpolar Biodiversity Monitoring Program), 49–50

CCAMLR (Convention on the Conservation of Antarctic Marine Living Resources), 20, 21, 22, 63, 66, 81, 95, 100, 153
Center for Circumpolar Studies, 232
Center for Northern Studies (CNS), 227–228
Certification, nongovernmental, 16–17
Chandler, Jo, 156
Charcot, Jean-Baptiste, vi
Chile, 22, 62, 103, 151–152
Chile-Escudero Proposal, 62
Chilingarov, Arthur, 164
China, 22; and Antarctic resource exploitation, 153–154, 156–157; in Arctic Council, 154; and Arctic resource exploitation, 153; climate change policy of, 152; -Greenland relations, 156, 157; -Iceland relations, 155–156; and Russian oil pipeline proposal, 204; -Russia relations, 163–164
Chinese Arctic and Antarctic Administration, 153
CHM (Biodiversity Clearing House Mechanism), 48
Chukchi Sea, 173
Church, Frederic, 225
Circumpolar Biodiversity Monitoring Program (CBMP), 49–50
Circumpolar business forum, 31
Circumpolar studies: academic programs, 227–228; Center for Circumpolar Studies, 232; Center for Northern Studies, 228–229; historical background to, 224–227; importance of, 232–233; and internet technology, 231–232; University of the Arctic, 229–231
CITES (Convention on International Trade in Endangered Species of Wild Fauna and Flora), 80–81, 85
Clark, Wesley, 3
CLCS (Commission on the Limits of the Continental Shelf), 66, 70, 132, 137
Climate change, Antarctic, 61; consequences of, 27; cooperative approach to, 2; international cooperation on, 151–152, 158; media coverage of, 235, 236; melting of sea ice, 153–154; and regulation, 67; speed of, 1, 236
Climate change, Arctic: Arctic Climate Impact Assessment recommendations, 44–45; consequences of, 27, 41, 171, 186; cooperative approach to, 2; data on, 152; and greenhouse gas emissions,

129–130; as human rights issue, 175–176, 182–183n28; international cooperation on, 151–152, 158; and invasive species, 72–74, 76–77, 84; media coverage of, 235, *236*; melting of sea ice, 76, 128, 129, 136, 161, 166, 172–173, 186; and scientific collaboration, 50–51; and sea route opening, 76, 130, 153; speed of, 1, 72, 236; and U.S. policy, 164–168

Coalition of Legal Toothfish Operators (COLTO), 22

Coast Guard, U.S., 166

Codex Alimentarius Commission, 83, 97

Cold Response *2012*, 2

Cold War, 2, 3, 4, 5, 13, 23, 62, 226

Collings, P., 188

COLTO (Coalition of Legal Toothfish Operators), 22

Commission for the Conservation of Antarctic Marine Living Resources, 100, *102*

Commission on the Limits of the Continental Shelf (CLCS), *66*, 70, 132, 137

Committee for Environmental Protection (CEP), 21

Committee on Trade and the Environment (CTE), 82

Common heritage of mankind, principle of, 14

Community-level food sharing, 189–197

COMNAP (Council of Managers of National Antarctic Programs), 100, 101, *102*, 103

Conference of Parties (CoPs), 80

Conoco Phillips, 210

Conservation of Arctic Flora and Fauna (CAFF) Working Group, 49, 50, 86

Continental shelf claims, *66*, 132–133, 163

Contingent sharing, 188

Convention on Biological Diversity (CBD), 41–42; and Arctic issues, 48–50; and climate change, 50–51; definition of biodiversity, 47; and indigenous rights, 51–52; and information exchange, 52–54; intertreaty linkages of, 47–48; and invasive species, 77, 78–79, 83–84, 85; mainstreaming biodiversity, 49; and marine biodiversity initiatives, 48; sovereign rights of states under, 45–46; and UNCLOS Convention, 47, 48

Convention on the Conservation of Antarctic Marine Living Resources (CCAMLR), 20, 21, 22, 31–32, 63, *66*, 81, 95, 100, 153

Convention for the Conservation of Antarctic Seals (Seal Convention), 19–20, 31, 32–33, 63, 95, 100

Convention on Human Rights, 178

Convention on International Trade in Endangered Species of Wild Fauna and Flora (CITES), 80–81, 85

Convention on the Law of Non-navigational Uses of International Watercourses, 80

Convention on the Law of the Sea. *See* United Nations Convention on the Law of the Sea

Convention on Migratory Species of Wild Animals, 81, 85

Convention on the Protection of the Marine Environment in the Baltic Sea Area, 86

Convention for the Protection of the Marine Environment of the North-East Atlantic. *See* OSPAR Convention

Convention on the Regulation of Antarctic Mineral Resource Activities (CRAMRA), 21, 63

Convention on Wetlands of International Importance (Ramsar Convention), 80

Cooperation strategies, food sharing, 169; agent-based model of, 187, 193–196, *194*, *195*; benefits of, 187–189; community-level *vs* household-level, 189–197, *192*, *194*; contingent sharing, 188; with elders, 192, *192*; and social resiliency, 189, 191

Copenhagen Climate Change Summit of 2009, 152

Corporate Social Responsibility (CSR), 30–31

Costa Concordia disaster, 104

Coston, Jacqulyn, 132

Council of Europe, 178

Council of Managers of National Antarctic Programs (COMNAP), 100, 101, *102*, 103

CRAMRA (Convention on the Regulation of Antarctic Mineral Resource Activities), 21, 63

Creative diplomacy concept, 151, 158n2

Crude Oil Windfall Profit Tax Act, 6

Cruise ships: large-capacity, 105–107; oil pollution from, 98, 104–107; safety hazards to, 103–104; sinking of, 105

CTE (Committee on Trade and the Environment), 82

Cultural differences, and strategic preferences, 3

Cutter, S., 187

Dana, L.P., 199, 208, 211
Dartmouth College, 227
Degeorges, Damien, 111, 151–160
Deggim, Heike, 108
Dehcho people, and Mackenzie Valley pipeline project, 209–210
DeMarban, Alex, 220
Denmark, 174; Greenland as territory of, 113, 122, 155; in Hans Island dispute (Greenland), 135–136; Iceland as territory of, 113; Ilulissat Declaration, 138; in OSPAR Convention, 46; resource extraction policies of, 207; seabed claims of, 132
Department of Energy Organization Act, 6
Department of the Interior, U.S., 215
Department of Wildlife Management, 222
Dickinson, Mark, 104–105
Distant Early Warning sites (DEW line), 226
Dittmer, Jason, 136
Dodds, K., 64, 65, 66, 67, 68, 69
Dodds, Klaus, 136
Doyle, J., 68
Drezner, Daniel, 97–98
Drucker, P.F., 114
Duerden, F., 186
Duyck, Sébastien, 11, 13–40

Eastern Siberia–Pacific Ocean (ESPO) oil pipeline, 199, 203–207
Ebinger, Charles K., 164
Economy of knowledge, 114
Education: in Alaska Native villages, 218. *See also* Circumpolar studies
Eemian period, 1
EEZ (Exclusive Economic Zone), 46, 136
Egeland, G.M., 187
EIS (Environmental Impact Statement), 216–217, 221
Elden, S., 136
Elders, food sharing with, *192*, 192
Electrowatt Engineering, 119
Elk, breeding decline of, 198
Elkem company, 119
Elkind, Jonathan, 6
Emmerson, C., 136, 207, 208
Energy consultants: and growth imperative, 145–150; as intermediary actors, 142–143; market forecasting by, *143*, 143–145
Energy crisis, 149
Energy deposits. *See* Natural gas; Oil and gas deposits; Resource extraction

Energy security: defined, 6; and national security, 5–7
Energy Security Act, 6
Enterprise Resource Planning Systems, 143
Environmental governance. *See* Antarctic Treaty System; Arctic Council; Arctic governance; International environmental governance
Environmental Impact Statement (EIS), 216–217, 221
Environmental law. *See* International law
Environmental protection, and human rights, 178
Environmental Protection Agency (EPA), 215
Equation-based models (EBM), 193
Espersen, Lene, 156
ESPO (Eastern Siberia–Pacific Ocean) oil pipeline, 199, 203–207
Ethnographic studies, 226
Etzkowitz, H., 114
European Court of Human Rights, 178
European Union (EU): and Arctic Council, 154; Arctic Window policy of, 178; seal hunting ban of, 29
Evenki people, and Russian oil pipeline project (ESPO), 205–207
Evolution and Culture (Sahlins and Service), 147
Exclusive Economic Zone (EEZ), 46, 136
Explorer, sinking of, 105, 108
Exxon, 210

Falklands conflict, 67
Faroe Islands, 174
Farrington, Aaron, 223
Financial analysis, and growth imperative, 145–150
Finland, 23, 27, 46, 172, 174
First Nations. *See* Indigenous peoples
Fisheries, Antarctic, 1; illegal, 65, *66*; regulation of, 22
Fisheries, Arctic, 28, 173; Alaska, 215; and climate change, 74; Greenland, 113, 122; history of, 225; Iceland, 113, 115
Food and Agriculture Organization (FAO), 20, 48, 84, 97, 200
Food sharing. *See* Cooperation strategies, food sharing
Ford, J.D., 187
Forest Stewardship Council (FSC), certification of, 17

Fossil fuel consumption, 129

France, 21, 62

Freeman, L.C., 190

Free trade, and introduction of invasive species, 74–75

French, D., 67

Friðleifsson, I.B., 115, 122

FSC (Forest Stewardship Council), certification of, 17

Furgal, C., 186

G.A.P. Adventures, 105

Gardiner Line, 133

Garud, R., 142

General Agreement on Tariffs and Trade (GATT), invasive species regulation under, 82

General Guidelines for Visitors to the Antarctic, 96

Giddens, Anthony, 136, 144

Gilbert, N., 193

Gilchrist, A., 187, 189

Girvan, M., 190

Girvan-Newman algorithm, 190–191, *191*

GISP (Global Invasive Species Program), 83

GIWA (Global International Waters Assessment), 75

Glantz, Michael H., 128–140

Global International Waters Assessment (GIWA), 75

Global Invasive Species Program (GISP), 83

Globalization: and environmental standards, 99–100; and introduction of invasive species, 74

Global Strategy on Invasive Alien Species, 84

Global warming. *See* Climate change, Antarctic; Climate change, Arctic

Gomez, E.T., 200

Gorbachev, Mikail, 23

Governance Triangle (Abbott and Snidal), 98

"Green growth", 151, 154, 156, 158, 159n19

Greenhouse gas (GHG) emissions: and fossil fuel consumption, 129; rate of, 128–129, *129*, 130

Greenland: -China relations, 156, 157; and climate change cooperation, 152–153; under Denmark, 113, 122, 155, 226; economy of, 113, 114, 122; energy-intensive industry in, *124*, 124–125; in Hans Island dispute, 135–136; historical background of, 113;

hydroelectric power in, 123–124, *124*, 127; labor force in, 125–126, 127; natural resources of, 154–155, 156; oil deposits in, 130; in OSPAR Convention, 46; rare earth mining in, 154, 156; Self Rule Act, 155, 158n1; technology transfer to, 115; during World War II, 226

Greenland Technological Organization (GTO), 123

Greenpeace, 20, 21

"Grolar bear" hybrid, 77

Grover, Richard, 198–212, 206

Groves, S., 137

Growth imperative, in natural gas industry, 145–150

Guardian, 76, 235

Gurven, M., 188

Gwich'in people, and Mackenzie Valley pipeline project, 209, 210

Habitat modification, and introduction of invasive species, 75

Hálfdanarson, G., 116

Hamilton, W.D., 188

Hansen, Klaus Georg, 111, 113–127

Hans Island dispute (Canada-Denmark), 135–136

Hardie, I., 145

Harðarson, P., 121

Harza Engineering International, 117, 118

Hawkes, K., 188

Heal, Bill, 230

Heap, J.A., 62, 63

Hedberg Line, 133

Heinämäki, Leena, 25

Helsinki Commission, 86

Hemmings, A.D., 61, 63, 64, 65, 66, 67, 68, 70

Henriksen, G., 188

Hepa, Taqulik, 222

Herber, B.P., 64, 65

Herr, Richard A., 19, 33

Hess, Bill, 214, 221

Higuchi, Kaz, 186–197

Hipwell, W., 199

Hirsch, Rachel, 186–197

Hoekman, B.M., 115

Hoel, A.H., 134

Hoffman, P., 146

Hong, Nong, 138

Hossain, Kamrul, 12, 72–93

Household-level food sharing, 189–197
Howard, Roger, 138
Howkins, Adrian, 151
Hrauneyjarfoss power station, Iceland, 119
Huber, J., 68, 69
Hudson Bay Company, 225
Hughes, D.M., 219
Human rights, 41, 42; and climate change,
    175–176, 182–183n28; environmental
    protection as, 178; norms of, 176–177;
    and public participation, 177–178
Hunting, subsistence, 188, 189–190,
    214–215, 216, 217, 219
Huntington, Samuel P., 4
Hurley, M.C., 209
Hvalfjörður aluminum smelter, Iceland, 120
Hydroelectric power: in Greenland,
    123–124, *124*, 127; in Iceland, 115–117, 119,
    120–122, 126

IAATO (International Association of Antarc-
    tic Tour Operators), 22, 95, 96, 97–98,
    99, 101, *102*, 104
IASC (International Arctic Science Commit-
    tee), 44, 50
ICC (Inuit Circumpolar Council), 28, 52
ICCPR (International Convention on Civil
    and Political Rights), 175, 176
Icebreakers, 2, 166
Iceland, 174; and Arctic Ocean management,
    27, 28; -China relations, 155–156; econ-
    omy of, 113, 114, 121; energy-intensive
    industry in, 118–120, 121; historical back-
    ground of, 113, 115; hydroelectric power
    in, 115–117, 119, 120–122, 126; knowl-
    edge-based sector in, 126, 127; labor force
    in, 114, 125–126; in OSPAR Convention,
    46; technology transfer to, 115
Ice mass, Antarctic, 95
Ice melting, Arctic, 76, 128, 129, 136, 161,
    166
ICESCR (International Convention on
    Economic, Social and Cultural Rights),
    175, 176
IGOs (international governmental organiza-
    tions), 97, 98, 101
IGY (International Geophysical Year), 61,
    62–63, 70n1
ILO (International Labor Organization),
    200–201, 203
Ilulissat Arctic Conference, 28
Ilulissat Declaration, 84, 92n104, 138

Ilulissat Icefjord, 153
IMO. *See* International Maritime
    Organization
Imperial Oil, 210
Indigenous Minorities of the North, Siberia,
    and Far East, 212n8
Indigenous peoples: in Alaska North Slope,
    213–223; art of, 225; and Canadian gas
    pipeline project, 209–212; and climate
    change, 176, 183n28; cooperative strate-
    gies of (*See* Cooperative strategies, food
    sharing); cultural resiliency of, 220–223;
    governance role of, 24, 25, 26–27, 33,
    38n94, 43, 178, 229, 237; invasive spe-
    cies impact on, 73; land claim rights of,
    186–187, 199–203, 202, 208–210; and
    national sovereignty, 14; resource extrac-
    tion impact on, 169, 179–180, 199, 200,
    201, 208; rights of, 51–52, 179, 211; and
    Russian oil pipeline project, 205–207,
    211; sacred sites of, 86; traditional
    economic activities of, 206, 213, 214–215,
    217; transition from traditional life,
    213–214
Indigenous people's organizations (IPOs),
    24, 27, 28
Indigenous Peoples' Secretariat, 25
Information access on environmental risks,
    178–179
Information exchange, 52–54, 69
Information technology (IT), and Arctic
    energy futures, *143*, 143–144
Innu people, food sharing among, 187–193
Inter-American Development Bank, indig-
    enous peoples' policy of, 203
Intergovernmental Panel on Climate Change
    (IPCC), 1, 50, 74, 128, 129, 152
Intergovernmental Platform on Biodiversity
    and Ecosystem Services (IPBES), 50
International Arctic Science Committee
    (IASC), 44, 50
International Association of Antarctic Tour
    Operators (IAATO), 22, 95, 96, 97–98,
    99, 101, *102*, 104
International Conservation Union (IUCN),
    73, 83
International Convention on Civil and Politi-
    cal Rights (ICCPR), 175, 176
International Convention for the Control and
    Management of Ships' Ballast Water and
    Sediments, 78, 79, 85, 86–87

International Convention on Economic, Social and Cultural Rights (ICESCR), 175, 176
International Convention for the Prevention of Pollution from Ships (MARPOL), 23, 85, 98
International Convention for the Regulation of Whaling, 85, 215
International Court of Justice, 136
International environmental governance: and Antarctic tourism, 96–98; cooperation among intergovernmental organizations, 18–19; invasive species related, 77–84; local/regional role in, 17–18; and national sovereignty model, 15; new forms of, 13–14; nongovernmental organizations (NGOs) in, 15–16; in polar regions, 14–15; private sector in, 16–17. *See also* Antarctic Treaty System; Arctic Council; Arctic governance
International Geophysical Year (IGY), 61, 62–63, 70n1
International governmental organizations (IGOs), 97, 98, 101
International Hydrographic Organization (IHO), 101, *102*
International Labor Organization (ILO), 200–201, 203
International law: categories of, 42, 44; and invasive species regulation, 77, 78; and land claims, 200; principles of, 90n66; of territory, 45–47. *See also specific laws*
International Maritime Organization (IMO): and ballast water regulation, 79, 84; and oil pollution regulation, 85, 106; and Polar Code, 23, 107–109
International Organization for Standardization (ISO), 97
International Plant Protection Convention (IPPC), 79–80, 83, 90n69
International Polar Year, 50
International Politics (Art and Jervis), 3–4
International trade: and Arctic sea routes, 162, 164; environmental impact of, 82; and introduction of invasive species, 74–75; regulation of, 81–82
International Whaling Commission (IWC), 215–216, 221
Inuit, 14, 176; land-claim rights of, 186–187
Inuit Circumpolar Council (ICC), 28, 52, 219
Inuit Tapiriit Kanatami (ITK), 186
Inupiat people, 213–214, 220–223

Inuvialuit people, and Mackenzie Valley pipeline project, 209, 210
Invasive species, Antarctic, international regulations related to, 81
Invasive species, Arctic: adverse effects of, 72, 73, 75–77; animals, 76–77; and Arctic Council, 86–87; and Arctic governance, 84–85; and biodiversity loss, 77; and climate change, 72–74, 76, 84; holistic approach to, 87; and indigenous peoples, 73; international regulations related to, 77–84; introduction of, 72, 73–75, 87; and multilateral environmental agreements, 84, 85–86; positive effects of, 76; tracing presence of, 73
IPBES (Intergovernmental Platform on Biodiversity and Ecosystem Services), 50
IPCC (Intergovernmental Panel on Climate Change), 1, 50, 74, 128, 129, 152
IPOs (Indigenous people's organizations), 24, 27, 28
IPPC (International Plant Protection Convention), 79–80, 83, 90n69
Ironside, R.G., 208
Ísleifsson, S.R., 116, 117
IWC (International Whaling Commission), 215–216, 221

Jabour, J., 64
Jacobsson, M., 62, 63, *66*
Janssen, M.A., 189, 191, 196
Japan, 164
Japanese tourists, in Antarctic, 95
Jensen, Anne M., 213–223, 237
Jervis, Robert, 3–4
Johnston, Alastair Iain, 3
Jolly, D., 141, 186
Jónsson, B., 116, 117, 119
Joyner, C.C., 63, 65, *66*, 67

Kankaanpää, Paula, 30, 31
Kárahnjúkar power station, Iceland, 120–121, 126
Karlsdóttir, U.B., 116, 117, 118, 120
Katzenstein, Peter J., 3
Kelly, John J., 222
Kelman, Ilan, 128–140
Kingsbury, Benedict, 16
Kirkenes Declaration of *1993*, 26
Kirsch, S., 199
Kiruna ministerial meeting, 24, 28, 31, 43
Knott, Catherine, 219

Knowledge-based economy, 114, 126–127
Knox, H., 143
Koivurova, Timo, 25, 30, 33n5
Krisch, Nico, 16
Kristinsson, G.H., 116
Kristjánsson, H. Birta, 115, 116, 117
Kristjánsson, Svanur, 118
Krupnik, I., 141
Kurth, James, 163
Kyoto Protocol, 50, 79, 85

Labrador, food sharing in, 189–197
Labrador Inuit Association, 186–187
Lake Baikal, and oil pipeline route, 204
Land rights, of indigenous peoples, 186–187,
    199–203, 202, 208–210
Lassuy, Dennis R., 76
Law. *See* International law
Law of the sea, 47
Law of the Sea Convention. *See* United Na-
    tions Convention on the Law of the Sea
Leary, D., 66
Lee, B., 143
Lee Myung-bak, 155
Leins, Glen, 186–197
Lewis, C.S., 225
Lewis, Patrick N., 76
Liaison Group of Biodiversity Related Con-
    ventions (LGB), 48
Liggett, Daniela, 11–12, 61–71
LiPuma, E., 143
Local governments, and environmental
    governance, 17–18
Lomoosov Ridge controversy, 136
Lopez, Barry, 224, 237
LOS Convention. *See* United Nations Con-
    vention on the Law of the Sea (UNCLOS)
Low, Tim, 88n17

Machlup, F., 114
MacKay, Peter, 128
Mackenzie, Alexander, 207
MacKenzie, D., 145
Mackenzie Valley Aboriginal Pipeline Lim-
    ited Partnership, 210–211
Mackenzie Valley gas pipeline (Canada), 199,
    208–211
Mackinder, H.J., 162–163
Madrid Protocol, 63–64, 65, 70n2, 71n5,
    100, 151, 157
Mahan, Alfred, 162
Makarov, A., 203

Malinowski, B., 187
Mallard, A., 145
Marauhn, Thilo, 50
Marecic, C.J., 186, 187
Marine Mammal Protection Act (MMPA),
    215
MARPOL Convention, 23, 85, 98, 106
Marshall Plan, 117
Maskus, K.E., 115
Mason, Arthur, 111, 141–150
Mattli, Walter, 96, 97
Mauss, M., 187
McGhee, Robert, 235–236
McMurdo research station, 95
MEAs. *See* Multilateral environmental
    agreements
Mel'nikova, E., 204
Melting of Arctic ice, 76, 128, 129, 136, 161,
    166, 186
Memolli, Mariano, 103
Mercer, D., 200
Merkel, Angela, 153
Middlebury College, 228–229
Migratory species, endangered, 81
Military bases, in Arctic, 226
Milov, V., 203, 205
Minerals Management Service (MMS), 220
Missionaries, in Arctic, 225–226
Molenaar, E.J., 65
Monteiro, S., 114
Moose, breeding decline of, 198
Müller-Wille, Ludger, 227
Multilateral environmental agreements
    (MEAs): and invasive species, 84, 85–86;
    priorities for, 47
Munday, M., 206

Nares Strait, Hans Island dispute in,
    135–136
Nasu, H., 62, 63, 64, 66, 67, 68
National Energy Act, 6
National Marine Fisheries Service (NMFS),
    215
National Oceanic and Atmospheric Adminis-
    tration (NOAA), 215
National Ocean Service (NOS), 215
National Park Service (NPS), 215
National Science Foundation, 228; Office of
    Polar Programs, 95, 96, 98
National security: and climate change, 164–
    168; and energy security, 5–7; historical
    overview, 3–5

National Security Presidential Directive (NSPD-66), 164–165

National sovereignty. *See* Sovereignty claims

National Strategy for the Arctic Region (U.S.), 166–167

Natural gas: consumption, 129; growth imperative for, 146–150; Mackenzie Valley pipeline project, 199, 208–211; price rise, 209. *See also* Oil and gas deposits

Natural resources: in Greenland, 154–155, 156. *See also* Animal species, Arctic; Fisheries, Arctic; Resource extraction

Naval Arctic Research Laboratory (NARL), 222

Navy, U.S. *See* United States Navy

Nenets people, 26

Neumann, Thilo, 134

Newman, M.E.J., 190

New York Times, 235

New Zealand, 22, 70, 104, 105, 201

Nickel mine, 173

Noatak River Valley survey, 228

Nongovernmental organizations (NGOs): in Antarctic governance, 20–22, 31–32, 64, 100; in Antarctic tourism, 97–98, 101; and Arctic observer status, 24–25, 37n89; role in international environmental governance, 15–16

NORAD (North American Aerospace Defense Command), 165

Nordal, Jóhannes, 126

Nordnorge, 106

Norsk Hydro, 120

North Atlantic Treaty Organization (NATO), Arctic activities of, 2

Northern Sea Route, 76, 155, 164, 172–173

Northern Studies. *See* Circumpolar studies

North Slope Borough (NSB), regulation of, 214–217, 221

Northwest Passage, 76, 137, 164, 172–173, 225

Norway, 174; Antarctica claim of, 62; in Barents Sea conflict, 133–134, *134*; disappearance of *Berserk*, 104; Ilulissat Declaration, 138; in OSPAR Convention, 46; seabed claims of, 132

Norway rats, 89–90n61

Nuclear weapons, 4, 221, 226

Nunavit, 186

Nuuk, hydroelectric plant at, 123

Nuuk Observer Rules, 44

Obama, Barack, 166, 167

Observer status, Arctic Council, 24–25, 28–29, 37n89, 44, 55n8, 55n13

O'Faircheallaigh, C., 199

Office International des Épizooties (OIE), 79, 83

Office of Surface Mining (OSM), 215

Ohio State University, 227

OIE (Office International des Épizooties), 79, 83

Oil consumption, 129

Oil dependency, 6

Oil and gas deposits: areas of, *131*; in Barents Sea, 133–134, *134*; and consultant advisory services, 142–145, *143*; indigenous voice in decision making, 179–180; and national security, 5–7; offshore, 54, 130, 173, 214; regulating development of, 174–175; risks of extraction, 175, 237; in Russia, 203; size of, 130, 172; sovereignty questions in, 2, 130–131, 138

Oil and gas pipelines: Eastern Siberia–Pacific Ocean oil pipeline (Russia), 199, 203–207; Mackenzie Valley gas pipeline (Canada), 208–211; Trans-Alaska Pipeline, 208

Oil pollution, from cruise ships, 85, 98, 104–107

Oil Spill Response and Preparedness Agreements, 45

Oil spills, 98–99, 173, 175, 204, 221

O'Neill, Dan, 221

Orheim, O., 67

Osgood, Kathleen, 224–233

OSPAR Convention, 86; principles of, 46; states party to, 44, 46

Ostebo, Rear Admiral, 220

Ostrom, E., 68

Ottawa Declaration of *1996*, 24, 25, 38n94, 43, 45, 55n8, 229

Ozone hole, Arctic, 171, 180n1

Pálsdóttir, S., 116, 117, 118, 119, 120, 126

PAME (Protection of Arctic Marine Environment), 86, 175

Panama Canal, 162

Pastean, T., 189

Peary, Robert E., 161

Pelosi, Nancy, 152–153

Permafrost, temperature rise in, 128

Permanent participants status, Arctic Council, 25–26, 28, 29, 33, 43, 44

Pests, invasive, 76
Petroleum consumption, 129
Phillips oil, 210
Pincus, Rebecca, 1–9, 111, 161–170, 235–238
Polanyi, K., 187
Polar Code, 23, 107–109
Polar governance, 11–12; differences/common patterns in, 14. *See also* Antarctic Treaty System; Arctic Council; Arctic governance
Polivanov, A., 204
Polk, W.A., 63, 68
Pollution: from ballast water, 79, 86; biological, 75; carbon dioxide (CO2) emissions, 74, *129*, 129, 238; greenhouse gas emission, 128–129, *129*, 130; MARIPOL Convention on, 85, 98; and oil spills, 98–99, 173, 175, 204, 221; polluter-pays approach to, 99
Port state control, on ships to Antarctic, 105–106
Potapov, E., 136, 208
Power, E.M., 188
Princess Cruise Line, 105, 106
Prior informed consent, and indigenous rights, 179
Private sector: in Antarctic governance, 22–23, 32; in Antarctic tourism regulation, 96, 97–98; in Arctic governance, 30–31; role in environmental governance, 16–17
Project Chariot, 221, 226
Protection of Arctic Marine Environment (PAME), 86, 175
Protocol on Environmental Protection to the Antarctic Treaty (Madrid Protocol), 63–64, 100, 151, 157
Prudhoe Bay (Alaska), oil and gas deposits in, 141–142, 149, 207–208
Public participation, as human right, 177–178
Putin, Vladimir, 204

Quadrennial Defense Review Report (QDR), 165
Quadruple helix, 114, 115
Qu Tanzhou, 156

"Race-to-the-bottom" theory of environmental regulation, 99–100
"Race-to-the-top" theory of environmental regulation, 99

Ragnarsson, S., 116
Ramsar Convention, 80, 85
Raphael, Sam, 6
Rare earth elements (REE), 151, 154, 155, 156, 159n3
Rasmussen, J., 146
Rational models, 3
Rats, invasive alien, 77, 89–90n61
Raupach, Michael R., 129
Raz, Joseph, 180
Regional cooperation: in Arctic governance, 23–33; between intergovernmental organizations, 18–19
Regulatory standard-setting (RSS), defined, 97
Reindeer, breeding decline of, 198
Reineke, Manfred, 104, 107
Resource extraction: cost of, 236; environmental consequences of, 173, 204, 237–238; and indigenous peoples, 179–180, 199, 200, 201, 208–209, 211–212, 214; nickel and zinc, 173; in North America, 207; rare earth, 154, 156; transport infrastructure for, 198. *See also* Hydroelectric power; Oil and gas deposits; Oil and gas pipelines
Reykjavik (Iceland), 115, 117, 120, 155
Rice, Condoleezza, 5
Rio Conference on Sustainable Development, 13, 17, 40n143, 46
Rio Declaration on Environment and Development, 15–16, 25, 45, 77, 178
Rio Plus 20 Conference, 13, 16, 32
Robinson, T., 146
Rodents, invasive alien, 77, 89–90n61
Rothkopf, David J., 4
Rothwell, D.R., 62, 63, 64, 65, 66, 67, 68
Rovaniemi Conference of 1989, 23
Rubel, Robert C., 167
Rudd, Kevin, 158n2
Russia, 2, 44, 174; and Antarctic claims, 63; and Antarctic fisheries, 22; and Arctic governance, 28; Arctic strategy of, 163; in Barents Sea conflict, 133–134, *134*; -China relations, 163–164; flagging incident at North Pole, 130, 136, 137, 164; Ilulissat Declaration, 138; indigenous peoples' rights in, 211; oil pipeline project (ESPO), 199, 203–207, 211; oil reserves of, 203; seabed claims of, 132, 136, 163; in World Trade Organization, 85
Rwin, 209

Saami people, 26
SAC (Science Advisory Committee), 221–222
Sagers, M.J., 204
Saggi, K., 115
Sahlins, Marshall, 147, 187
Sahtu people, and Mackenzie Valley pipeline project, 209, 210
St. John, Courtney, 167
Sakha, Republic of (Yakutia), and ESPO oil pipelines, 204–206
Sale, R., 138, 208
Salt, G.W., 187
SAOs (Senior Arctic Officials), 24, 29, 31, 229–230
Saro-Wiwa, Ken, 182n16
SARS epidemic, 152
Sawyer, S., 200
SCAR (Special Committee on Antarctic Research), 10, 19–20, 31, 101, 102
Schelling, Thomas C., 4
Science Advisory Committee (SAC), 221–222
Scientific Committee on Antarctic Research, 100
Scientific Committee on Problems of the Environment (SCOPE), 83–84
Scientific research: in Alaska's North Slope, 221–222; and Antarctic Treaty System, 19–20; public funding of, 142. *See also* Circumpolar studies
Scientific visitors, to Antarctic, 94–95, 96
SCOPE (Scientific Committee on Problems of the Environment), 83–84
Scott, K.N., 66(tab.), 67, 69, 70, 71n5
SDWG (Sustainable Development Working Group), 30–31
Seabed claims, 66, 132–133
Sea ice, melting of, 76, 128, 161, 186
Seal Convention, 19–20, 31, 32–33, 63, 95, 100
Sea level rise, global, 152
Seal hunting, EU ban on, 29
Search and rescue (SAR): in Antarctic, 103–104, 106; in Arctic, 45
Sea routes, polar, and global warming, 76, 130, 153
Seguin, J., 186
Self-regulation approach to Antarctic tourism, 23
Senior Arctic Officials (SAOs), 24, 29, 31, 229–230
Senkpiel, Aron, 230–231
Service, Elman, 147

Shackleton, Ernest, 62
Shadian, J., 186, 187
Sheehan, Glenn W., 213–223, 214, 237
Shell Oil, 182n16, 210
Sheshatshiu Innu First Nation (SIFN), 189–190
Ships: ballast water regulation, 78, 79, 84, 85, 86–87; and extraction industries, 173; invasive species introduced by, 75, 76; large-capacity cruise ships, 105–107; oil pollution from, 85, 98, 104–107; and Polar Code (IMO), 107–109; port state control over, 105–106; safety and authorization protocol in Antarctic, 103–104; sea routes opened by Arctic warming, 76, 130, 153, 171, 172–173; sinkings of, 104, 105, 108
Siddon, T., 209
Sigalda hydropower plant, Iceland, 119
Sigurðson, H.M., 116, 117
Snidal, Duncan, 98
Snow, Donald, 5
Snow cover, melting of, 128
Social resiliency, connectivity related to, 189
Sovereignty claims, Antarctic, 61, 62, 65, 69–70
Sovereignty claims, Arctic: to continental shelf, 132–133, 163; and oil and natural gas deposits, 130–131, 138; Russian flagging incident, 130, 136, 137–138; territorial dispute resolution under UNCLOS, 46, 66, 132–139
Sovereignty concept, 14–15
Special Committee on Antarctic Research (SCAR), 19–20, 31, 101, 102
Spectar, J.M., 31
Spielman, Brian, 136
Spykman, Nicholas, 161
Stammler, F., 199, 203
Star Princess, 105, 106
Stefánsson, Vilhjálmur, 227
Sterling College, 229
Stevenson, Christopher, 136
Stewart, Richard, 16
Stockholm Convention on Persistent Organic Pollutants, 85
Stockholm Declaration of 1972, 17, 46, 47
Stoilkova, M., 141
Stokes, Doug, 6
Straumsvík aluminum smelter, Iceland, 119, 120
Stroeve, J., 186

Sturluson, J., 121

Summerhayes, C., 62, 63

Sunstein, 99

Sustainable development conferences, UN, 13, 32

Sustainable Development Working Group (SDWG), 30–31

Svalbard station, 163

Svalbard Treaty of 1920, 133, 134

Svanbjörnsson, A., 115, 122

Sweden, 172; and Arctic governance, 27, 30–31; in OSPAR Convention, 46

SWIPA (Snow, Water, Ice, and Permafrost in the Arctic) project, 152

Taking Control: The Story of Self Determination in the Arctic (Hess), 214

Task Force on Sustainable Development and Utilization (TFSDU), 24

Technical Barriers to Trade (TBT) Agreement, 82

Terrestrial Animal Health Code, 79

Territorial disputes, Arctic, 46, *66*, 132–137

Territory, international law of, 45–47

Terrorism, and energy security, 6–7; global, 5

Thomas, D.S.G., 187

Thompson, M., 114

Thorsteinsson, L., 115, 122

Titley, David W., 167

Tolkein, 225

Toolie, Mabel, 141

Tourism, Antarctic, 1; and environmental standards, 99–100; growth of, 94; international organizations' role in, *102*; from Japan, 95; large-capacity cruise ships in, 104–107; and Polar Code, 23, 107–109; pollution liability in, 98–99; regulatory framework for, 22–23, *67*, 96–98; and regulatory implementation, 100–103; safety hazards in, 95, 103–104; scientific visitors, 94–95, 96

Tracey, P.J., 65

Trade. *See* International trade

Trans-Alaska Pipeline, 208

Transportation, for resource extraction, 198. *See also* Ships

Treaties: Arctic-relevant, 41, 44; and indigenous peoples, 202; interlinkages, 47–52

Treaty of Münster of *1648*, 15

Trenin, Dmitri, 164

Triggs, G., 62, *66*, 67

Triple helix, 114, 115

Trivers, R.L., 188

Truman, Harry S., 4

Tshash Petapen Agreement of 2008, 187

Twyman, C., 187

UNCLOS. *See* United Nations Convention on the Law of the Sea

UNDRIP (UN Declaration on the Rights of Indigenous Peoples), 51–52, 176, 179, 180, 182n20, 201–202

UNEP (UN Environment Program), 47, 75, 84

UNESCO Convention on the Protection of the World Cultural and Natural Heritage, 85

UNFCCC (UN Framework Convention on Climate Change), 50, 79, 85, 158, 172, 184n46

Union Carbide, 119

United Kingdom: Antarctica territorial claims, 62; Falklands conflict, *67*; in Iceland occupation, 118

United Nations Commission on Sustainable Development, 13

United Nations Conference on Human Environment, 20

United Nations Conference on Sustainable Development (Rio Plus 20) of 2012, 13, 16

United Nations Convention on the Law of the Sea (UNCLOS), 42, 44, 84, 111, 172, 174, 176; comparison to Convention on Biodiversity, 47; and continental shelf claims, 66 (tab.), 132, 133, 163; Ilulissat Declaration on, 84, 92n104, 138; invasive species under, 78; limitations of, 136–138, 139; objective of, 92n105; and sovereignty rights, 46; and territorial dispute resolution, 133–136, 138–139; U.S. rejection of, 137

United Nations Declaration on the Rights of Indigenous Peoples (UNDRIP), 51–52, 176, 179, 180, 182n20, 201–202, 203

United Nations Development Group, 18

United Nations Economic Commission for Europe (UNECE), 16

United Nations Environment Program (UNEP), 47, 75, 84

United Nations Framework Convention on Climate Change (UNFCCC), 50, 79, 85, 158, 172, 174, 184n46
United Nations Universal Declaration of Human Rights, 203
United States: and Antarctic Treaty, 63; Arctic activity of, 2, 173; Arctic policy of, 164–168; in Beaufort Sea dispute, 135; energy security of, 5–7; Iceland occupation by, 118; Ilulissat Declaration, 138; and indigenous peoples' rights, 201; national security policy overview, 3–5; resource extraction policies of, 207; and UNCLOS, 132, 137. *See also* Alaska
United States Army War College, 2
United States Coast Guard, 165, 166, 220
United States Fish and Wildlife Service, 215
United States Geological Survey (USGS), 130, 172
United States Navy: Arctic Roadmap of, 2, 165, 167; and Arctic security, 165–166
Universal Declaration of Human Rights, 176
University of Alaska Fairbanks, 227
University of the Arctic, 170, 229–231
Uruguay, 22
Uruguay Round, 82
USGS (United States Geological Survey), 130, 172

Van Lente, H., 143
Vespian people, 26
Vietnam War, 5
Virkis Hlutafélag, 119
Vondracek, T.J., 206

Wagner, Andrew Van, 133, 137
Wagnerian Ring Cycle, 225
Wallace, D., 144
Weber, M., 64, 66(tab.)
Weeramantry, 177
Westphalian system of world order, 15
Wetlands, international regulation of, 80

WGIP (Working Group on Indigenous Peoples), 26
Whales, killer, 76, 77
Whaling: Antarctica, 66; Arctic, 214, 215, 221–222
Wilson, E., 199, 203
Wilson, Woodrow, 111
Wily, L.A., 208
Wolves, breeding decline of, 198
Wood Mackenzie, Global Economic Model of, 143, 144
Woods, Ngaire, 96, 97
Wooldridge, M., 193
Working Group on Indigenous Peoples (WGIP), 26
World Bank: and Iceland power station funding, 118–119; indigenous peoples policy of, 202–203
World Commission on Environment and Development, 15
World Health Organization, 97
World Summit on Sustainable Development, 13
World Trade Organization (WTO): and invasive alien species regulation, 78, 82–83, 85; objectives of, 81–82; Uruguay Round, 82
World War II, 3, 4, 226
WTO. *See* World Trade Organization

Xu Shaoshi, 156

Yakovleva, Natalia, 198–212, 203, 206, 207
Young, Oran R., 30, 31, 68, 95–96, 138, 186, 187
Young, Steven B., 224–233
Yukon-Alaska boundary dispute, 133

Zambetakis, Evie, 164
Zebich-Knos, Michele, 12, 94–110
Zebra mussels, 75
Zia, Asim, 128–140, 139
Zinc mine, 173